Creating Lively Passover Seders

A Sourcebook of Engaging Tales, Texts & Activities

DAVID ARNOW, Ph.D.

JEWISH LIGHTS Publishing
Woodstock, Vermont

Creating Lively Passover Seders:
A Sourcebook of Engaging Tales, Texts & Activities

2004 Second Printing
2004 First Printing
© 2004 by David Arnow, Ph.D.

For information regarding permission to reprint material from this book, please mail or fax your request in writing to Jewish Lights Publishing, Permissions Department, at the address / fax number listed below, or e-mail your request to permissions@jewishlights.com.

Page 372 constitutes a continuation of this copyright page.

Library of Congress Cataloging-in-Publication Data

Arnow, David.
Creating lively Passover seders : a sourcebook of engaging tales, texts, and activities / David Arnow.
      p. cm.
Includes index.
ISBN 1-58023-184-5 (pbk.)
1. Seder. 2. Haggadah. 3. Passover—Customs and practices. I. Title.
BM695.P35A76 2004
296.4'5371—dc22

                                                    2004001686

About the Cover Art:

Plates 58–59 "When Israel Went Out of Egypt" from the Moriah Haggadah™

Avner Moriah was born in Jerusalem in 1953. He received his BFA from the Bezalel Academy of Art and Architecture in Jerusalem and his MFA from Yale University's Graduate School of Art and Architecture. His paintings have been acquired by the Metropolitan Museum of Art and the Jewish Museum in New York, the Israel Museum in Jerusalem, the Holocaust Museum in Washington, the Skirball Museum in LA, and private collections throughout the world. The artist can be reached in Israel at Rehov Elqahi 57/8, Jerusalem 93807; phone: 972-2-6732688.

The image "When Israel Went Out of Egypt" is comprised of ten panels visualizing text from the Limited Edition of the Moriah Haggadah™, arranged in pairs from right to left: The Hand of God delivering Israel from Egypt; the sea fleeing and the Jordan turning back; the mountains skipping like rams, the hills like lambs; God's presence on Mount Sinai; and Moshe tapping the rock for water.

10   9   8   7   6   5   4   3   2

Manufactured in Canada

Published by Jewish Lights Publishing
A Division of LongHill Partners, Inc.
Sunset Farm Offices, Route 4, P.O. Box 237
Woodstock, VT 05091
Tel: (802) 457–4000 Fax: (802) 457–4004
www.jewishlights.com

To my parents, Joan and Robert, who showed me the way.

To Madeleine, my wife and beloved partner
on the journey for now twenty-eight years.

CONTENTS

—

Acknowledgments   xi

Preface   xiii

Introduction   xv

How to Use This Book   xix

A Few Words for Seder Leaders   xxi

A Note on Rabbinic Literature, the Haggadah, and Translations   xxiii

1

The Long Road from Slavery to Freedom: From Ancient Egypt to Our Time   1

Slavery in Ancient Times • Exodus and the American Ethos •
Vengeance versus Empathy • The Great Seal of the United States: Israelites
Crossing the Red Sea versus a Pyramid • Former Slaves Speak •
Let Freedom Ring: Historic Words on Freedom • Jewish Values
and Social Justice: American Jews in the Antebellum South •
Slavery in Our Time

2

The Four "Questions": Who's Asking What and Why?   25

Engaging Children during the Seder: An Ancient Lesson • Questions
about Questions • The Greek Symposium and the Jewish Seder •
Why These Particular Questions?

3

Two Haggadot in One: The Haggadah's Early Development   33

When Two Sages Disagree: A Story about the Haggadah's Early Development
• Art Midrash: "Begin with Disgrace and End with Praise"
• Crossing Rivers and Taking Responsibility

4

The Five Sages' Seder: Who Were They and What Kept Them So Late?   43

Five Super-Sages: Their Times and Teachings • Banning Rabbi Eliezer
• The Seder in B'nei B'rak: Reconstructing the Conversation

5

The Four Children: A Seat at the Table for Everyone   57

The Four Children • Torah versus Haggadah • The Wise versus the
Wicked: A Recipe for Conflict or Conflict Resolution? •
Four Voices on Four Children

6

Hardening Pharaoh's Heart: The Toughest Part of the Story   71

The Bible and the Hardening of Pharaoh's Heart • The Commentators'
Struggle • "I Will Send All My Plagues into Your Heart . . . "
• The Softening of God's Heart

7

The Festival of Spring: Reconnecting Passover and Nature   85

On Spring and Time • The Origins of Passover: Two Views •
History Trumps Nature • Activities, Blessings, and Readings

8

The Exodus as a Personal Spiritual Journey   103

Exodus: The Spiritual Journey • Milestones along the Road •
Crossing the Sea and the First Song • The Journey's Ultimate Purpose

9

Enslaved in Egypt: Why?   115

The Covenant of the Pieces • Israel Enslaved: Many Questions,
Many Answers • Joseph and the Enslavement? •
The Self-Critical Voice: Benefits and Dangers

10

"Strangers in a Land Not Theirs": Remembering to Treat the Strangers among Us Justly   129

Knowing the Heart of the Stranger • A Blessing: Treating Strangers Justly • Israel and Its Minority of Arab Citizens

11

"In Every Generation . . ."? God's Role in History and the Jewish People's History among the Nations   137

God: The Elephant, as It Were, at the Seder • Arguing with God • The Sages on Innocent Suffering • Modern Voices

12

"Go Out and Learn . . .": How the Haggadah Tells the Story of the Exodus   153

How the Haggadah Tells the Story • The Pilgrims' Prayer and the Haggadah • Jacob in the House of Laban • A Much-Interpreted Phrase • Moses in the Haggadah • Deuteronomy's Israelite History without Sinai

13

Women of the Exodus: Redeemed by Their Righteousness   169

Passover in an Upside-Down World • Women and the Haggadah: Missing in Action • Women of the Exodus in Midrash • Eden and Egypt: Two Tales of Exodus • Serakh bat Asher and the Exodus • The Legend of Miriam's Well • The Ritual of Miriam's Cup • Redeemed through Blood and Water: Balancing Elijah's Cup with Miriam's Cup

14

The Ten Plagues: Who Suffered and Why?   189

Plagues Against the Israelites? • Why Spill Wine from Our Cups? • When Our Enemies Fall • The Plagues and Knowing God • Signs, Wonders, and Faith: Or Did the Plagues Fail? • Measure for Measure • Revealing the Creator through Anti-Creation

15

Rabban Gamaliel: An Embattled Leader   205

Who Was Gamaliel? • Deposed and Reinstated • Fingerprints on the Haggadah

16

Reliving the Exodus: The Story of the Last Night in Egypt   213

Setting the Stage • The Last Night in Egypt • Bibliodrama: Knocking
in the Night • Bibliodrama: To Stay or to Leave? • A Prayer for the Journey
• Marching from Egypt to the Promised Land

17

Israel and the Haggadah   225

The Fruits of Israel versus Egypt: A Puzzle • Israel's Absence from
the Heart of the Haggadah • Whither Israel? • The Fifth Cup •
Readings for the Fifth Cup • Passover, Messianism, and Israel

18

The Restoration of Wonder: The Miracles of Egypt and Our Day   241

The Bible and the Dictionary • The Sages on Miracles • The Restoration of
Wonder • Jewish Voices on Miracles • At the Red Sea: Two Midrashim •
Between Pharoah and the Red Sea • The Horse and Driver

19

"From Darkness to Great Light": What Do These Words Mean to Us Today?   259

An Art Midrash Project • Variations on a Theme • Four Interpretations
of Five Phrases • A Deeper Look at a Memorable Passage •
The Cultural Milieu

20

"Blessed Are You . . . Who Redeemed Us": The Seder of Redemption   271

The Seder of Hope: Tuning in to Themes of Redemption • Redemption
in the Bible and the Ancient Near East • An Age-Old Question: Why Did
God Redeem the Israelites? • The Four Cups of Redemption • A Quartet
of Twentieth-Century Voices on Redemption • On Faith in Redemption

21

"A Remembrance of the Temple": The Life and Times of Hillel   287

The Meaning of Hillel's Sandwich • A Legendary Leader • Hillel's Teachings
• The Talmud on the Destruction of the Temple

22
Elijah's Transformation: From Zealot to Folk Hero   301
Elijah Comes to the Seder • Elijah's Cup • The Biblical Elijah •
The Elijah Puzzle • Modeling the Potential to Change • A Mirror: A Tale of
Elijah and the Seder • "Pour Out Your Wrath" versus "Give Up Anger"

23
The Exodus from Egypt: The Question of Archeology   315
History and Story • Five Sage Perspectives on the Exodus and History

Appendix I: Chapter Ten of the Mishnah Pesachim, the Night of Passover   **323**

Appendix II: What Is Midrash?   **325**

Appendix III: Directions for Art Midrash Projects   **326**

Appendix IV: Blessing for the New Moon   **327**

Abbreviations and Abbreviated Titles Used in This Book   **329**

Notes   **331**

Select Bibliography   **360**

Index   **365**

ACKNOWLEDGMENTS

—

This book would never have been written were it not for the New Israel Fund's interest in publishing a series of eight Haggadah supplements I wrote, which represent a significant portion of the present volume.

The following individuals were kind enough to review chapters of the book: Rabbis Lester Bronstein, Lawrence Kushner, Hillel Levine, Michael Paley, Nahum Shargel, Gordon Tucker, and Abraham Unger, and Professors Judith Hauptman, John Healey, and Lee Levine. Rabbis Gilbert Rosenthal and Burton Visotzky merit extra thanks for reviewing extensive material and for quickly responding to queries. Thanks to Hershel Shanks for his helpful comments. This book has also benefited from many of Riva Silverman's insights on a broad range of topics. Each of these individuals' wisdom has vastly improved the book.

Several conversations with David Goshen also proved extremely enlightening. Robert Friedland; Elliott Malki; Egon Mayer; Joshua Sherman; and Tatiana Light, my Hebrew teacher for many years; served as ready sounding boards for testing out ideas. Madeleine, Adam, and Noah Arnow; Tammy Reiss; and Ariella Sidelsky provided unstinting editorial assistance. For their comments on the entire manuscript, special appreciation goes to Kathleen Peratis and to the director of Hazon, Nigel Savage. Co-led by Basmat Hazan Arnoff, Hazon's Beit Midrash on the Exodus from Egypt introduced me to wonderfully creative approaches to the story.

Weekly study sessions with Elie Kaunfer, a gifted rabbinical student at the Jewish Theological Seminary of America, provided invaluable assistance for translations and deepening my understanding of numerous texts.

Thanks also to Ruth Abram; Michael Balick; E. Robert Goodkind; Betsy Lewittes; John D. MacArthur; Joseph B. Moskaluk; Dina Shargel Projansky; Elliott Rabin; Peter Reimold; Sharon Zoffness; Rabbis Shlomo Riskin and Neil Zuckerman; and Professors Robert Brody, Daniel J. Lasker, and Israel J. Yuval for their help with particular questions or bringing important material to my attention.

My teachers in the Wexner Heritage Leadership Program helped me learn what it means to make a Jewish text come to life. I owe them and all those associated with that program an enormous debt of gratitude.

The librarians of the Dorot Jewish Division of the New York Public Library—Anne-Marie Belinfante, Faith Jones, Roberta Saltzman, and Eleanor Yadin—are simply among the most dedicated, helpful professionals I've ever encountered. And the Jewish Division's collection is one of the best in the world. Thanks also to Laura Schraeger for her tireless assistance. In addition to their time and varied expertise, these individuals have contributed something equally important: unflagging encouragement.

The staff of Jewish Lights has been a pleasure to work with. Thanks to Stuart Matlins, publisher, for his confidence in the concept for this project. Emily Wichland, managing editor, unflappable and pleasant throughout, has provided endless guidance. Alys Yablon's wise editing contributed enormously to the book. Amanda Dupuis, project editor, did a superb job turning the manuscript into a book.

My sons Noah and Adam have blessed me with unlimited opportunities to fulfill the injunction that "You shall tell your children . . ." about the Exodus from Egypt. I thank them for their patience and wise counsel.

Madeleine J. Arnow, my wife, has endured living through something of a nonstop Passover for more than a solid year. For that, along with helping in countless ways, she deserves all my gratitude.

PREFACE

—

Memories of Passover Seders in my grandparents' Manhattan apartment are among the most treasured of my childhood—the smells, tastes, and songs; the faces of friends seen only at Seders year after year; and the dramatic storybook illustrations of the vintage 1952 Haggadah we used, a copy of which sits open to the left of my computer screen as I write this now. The cover is unforgettable: a young wide-eyed boy with a kindly, white-bearded man—who may as well be Moses—gazing together toward the heavens over an open book. But for a child raised in the suburbs, spending two consecutive nights in a building with an elevator also made those nights different from all others.

In March of 1988 I traveled to Israel with Jonathan Jacoby, then executive director of the New Israel Fund, to investigate the implications of the first *intifada*. Following that disturbing visit, I composed a short reading for our family Seder. Each subsequent year I wrote something else. My family liked these and in 1994 the New Israel Fund, with which I had long been involved, published the first of what would become a series of eight Haggadah supplements that comprise about one-third of this book.

I'm neither a rabbi nor formally trained in any area of Jewish studies, so I approach this undertaking with a combination of excitement, trepidation, and *chutzpah*. My formal training was in clinical psychology, but I've pursued Jewish learning in various formats over the years and have picked up things along the way. Passover has been on my mind for a long time. The holiday fascinates me. I've come to love the Haggadah for itself and because it provides such a perfect doorway into virtually every aspect of Jewish thought and experience. If this book transmits some of that love and fascination to you and your Seder participants, it will have succeeded.

INTRODUCTION

—

THE GOAL OF THE SEDER AND OF THIS BOOK

For almost two thousand years, Jews have gathered with family and friends to celebrate the festival of Passover with a Seder-like meal featuring matzah, wine, and questions about the story of the Exodus from Egypt. Today we conduct Passover Seders in almost every country on earth and in scores of different languages. Among the common ingredients at all these Seders is a book recounting the Exodus saga. That book, the Passover Haggadah (which means "the telling"), might be "traditional," "modern," Ashkenazic, Sephardic, Yemenite, Conservative, Orthodox, Reconstructionist, Reform, Post-Denominational, Hasidic, Kabbalistic, New Age, Feminist, Gay, Environmental, Vegetarian, Civil Libertarian, and so on.

But behind the symbols, rituals, and countless Haggadot lies one aim: to help us draw inspiration from the ancient tale of our ancestors' liberation from Egypt as we wage our own struggles against physical and spiritual oppression.

The Haggadah itself expresses this goal in a single sentence.

In every generation, each individual should feel as though he or she had gone out of Egypt.

This book will help you create that feeling at your Seder.

The sages who composed the oldest parts of the Haggadah realized that breathing life and meaning into Judaism's central story required more than annually rereading the eternally fixed biblical account of the Exodus, regularly reciting liturgical evocations of the story, and diligently reading the Haggadah.

In fact, the sages conceived of a Seder with a radically different approach. The Mishnah, a law code or teaching manual compiled around 200 C.E., contains the first outline for a Seder-like ritual. The relevant section (Pesachim, chapter 10) includes just 435 Hebrew words, and a chunk of that involves differences among sages over details. Some of the oldest manuscripts of that chapter of the Mishnah are even shorter.

Sometimes the Mishnah gives us the precise words for the Seder, but more importantly it points to a general method. After illustrating the kinds of questions the Mishnah hopes children will be prompted to ask about the evening's unusual proceedings, it adds, "And according to the understanding of the son his father teaches him. He begins with disgrace and ends with glory; and he expounds from *My father was a wandering Aramean . . .* (Deut. 26:5) until he finishes the whole section."

The Mishnah's instructions reflect two central principles. First, telling the story of the Exodus must be geared to the level of understanding of the younger generation—and I would broaden that to include the interests of adult participants as well. Remember, the Haggadah alludes to the Seder of five illustrious sages who discuss the Exodus all through the night. Children should participate in the Seder, but it's also important for them to observe their parents and other adults seriously engaging the issues the story raises.

Second, the story is not to be read but to be told through the process of expounding, *drasha*—literally "drawing out meaning"—or making midrash on a passage in the Book of Deuteronomy. The alternative of simply reciting particular verses from the Book of Exodus highlights the uniqueness of the Mishnah's approach. The story is to be made meaningful to those gathered around the table through an interactive, creative process. The Mishnah implies that no two Seders should be the same.

Rather than "slavishly" reading a prescribed text, the Mishnah encourages us to take liberties, using its example as a core and a guide. Back in the 1960s, Marshall McLuhan, the great critic of culture and the media, famously observed that "the medium is the message." In the liberty with which we elaborate on the Exodus, we taste freedom and celebrate it. We experience ourselves as free, independent creators, the very antithesis of our ancestors mired in the mind-numbing pits of slavery. In so doing, we renew the divine sparks within, which mark us each as images of God, the paradigmatic free creator.

Over the centuries, the Seder continued to evolve, but in an ironic direction. The passion for creative elaboration persisted; the Haggadah grew and grew. The text of the traditional Ashkenazic Haggadah now runs more than 5,500 Hebrew words, and that's without a single word of commentary.

Today's "traditional" Haggadah preserves elaborations and additions that evolved over more than a thousand years.

You can *read* that "everyone who elaborates on the story of the Exodus deserves praise."

You can *read* about Rabbis who did just that as they discussed the Exodus all through the night.

You can *read* a complete midrashic exposition on *My father was a wandering Aramean* mostly composed in the late third century.

You can *read* how Rabbi Akiva managed to cleverly recalculate the number of plagues from 10 to 50 in Egypt and 250 at the Red Sea.

You can *read* about how *others* freely and creatively played with the Exodus story and made it come alive for *them*. For them, but not necessarily for us!

For most of us, simply reading the Haggadah no longer helps us feel as if *we* had been redeemed from Egypt. Instead, the experience of reading more than few pages of the Haggadah often makes us feel as if we are oppressed, saddled with an ancient, confusing text that never quite tells the story we expect to hear. Further complicating the matter, the Haggadah lauds a God who saved the Israelites but whose strong hand and outstretched arm seems so very distant from the world as many of us experience it.

Don't get me wrong. I love the Haggadah. But I probably wouldn't if I opened it just for Seders once or twice a year.

The positive feedback I've received from people who have used the texts, tales, and activities that I've put together in Haggadah supplements over the past ten years have convinced me that the Haggadah *can* serve as the basis for great Seders that can give you a taste of leaving Egypt.

At its core, the Passover Seder embodies a dialogue that began millennia ago and continues to this very day. The dialogue reflects the encounter between the Jewish people and our founding story, sacred texts, evolving ritual practice, changing political circumstances, and a shifting cultural milieu. You can get a hint of that dialogue if you consider three things: the Seder developed as a response to the destruction of the Second Temple in 70 C.E.; it found much of its form in the Greek symposium; and it evolved over an extended period when Jews were exiled from the land of Israel, sometimes living under circumstances in which oppression was very real.

For the Haggadah, reliving the Exodus is not about remembering an event long ago, but about participating in a conversation that aims to shore up our hope and strength for the struggle to make tomorrow brighter than today.

With some background, virtually every passage in the Haggadah provides a springboard for activities and discussions that can help you bring that conversation to life.

HOW TO USE THIS BOOK

—

U nless you have a special interest in the Haggadah or the Exodus story, this is probably not a book you'll want to read from beginning to end. I would suggest looking through it three or four weeks before Passover. Just after Purim would be a good time. Choose one or maybe two chapters to read leisurely. That will help you get in the Passover spirit and give you some ideas you may want to take up during your Seder.

As you'll see, each chapter begins with a passage from the Haggadah, and the chapters are arranged in the order in which those passages appear in the Haggadah. Generally you'll find material you can bring into the Seder when you reach the passage in the Haggadah with which a particular chapter begins. But keep in mind that most chapters also contain material that would be better used at other points during the evening. For example, chapter 16, "Reliving the Exodus: The Story of the Last Night in Egypt," includes a package of activities to do before the Seder begins. Similarly, chapter 13, "Women of the Exodus: Redeemed by Their Righteousness," includes the ritual of Miriam's Cup, elements of which occur toward the beginning and end of the Seder.

Over the years, my family has used some of the material in this book to help set the mood for our Seders. We invite people to arrive about an hour and a half before we plan to sit down at the table. We gather in the living room for about an hour before the Seder begins for an activity or conversation like those suggested in this book.

Alternatively, you might consider beginning your Seder on the early side (depending on your observance of Jewish law), making Kiddush, washing hands, and then dipping parsley (*karpas,* Greek for *"hors d'oeuvre"*). Then you might serve more substantial dips. These will take the edge off your participants' appetites and create a good atmosphere for discussion.

We've also sometimes divided into small groups, moving into opposite ends of the living room and an adjacent library for small group discussions. Later, during the Seder, each group gets a chance to share *briefly* the highlights of its conversation with the entire group. (If you plan to do this, ask someone in advance to be the group's "reporter.") You'll be surprised how engaging these conversations can become.

If you plan to lead a discussion based on a particular passage from the Haggadah or another selection from this book, it is important to make a copy for each of your participants. That really helps keep things focused.

Another reason for dividing into small groups is that you can devote one group to activities that are particularly suitable for children. For example, "The Last Night in Egypt" includes a version of the Passover story for reading aloud to children (it's fine for adults, too). On the other hand, you'd be surprised how well even five- and six-year-olds can participate in most of the other activities along with adults, especially in small groups.

We then begin the Seder itself, which for our family does include a fair amount of reading from the Haggadah, interspersed with brief questions and occasional discussions.

How long you want your Seder to run and how much you read from the Haggadah will determine how much time you have to bring additional activities into the Seder.

I've found that once people are seated at the table it's easier to read things and to take a few comments that may evolve into short conversations, rather than to plan on numerous extended discussions. Those conversations are best held before the Seder.

Your Seder will also work better if you involve others in leading parts of it. If you do this and want them to work with the material in this book, be sure to make them a copy and send it to them in advance! When copying material from this book for your Seder, please be careful to cite Creating Lively Passover Seders. For public uses, please be respectful of copyrights and the requirement for permission (see page ii). To find a list of the permissions required for reprinting previously published materials included in this volume refer to page 372.

A FEW WORDS FOR SEDER LEADERS

—

As anyone who has led a Seder knows, the Passover gathering generates a range of expectations, joys, and sometimes a few disappointments. Year after year, you hear the grumbling whispers: "When do we eat?" "How long is this going to last?" "It's getting late!" Some come to the Seder hungry for spiritual sustenance, and others are simply famished for a dinner that seems as if it will never arrive. Some find great meaning in the holiday. For others it seems paradigmatic of that rather sad nine-word version of Jewish history. "They tried to kill us. We won. Let's eat." Some would never miss a Seder. Others come because they would be embarrassed not to. For some, it's all about being with family. For others, that's just the beginning.

Many arrive at the Seder vaguely expecting to hear the great tale of the Jewish people's struggle for freedom. Year after year they leave with a gnawing sense of disappointment. The Haggadah comes close to telling the story, but it does so in a way that creates confusion, if not frustration.

Instead of a heroic battle for liberation, the Haggadah recounts an all-powerful God's triumph over an evil, but comparatively impotent, Pharaoh. There's barely even a word about Moses!

Although the activities in this book can help overcome some of these challenges, it's also important to understand the underlying dynamics that contribute to them. Even if a problem cannot be entirely solved, often just having a better grasp of what causes the difficulty changes the way you experience it.

To one degree or another, the difficulties of creating an "ideal Seder," in which all participants actually *feel as though they have gone out of Egypt,* recapitulate the original Exodus.

We know that many of those slaves who *physically* left Egypt remained there *psychologically.* Taking the slaves out of Egypt turned out to be easier than taking Egypt out of the slaves. No sooner did the slaves leave than they yearned to return. The leader of the Seder gets to taste Moses' frustration. His unruly followers were a lot better at lamenting the good old days in Egypt than at celebrating their newfound freedom. The grumbling at the Seder comes straight from the story of the Exodus! Three days after crossing the Red Sea, the Israelites start complaining about the quality of the water. A while later, they whine about being starved for the "fleshpots" of Egypt.

What makes it so hard to stay focused on celebrating the fact that we are free? In part because we take freedom for granted. But maybe on a deeper level we really *don't* feel free. So we find it hard to wholeheartedly celebrate a condition that still eludes us.

The Hebrew word for Egypt, *Mitzrayim,* can also be read *maytzarim,* "narrow straits." To the extent that all of us feel stuck in our own narrow, familiar places—our own private Egypts—we all resist the Seder. We want to leave, but we're afraid. Of course, this is exactly why the festival is so important.

The Haggadah tells it like it is: "Now we are slaves." We all need to confront the enslaved parts of ourselves with hope that "next year we will be free."

An element of tension at the Seder seems to pit those who want to make this night "different from all other nights" against those who want it to remain an ordinary night—an evening that ends "on time" and includes all the regular topics of conversation. This is only part of the picture. The rest is that each of us feels both poles of ambivalence—wanting to make the night different from all others, wanting to become free, and at the same time not wanting to leave our own Egypts. This helps explain why making a "successful" Seder is not such a simple matter.

There's another angle we need to consider. *Seder* literally means "order." In fact, many begin the Seder by chanting a rhymed mnemonic list of the Seder's fifteen traditional elements. Here the tension lies between the urge for freedom in the sense of total absence of limits versus freedom that comes from acting within the bounds of an externally imposed structure. The chaos that sometimes invades the Seder represents the newly freed slave's yearning for unbridled liberty. Anyone who saw the news footage of the looting in Iraqi cities immediately following the fall of Saddam Hussein's regime in the spring of 2003 witnessed an example of the chaos of sudden freedom without order.

It is as if the Seder represents Torah and we are not really sure that we want to accept it. We'd rather enjoy anarchy than constraints upon our personal freedom. If Sinai is the ultimate destination of the Exodus, each of us along the way is tempted by our own golden calves, by our own false gods.

Another challenge involves the dissonance between the comfort of celebrating liberation and the distance, if not alienation, from God the Liberator as depicted in the Haggadah. The truth is that the God of Jewish liturgy (at least of most liturgy) poses a serious obstacle for many Jews today. Without tools to reframe the concept of God, that dissonance often leads to disappointment and frustration with prayer and ritual. For many, the God of the Haggadah has become the elephant, as it were, at the Seder—present in virtually every passage, but ignored by everyone. Neglecting this "disconnect" can seriously undermine the Seder's potential.

Finally, remember the Haggadah's four children. Each has a seat at the table. That makes the Seder's diversity something of a microcosm of the Jewish world. Working to create a space in which all can feel comfortable during the Seder gives us a taste of what life in today's pluralistic Jewish world is sometimes like and of the unfinished work that lies ahead for the Jewish people when it comes to living with our differences.

As a Seder leader, the more you're aware of these issues, the better you can handle them with grace and sensitivity.

Finally, Seder leaders should realize that having two Seders—with the possibility of two kinds of Seders with different participants—can be a real opportunity! Our second Seder is smaller than the first and often more experimental.

A NOTE ON RABBINIC LITERATURE, THE HAGGADAH, AND TRANSLATIONS

This book includes a good number of passages from rabbinic literature. Dating of rabbinic literature, often an issue of scholarly debate, follows the *Introduction to the*

Talmud and Midrash, by H. L. Strack and Gunter Stemberger, translated and edited by Markus Bockmuehl (Minneapolis: Fortress Press, 1996).

This vast body of literature has much to teach us, but not necessarily about the "facts" of Jewish history or the actual biographies of the sages who appear in its texts. The material was virtually always compiled by redactors over long periods of time, often hundreds of years after the events described. The deeds and even particular teachings of rabbinic figures all reflect the complex motivations of redactors who sometimes sought to elevate a particular idea by putting it in the mouth of a beloved or highly respected sage. These are the texts our tradition has handed down. Like the Bible, they represent a treasure of wisdom about how to live our lives; they are not meant to be history books. The question is not whether events occurred literally as these texts describe them, but what deeper lessons our tradition wants us to learn from a particular story.

All this applies to the Haggadah with the added complication that it has evolved over a longer period of time and exists in more versions than possibly any other Jewish text. The Haggadah, of course, includes many verses from the Bible. But the core of the Haggadah's treatment of them as well as its nonbiblical material derive first from the Mishnah and secondarily from the Jerusalem and Babylonian Talmuds as well as various midrashim.

Our oldest Haggadot are manuscripts written in Israel that were found in the Cairo Geniza. They date from between the tenth and eleventh centuries and differ recognizably from contemporary Haggadot. They include three, rather than four, questions, for example, and lack the midrashic elaboration of Deuteronomy 26:5–8. Fourteenth century "copies" of Haggadot attributed to ninth century Geonim—leaders of the great centers of learning in what is now central Iraq— are relatively similar to those of today with the exception that they lack the rituals associated with Elijah and the familiar Seder songs, which were added in the Middle Ages. Beyond this, it is difficult to be more precise about the sources and dates of some of the Haggadah's nonbiblical passages. Take for example: "In every generation, each individual should feel as though he or she had gone out of Egypt." This passage appears in today's "standard" Mishnah but not in earlier manuscripts from the twelfth and thirteenth centuries. Some of the "standard" Mishnah's language about the night of Passover may actually reflect the influence of the textual traditions found in early Haggadot. References to the Mishnah's treatment of the night of Passover (Pesachim, chapter 10) are based on the text of the Kaufmann manuscript, thought to be relatively free of these influences. It was published in facsimile by George Lewis Beers in 1929 (Haag, M. Nijhoff). A translation of this appears in Appendix I.

I've used the Ashkenazic text of the Haggadah, variations of which are likely used by a majority of American Jews. My "standard" Hebrew version of this text is found in the *The Passover Haggadah* (Schocken Books, 1984), edited by Nahum N. Glatzer with commentaries based on the studies of E. D. Goldschmidt, one of the great Haggadah scholars of the last century. This text, or very similar versions of it, is widely used. It appears, for instance, in the Maxwell House Haggadah, the Silverman Haggadah (Media Judaica, 1979), and the many Haggadot published by Artscroll/Mesorah Publications. Translations of this basic text are based on various Haggadot.

In most cases, I've used the Second (1999) Jewish Publication Society's translation of the Bible. When the Talmud, for example, quotes a biblical passage, I've generally retained the translation contained in that passage, because in such cases, the translation of a Talmudic passage and the rendering of biblical verse are often closely related. Unless otherwise noted, quotations from the Mishnah, Talmud, Midrash Rabbah, and Zohar are from the Soncino translation, Davka CD-ROM version. In an attempt to preserve the flavor of these works spanning thousands of years of Jewish history, their original language has been maintained whenever possible, including instances of "masculine God language."

1

The Long Road from Slavery to Freedom:
From Ancient Egypt to Our Time

הָשַׁתָּא עַבְדֵי, לְשָׁנָה הַבָּאָה בְּנֵי חוֹרִין:

Now we are slaves. Next year we will be free.
—THE PASSOVER HAGGADAH

Near the beginning of the Seder we come upon this extraordinary statement. The Haggadah asks us to look within ourselves and to question how we remain enslaved by the fears that plague us or the false gods we worship. But the Haggadah also wants us to think about slavery in the physical sense, to remember what it was like, to bear in mind that, for some, those memories are not so distant, that, for too many, slavery still persists.

Scholars believe that this Aramaic passage dates from the Talmudic period, between 200 and 500 C.E. It clearly refers to a period of Jewish subjugation.[1] When this passage was composed, the fortunes of the Jewish people had fallen disastrously. In the year 70 C.E., the Romans crushed a Jewish rebellion and destroyed the Second Temple. Sixty-two years later, rebellion erupted again, this time led by Bar Kochba, a Jewish general whose followers believed him to be the Messiah. The rebellion ended with the death of hundreds of thousands of Jews and the exile of most of the Jewish population. The composers of this passage identified their fate with that of their exiled, enslaved ancestors.

1

"Now we are slaves. Next year we will be free." Given the tenor of their times, we can understand these words both literally and metaphorically—literally in the sense that once again the Jewish people experienced oppression and exile, and metaphorically in the sense that they interpreted their current circumstances as a *recurrence* of the familiar Exodus pattern.

This chapter explores the themes of slavery and freedom on the political plane through a series of readings and topics for discussion during your Seder.

CHOOSE ONE OF THESE THREE SELECTIONS TO READ ALOUD DURING YOUR SEDER OR ON YOUR OWN

- Slavery in Ancient Times

- Exodus and the American Ethos

- Vengeance versus Empathy

CHOOSE ONE OF THE ACTIVITIES BELOW FOR YOUR SEDER

- The Great Seal of the United States: Israelites Crossing the Red Sea versus a Pyramid

- Former Slaves Speak

- Let Freedom Ring: Historic Words on Freedom

- Jewish Values and Social Justice: American Jews in the Antebellum South

- Slavery in Our Time

QUESTIONS FOR DISCUSSION

- Consider beginning the section of the Seder called Maggid with a discussion of this passage: "Now we are here. Next year in the land of Israel. Now we are slaves. Next year we will be free." Ask your guests to discuss what this means to them.

- To whom does this statement apply? In what ways might we, today, be enslaved?

• What do you think the Haggadah means when it says, "Next year we will be free"?

• Later in the Haggadah we read, "In every generation they rise up to destroy us, but the Holy One, Blessed be He, saves us from their hand." How does this passage's vision of history contrast with "Now we are slaves. Next year we will be free"?

• Imagine that you have been asked by a journalist to explain why you oppose slavery. What moral arguments might you make? Can you make a compelling moral argument without invoking religious traditions? Would you feel comfortable making your case on purely pragmatic grounds? For example, would you be willing to argue that slavery ultimately produces political instability or that slave labor is less efficient than hired labor?

SLAVERY IN ANCIENT TIMES

Any of the following three selections may be read during the Maggid section of the Seder or as a reading before you sit down at the table. Together these three short essays explore slavery in the ancient world, the role of Exodus imagery in America's founding and battle against slavery, and finally the often-repeated cycle in which the struggle for freedom only leads to the replacement of one oppressive regime with another.

The road from slavery to freedom stretches back a long way. The history of slavery began with the earliest days of civilization and the discovery that one group of people was able to dominate another. Indeed, slavery may be as old as war itself: Those whom the victor did not kill were enslaved and brought home as a ready source of cheap labor.

But war was hardly the only source of slaves. They could be bought at markets in the larger cities or from traveling dealers. In times of economic distress, parents unable to care for their infants would lay them in a pit. The lucky ones might be rescued by passersby and raised as slaves. Desperate parents might also be forced to sell their children in exchange for food or clothing. If unemployment persisted or debts rose too high, fathers or mothers resorted to selling themselves in order to survive.[2] Kidnapping children provided another source of slaves.

Massive exploitation of slave labor actually came to Egypt rather late. Archeologists tell us that the pyramids (most were constructed between 2600 and 2300 B.C.E.) were not built by slaves, but by peasants forced into servitude for a few years and then released. But centuries later, when slavery did become widespread there, the Egyptians "perfected" it, just as they had done with everything from building to making war to cultivating crops. In its imperial heyday, Egypt became the largest consumer of slaves in the Near East.[3] An Egyptian general's letter to Ramses III (1186–1154 B.C.E.) after one of Egypt's frequent victories over the Canaanites paints a graphic but typical picture:

> I have brought back in great numbers those that my sword has spared, with their hands tied behind their backs before my horses, and their wives and children in tens of thousands, and their livestock in hundreds of thousands. I have imprisoned their leaders in fortresses bearing my name . . . branded and enslaved, tattooed with my name and their wives and children have been treated in the same way.[4]

As part of their homage to Egypt, Canaanite leaders regularly shipped boatloads of slaves off to Egyptian ports.[5] Most slaves in Egypt were foreigners or Asiatics, as they were called there. But often Egyptians themselves who had fallen on hard times had no choice but to sell themselves into slavery.[6]

The demand for slaves became so great that enterprising Egyptians created special "houses of female settlement" where slaves could be conveniently bred in large numbers. For those unable to acquire their own slave, it was possible to rent one to work for just a day or two.

Egyptian law *did* include procedures for freeing slaves, as did biblical law. But the vast majority of these unfortunate people died as slaves, passing their lowly status down to their children and their children's children. In the end, Egyptian society grew increasingly dependent on slavery, more so than other ancient Near Eastern empires. Elsewhere, newly crowned kings often freed prisoners, rebels, and slaves in order to bolster their popularity: In Egypt, these freedom proclamations generally excluded slaves.[7]

Against this background, the Bible's legislation represents a significant step toward humanizing, if not eliminating, bondage. The Ten Commandments begin by invoking the Israelites' redemption from slavery: "And God spoke all these words, saying: 'I am the Lord your God who brought you out of the land of Egypt, the house of bondage'" (Ex. 20:1–2). The fourth commandment explicitly includes slaves: "But the seventh day is a sabbath of the Lord your God; you shall not do any work—you, your son or your daughter, your male or female slave, or your cattle, or the stranger within your settlements" (Ex. 20:10). And the laws given immediately after the Decalogue further regulate slavery. A Hebrew slave was to serve a maximum of six years.

But in Israel, as in Egypt, most slaves were foreigners and their lot remained bleak: "You may keep them as a possession for your children after you, for them to inherit as property for all time" (Lev. 25:46).

The laws of Hammurabi, a Babylonian king who ruled from 1792 to 1750 B.C.E., placed no limits on how a master could treat his slaves. The Bible punished cruelty toward all slaves: "When a man strikes the eye of his slave . . . and destroys it, he shall let him go free on account of his eye. If he knocks out the tooth of his slave . . . he shall let him go free on account of his tooth" (Ex. 21:26–27). And if a master struck his slave and killed him on the spot, he was guilty of murder and punished by death.

But the Bible's treatment of fugitive slaves, Hebrew or foreigner, was without a doubt its most revolutionary advance. In the Code of Hammurabi, the penalty for harboring a fugitive slave was death.[8] Compare this with Deuteronomy 23:16–17: "You shall not turn over to his master a slave who seeks refuge with you from his master. He shall live with you in any place he may choose among your settlements in your midst, wherever he pleases; you must not ill-treat him."[9]

The Bible did not outlaw slavery, but it tried to humanize the practice. And Deuteronomy's treatment of fugitive slaves represents a giant step down the road toward freedom.

EXODUS AND THE AMERICAN ETHOS

Almost three thousand years after the Israelites crossed the Red Sea in pursuit of freedom, Europeans seeking greater religious liberty sailed across the Atlantic Ocean to build a "New Israel" in the New World. In the spring of 1630, as his ship approached the shores of Massachusetts, John Winthrop preached a sermon to his Puritan disciples befitting the travails of a group who felt as if they had relived the journey from Egypt to the Promised Land:

> Now the only way to avoid this shipwreck and to provide our posterity is to follow the counsel of Micah, *to do justly, to love mercy, and to walk humbly with our God* . . . The Lord will be our God and delight to dwell amongst us as His own people, and will command a blessing upon us in all our ways . . . We shall find the God of Israel is among us, when ten of us shall be able to resist a thousand of our enemies . . . For we must consider that we shall be as a City upon a hill. The eyes of all the people are upon us. So that if we deal falsely with our God in this work . . . [we will be] consumed out of the good land where we are going.[10]

But the long arm of oppression proved difficult to escape. In their demand for freedom, the colonists identified with the struggle against Pharaoh. The English King George III and the Egyptian Pharaoh were both freedom's enemies. When the British hastily repealed the hated Stamp Act in 1766 ("No taxation without representation!") it was as if Pharaoh had been defeated. One patriotic pastor preached:

> [The colonists feared that] they should gradually be brought into a state of the most abject slavery. This it was that gave rise to the cry, which became general throughout the colonies, "We shall be made to serve as bond-servants; our lives will be bitter with hard bondage." Nor were the Jews more pleased with the royal provision in their day, which, under God, delivered them from their bondage in Egypt, than were the colonists with the repeal of that act which had so greatly alarmed their fears and troubled their hearts. It was to them as "life from the dead." They "rejoiced and were glad."[11]

Eventually, the bitterness of British tyranny led the colonists to revolt and declare independence. On July 4, 1776, the Continental Congress charged Thomas Jefferson, Benjamin Franklin, and John Adams with recommending a design for the new nation's Great Seal. Franklin proposed Moses parting the Red Sea with Pharaoh's armies drowning as their chariots were overwhelmed by the waters. Jefferson preferred an image of the children of Israel in the wilderness, led by a cloud by day, and a pillar of fire by night. As a motto they proposed, "Rebellion to tyrants is obedience to God" (see page 12).[12]

Despite their infatuation with the Exodus, America's early leaders held a wide range of opinions about slavery. Indeed Jefferson, Washington, and many others owned slaves. And ratification of the nation's Constitution rested on uneasy compromises. One provided that slaves would be counted as three-fifths of a free person when it came to apportioning seats in the House of Representatives. Another forbade harboring fugitive slaves.[13]

In the end, the Great Seal did include an image from Egypt—a pyramid, then thought to have been built by slaves—a monument to a king!

In 1790, there were fewer than 700,000 slaves in the United States. Samuel Elliot Morrison, one of America's great historians, spoke of the terrible contradiction:

> The emancipation of these blacks, their becoming domestic servants, common laborers and small farmers, even the return of many to Africa, would then have been possible. But the revolutionary generation lacked the imagination to foresee the tragic consequences of perpetuating an institution which denied the very premises upon which American independence was based.[14]

Pharaoh learned the hard way that building a country on the backs of slaves is dangerous business. It cost many Egyptians their lives. Americans learned the same lesson and paid the same price.

Abolishing slavery required a civil war and the death of 600,000 Americans, more than have been killed in all our subsequent wars combined. And if ever an American president has been compared to Moses it is Abraham Lincoln. His condemnations of slavery ring out as strongly today as they did in the days of the Civil War:

This is a world of compensations; and he who would be no slave must consent to have no slave. Those who deny freedom to others deserve it not for themselves, and under a just God, cannot long retain it.[15]

More than a hundred years later, African Americans still had not fully won their freedom and rights as equal citizens. Imagery of the Exodus fueled their struggle. When he accepted the Nobel Peace Prize in 1964, Martin Luther King Jr. said, "Oppressed people cannot remain oppressed forever. The yearning for freedom eventually manifests itself. The Bible tells the thrilling story of how Moses stood in Pharaoh's court centuries ago and cried, 'Let my people go.'"[16]

Just as discrimination against African Americans did not end with the Emancipation Proclamation in 1863, it didn't end for women when they finally won the right to vote in 1920.

Changing a nation's laws is often just the first step in changing people's stubborn and unfair "habits of the heart."

The Seder is the time to explore the contradictions between the principles we preach and the realities we perpetuate.

Have we turned our backs on oppression when it stares us right in the face? Do we pretend that victims of hatred somehow deserve their plight? Have we treated those fairly over whom we have power? Among those closest to us, do we encourage the freedom to grow and change?

VENGEANCE VERSUS EMPATHY

The Haggadah teaches that "in every generation, each individual should feel as though he or she had gone out of Egypt." Now comes the tough question: "What will we do with our memories of slavery?" Will we use them to renew empathy or vengeance? As free people, the choice remains ours, but history suggests that the urge for vengeance often proves irresistible. Passover should renew our capacity for empathy.

Martin Luther King Jr. said, "Oppressed people cannot remain oppressed forever." But it is also true that oppression has been with us *forever*. In fact, the fight for freedom often ends with one repressive regime's replacement by another. The French

Revolution, with its slogan of "liberty, fraternity, equality," produced a reign of terror more brutal than even that of the worst French kings. The Russian Revolution gave birth to a totalitarian state more coercive than most autocratic czars. And in Africa, the struggle against colonialism brought to power a slew of regimes that ultimately proved more abusive than the most domineering colonial overlords.

Why does this disillusioning pattern recur throughout history? Part of the answer lies in the fact that liberation rarely frees us from the desire or the emotional capacity to oppress others. The fiery cauldron of revolution, seething with moral contradictions, stands far from the cool ideal of justice. By the time the freedom fighters have finally won, their moral integrity has often dwindled to that of the overturned regime. Principles become the rebellion's first casualty, the human rights of those on the other side are the next casualties. Locked in a spiral of brutal strife, the tactics of the oppressed and the oppressor become increasingly difficult to distinguish. And then the liberation movement turns inward, purifying itself, silencing the murmuring, divisive voices within its own ranks.

Let's look at elements of this pattern within the Exodus story itself.[17] With God fighting the war against Pharaoh, the Israelites themselves were spared from violently rebelling against the Egyptian king. But they must surely have observed that the forces for and against oppression, Pharaoh and God, ultimately resorted to similar tactics: the slaying of children. To prevent the Israelites from becoming too numerous, Pharaoh orders the murder of their newborn sons. To persuade Pharaoh to let the Israelites go, God slays the Egyptians' firstborn sons.

The murmuring against God, Moses, and Aaron begins in Egypt but increases after the Exodus. Unable to find water for three days after the miraculous parting of the Red Sea, the Israelites yearn for Egypt:

> The Israelites said to them, "If only we had died by the hand of the Lord in the land of Egypt, when we sat beside the fleshpots, when we ate our fill of bread! For you have brought us out into this wilderness to starve this whole congregation to death."
>
> —EXODUS 16:2–3

The height of the murmuring comes when the Israelites build the Golden Calf. Moses smashes the Ten Commandments and sentences the counterrevolutionaries.

9

Moses stood up in the gate of the camp and said, "Whoever is for the Lord, come here!" And all the Levites rallied to him. He said to them, "Thus says the Lord, the God of Israel: Each of you put sword on thigh, go back and forth from gate to gate throughout the camp, and slay brother, neighbor, and kin." The Levites did as Moses had bidden; and some three thousand of the people fell that day.

—EXODUS 32:26–29

To enforce the first commandment against idol worship, Moses violates the sixth—"Thou shalt not kill." So revolutions go. The sanctity of human life pales in the blinding light of more exalted ideals.

Liberation struggles often whet an evil appetite: Revenge is sweet. Frantz Fanon was a French psychiatrist who studied the effects of oppression. Descended from African slaves, Fanon found himself irresistibly attracted to the Algerian fight to end 132 years of French colonial occupation. In 1961, a year before the end of the bloody war between France and Algeria, he described the circumstances and inner feelings of oppressed peoples:

The town belonging to the colonized people . . . is a hungry town, starved of bread, of meat, of shoes, of coal, of light. The native town is a crouching village, a town on its knees, a town wallowing in the mire.

The colonized man is an envious man. And this the settler knows very well; when their glances meet, he ascertains bitterly, always on the defensive, "They want to take our place." It is true, for there is no native who does not dream at least once a day of setting himself up in the settler's place.

He is in fact ready at a moment's notice to exchange the role of the quarry for that of the hunter. The native is an oppressed person whose permanent dream is to become the persecutor. . . .[18]

This is Pharaoh's Egypt and it is all around us, from the grinding decay of America's worst inner cities to the brutal dictatorships that still dominate much of Africa and the Middle East.

10

But the desire to humiliate one's former master explains only part of the cycle in which the oppressed become the oppressors. Subjugation of another reflects more than quenching an old thirst for revenge. The capacity to oppress another human being represents a fundamental rupture of human empathy, the bond of understanding that links us with our brothers and sisters and enables us to put ourselves in their shoes. Eliminate empathy and one group begins to treat another as inhuman objects—as machines to build cities in Egypt, as beasts to be captured in Africa, as insects to be exterminated in Nazi concentration camps. Expose a people to a world without empathy and you forge the next link in the chain of oppression. Nations respond this way and so do individuals. Scratch a parent who abuses a child and you will usually find someone who suffered abuse as a child.

If vengeance and a lack of empathy are the germs that breed oppression, neither the Israelites who left Egypt nor we today are immune from the disease.

At the very climax of their struggle for freedom, the children of Israel rejoice when Pharaoh's soldiers drown in the Red Sea. A tide of other emotions submerged what compassion they may have had—revenge, relief, and the joy of salvation: "Then Moses and the Israelites sang this song to the Lord. They said: I will sing to the Lord, for He has triumphed gloriously; Horse and driver He has hurled into the sea" (Ex. 15:1). For the Israelites dancing on the shore of the Red Sea, the Egyptians were hardly the object of human concern. They were the enemy, not young men whose mothers would mourn them, whose firstborn brothers had just been slain by God, soldiers following orders of a Pharaoh whose heart had repeatedly been hardened by the Lord of Israel.

In reminding us of our experience as slaves, Passover renews our collective empathy. We are neither slaves stripped of our dignity, nor are we fully free to rejoice in the fall of our enemies. We must remember their humanity, even when they have forgotten ours.

So, before we sing *Dayyenu,* we spill a drop of wine from our glasses for each of the ten plagues. A common interpretation explains that our joy cannot be complete because our redemption was achieved at the cost of great suffering to the Egyptians.

The passion for vengeance cools slowly. Dignity destroyed takes years to rebuild. The scars of slavery take generations to heal. That is why we needed forty years in the desert before entering the Promised Land. But time alone does not heal all wounds. If they are deep enough, active intervention and treatment are essential. And for the Jewish people, that intervention came in the form of the Torah, a code for transforming the bitter memories of oppression into a commitment to building a more just and humane society.[19]

As the Rabbis of the Talmud wisely observed, the commandment to respect the rights of minorities appears thirty-six times in the Torah, a reminder that with power, the oppressed themselves often become oppressors. It is the Jewish people's responsibility to remain strong and to help break this tragic cycle. When Hillel, the great sage, was asked to teach the entire Torah to a man while standing on one foot, this is what he said: "What is hateful to you, do not do to others. All the rest is commentary. Now go and study."[20]

Let your bitter memories enlarge the well of human empathy. Overcome your lust for vengeance. Overcome your readiness to deny others their humanity. For who has not dreamed—at least once—of sitting on Pharaoh's throne?

THE GREAT SEAL OF THE UNITED STATES: ISRAELITES CROSSING THE RED SEA VERSUS A PYRAMID

Copy these two images for each of your guests. Discuss the differences between them, and ask your guests which they prefer and why. You might pair this activity with the earlier reading, "Exodus and the American Ethos," which also mentions the original proposal for the Great Seal.

(Left) The image created by Benson J. Lossing (1813–1891) to illustrate the original proposal for the reverse side of the Great Seal by Jefferson, Adams, and Franklin in 1776. It depicts the Israelites, crossing the Red Sea protected by a pillar of fire, and Pharaoh's drowning army. The motto first appeared on the tombstone of John Bradshaw, head of the English court that condemned King Charles I to death in 1649. Thomas Jefferson also adopted the motto for his personal seal. *(Right)* The seal adopted by the Continental Congress in 1782, which appears on the one-dollar bill. *Annuit Coeptis* means, "He (God) has favored our undertakings." *Novus Ordo Seclorum* means "A new order of the ages (is born)." Both Latin inscriptions paraphrase verses by the Roman poet Virgil.

The Exodus has been a powerful symbol for many peoples engaged in the struggle for liberation. On July 4, 1776 the Continental Congress appointed a committee to make recommendations for a "Great Seal" befitting the new confederation. A small committee, it included just Thomas Jefferson, Benjamin Franklin, and John Adams! Adams described the group's emerging recommendations in a letter to his wife Abigail on August 14, 1776:

> I am put on a committee . . . to prepare devices for a Great Seal of the confederated States . . . Doctor F. proposes . . . Moses lifting up his wand, and dividing the Red Sea, and Pharaoh in his chariot overwhelmed with the waters. This motto: 'Rebellion to tyrants is obedience to God.' Mr. Jefferson proposed, the children of Israel in the wilderness, led by a cloud by day, and a pillar of fire by night. . . .[21]

In 1782, the Continental Congress finally approved the recommendations of another and far less distinguished committee. Again they chose imagery associated with the Exodus—the pyramid, a monument built to a king, then thought to have been built by slaves. You can find it on the back of a one-dollar bill. The all-seeing eye within a triangle proved to be the only image in the new seal that had been suggested by the previous committee of Jefferson, Adams, and Franklin. The eye within a triangle was to have appeared on the obverse of the seal above representations of liberty and justice.

Annuit Coeptis, the Latin inscription above the pyramid, means, "He (God) has favored our undertakings." The lower inscription, *Novus Ordo Seclorum,* means, "A new order of the ages [is born]." Both inscriptions paraphrase verses by the Roman poet Virgil.

FORMER SLAVES SPEAK

The Seder is not a time for the automatic repetition of a familiar old story. To the contrary, the Haggadah challenges us to make the remote experience of slavery in Egypt vivid and palpable. To accomplish this you might want to bring to your Seder the words of individuals who actually lived as slaves. Below you will find excerpts from three "slave narratives"—one from the early nineteenth century, another from the Holocaust, and a third from man who had been a slave in Sudan and obtained his freedom in 1999. Consider the following questions before delving into the "slave narratives."

- We Jews trace our ancestry back to slavery in Egypt and have suffered inordinate persecution over the ages. Some would say, "That was a long time ago," and that Jewish interests now dictate that our community's historic commitment to fighting for equality and social justice should be a lesser priority. Do you agree? Why or why not?

- To what extent, if any, do you believe that Jews have a special responsibility to the cause of social justice?

Mary Prince dictated her story to an Englishman active in the antislavery movement who published her narrative in 1831. This was the first such published work written by a woman, and it exerted a great influence on subsequent narratives. Mary was born to a family of slaves in Bermuda. She later lived in Antigua, where she married a former slave who had managed to buy his freedom. Soon afterward, her master's family moved to England, promising to free her in a few years. The separation from her husband pained Mary terribly. Increasingly arthritic, she was unable to perform heavier housework. Her master threw her out of the house penniless. Eventually she contacted the Moravian Church with which she had become active in Antigua. Moravians and Quakers gave her work and encouragement, but the story ends with Mary languishing in England, pining for her beloved husband. Here she describes her sale as a young girl.

At length . . . the master who was to offer us for sale like sheep or cattle, arrived, and asked my mother which was the eldest. She said nothing, but pointed to me. He took me by the hand, and led me out into the middle of the street, and, turning me slowly round, exposed me to the view of those who attended [the sale]. I was soon surrounded by strange men, who examined and handled me in the same manner that a butcher would a calf or a lamb he was about to purchase, and who talked about my shape and size in like words—as if I could no more understand their meanings than dumb beasts. I was then put up to sale. The bidding commenced at a few pounds, and gradually rose to thirty-eight sterling [today about $2,600] when I was knocked down to the highest bidder; and the people who stood by said that I had fetched a great sum for so young a slave. I then saw my sisters led forth, and sold to different owners; so that we had not the sad satisfaction of being partners in bondage . . . All slaves want to be free—to be free is very sweet . . . I have been a slave myself—and I know what slaves feel . . . The man that says the slave is quite happy in slavery—that they don't want to be free—is either ignorant or lying.[22]

During World War II, slave labor contributed significantly to the German war effort. As manpower grew short and the supply of armaments began to run low, Hitler agreed to build factories in concentration camps. By 1944, more than half a million concentration camp inmates had been leased out to German companies that would in turn pay fees back to the camps.

Betty Lissing's family had lived in Holland since 1650. At age twenty-one, she arrived in Auschwitz in January of 1944. Her grandfather, parents, and two brothers had already been killed there. Until the war ended about eighteen months later, she worked in the control section of a plant, the Union, that manufactured artillery shell casings and cone-shaped metal pieces (korpers) used elsewhere in the shells. Betty's husband also survived the war and the couple eventually settled in Australia.

During my second week at the Union I came down with typhus, had a tremendously high fever and became very ill. I felt I could not go on. My cousin forced me not to go to the [inmate's hospital]. She warned me that I would be gassed there. I don't remember how I survived, since I was mostly delirious. The night shift workers received an extra dish of soup at the Union, which helped us not to be completely starved. However, the work was very hazardous because everything was called sabotage; for example, stopping work a minute before the alarm went off or letting defective [parts] pass the control. As a matter of fact, I attempted to let faulty items go through on purpose as often as I was able to do so . . . I recall one incident when all girls working at a particular table were severely punished for sabotage. Then the entire work squad of the Union had to assemble in the hall. Camp commandant Hoessler screamed and whipped the girls in front of us and condemned them to be gassed. The whole work detail was in shock and I could not speak . . . The bruised and bleeding girls were taken away and we could do nothing at all to help them. Two days later, when we had assumed that they had been killed, they all suddenly returned to the block. Such things happened constantly. We were always in a state of terror. . . .[23]

Francis Bok was enslaved in Sudan for ten years. He escaped in 1999 and now works with the American Anti-Slavery Group in Boston. In September 2000 he gave this testimony before the Senate Foreign Relations Committee.

I was born in Southern Sudan, near Nyamllel. When I was seven, my mother sent me to the market to sell eggs and beans. I never saw my mother again. At the market, militia soldiers attacked. Hundreds of Arabs on horses came into the market shouting. They shot people in the head. They cut off heads with swords. The streets were a river of blood.

They took me and many children as slaves. They put me in a big basket, tied to a donkey and they took us north.

One girl had seen her parents killed, and she would not stop crying. So they shot her in the head. Her younger sister started crying. So they cut off her foot. I was quiet.

In the north, I was given as a slave to Giema Abdullah. He took me to his family, and they beat me with sticks. All of them—the women and children, too. They laughed and called me *"abeed"*— "slave." [The Arabic *abeed* is a cognate of *eved,* Hebrew for "slave."]

For ten years, they beat me every morning. They made me sleep with the animals, and they gave me very bad food. They said I was an animal. For ten years, I had no one to laugh with. For ten years, nobody loved me. But every day I prayed to God.

One day, I asked my master a question: "Why do you call me 'abeed'? And why do you feed me bad food all the time and make me sleep with the animals? Is it because I am black?" My master was very angry. "Where did you learn to ask this question?" he said. "Never ask me this again." And he beat me and beat me. When I was 17, I decided to escape. I would rather die than be a slave.[24]

LET FREEDOM RING: HISTORIC WORDS ON FREEDOM

Below you will find a collection of historic statements on freedom spanning three thousand years. Copy this section and ask each guest to read a selection. As you read them, keep the following questions in mind.

• Do you think that the world is moving in the direction of greater freedom or greater oppression?

• Is the vision of a world with substantially less oppression realistic or hopelessly messianic?

• What light does the story of the Exodus from Egypt shed on this question?

• Which selection do you find to be the most personally moving and why?

• Which ones strike you as particularly relevant this year?

Thus says the Lord, the God of Israel: Let my people go. . . .

—EXODUS 5:1

Proclaim liberty throughout the land unto all the inhabitants thereof. . . .

—LEVITICUS 25:10 (INSCRIBED ON THE LIBERTY BELL IN 1752)

If liberty and equality, as is thought by some, are chiefly to be found in democracy, they will be best attained when all persons alike share in the government to the utmost.[25]

—ARISTOTLE (384–322 B.C.E.)

Those who would give up essential liberty to purchase a little temporary safety deserve neither liberty nor safety.[26]

—BENJAMIN FRANKLIN (1706–1790), 1759

We hold these truths to be self-evident, that all men are created equal; that they are endowed by their Creator with certain inalienable rights; that among these are life, liberty and the pursuit of happiness.

—THE DECLARATION OF INDEPENDENCE, 1776

Familiarize yourselves with the chains of bondage and you prepare your own limbs to wear them. Accustomed to trample on the rights of others, you have lost the genius of your own independence and become the fit subjects of the first cunning tyrant who rises among you.[27]

—ABRAHAM LINCOLN (1809–1865), 1858

It was we, the people, not we, the white male citizens, nor we the male citizens; but we, the whole people, who formed this Union. We formed it not to give the blessings of liberty but to secure them; not to the half of ourselves and the half of our posterity, but to the whole people—women as well as men. It is downright mockery to talk to women of their enjoyment of the blessings of liberty while they are denied the only means of securing them provided by this democratic-republican government—the ballot.[28]

—SUSAN B. ANTHONY (1820–1906), 1872

Give me your tired, your poor,
Your huddled masses, yearning to breathe free,
The wretched refuse of your teeming shore,
Send these, the homeless, tempest-tossed, to me:
I lift my lamp beside the golden door.

—EMMA LAZARUS (1849–1887), 1883, FROM *THE NEW COLOSSUS*,
INSCRIBED ON THE BASE OF THE STATUE OF LIBERTY

Complete Civil Disobedience is rebellion without the element of violence in it . . . Submission to the state law is the price a citizen pays for his personal liberty. Submission, therefore, to a state wholly or largely unjust is an immoral barter for liberty . . . Civil resistance is a most powerful expression of the soul's anguish and an eloquent protest against the continuance of an evil state . . . Freedom is like a birth. Till we are fully free we are slaves. All birth takes place in a moment.[29]

—MOHANDAS K. GANDHI (1869–1948), 1921

The State of Israel will be open to the immigration of Jews from all countries of their dispersion; will promote the development of the country for the benefit of all its inhabitants; will be based on the principles of liberty, justice, and peace as conceived by the Prophets of Israel; it will uphold the full social and political equality of all its citizens, without distinction of religion, race, or sex. . . .

—ISRAEL'S DECLARATION OF INDEPENDENCE, 1948

The use of force by powerful states—even when initially propelled by worthy objectives—naturally turns from a means to an end . . . Many conquerors . . . indeed provided the peoples they ruled with improved government and a higher culture . . . But history does not know of a single case where such "benign" conquest did not eventually turn to oppression and subjugation. Government by force—one which does not rest on the free will of the governed—assumes inevitably a logic of its own: maintaining government under such conditions is impossible without means of oppression, and the desire to maintain control eventually subordinates all other requirements.[30]

—DAVID BEN-GURION (1886–1973), 1964, ON THE BRITISH OCCUPATION OF PALESTINE DURING THE YEARS OF THE MANDATE, 1922–1948

There is something in the soul that cries out for freedom . . . Men cannot be satisfied with Egypt. They tried to adjust to it for a while . . . And eventually they rise up and begin to cry out for Canaan's land . . . Moses might not get to see Canaan, but his children will see it. He even got to the mountaintop enough to see it and that assured him that it was coming. But the beauty of the thing is that there's always a Joshua to take up his work and take the children on in. And it's there waiting with its milk and honey, and with all of the bountiful beauty that God has in store for His children.[31]

—MARTIN LUTHER KING JR. (1929–1968), 1957

Freedom is indivisible; the chains on any one of my people were the chains on all of them, the chains on all of my people were the chains on me . . . The oppressor must be liberated just as surely as the oppressed. A man who takes away my freedom is a prisoner of hatred. He is locked behind the bars of prejudice and narrow-mindedness. I am not free if I am taking away someone else's freedom, just as surely as I am not free when my freedom is taken away from me. The oppressed and the oppressor alike are robbed of their humanity.[32]

—NELSON MANDELA (1918–), 1994

JEWISH VALUES AND SOCIAL JUSTICE: AMERICAN JEWS IN THE ANTEBELLUM SOUTH

The Passover Seder ought to renew our dedication to the fight for social justice. But we know that does not always happen. Why? To probe this question, let's take a look back at the difficult question of Jewish support for slavery in the South before the Civil War. Read aloud what follows and discuss one or two of these questions:

- How do you feel about the fact that American Jews in the South participated in the institution of slavery?

- Can one generation judge another about what in hindsight appears to be its failure to speak out?

- What are the moral issues today about which Jews should protest more vigorously? What do you think is stopping us?

- How do you react to the two passages from the Talmud below?

Along with many passages from the prophets, the Talmud would seem to make it clear that when Jews witness social injustice, we belong on the barricades of protest.

Whoever is able to protest against the transgressions of his own family and does not do so is punished [liable, held responsible] for the transgressions of his family. Whoever is able to protest against the transgressions of the people of his community and does not do so is punished for the transgressions of his community. Whoever is able to protest against the transgressions of the entire world and does not do so is punished for the transgressions of the entire world.

—THE BABYLONIAN TALMUD, SHABBAT 54B

At the same time, the Talmud also lays down the principle of *dina demalkhuta dina,* "the law of the state is the law":[33]

Samuel [a Babylonian sage active from 220–250 C.E.] said: "The law of the state is the law." Said Rava [a Babylonian sage active about a century later]: "You can prove this from the fact that the authorities fell palm trees [without the consent of the owners] and construct bridges [with them] and we nevertheless make use of them by passing over them." [For if the rulings of the state were not binding by religious law, it would have been a sin to make use of the bridges constructed in such a way.]

—THE BABYLONIAN TALMUD, BABA KAMA 113B

Our tradition's call to justice and our history of oppression have inspired many Jews to fight for social justice. After the Second World War, American Jews played important roles in the civil rights movement. But in an earlier era, that of the Civil War for instance, few Jews opposed slavery. Jews in the South demonstrated attitudes toward slavery similar to those of their Christian neighbors. One of the pioneering studies—written by a Jewish historian—on Jewish involvement in slavery in the American South concludes: "Ante-bellum Southern Jews were more likely to quote the Talmudic maxim that 'the law of the land is the law [for Jews],' and to regard the institution of slavery as part of the law, which they were bound to uphold and follow, than they were to evaluate the failings of slavery in the light of the prophetic ethic."[34] American Jews in the South had generally risen to higher levels of social and economic status than their Northern brethren, because as whites they belonged to the dominant white "caste." In the South, blacks rather than Jews served as a ready target for prejudice. Notwithstanding how they benefited from it,

Jews nonetheless played a relatively minor role in the overall institution of slavery.[35]

SLAVERY IN OUR TIME

When you've finished reading the Four Questions at your Seder, ask a participant to read the following Fifth Question. Then either summarize or lead a short discussion on the information that follows. (Much of this has been taken from *Disposable People,* by Kevin Bales and The American Anti-Slavery Group's "Modern Day Slavery Fact Sheet.")[36]

- *A Fifth Question: Why is this night no different from all other nights?* Because on this night, millions of human beings around the world still remain enslaved, just as they do on all other nights. As we celebrate our freedom tonight, we remember those who remain enslaved.

Now either briefly summarize the information that follows or describe the four current forms of slavery and lead a discussion asking participants to define slavery, estimate how many slaves there are in the world today, define the factors that allow slavery to persist, etc.

- *Slavery, a definition:* The total control of one person by another for the purpose of economic exploitation. Slaves are controlled by violence and denied all of their personal freedom in order to make money or provide labor for someone else.

- *How many slaves are there today?* According to conservative estimates, 27 million, more than all the slaves shipped from Africa during the transatlantic slave trade.

Current forms of slavery:

- *Chattel slavery:* Closest form to the slavery practiced during the transatlantic slave trade. A person is captured, born, or sold into permanent servitude. Ownership is often asserted. Represents a small percentage of slaves. Practiced in northern and western Africa and some Arab countries.

- *Debt bondage:* The most common form of slavery. A person pledges him- or herself against a loan of money, but the length and nature of the service are not defined and the labor does not reduce the original debt. Ownership is not normally asserted, but there is complete physical control over the bonded laborer. Most common in India and Pakistan.

- *Contract slavery:* The most rapidly growing form of slavery. Contracts are offered that guarantee employment, perhaps in a workshop or factory, but when the workers are taken to their place of work they find themselves enslaved. Most often found in Southeast Asia, Brazil, some Arab states, and parts of the Indian subcontinent.

- *Sex slavery:* Girls are forced into prostitution by their own husbands, fathers, or brothers to earn money for the men in the family to pay back local money lenders. Others are lured by offers of good jobs and then beaten and forced to work in brothels. Most common in South Asia.

- *What kind of work do slaves do?* Simple, nontechnological, and traditional labor. Most slaves work in agriculture, but many also work in mining, quarrying, prostitution, and the manufacture of everything from charcoal and cloth to fireworks and chocolate.

- *Which factors allow slavery to persist?* The world's population explosion, which has produced a reservoir of poor and vulnerable people. The modernization of agriculture, which results in huge numbers of dispossessed farmers. Greed, corruption, and violence created by economic change in much of the developing world, and a breakdown of the social norms that protected potential slaves. Widespread ignorance about slavery. Generally, the kind of slavery most of us learned about in school was abolished in the nineteenth and early twentieth centuries. But we are unaware of the ways in which modern forms of slavery have evolved. Powerful nations often fear that taking a strong stand against slavery will jeopardize economic or military interests deemed to be more compelling national interests.

23

THREE THINGS YOU CAN DO TO HELP END SLAVERY

1. Learn more about slavery by contacting one of these organizations:

   The American Anti-Slavery Group
   198 Tremont Street #421, Boston, MA 02116
   (617) 426-8161 or www.anti-slavery.org

   Free the Slaves
   1326 14th Street NW, Washington, DC 20005
   (866) 324-FREE or www.freetheslaves.net

   Human Rights Watch
   350 Fifth Avenue 34th Floor, New York, NY 10118-3299
   (212) 216-1200 or www.hrw.org

2. Participate in ongoing social-action efforts to end slavery.

3. Encourage organizations with which you are involved to take a stand on the issue.

2

The Four "Questions": Who's Asking What and Why?

מַה נִּשְׁתַּנָּה הַלַּיְלָה הַזֶּה מִכָּל הַלֵּילוֹת?

Why is this night different from all other nights?
On all other nights we eat either leavened or unleavened bread.
On this night only unleavened bread.
On all other nights we eat all kinds of herbs. On this night only bitter herbs.
On all other nights we don't even dip once. On this night twice.
On all other nights we eat either sitting up or reclining. On this night we all recline.
—THE PASSOVER HAGGADAH

The Four Questions are doubtless among the most familiar and beloved elements of the Seder.[1] What could be more fitting for a child to ask than what makes the night of Passover different from all other nights?

But scratch the surface just a little and you'll find a tangle of questions of another sort. How many questions are there? Four, five, or one? Really just one! *Mah nishtanah ha-lailah ha-zeh mikol ha-leilot?* (Why is this night different from all other nights?) The Four Questions are actually four answers to that single query. Take a look at your Haggadah. Some Haggadot translate these as statements. Others take a bit of license with the Hebrew and make them into questions.

In Hebrew, the Four Questions are known as the *Arba Kushiot,* literally the "four difficulties." In rabbinic parlance, a *kushiya* refers to an observation of behavior or an idea that deviates from expectation and therefore poses a difficulty or challenge.[2]

As we'll see, the Four Questions provide an excellent window through which to take a brief look at the evolution of critical aspects of the Haggadah and the Passover Seder.

We begin with an activity for your Seder and follow that with a number of questions for discussion.

When you invite your guests to the Seder, ask a few families or individuals to bring along a question about Passover and a possible answer. If the questions are factual, in all probability they can be easily researched on the Internet. At an appropriate time during the Seder, your guests can present their questions, the group can discuss them, and then those who brought particular questions can share their answers.

ENGAGING CHILDREN DURING THE SEDER: AN ANCIENT LESSON

Read on your own.

Ancient sources stress the importance of the Seder as an educational opportunity for children and suggest introducing a bit of levity to the Seder in order to keep children involved. The Tosefta (Piskha 10:9), a law code from about the third century C.E., suggests that adults grab matzah from one another to astonish children so they won't fall asleep! The Talmud (Pesachim 109a) describes how Rabbi Akiva would distribute snacks of parched corn and nuts to children to help them stay awake.

Because matzah snatching and snacks during dinner were not regular dinner practices, these may also have been deliberate ways to provoke children to ask questions about why this night differed from others.

For instance, the Talmud (Pesachim 115b) relates a story about an old custom of suddenly removing the traylike tables before the meal had been eaten. When a child saw this and asked why, the Seder leader said, "You have exempted us from saying the *mah nishtanah!*" (A remnant of that custom survives today in some Ashkenazic Haggadot that instruct us to remove the Seder plate before the Four Questions.)

In ancient times, the goal was for children to ask their *own* questions. If for some reason the child did not or was unable to do so, the father would teach the child by asking and then answering a number of prescribed questions. The Mishnah (Pesachim 10:4) includes the oldest reference to questions—three questions, not four—during the Seder: "They mixed a second cup of wine [for the father] and here the son asks his father. And if the son has insufficient understanding his father instructs him. Why is this night different from all other nights? On all other nights we dip once, and on this night twice. . . ." And so on. Yes! Long ago, parents, not children, recited the *mah nishtanah*. "Why is this night different from all other nights" was the question the father posed if others had not already been asked.[3] That's why the Four Questions aren't really questions at all. They are answers to the father's rhetorical question about what distinguishes the night of Passover.

During the Middle Ages things began to change. An ambiguity in the Talmud's treatment of the questions led to different interpretations. Some scholars continued to teach that if a child asked spontaneous questions, there was no need to recite the Four Questions. Maimonides (1135–1204) instructed parents to engage in unusual behavior—matzah snatching, removing the tray that held the Seder plate before the meal, etc.—to provoke children to ask, "Why is this night different from all other nights?" But the father would still recite the *mah nishtanah*. In the thirteenth century, Ashkenazic rabbis concluded that *a young child* should ask the Four Questions. Parents should only do so if the child was unable to.[4]

Although reciting the Four Questions may have given children a special responsibility at the Seder, it also undermined the notion that the Seder should stimulate a child's spontaneous inquiry.

So what can we learn from the earliest designers of the Seder about how to engage children on the night of Passover? They hoped to create a Seder that would do at least three things, each of which relates to an important aspect of what's involved when a child asks a question. First, the elements of the Seder should involve activities that are sufficiently unusual or dramatic to evoke curiosity. Second, the Seder must be conducted with few enough distractions so a child can pay attention to what's happening. And third, the Seder must unfold in an atmosphere in which a child feels *free* to ask occasional questions even amidst a large group of adults. That's easier said than done! Just a few minutes after the Four Questions are asked, the Haggadah tells of four children who ask entirely different questions. A "wicked" child asks such a terrible question that he's told he deserves to have been left behind in Egypt!

Unless we create an atmosphere that welcomes *all* questions, the most important ones may never make it to the table. There's nothing wrong with reciting the beloved Four Questions. But we should remember that the designers of the Seder hoped to create an experience that would stimulate children's spontaneous questions. It's our job to create a lively Seder in which that kind of spontaneity can flourish.

QUESTIONS ABOUT QUESTIONS

- Ask the children at your Seder what they think makes the Seder night most different from other nights.

- Ask adults to share their memories of learning the Four Questions and how it felt to recite them at the Seder.

- What are the most important questions about Passover that you think should be discussed at the Seder?

- Soon after the Four Questions, three children ask three different kinds of questions and a fourth child "does not know how to ask." Why do questions play such an important role in the Seder?

- How would you compare these Four Questions to those asked by the Four Children?

THE GREEK SYMPOSIUM AND THE JEWISH SEDER

Depending on your group, read aloud or on your own.

Not long after the Four Questions, the Haggadah describes four kinds of children, three of whom also ask questions. Why are questions such an important component of the Seder? There are many reasons, but the most important one is that free people ask questions; slaves don't.

As with other elements of the Haggadah, the act of children asking their parents questions about their religious traditions fulfills an ancient biblical promise: "When, in time to come, your children ask you, 'What mean the decrees, laws, and rules that the Lord our God has enjoined upon you?' You shall say to your children, 'We were slaves to Pharaoh in Egypt . . .'" *"Avadim hayinu l'pharaoh b'mitzrayim . . ."* (Deut. 6:21). Those are the very words that follow the Four Questions.

In his commentary on the Haggadah, Abarbanel (1437–1508), the Spanish statesman and scholar, observed that these particular questions capture a certain paradox within the Seder. We simultaneously relive our enslavement and our redemption. Matzah represents both the bread of affliction and of liberation. Eating raw bitter herbs evokes the harshness of our suffering. By contrast, aristocrats dip hors d'oeuvres and recline during dinner.[5]

The Four Questions also embody the effort to adapt the Passover celebration to the loss of the Temple and the ability to perform the paschal sacrifice, the festival's central rite. Reliving the story of the Exodus and passing it down to the next generation in a lively, joyous atmosphere with questions and answers helped replace sacrifice.

The form, and to some extent even the content, of the post-Temple Passover celebration reflect what some might find a surprising influence: the Greek symposium, a structured banquet that featured a question-and-answer-style dialogue.

Typically, the symposium involved a small group of learned men who gathered to mark various occasions from birthdays to religious celebrations. The symposium began with a series of dipped hors d'oeuvres, served on small portable tables and eaten while reclining on benchlike couches. Discussion, interspersed with drinking wine, was wide ranging and touched on questions of philosophy, religion, and ancient history, and occasionally on the customs and peculiarities of various foods that had been served. Even secular symposia contained a religious component. In his *Symposium,* Plato describes a secular gathering: "Socrates took his place on the couch, and supped with the rest; and then libations were offered, and after a hymn had been sung to the god, and there had been the usual ceremonies, they were about to start drinking. . . ."[6] In Greek, *symposium* literally means "to drink with."

Plutarch (c. 45–120 C.E.), the Greek biographer, describes the interchange that followed the meal: "Even Plato did not prepare himself for the contest like a wrestler, that he may take the faster hold of his adversary . . . Questions should be easy, the problems known, the interrogations plain and familiar, not intricate and hard, so that they may neither vex the unlearned nor frighten them from disquisition . . . The discourse should be like our wine, common to all, of which everyone may equally partake."[7]

The symposium generally concluded with the inebriated guests carousing about town. To ensure that the Seder ended with appropriate dignity, the final Mishnah on Passover bans *afikomen,* often understood to mean "revelry."

Eventually, the symposium developed from an actual meal to a genre of literature structured around the dialogue accompanying a fictional meal. The Haggadah's description of the Seder of the five sages who "reclined" in B'nei B'rak seems to reflect a similar development, because it, too, was likely specially composed for the Haggadah.[8]

It's not clear whether women participated in Greek-style symposia. But we do know that the Rabbis believed women belonged at the Seder. The Tosefta (Pesachim 10:4), an ancient legal code, states that "a man is commanded to make his children and his wife happy on the holiday. With what does he make them happy? With wine. . . ." The Babylonian Talmud (Pesachim 116a) indicates that if a man's son cannot ask the questions, his wife should.

The sages who composed the earliest layers of the Haggadah worried deeply about what lay ahead for the Jewish people. To ensure a vital Jewish future, they were not afraid to borrow an approach from the broader culture with a proven track record of creating memorable evenings.

- How do you feel about the fact that the Seder reflects significant influences from Greek culture?

- What lessons can contemporary Jews learn from this example of cross-cultural influence?

WHY THESE PARTICULAR QUESTIONS?

Depending on your group, read aloud or on your own.

How these particular questions came to the Haggadah also remains a bit of a mystery.

The original three "questions" presented in the Mishnah (Pesachim 10:4) were compiled around 200 C.E. They are:

- On all other nights we dip *once.* On this night twice [i.e., once before the formal meal, and again during the meal when bitters are dipped in *charoset*].

- On all other nights we eat leavened or unleavened bread. On this night only unleavened bread.

- On all other nights we eat meat that is roasted, stewed, or boiled. On this night only roasted.

Because the Mishnah suggests that in ancient times the meal preceded the telling of the Passover story, these questions made sense. The child would have observed two rounds of dipping (first the common dipping of hors d'oeuvres and later the special dipping of mandated bitter herbs), matzah rather than bread, and roasted rather than stewed or boiled meat. These three questions correspond to Rabban Gamaliel's injunction (which we arrive at later in the Seder) to explain the meaning of three things eaten on the night of Passover during Temple times: the paschal offering, matzah, and bitter herbs.[9] Only the Mishnah's second question about matzah survived without modification.

The Mishnah's first question was changed in a subtle but revealing manner. Our current question about dipping derives from the observation of Rav Safra recorded in the Talmud (Pesachim 116a): "On all other nights we don't dip *even once;* on this night we dip twice." What had been a widespread custom of dipping hors d'oeuvres before dinner had apparently been forgotten. In earlier times, when the ways of the Greek symposium were still current, dipping a course of hors d'oeuvres—dipping once—was natural. Dipping again *during* the meal was noteworthy. The original question about dipping seems to have been divided in two, one focusing on the act of dipping and the other on the items dipped—that is, bitter herbs (nowadays often horseradish) dipped into *charoset.*

The question about how to cook meat on the night of Passover reflected the fact that in Israel (and apparently elsewhere) it remained customary to eat roasted meat at the Seder in memory of the Temple sacrifice. The yearning to eat roasted meat to recollect or substitute for the Passover sacrifice often proved irresistible. The Rabbis generally permitted this if the meat was not prepared exactly as it had been in Temple times—it could no longer be roasted whole on a metal spit or grill. But according to the Mishnah (Betzah 2:7), none other than Rabban Gamaliel himself, the leader of Jewish community between 80 and 110 C.E., ordered a whole young goat roasted on a grill for Passover!

This marks a transition in the development of the post-Temple Passover. The rituals designed to replace the paschal sacrifice had yet to become sufficiently meaningful in their own right. A more tangible link with the ancient sacrifice remained necessary.[10]

Some scholars believe that the custom of eating roasted meat on the night of Passover persisted until at least the late seventh century. In Palestine, this act was accompanied by a blessing praising God "who has commanded us to eat *matzah*, bitter herbs, and roasted meat to remember his great deeds. Blessed are You who remembers the covenant."[11] Our oldest extant Haggadah, a manuscript from the tenth or eleventh century, reflects the Palestinian rite and still includes this query.[12] By the twelfth century, Maimonides listed this question but added that it was no longer recited "for we do not have sacrifice" (*Laws of Chametz U'Matzah* 8:3).

Nowadays, roasted meat on the night of Passover is widely forbidden, lest one convey the impression of consuming the paschal sacrifice, an act that would only be permitted with the rebuilding of the Temple. What began as a common practice to evoke the memory of the Temple has now become a virtual taboo.

The fourth question, about why we recline on Passover, seems to have been added between the end of the Talmudic period (500–600 C.E.) and the ninth century. It derives from the opening Mishnah (10:1) about the night of Passover: "Even a poor person in Israel may not eat unless he reclines." The Haggadah tells us that the five sages who celebrated a Seder were "reclining in B'nei B'rak." Reclining had been a standard feature of the Greek symposium and the Mishnah envisioned its incorporation into the Passover meal even for those not accustomed to such luxury. But in Mishnaic times, reclining during festive meals had been so common that it hardly distinguished Passover. Only after the custom of reclining had lapsed did the Mishnah's instruction become the basis for a question distinguishing Passover from all other nights.

3

Two Haggadot in One:
The Haggadah's Early Development

עֲבָדִים הָיִינוּ לְפַרְעֹה בְּמִצְרָיִם.

וַיּוֹצִיאֵנוּ יְיָ אֱלֹהֵינוּ מִשָּׁם בְּיָד חֲזָקָה...

מִתְּחִלָּה עוֹבְדֵי עֲבוֹדָה זָרָה הָיוּ אֲבוֹתֵינוּ.

וְעַכְשָׁו קֵרְבָנוּ הַמָּקוֹם לַעֲבוֹדָתוֹ.

We were slaves to Pharaoh in Egypt and the Lord took us out from Egypt with a mighty hand (Deut. 6:20) . . . In the beginning our ancestors worshiped idols, but now, the Omnipresent has brought us close to His service.
—THE PASSOVER HAGGADAH

A few minutes after the Seder starts, many people begin to feel lost. We make Kiddush, wash our hands, dip parsley in saltwater, break the middle matzah and set part of it aside for the *afikomen*. We continue with the Four Questions and *avadim hayinu l'pharaoh b'mitzrayim* . . . "We were slaves to Pharaoh in Egypt." So far, so good. But soon the confusion begins. Four children ask four different questions followed by what seems to be a brief retrospective of patriarchal history from the Book of Joshua that begins with Abraham's idol-worshiping ancestors and ends with Jacob, Abraham's grandson, going down to Egypt.

33

Here we'll try to reduce some of the confusion with a story, *When Two Sages Disagree.* You can read it aloud to your guests before the Seder begins. It's written in fairly simple language and explains a bit about the Haggadah's early development. We follow that with a brief look at the passage from the Book of Joshua on page 39. We also include a brief art midrash project. You'll find questions for discussion throughout. As we'll see, the transition from "disgrace" to "praise" is a motif that recurs throughout the Haggadah. When you read portions of the Haggadah, ask your guests to point out every time they see an example of this transition.

WHEN TWO SAGES DISAGREE: A STORY ABOUT THE HAGGADAH'S EARLY DEVELOPMENT

Invite your guests to take turns reading this story about how the Haggadah developed.

Once, long, long ago—about eighteen hundred years ago—there lived a man named Judah the Prince. Judah lived in the north of Israel in a town called Tzippori, in a fancy stone house up on a hill. It was a very hard time for the Jewish people. About seventy years before Judah was born, the mighty Romans destroyed the great Temple of the Jews in Jerusalem. Near the time Judah was born, the Jewish people started a war against the Romans to try to throw them out of Israel. But the Romans won. They forced most of the Jews to leave the country. Jews moved to many different countries, near and far.

Some, like Judah's family, stayed in the hills, far from Jerusalem. Judah was called "the Prince" because he became the leader of the Jewish community that remained in Israel. He was one of the wisest rabbis in the country. Judah was afraid that without their Temple, without their country, and scattered around the world, the Jewish people would forget how to observe their traditions. He worried that they would not know how to celebrate Passover and would not remember its meanings.

The Jews *did* have their ancient Torah scrolls. But since the Torah had been written, all sorts of new traditions had grown up. For several centuries before Judah was born, great rabbis and teachers had had long conversations about what the Torah and all those new traditions meant. Besides, when it came to the holidays, the Torah mostly told you about how to celebrate them by making special sacrifices at the Temple. With the Temple then just a pile of smashed-up stones, what could Jews do to celebrate Passover?

The Rabbis who lived after the Temple's destruction finally decided that *talking* about what Passover meant—asking and trying to answer lots of questions about it—might work. Instead of sacrifices, words would have to do, and maybe they were better anyway.

So Judah decided to collect stories of the Rabbis' conversations about what they thought the Torah *really* meant and about how Jews could practice their religion without sacrifices in the Temple.

Some say Judah wrote all this down in a big book that he finished around the year 200 C.E. Others say Judah taught it to his students and they memorized his teachings. Judah's teachings were called the Mishnah, which means something like teaching and repeating. One part of Judah's teachings described the Passover Seder:

> They filled a second cup [of wine] . . . At this stage, the son questions his father; if the son is unintelligent, his father instructs him [to ask]: "Why is this night different from all [other] nights? On all other nights we dip *once*. On this night twice. On all other nights we eat leavened or unleavened bread. On this night only unleavened bread. On all other nights we eat meat that is roasted, stewed, or boiled. On this night only roasted." And according to the son's intelligence his father instructs him. He begins with disgrace [or shame] and concludes with praise; and expounds from "My father was a wandering Aramean. . . ."
> —MISHNAH, PESACHIM 10:4, CIRCA 200 C.E.

Collecting the Passover traditions turned out to be a great idea. On this Passover night, Jews all around the world are following many of the same customs that Judah described in the Mishnah about eighteen hundred years ago. Some of the details may have changed, but the Seder remains a night of questions. And we spend a long time discussing a section from the Bible (Deut. 26:5–8) that begins, "My father was a wandering Aramean."

One difference between Judah's Seder and ours is that tonight, most of us don't focus exclusively on fathers and sons at the Seder table. Mothers and daughters can do everything that fathers and sons do.

But, of course, just as people weren't always exactly sure what the Torah meant, discussions immediately began about what Judah's Mishnah meant. In fact, some people believe that Judah wrote the Mishnah in a style that would be sure to keep the conversations about Jewish tradition going for a long time.

So it was no surprise when Rav and Shmuel, two famous Rabbis active from about 220 to 250 C.E., often disagreed with one another about what the Mishnah meant. They lived in Babylonia, not far from what is now the city of Baghdad, the capital of Iraq. Rav visited Israel, and Judah the Prince became one of his teachers. He was called "Rav," which means "master," because he was among the greatest scholars who brought the teachings from the homeland to communities living outside of Israel. Rav earned a living by making beer; he wrote many prayers and built one of the greatest centers for Jewish learning of all time. Shmuel was a wealthy farmer, an astronomer, and a doctor. Once, he sent medicine to Judah that cured him of an eye infection. Shmuel also helped create the Jewish calendar.

Both Rav and Shmuel were great teachers and leading judges in the Jewish courts. Sometimes they studied together. The two sages respected one another even though they thought about Jewish laws and customs in very different ways. Not too long after Judah finished putting together the Mishnah, Rav and Shmuel disagreed about what Judah meant about the Seder when he wrote, "He begins with disgrace and concludes with praise." The Talmud, written down between 200 and 500 C.E., records their disagreement: "What is 'with disgrace?' Rav said: *'In the beginning our ancestors worshiped idols'*; while Shmuel said: *'We were slaves.'*"[1]

Rav thought that the most disgraceful thing for the Jewish people was that our ancestors believed that statues were gods. For Rav, the most important way to be free was to know that statues made out of stone or wood or metal did not control your life. Even after God had taken the Israelites out of Egypt with a mighty hand and an outstretched arm, they soon made a statue of a Golden Calf and started praying to it as if *it* were God. They were slaves to silly ideas.

But according to Shmuel, the disgrace was slavery itself. The wicked Pharaoh treated us as if we were more like machines or animals than people.

Shmuel thought that the worst thing we suffered was not to be treated like human beings created in the image of God, like real people, with feelings, fears, and hopes for a better life. To be free, we first had to escape from the tyrannical Pharaoh.

Later, the Rabbis who wrote down the Haggadah decided that Rav and Shmuel were both right. So, one part of the Haggadah describes the Israelites' experience when *"we were slaves,"* as Shmuel said. The other part reminds us that *"in the beginning our ancestors worshiped idols,"* as Rav believed.

If you remember that the Haggadah really includes two Haggadot in one, the Seder may not seem quite as confusing as it sometimes does! Each Rabbi's part of the Haggadah begins with a set of four questions that are followed by an explanation.

Shmuel's version of the Haggadah begins with the famous Four Questions. These questions all refer to elements of the Seder connected with physical enslavement. As an answer, the Haggadah says, *Avadim hayinu . . .* *"We were slaves to Pharaoh in Egypt, and the Lord our God brought us forth from there with a mighty hand and an outstretched arm. . . ."*

Rav's version comes next. It begins with the Four Children, who ask questions about why the Passover traditions should be important to us, so long after our ancestors left Egypt. Rav's answer begins, *"In the beginning our ancestors worshiped idols, but now the Omnipresent has brought us to God's service."* Rav tells us about our ancestors' spiritual journey from believing in idols to feeling that they had a relationship with the true God.

Tonight, we continue to celebrate Passover in the spirit of Judah the Prince, Rav, and Shmuel. We keep the conversation going about what the Exodus from Egypt means to our people and to each one of us. We try to reexperience the pain of slavery so we never take freedom for granted. We remember when we were down so we can help others up. We struggle to free ourselves from the false gods that bit by bit enslave us and lead us to forget our most important dreams. And we keep asking questions.

- Shmuel's part of the Haggadah (about redemption from slavery) comes before Rav's (about evolving beyond idolatry). Why do you think Shmuel's comes first and Rav's comes second?

- According to the Babylonian Talmud, "The law is in accordance with the opinions of Rav in ritual matters and of Shmuel in civil matters" (Bekhorot, 49b). Their views on the world to come further distinguish these two sages. Rav: "In the future world there is no eating nor drinking, no procreation nor business, no jealousy nor hatred nor competition, but *the righteous sit with crowns on their heads and delight in the radiance of the Shekhinah*" (Berachot 17a). (The italicized words appear in many Ashkenazic Haggadot in the Grace after the Seder meal.)[2] Shmuel: "The only difference between this world and the days of the Messiah is political oppression [in messianic days oppression will cease]" (Berachot 34b). What light do these statements shed on Rav and Shmuel's interpretation of "disgrace"?

• Judah's Mishnah includes a statement by Rabbi Elazar ben Azariah, one of the sages mentioned in the Haggadah, that at first might sound strange: "Where there is no flour, there is no Torah. Where there is no Torah, there is no flour" (Mishnah, Avot 3:21). How does this relate to Rav and Shmuel's opinions about the Seder?

Although the Haggadah may often seem confusing, there's one theme that recurs in many, many variations throughout: what the Mishnah called the transition from shame or disgrace to praise. As we've seen, the Mishnah (Pesachim 10:4, c. 200 C.E.) says: "And according to the son's intelligence his father instructs him. He begins with disgrace (*g'nut*) and ends with praise (*shevach*)."

• What might "disgrace" or "shame" mean? What about "praise"?

• What do you think this transition might represent and why is it so central to the Haggadah?

• Why do you think we end with "praise" rather than "joy"?

ART MIDRASH: "BEGIN WITH DISGRACE AND END WITH PRAISE"

Create an art midrash project based on the Mishnah's instructions that, when telling the story of the Exodus at the Seder, you should "begin with disgrace and end with praise."

Explain that the Mishnah is a collection of teachings and laws compiled about eighteen hundred years ago. It contains the oldest directions for a Passover Seder as we have come to know it. Also mention that the transition from disgrace to praise recurs throughout the Haggadah. Ask each of your guests to make a collage that illustrates his or her feelings and ideas about beginning with disgrace and ending with praise. See Appendix III (page 326) for general directions for art midrash projects.

CROSSING RIVERS AND TAKING RESPONSIBILITY

Now let's take a look at how the Haggagah elaborates upon Rav's interpretation of disgrace. We'll focus on the theme of taking responsibility as it relates to Passover and the imagery of crossing from one side of the river to the other. Although crossing the Red Sea certainly represents the Bible's paradigmatic story of rebirth, other less well-known tales of crossing through waters also teach important lessons about the meaning of Passover. Take turns reading the following selections. Then discuss the accompanying questions.

In the beginning our ancestors worshiped idols, but now the Omnipresent has drawn us close to His service, as it is written, "And Joshua said to all the people, 'Thus said the Lord God of Israel: Your fathers lived on the other side of the river in olden times, Terah, the father of Abraham, and the father of Nahor; and they served other gods. And I took your father Abraham from the other side of the river, and led him throughout all the land of Canaan, and multiplied his seed, and gave him Isaac. And I gave to Isaac Jacob and Esau; and I gave to Esau Mount Seir, to possess it; but Jacob and his children went down to Egypt'" (Joshua 24:2–4).[3]

—THE PASSOVER HAGGADAH

This is the beginning of the Haggadah's answer to the questions posed by the Four Children about Passover's meaning. It begins with Rav's words and concludes with Joshua's farewell speech to the Israelites just before his death, years after they had conquered the Promised Land. (Joshua was Moses' successor.) The text is well chosen. Near the beginning of the Book of Joshua, the Israelites crossed over the Jordan into the land of Canaan:

When the people set out from their encampment to cross the Jordan, the priests bearing the Ark of the Covenant were at the head of the people. Now the Jordan keeps flowing over its entire bed throughout the harvest season. But as soon as the bearers of the Ark reached the Jordan, and the feet of the priests bearing the Ark dipped into the water at its edge, the waters coming down from upstream piled up in a single heap a great way off . . . all Israel crossed over on dry land, until the entire nation had finished crossing the Jordan.

—JOSHUA 3:14–17

- The Bible first uses the term "Hebrew" (*ivri*) to identify Abraham. Five evil kings were on the warpath and they captured Lot, Abraham's nephew. Someone escaped and warned "Abraham the Hebrew" (Gen. 14:13). Abraham's army immediately set out, defeated the kings, and rescued Lot. What was Abraham doing when he learned of Lot's capture? According to the midrash, which imagined that the patriarchs fulfilled all the precepts of the Torah even before the revelation at Sinai, Abraham was baking cakes of unleavened bread to celebrate Passover. Next, the midrash explains that "Hebrew" derives from the word *ever* and means "the one who came from the other side of the river" and that *ha-ivri,* "the Hebrew," signifies that "the whole world was on one side while he [Abraham] was on the other side."[4]

- What are some of the different meanings suggested by "crossing over" and why is it stressed in the above texts? How do these relate to the notion of moral or spiritual development?

- How does the theme of "crossing over" relate to Passover?

Immediately after crossing the Jordan into the Promised Land, Joshua oversees the reinstitution of the Passover celebration. This had apparently lapsed during the years in the desert.

Encamped at Gilgal, in the steppes of Jericho, the Israelites offered the Passover sacrifice on the fourteenth day of the month toward evening. On the day after the Passover offering, on that very day, they ate of the produce of the country, unleavened bread and parched grain. On that same day, when they ate of the produce of the land, the manna ceased. The Israelites got no more manna; that year they ate of the yield of the land of Canaan.

—JOSHUA 5:10–12 (READ IN SYNAGOGUE ON THE FIRST DAY OF PASSOVER)

• How do you interpret the fact that the celebration of Passover lapsed within a few years after the Israelites left Egypt?

• Why was it important to renew the celebration of Passover when the Israelites entered the Promised Land?

• How does Joshua 5:10–12 let you know that there are important relationships among the renewal of Passover, entering the Promised Land, the cessation of manna, and eating the "yield of the land"? What do these relationships mean? What might this text be trying to teach us by making such an explicit connection between entering the Promised Land, and assuming new responsibilities, on both the spiritual and the material levels? What are the implications of this text for contemporary Israel?

4

The Five Sages' Seder: Who Were They and What Kept Them So Late?

מַעֲשֶׂה בְּרַבִּי אֱלִיעֶזֶר וְרַבִּי יְהוֹשֻׁעַ
וְרַבִּי אֶלְעָזָר בֶּן־עֲזַרְיָה וְרַבִּי עֲקִיבָא וְרַבִּי טַרְפוֹן
שֶׁהָיוּ מְסֻבִּין בִּבְנֵי־בְרַק...

A tale is told about Rabbi Eliezer, Rabbi Joshua, Rabbi Elazar ben Azariah,
Rabbi Akiva, and Rabbi Tarfon. They were reclining in B'nei B'rak, discussing the
Exodus from Egypt all through the night, until their students came to them and said,
"Masters, the time has come to recite the morning Sh'ma."
—THE PASSOVER HAGGADAH

Read the paragraph above from the Haggadah and then take turns reading
aloud the story beginning on page 44 that is based on the Talmud and the Midrash.
The story will give you a feeling for the period during which key elements of the Seder
evolved and the way our tradition remembers some of the individuals who helped
shape Judaism's development after the destruction of the Second Temple in 70 C.E.
The story also includes a wrenching conflict among the sages that led to the banning
of Rabbi Eliezer from the community. Discuss the questions that follow.

Note: This will make an excellent pre-Seder activity and is best suited for older children and adults. If you have young children at your Seder, you may want to consider inviting them to a reading of *The Last Night in Egypt* in a separate room (see page 216) while others read and discuss this section.

FIVE SUPER-SAGES: THEIR TIMES AND TEACHINGS

About nineteen hundred years ago, during some of the Jewish people's darkest days, there lived five very famous Rabbis—Eliezer, Joshua, Elazar ben Azariah, Tarfon, and Akiva.

For as long as he could remember, Eliezer had dreamed of studying with the most famous Rabbi of the time, Yochanan ben Zakkai. But his father, a wealthy farmer, insisted that he work the land and enjoy a simple, comfortable life. When he was twenty-eight years old, Eliezer ran away to Jerusalem. Nearly starving, he found Yochanan and explained his dream of studying with the great master. Yochanan took pity on Eliezer and was soon impressed by how fast he learned.

Eliezer too became a great teacher. Yochanan said, "If all the sages of Israel were on one pan of a balance scale, and Eliezer were on the other, he would out-weigh them all."[1] Eliezer used to say: "Let the honor of your fellow man be as precious to you as your own. Do not be quick to anger, and repent one day before your death." His students asked, "But does a person know the day of his death?" Eliezer answered, "Let him then repent today for perhaps he will die tomorrow."[2]

Eliezer taught that three things could annul God's decrees—prayer, charity, and repentance, *tefillah, tzedakah, u-teshuvah*.[3] (Eliezer's words inspired the *Unetaneh Tokef* prayer recited during Rosh Hashanah and Yom Kippur.)

Rabbi Joshua was another of Yochanan ben Zakkai's most important disciples. His teacher compared him to a "threefold cord that cannot be easily broken" (Eccl. 4:12).[4] Despite a great knowledge of science and mathematics, Joshua lived a life of poverty and earned his living as a blacksmith making needles.

These were the days when Israel was controlled by the mighty Roman empire. Rome collected heavy taxes, and most Jews were very poor. The Jews wanted to be free. Some thought that just as they had escaped from Egypt, and as the Maccabees had defeated the Greeks, so too could they win a war against Rome. Others believed such a war would be foolish. Hoping for a miracle, a group of zealots attacked the Romans in the year 66 C.E. Four years later, the Romans had almost won and demanded the surrender of Jerusalem. If the fighting continued, the Romans threatened to burn the city and destroy the great Jewish Temple.

Yochanan ben Zakkai opposed the war and pleaded with the zealots to make peace with Rome. But the zealots only fought harder, declared the Rabbi a traitor, and continued killing Jews who called for peace.

Yochanan realized that if the Jews lost both their Temple in Jerusalem and all the city's great teachers, Judaism might not survive. He decided to escape and arranged for two of his disciples to smuggle him out of Jerusalem in a coffin. Eliezer carried him by the head and Joshua carried him by the feet.

When they had left Jerusalem, Joshua turned to look back at the Temple's ruins and cried to his teacher, "Woe unto us, that this, the place where the sins of Israel were atoned for, is laid waste." Yochanan said to him, "Do not grieve. We have another source of atonement as effective as this. And what is it? Acts of loving-kindness, as it is said, 'For I desire goodness, not sacrifice'" (Hosea 6:6).[5] Prayer, study, and the observance of Jewish law would also help take the place of the destroyed Temple.

The Temple was gone, but Rabbi Yochanan and his students kept Jewish tradition alive by founding a center for Jewish learning at Yavne (today a small town not far from Tel Aviv). Yavne attracted the most brilliant scholars, including Elazar ben Azariah. He came from a wealthy family and traced his lineage back almost five hundred years to Ezra, who had led the Jewish people back to Jerusalem after the Babylonian exile. At the age of eighteen, Elazar ben Azariah became the head of the Sanhedrin, the highest court in the land. Whether from anxiety about his new responsibilities or to help him look more suitable for the job, his hair turned white overnight. In the morning he said, "I am like a man of seventy."[6] (We read those very words in the Haggadah itself.)

Rabbi Tarfon also taught at Yavne. His mother, while out walking, once lost her shoe. Tarfon placed his hand under her bare foot so she would not hurt it while she walked home. Rather than benefit from his fame as a teacher, Tarfon traveled in disguise. Once he had to reveal his identity when a watchman beat him for taking grapes from his own vineyard! Rabbi Tarfon used to say, "You are not required to complete the task, but neither are you free to avoid starting it."[7]

Elazar ben Azariah used to say that a court that executes a person once in seventy years is a cruel court. Tarfon and Akiva said that if *they* had been members of the court, it never would execute anyone![8]

Eliezer, Joshua, and Tarfon taught many students, but Akiva became their most important disciple. Akiva worked as a shepherd for a wealthy farmer until he was forty, and he fell in love with Rachel, his boss's daughter. They married against her father's will, but Rachel insisted that the ignorant shepherd had promised to study at Yavne. Years of study kept him away from Rachel, but he finally returned—a great scholar followed by droves of students.

Akiva developed a new way of interpreting the Torah. He discovered meaning in every word. He also began to write down many of the oral traditions that had grown up over the centuries. Akiva used to say, "'Love your neighbor as yourself' is the Torah's fundamental principle" and "He who sheds blood is regarded as though he had impaired the Divine image . . . What is the reason? *'For in His image did God make man'*" (Gen. 1:27).[9]

Once Tarfon and Akiva argued before a group of sages about which was more important, study or religious observance. Tarfon said, "Observance is more important." Akiva answered, "Study is more important." The sages all agreed that study is more important because it leads to observance.[10]

Some years later, the Romans once again began to oppress the Jews in Israel. They tried to put an end to Judaism by preventing Rabbis from teaching and by banning circumcision and the observance of Shabbat. A Jewish general named Bar Kochba led another unsuccessful revolt against Rome (132–135 C.E.). Rabbi Akiva, the greatest sage of his time, refused to stop teaching and threw his support behind Bar Kochba, declaring him to be the Messiah. Other Rabbis opposed the rebellion.

Akiva was tortured and died with the *Sh'ma* on his lips. The angels asked God, "Is this the reward for studying Torah?" A Heavenly Voice declared, "Blessed are you, Rabbi Akiva, for you are destined for life in the World to Come."[11] According to legend, Elijah the Prophet carried his body for burial.

BANNING RABBI ELIEZER

The Talmud (Baba Metzia 59b) tells the story about one dispute between Eliezer and his colleagues, which led to banning him from the community. That meant that his rulings could not be taught and that except for business dealings, only his family could spend time with him. It seems that Eliezer, himself a judge in an important court, was unwilling to follow the ruling of a higher court. He also believed that human reasoning alone could not be the basis for legal decisions.

Once Rabbi Eliezer tried to prove that a particular oven was kosher or clean. He tried every imaginable argument, but everyone still disagreed. So he said, "If halakhah [Jewish law] agrees with me, let this carob tree prove it." And the tree was torn from its roots and moved twenty-five feet. "No proof can come from a tree," they argued. "If the halakhah agrees with me, let this stream of water prove it," Eliezer said. And the stream of water flowed backwards. "No proof," they said, "can come from a stream of water." Then Eliezer said, "If the halakhah agrees with me, let the walls of this building prove it." And the walls leaned in toward each other and almost collapsed. But Joshua scolded the walls, saying: "When scholars are engaged in a halakhic dispute, why are you interfering?" Hence the walls did not fall, in honor of Joshua, nor did they become upright in honor of Eliezer. And they are still leaning that way.

Then a heavenly voice cried out, "Why do you argue with Rabbi Eliezer, since in all matters the halakhah agrees with him!" But Rabbi Joshua arose and quoted the Torah [Deut. 30:12]: "[The Torah] is not in the heavens." What did he mean by this? That the Torah had been given at Mount Sinai. So now we pay no attention to a heavenly voice because the Torah itself says, *"One must follow the majority"* [Ex. 23:2].

Later, a rabbi met Elijah the Prophet and asked him: "What did the Holy One, Blessed be He, do in that hour?"—"He laughed [with joy]," Elijah replied, saying, "My children have defeated Me, My children have defeated Me" [since they showed such a commitment to their own creative thinking].

After they voted to ban Eliezer, Rabbi Akiva dressed in black mourning garments to bring his friend and teacher the news. "Master, it appears to me that your companions have distanced themselves from you." Then Eliezer too rent his garments, took off his shoes, got up from his chair, and sat on the earth, while tears streamed from his eyes.

The story has a perplexing conclusion. After the ban on Eliezer, "the world was then smitten: a third of the olive crop, a third of the wheat, and a third of the barley crop [withered and died]. . . ." Rabban Gamaliel, also of Seder fame, is generally thought to have initiated the action against Eliezer, his brother-in-law.

Gamaliel was traveling in a ship, when a huge wave arose to drown him. "It appears to me," he reflected, "that this is on account of none other than Rabbi Eliezer." He arose and exclaimed, "Sovereign of the Universe! You know full well that I have not acted for my honor, nor for the honor of my paternal house, but for Yours, so that strife may not multiply in Israel!" At that, the raging sea subsided.

Many years later, when Eliezer was near death, Akiva, Joshua, Elazar ben Azariah, and Tarfon went to visit him. Because of the ban they didn't enter his room. His friends praised him greatly, but Eliezer was angry that they had neither visited nor studied with him for so many years. Finally, the Rabbis asked his opinion about whether a certain item was kosher, clean or unclean. Eliezer's last word was "clean," which convinced Rabbi Joshua that Eliezer himself was "clean" and that the ban should finally be lifted.[12] Aside from their famous Seder in B'nei B'rak, this is the only story in rabbinic literature in which all five sages appear together.

Depending on your group, you might consider assigning people to play the roles of Rabbi Joshua, Rabbi Eliezer, and God. The rest of your participants can play the role of the Sanhedrin, the court, and render a verdict. Encourage your "actors" to think freely in framing their arguments to convict or exonerate Rabbi Eliezer.

- Rabbi Joshua and Rabbi Eliezer disagreed over the ultimate source of religious authority—the "objective," direct word of God versus human interpretation of divinely inspired religious law. Which side would you take and why?

- Note, Rabbi Eliezer's punishment (niddui) required expulsion from the community except for purposes of business. Otherwise, his social contact was limited to his family. Beyond family, no one could greet him, eat or drink with him, or bring him any enjoyment.[13] Neither was he counted in a prayer *minyan*. Does the punishment fit the crime? Why or why not?

- How would you describe God's reaction during this dispute? Whose side does God seem to take?

- What parallels do you see between the political situation in the time of these Rabbis and Israel's situation today?

- Aside from the Haggadah, the story of the five Rabbis' Seder occurs in no other Jewish sources. Why do you think the compilers of the Haggadah created or included it?

Many interpret the five Rabbis' Seder as the meeting at which they decided to support the Bar Kochba rebellion (132–135 C.E.). It is said that they didn't realize the time had come to say the morning *Sh'ma* because the Rabbis were hiding from the Romans in a dark cave. This is unlikely, because Joshua and Eliezer died before the revolt and the ban on Eliezer would likely have excluded him from such a Seder.

Perhaps the authors of the Haggadah wanted to teach us a subtle but important lesson by fashioning a story that would reunite the five Rabbis at the Seder year after year. The compilers of the Haggadah created a scene of harmony to repair the fractured relationships among the sages, particularly between Joshua and Eliezer.

Remember, these were the two disciples of Yochanan ben Zakkai who had conspired to smuggle their master to safety outside of Jerusalem as he feigned death in a coffin. Eliezer carried the head, Joshua the feet. The compilers of the Haggadah created a text that will eternally bring Eliezer and Joshua to the same Seder table. The message is that peace and fraternity are ultimately more important than ideology or winning an argument. The Haggadah underscores the point through its placement of this passage. The story of the five sages has been sandwiched between the Four Questions and the questions asked by the wise, the wicked, and the simple children.

The Seder is a night when *all* questions are welcome. The Seder is a time for renewing sundered relationships and interrupted dialogue over the toughest questions. Even the skeptical "wicked" child and the banned Rabbi Eliezer participate in the Seder. The Seder is a table from which *none* should feel excluded.

THE SEDER IN B'NEI B'RAK: RECONSTRUCTING THE CONVERSATION

The Haggadah alludes briefly to the tale of a Seder in B'nei B'rak attended by five sages who lived during the first and second centuries C.E. Alas, aside from describing the depth of their absorption, the Haggadah tells us nothing about their conversation. This story was probably created especially for the Haggadah, because it is not mentioned elsewhere in rabbinic literature. In that spirit, I've reconstructed a midrashic version of some of that evening's discussion, beginning on page 52. The conversation includes passages from rabbinic literature (compiled between the third and thirteenth centuries) actually attributed to these sages. The wives of two sages and two students participate as well!

I've tried to maintain the often spare style of rabbinic discourse. Ancient rabbinic literature preserves a few statements of Rachel and Imma Shalom, the respective wives of Akiva and Eliezer. Some of the Rabbis opposed teaching women Torah, while a more moderate view held that "a man is under the obligation to teach his daughter Torah" (Mishnah, Sotah 3:4). Regrettably, in rabbinic times women would have played a more limited role in such a conversation. However, the Talmud does indicate that if a son is unable to ask the Four Questions, a wife should ask them of her husband (Babylonian Talmud, Pesachim 116a).

A few words of context introduce the conversation in B'nei B'rak. Depending on your group, you may want to read this aloud, summarize it, or omit it entirely. Before your Seder formally begins, you can read the entire B'nei B'rak conversation aloud and discuss the questions below. Or, depending on your group's interests and attention span, you might select one or two passages from it for discussion during the Seder itself.

As depicted in the Haggadah, God directs human history, redeeming the oppressed and punishing the wicked. Although our concepts of God may have evolved, typically this is the God we first learned about and for whom, on some level, we understandably still yearn. Who has not felt a pang of longing for a just, interventionist God, a wave of anger because the interventionist God's face remains so deeply hidden precisely when evil roams so brazenly about? Yet, the very name "Israel" means "to wrestle with God," so tension between the people of Israel and God is hardly new: We simply feel it more acutely in times of darkness and loss.

In recent times, many of us have enjoyed the luxury of looking back on Egypt from the vantage point of ever-expanding freedom. But in America after September 11, and in Israel since the second *intifada*, "freedom from fear" has palpably diminished. The plague of terrorism, with all its manifold consequences, has struck both nations with devastating ferocity. And so, on the night of Passover, we wrestle with difficult questions. Why do the innocent suffer? And why would a just, all-powerful God allow evil in the world?

Our current situation provides but a pale shadow of what the sages experienced. Indeed, they lived through one of the Jewish people's bleakest periods. Two failed rebellions (66–70 C.E. and 132–135 C.E.) against Rome's oppressive rule proved disastrous. More than a million Jews were killed, the Temple lay in ruins, most survivors were exiled, and many of Judaism's foremost sages were savagely martyred.

The sages who shaped the oldest portions of the Haggadah used the saga of the Exodus to express their own search for hope amidst oppression. As much as the Seder celebrated the liberation from Pharaoh, it was also a plea for God to return once more to the stage of history with signs, wonders, and a mighty hand to execute judgment upon Israel's enemies. When the sages said, *"Now we are slaves, next year we will be free,"* they meant it—almost literally. In dark times, the Haggadah stands as a beacon of faith that evil, no matter how deeply entrenched, shall be overcome.

Despite their travails, the sages were unwilling to renounce their faith in a just, omnipotent God who would respond to their cries. But many had trouble accepting the common biblical explanation that affliction necessarily reflected God's punishment for sin. Instead, they developed the concept that agony in *this* life would ensure reward in the next, where the righteous and the sinful would ultimately get their just desserts. And at least some of the sages and their students continued the ancient tradition of arguing with God, which they had inherited from the likes of Abraham and Moses.

Read the following aloud or choose one or two passages to read aloud and discuss.

(Note: Passages in bold represent quotations from rabbinic literature, many of which are attributed to these particular sages.)[14]

> A tale is told about Rabbi Eliezer, Rabbi Joshua, Rabbi Elazar ben Azariah, Rabbi Akiva, and Rabbi Tarfon. They were reclining in B'nei B'rak, discussing the Exodus from Egypt all through the night, until their students came to them and said, "Masters, the time has come to recite the morning Sh'ma."
>
> —THE PASSOVER HAGGADAH

Rabbi Akiva began. **"Israel was redeemed from Egypt because of the righteousness of the women of that generation.** [Despite grave dangers, women smuggled food to their husbands, who were oppressed under hard labor, and they insisted on bearing children.] **When God revealed Himself at the Red Sea, they were the first to recognize Him, as it is said, 'This is my God and I shall enshrine Him'"** (Ex. 15:2).

Rachel, Akiva's wife, answered, "Does the righteousness of this generation of our women not merit redemption from the heel of Rome? As it is written, '*Why, O Lord, do You stand aloof, heedless in times of trouble?*' (Psalms 10:1). '*The earth is handed over to the wicked one; He covers the eyes of its judges. If it is not He, then who?*'" (Job 9:24).

Rabbi Eliezer lamented: **"O God, heathens have entered your domain (Psalms 79:1). He applied the verse to the Emperor Trajan, who came and seized Alexandria** [in Egypt, 117 C.E.] **in which there were one hundred and twenty thousand Jews, and he butchered them until not one was left alive; as Scripture says, 'Their blood was shed like water . . .'"** (Psalms 79:3).

"*The Lord will take Judah to Himself as His portion in the Holy Land,*" Akiva said, "*and He will choose Jerusalem once more*" (Zechariah 2:16). **Akiva continued,**

"The Rabbis say, 'From the way I gave the children of Israel food in the wilderness, food sweeter than milk and honey, you may know what I shall do for them subsequently, as it says, *And in that day the mountains shall drip with wine*'" (Joel 4:18). "Now we are slaves. Next year we will be free" (the Passover Haggadah).

"Since the day that the Temple was destroyed [in 70 C.E.] there has been no day without its curse, the dew has not fallen to the good of the crops, and the fruit has lost its taste." So said Rabbi Joshua.

Imma Shalom, the sister of Rabban Gamaliel and wife of Rabbi Eliezer, spoke next. "It is written that *'The Lord stiffened the heart of Pharaoh'* (Ex. 9:12). Scripture says, *'I am the Lord, and there is no one else. I form the light and create darkness; I make peace and create evil; I the Lord do all these things'* (Isaiah 45:6–7). Is the Lord also stiffening Rome's heart? Is God using Rome to punish us? Has Rome any more choice in its actions than did Pharaoh?"

"Come and listen," said Akiva. "Suffering is precious. Still, Rome will be judged for its actions. We are all responsible for our actions. Everything is foreseen but the right [of choice] is granted, and the world is judged with goodness, and everything is in accordance with the preponderance of [humanity's] deed[s]."

"But how long will that Judge sleep?" asked Rachel. "As it says, *'It is for Your sake that we are slain all day long, that we are regarded as sheep to be slaughtered. Rouse Yourself; why do You sleep, O Lord? Awaken, do not reject us forever! Why do You hide Your face, ignoring our affliction and distress? . . . Arise and help us, redeem us, as befits Your faithfulness'*" (Psalms 44:23–27).

Rabbi Eliezer explained, "Because God loves the righteous, he chastises them in this world, as it is said, *'But He who loves him disciplines him early'*" (Proverbs 13:24). He said further, "Because God loves Israel, He disciplines them by handing them over to enslavement by the kingdoms in this world [Assyria, Babylonia, Greece, and Rome], so that they will thereby achieve atonement for their sins in the coming future."

Rabbi Tarfon said, "The day is short and the work is great . . . You are not required to complete this task, but neither are you free to avoid starting it. If you have studied much Torah, your reward will be abundant.

Your employer [God] **can be relied upon to reward you for your labors. Know, however, that the reward of the righteous is in the time to come."**

"But does not God punish the wicked in this world?" **argued Rabbi Elazar ben Azariah. He said, "The entire Torah is based on justice. God purposely gave the laws after having given the Ten Commandments to teach the world that He punishes those who transgress the laws.** As it is written, *'God of Israel, bestir Yourself to bring all nations to account'"* (Psalms 59:6).

One of the students who had been listening carefully to the discussion spoke up. "Masters," he said, "a student from one of the other houses of study related a teaching he had learned. When Moses first asked Pharaoh to let the Israelites go, Pharaoh made them work even harder. He refused to give them straw to make bricks. It is written, **'Then Moses returned to the Lord, and said: *O Lord, why did you bring harm upon this people? Why did You send me? Ever since I came to Pharaoh to speak in Your name, he has dealt worse with this people; and still You have not delivered Your people'* (Ex. 5:22–23). It was then that Moses exchanged words with God, by asking Him: *'Why did you bring harm?'* Usually, when one man asks another that question, he is angry with him. And yet Moses said to God: *'Why did you bring harm upon this people?'* . . . This people, what has it done to be more enslaved than all the preceding generations?"**

Rabbi Akiva then said something astounding. **He asked, "What is the meaning of** [the phrase we have just heard] *'and still You have not delivered Your people?'"* (Ex. 5:23). **"This,"** he explained, **"is how Moses argued: 'I know that one day You will deliver the people, but what about those who have been buried in the buildings** [while engaged in Pharaoh's construction projects]?'"

Another student recited a teaching that he had heard. **"Master of the Universe! . . . What wonders You performed in bringing them forth out of Egypt and dividing the sea for them! . . . You did it for them, but not for us. How does what You did for our ancestors benefit us?"**

The darkness had grown so thick that **Rabbi Joshua's** thoughts drifted to the Messiah. **He said, "Elijah will not come to judge between those who are ritually clean or unclean, but to remove those who have come to power through force and to bring near those who have been cast away**

by force . . . The sages say neither to remove nor to bring near, but to make peace in the world. For it is said, '*Lo, I will send to you Elijah the Prophet before the coming of the awesome, fearful day of the Lord. And he shall turn the heart of the parents to the children and the hearts of the children to their parents . . .*'" (Malachi 3:23–34).

The night had passed and their students came to them and said, **"*Masters, the time has come to recite the morning* Sh'ma"** (the Passover Haggadah).

- What questions does this conversation raise in light of recent events?

- Which statements or questions come closest to your own beliefs?

- Which ones do you find most disturbing or furthest from your views?

- How do you reconcile the image of God portrayed in the Haggadah with the historical suffering of the Jewish people and the travails of other peoples?

5

The Four Children:
A Seat at the Table for Everyone

בָּרוּךְ הַמָּקוֹם. בָּרוּךְ הוּא.
בָּרוּךְ שֶׁנָתַן תּוֹרָה לְעַמוֹ יִשְׂרָאֵל. בָּרוּךְ הוּא.
כְּנֶגֶד אַרְבָּעָה בָנִים דִּבְּרָה תוֹרָה.
אֶחָד חָכָם, וְאֶחָד רָשָׁע, וְאֶחָד תָּם,
וְאֶחָד שֶׁאֵינוֹ יוֹדֵעַ לִשְׁאוֹל:

Blessed be the Omnipresent. Blessed be He. Blessed be He
who gave the Torah to His people Israel. Blessed be He.
The Torah alludes to four children: One wise, one wicked,
one simple, and one who does not know how to ask.
—THE PASSOVER HAGGADAH

This is one of the passages of the Haggadah that contemporary interpreters have labored hard to make more attractive. The problem is, of course, the notion of "wicked" children and the pointed comparison between the "wise" and the "wicked."

The passage follows two short sections in the Haggadah: the Seder of the sages who discussed the Exodus all night long, and a rabbinic question about whether or not one should include a reference to the Exodus in the evening prayers. Then we come to the Four Children. It's as if these children had been sitting quietly at the sages' Seder and now pipe up with their reactions. These children amplify the motif of asking questions, but here their inquiries focus not on tangible symbols, as did the Four Questions, but on deeper issues of content, meaning, and their own relationship to Jewish tradition.

THE FOUR CHILDREN

Turn to your Haggadot and ask your guests to read the passage about the
Four Children aloud and discuss the following questions. I'd suggest reading each
question from the Haggadah, talking about it, and then discussing the answer and so
on. You may want to begin by reading aloud the introductory paragraph below.
(You can also make a copy for each of your guests of the section below that
includes the Haggadah's questions and answers. For the purpose of this discussion,
feel free to ignore the accompanying questions and answers from the Torah.)

The Haggadah's treatment of the Four Children seems straightforward enough. But nothing could be further from the truth. For starters, in only one case do the Haggadah's questions and answers match up with those given in the Torah. The story of the Four Children in the Haggadah is actually one of at least three ancient treatments of this parable. All of them were probably based on the Mishnah, a rabbinic text compiled around 200 C.E. It spoke about children who were able to ask questions and those who were unable to do so.[1] Over time, two children became four, generally thought to correspond to the four instances in the Torah that address the instruction of future generations about the Exodus.[2] The oldest version of our passage, from the *Mekhilta of Rabbi Ishmael,* a third-century C.E. midrash, is somewhat similar to the Haggadah, but the children are listed in a different order.[3] The Jerusalem Talmud's rendering, from the early fifth century, differs dramatically from the Haggadah. The Jerusalem Talmud gives more or less the Haggadah's answers, but to different children. There, the wise child gets the simple child's answer. And a "stupid" child gets the wise child's answer. Behind a passage that seems so simple lies a long and complicated process of evolution and very careful editing.[4]

• What might be the purpose of the blessing that introduces the Four Children?

• How do you feel about the Haggadah's comparison among the Four Children? How do you explain the order of the Four Children?

• What do you make of the answer the wise child receives and why is he told about *afikomen*?

• Some scholars believe that the Haggadah's treatment of the wise versus the wicked child reflects a response to the development of religious sects, including Christianity, which rejected many aspects of Jewish law. What kinds of questions asked at the Seder, if any, would you call "wicked"? The answer to the wicked child concludes that he rejects a major principle of faith (*kafar ba-ikar*). Comparing his question with that of the wise child and the answer given to the wicked child, what major principle(s) of faith may he have rejected?

A Note on the Questions of the Wise versus the Wicked Child: The wise child's question comes from the Book of Deuteronomy (6:20): "What mean the decrees, laws, and rules that the Lord our God has enjoined upon *you*?" Now take a look at your Haggadah. Is the pronoun at the end of this question "you" or "us"? According to the accepted text of the Bible and to standard versions of the Haggadah, the Hebrew should read *"etkhem,"* "you" in the plural. But in ancient texts, such as the Septuagint (the Greek translation of the Bible from the third century B.C.E.), and the versions of the Four Children found in the Jerusalem Talmud and the *Mekhilta,* that pronoun reads *"otanu,"* "us," instead of *"etkhem."* It's not clear whether those renderings were simply based on variant manuscripts of the Bible or whether they introduced a subtle change into the biblical text. In any case, some ancient Haggadot adopted this variant, which sharpens the difference between the wise and the wicked children. There seems to have been a concern that if the questions of both the wise and the wicked children ended with "you," some might argue that there was not such a big difference between them. Despite efforts to correct this over the centuries, you'll still find some Haggadot that use "us" in place of "you." There are also many Haggadot where the Hebrew is *"etkhem"* but the translation reads "us."[5]

- How does changing this pronoun affect your understanding of the difference between the wise and the wicked children?

A Note on Afikomen: The response to the wise child refers to the *afikomen,* the meaning of which seems to have been lost by the Talmudic era. It is now thought to mean "dessert," "dinner music," "after-dinner revelry, such as going from house to house," or "entertainment," all of which would have diverted attention from the paschal offering. However, some suggest that the *afikomen* is a messianic symbol, the reappearance of the hidden matzah representing the return of a messianic figure such as Elijah. Only the truly wise would merit such an explanation.[6] After the Temple's destruction, it was indeed traditional to conclude the meal with matzah in place of, or as a reminder of, the paschal offering. But this matzah was not called the *afikomen.* Designating the matzah eaten at the meal's conclusion as the *afikomen* seems to date back to the time of Rashi (1040–1105). He once told his students that he forgot to eat the "matzah of *afikomen*" after the meal. The expression stuck.[7]

TORAH VERSUS HAGGADAH

The Haggadah's story of the Four Children represents an interpretation, actually a midrash, on specific verses from the Torah that mention three different questions children will ask their parents about Passover and the Exodus from Egypt. The Torah also includes answers to those questions.

The contrasts between Torah and Haggadah—especially involving the "wise" (*chakham*) and the "wicked" (*rasha*) child—provide an illuminating commentary on the religious conflicts that have perennially plagued the Jewish people.

First, ask one of your Seder participants to read a question with its answer from the Torah and another to read the Haggadah's elaboration of the same exchange. After reading each pair of questions and responses, discuss the differences between them. When you have finished comparing each set, lead a discussion based on the questions at the bottom of page 62—or whatever else comes up in your group. (This will work best if you make a copy of page 61–62 for each of your guests.)

QUESTION ONE:

When, in time to come, your children ask you, "What mean the decrees, laws, and rules that the Lord our God has enjoined upon you?" you shall say to your children, "We were slaves to Pharaoh in Egypt and the Lord took us out from Egypt with a mighty hand. The Lord wrought before our eyes marvelous and destructive signs and portents in Egypt, against Pharaoh and all his household; and us He took out from there, that He might bring us and give us the land that He had promised on oath to our fathers. Then the Lord commanded us to observe all these laws, to revere the Lord our God, for our lasting good and for our survival, as is now the case. It will be therefore to our merit before the Lord our God to observe faithfully this whole instruction, as He has commanded us."

—DEUTERONOMY 6:20–25

What does the wise son say? "What mean the decrees, laws, and rules that the Lord our God has enjoined upon you?" You must tell him all the laws of Pesach, including the ruling that nothing should be eaten after the *afikomen* [the end of the Mishnah's discussion on Passover].

—THE HAGGADAH

QUESTION TWO:

And when your children ask you, "What does this service mean to you?" you shall say, "It is the Passover sacrifice to the Lord, because He passed over the houses of the Israelites in Egypt when He smote the Egyptians, but saved our houses."

—EXODUS 12:26–27

What does the wicked son say? "What does this service mean to you?" To "you" and not to "him." Since he excludes himself from the community and rejects a major principle of faith, you should set his teeth on edge and say to him: "It is because of what the Lord did for me when I went free from Egypt" (Ex. 13:8). "Me" and not "him." Had he been there he would not have been redeemed.

—THE HAGGADAH

QUESTION THREE:

And when, in time to come, your son asks you, saying, "What is this?" you shall say to him, "It was with a mighty hand that the Lord brought us out from Egypt, the house of bondage."

—EXODUS 13:14

What does the simple son say? "What is this?" You shall say to him, "It was with a mighty hand that the Lord brought us out from Egypt, the house of bondage" (Ex. 13:14). [The wise child's answer according to the Jerusalem Talmud.]

—THE HAGGADAH

THE FOURTH CHILD: (BECAUSE THIS CHILD IS UNABLE TO ASK A QUESTION, WE CAN ONLY INCLUDE THE RESPONSE HE RECEIVES IN THE HAGGADAH.)

As for the son who does not know how to ask, you should prompt him, as it is said: "And you shall explain to your son on that day, 'It is because of what the Lord did for me when I went free from Egypt'" (Ex. 13:8). [The Jerusalem Talmud: "With the child who does not know how to ask, you have to begin and start with him."]

—THE HAGGADAH

• What are the major differences between the texts from the Torah and the Haggadah?

• Does the Torah appear judgmental about the three types of questions it anticipates?

• What can we learn from the contrasting messages of the Torah and the Haggadah—especially those involving the wise and the wicked children—about how we might approach conflicts within the Jewish people today?

THE WISE VERSUS THE WICKED:
A RECIPE FOR CONFLICT OR CONFLICT RESOLUTION?

This can be used as an independent reading during your Seder or
as a conclusion for either of the previous activities.

What are we to learn from the Haggadah's Four Children? Is the passage a recipe for conflict or for conflict resolution? We can read it as a harmful text, at best offering a lesson of what *not* to do when we encounter Jews with whom we sharply disagree. But we can also read it as a useful framework for containing and possibly helping to resolve conflict.

Let's begin with text's problems.

According to the Haggadah, wisdom means uncritically embracing the study of Jewish law in all its intricacies—"the decrees, laws, and rules that the Lord our God has enjoined upon you." Wickedness involves questioning the *meaning* of those injunctions.

The parable's presence in the Haggadah indicates that the clash between those who eagerly accept the framework of Jewish law and those who question the meaning of our traditions goes back a long way. In recent times, that conflict has threatened to pull us apart.

The ancient argument for the wise son, the *chakham,* and against the wicked son, the *rasha,* uses tactics familiar to anyone who has followed the recent strife along the Orthodox/non-Orthodox divide.

It begins with an attempt to commandeer tradition: "The *Torah* alludes to Four Children"—as if those asking certain kinds of questions were singled out for praise or condemnation at Sinai itself. The Torah makes no mention of wise, wicked, or simple children. The truth is that in discussing the celebration of Passover, the Torah *expects* that children will ask their parents different questions about our traditions. The Torah casts no judgment on the comparative merit of these questions. Each one seems to have its place.

The Haggadah's argument continues by labeling the protagonists. Before we even hear their questions, the Haggadah tells us who is wicked, wise, or simple. And those labels color how we hear the children's questions. Having already been introduced to the *rasha,* we hear his question—"What does this ritual mean to you?"—as if "you" were angrily written in red. And so he receives an angry response "To *you* and not to *him.*"

The next step in the polemic involves polarization, attempting to destroy any shred of commonality among the disputants.

In the Torah, the questions of the wise and wicked children are not as different as you may think:

The wise child: "What mean the decrees, laws, and rules that the Lord our God has enjoined upon *you?*"

The wicked child: "What does this service mean to *you?*"

Both can be read as expressing a certain tendency to exclude oneself from the community.

To sharpen the distinction between the *chakham* and the *rasha,* some scholars believe that about sixteen hundred years ago the Jerusalem Talmud subtly altered the wise child's question. It changed the last word in his question from "you" to "us."

So, if we look back at the Torah itself, if we can see past the labels, the questions the Haggadah attributes to the *chakham* and *rasha* end on a similar note. Of course, their questions differ, but they have something in common, too. The Haggadah, however, wants to hide even this bit of potential common ground.

At the same time, by bringing the *chakham* and *rasha* to the Seder, the Haggadah implies that Judaism needs them both. The first speaks for the concept of law, halakhah, a guide to the how and when of Jewish life. The second wonders why, a quest of the spirit identified with *aggadah*—the tales, legends, anecdotes, and aphorisms that probe reasons and illuminate meaning. Abraham Joshua Heschel wrote: "Halakhah without *aggadah* is dead. *Aggadah* without halakhah is wild . . . We must neither disparage the body, nor sacrifice the spirit. The body is the discipline, the pattern, the law; the spirit is inner devotion, spontaneity, freedom. The body without the spirit is a corpse; the spirit without the body is a ghost."[8]

Yet, as the Haggadah demonstrates, our tradition sometimes speaks with a harsh voice to those who ask the "wrong" questions. Likewise, today many don't just *question* traditional observance. With little or no real understanding, they reject it out of hand as hopelessly primitive.

What is the bottom line? We can use the Haggadah's Four Children to flatter ourselves as wise and to smugly condemn those with whom we differ. And historically that's how the Four Children have been used. Centuries of illustrated

Haggadot have depicted the wicked child as the personification of everything wrong with modernity and acculturation. But in their heart of hearts, how many Conservative, Reconstructionist, and Reform Jews equate the wise child with what they perceive to be a hyper-legalistic form of Orthodoxy that substitutes blind adherence to law in place of the search for true wisdom?

Or we can read the Four Children as a plea that we sit at the same table with the people in our community—in our own families—with whom we differ most painfully. Whatever the "wicked children" may or may not believe, they deserve a seat at the table. And our answers to their questions had better not cause them to leave.

When the Jewish people are not united against a common enemy our internal conflicts become explosive. Animosity among those certain of their own wisdom, and of others' wickedness, has become dangerous. Both sides need to stop labeling and demonizing the other. Both sides need to appreciate that each has different questions. Both sides must remember that even the questions that seem to put some of us in different camps still speak the words of Torah. That's why this contentious passage begins with a fourfold blessing of God "who gave the Torah to God's people Israel"—all God's people.

From a practical point of view, both sides should spend part of a Seder discussing a stunning insight from the midrash: "If you estrange those who are distant from you, you will ultimately estrange also those who are near to you."[9]

FOUR VOICES ON FOUR CHILDREN

Below you will find four elaborations on the Haggadah's Four Children. Choose one or more to read aloud and react to at your Seder. Samson Raphael Hirsch's commentary may strike you as narrow-minded, especially in contrast with the other selections. Even if you reject Hirsch's message, consider how you might respond to someone expressing his position.

Four Children: the wise, the wayward, the simple, the sleeping.
Four worlds [of potential existence, according to the Kabbalists].
All are essential to the Divine Plan of Creation. Each manifests a different aspect of the Divine. All the children, all the Jewish souls, are

integral to the Jewish People. Symbolic of the four levels of Jewish Awareness. All are intrinsic to God's Plan for humanity. Each is imbued with a unique way of perceiving the Divine. Only together is the unity of the Jewish people complete . . . Rather than search in others, we must delve into ourselves. We all, to varying degrees, have aspects of the Four Children—Four Selves—within us. We must integrate the positive elements and rechannel the negative. As we hear the voices of the children, as we learn how to handle them, let us also learn how to deal with the voices of the different selves inside us. Only together is our Jewishness complete.[10]

—THE BRESLOV HAGGADAH, BASED THE TEACHINGS OF
THE HASIDIC MASTER REBBE NACHMAN
OF BRESLOV (1772–1810), PODOLIA AND UKRAINE

The wicked child: But what should be said to the members of this fallen generation who, in their apostasy, fancy themselves to be the "progressives," and deride their loyal elders as "backward"? *To them nothing should be said!* The Divine Word teaches in relation to the [three other children that their questions in the Torah are followed by the instruction that you should respond *to* your son]. But in relation to the scornful generation it does not say, "You should say *to* them" but simply, "You should say," because to *them* you have nothing to say. They expect no instruction from you. They have, indeed, "advanced" so far beyond you that they wish to instruct *you.* They wish to move you, by means of their "refined" mockery, from your stale "narrow" views, which appear to them to be burdensome encumbrances, up to their level, up to the bright, easy unrestraint of their "progressiveness." . . . The key to the hearts of the estranged generation rests in the Hands of God. Only experience can bring them back, the experience of the hollowness, the nothingness, the bleakness and emptiness of all those delusions into whose arms they have thoughtlessly thrown themselves. One day those hearts will once more be filled with

yearning for the happiness of possessing the ancient Truth which was
thrown away.[11]

—SAMSON RAPHAEL HIRSCH (1808–1888), GERMANY

*(Hirsch led the Modern Orthodox response to the spread of Reform Judaism in
Europe, though he also supported certain elements of reform within Orthodoxy,
such as congregational singing, the presence of a choir, and sermons twice
monthly in the vernacular.)*

The *order* of the four children, with the *rasha* (the wicked one) following right after the *chacham* (the wise one), seems rather odd . . .

   In the teachings of Rabbi Isaac Luria (the great sixteenth-century
Kabbalist from Safed) it is stated that the four cups drunk at the Seder
correspond to the four sons: the first cup relates to the *chacham;* the
second cup to the *rasha;* and so forth. The principal part of the
Haggadah is recited over the *second* cup [i.e., the second cup is poured
just before the Four Questions and is not drunk until shortly before the
meal]. Now, the *rasha* is the one of whom it is said that "If he had been
there, he would not have been redeemed"; why, then, is the principal
part of the Haggadah related to him? . . .

   The Talmud states: "Though one sinned, one remains *Yisrael,* i.e.,
an Israelite." Every Jew, regardless of his personal status, is possessed of
the essence of Judaism. My father-in-law, the Rebbe, thus commented
on the phrase "one is wise, and one is wicked . . .": Each one is possessed of *Echad* (the One), even the *rasha,* except that in him it is concealed and one must bring it out into the open.

   Yisrael is an acronym: *'Yesh Shishim Ribo Otiyot La Torah'* (there
are six hundred thousand letters to the Torah). The implication is clear:
Just as the totality of the Torah depends on every single letter . . . so,
too, the totality of the Jewish people depends on every single Jew.
Moreover, "You are children of God, your God" (Deut. 14:1); thus
even our Father in Heaven is, if one could say so, affected by every
individual Jew.

   The inclusion of the *rasha* in the Seder thus achieves the ultimate
purpose of everything . . . The *chacham* is the only one to uncover the

Echad inherent in the *rasha* . . . This is the reason for the juxtaposition of the *rasha* with the *chacham*. The *chacham* is taught not to argue: "Why should I bother with the *rasha*? Let him be lost through his wickedness!" He must be conscious of the fact that all of Israel are surety for one another.[12]

—MENACHEM MENDEL SCHNEERSON,
THE LUBAVITCHER REBBE (1902–1994), EUROPE AND AMERICA,
CHARISMATIC LEADER OF CHABAD HASIDISM

Recent generations have witnessed the development of many feminist Haggadot that seek to create a Seder more inclusive of women. Following is a thought-provoking selection from *The Journey Continues: The 1997 Ma'yan Passover Haggadah*.

The Four Daughters

The daughter in search of a usable past. *Ma hi omeret?* What does she say?

"Why didn't the *Torah* count women among the '600,000 men on foot, aside from children' who came out of Egypt? And why did Moses say at Sinai, 'Go not near a woman,' addressing only the men, as if preparation for Revelation was not meant for us as well?"

Because she already understands that Jewish memory is essential to our identity, teach her that history is made by those who tell the tale. If *Torah* did not name and number women, it is up to her to fill the empty spaces of our holy texts.

And the daughter who wants to erase her difference. *Ma hi omeret?* What does she say?

"Can't one just be a Jew? Why must you keep pushing your women's questions into every text? And why are these women's issues so important to you?"

"To you," and not "to me." Since she so easily forgets the struggles of her mothers and sisters, you must set her teeth on edge by saying, "I thank God every morning for the blessing of being a woman."

And the daughter who does not know that she has a place at the table. *Ma hi omeret?* What does she say?

"What is this?"

Because she doesn't realize that her question is, in itself, a part of the Seder tradition, teach her that the *Haggadah* is an extended conversation about liberation, and tell her that her insights and questions are also text.

And the daughter who asks no question.

You must say to her, "Your questions, when they come, will liberate you from Egypt. This is how it is and has always been with your mothers and grandmothers. From the moment Miriam and the midwives questioned Pharaoh's edict until today, every question we ask helps us leave Egypt farther behind."[13]

6

Hardening Pharaoh's Heart:
The Toughest Part of the Story

מַה זֹּאת? וְאָמַרְתָּ אֵלָיו:

בְּחֹזֶק יָד הוֹצִיאָנוּ יְהֹוָה מִמִּצְרַיִם מִבֵּית עֲבָדִים:

"What is this?" You are to say to him: "By strength of hand YHWH
brought us out of Egypt, out of a house of serfs" (Ex. 13:14).
—THE PASSOVER HAGGADAH, THE "SIMPLE CHILD'S"
QUESTION AND ANSWER

he Haggadah reminds us that "whoever elaborates on the story of the
Exodus deserves praise." In the spirit of elaboration and study, let's take a
look at one of the most troubling aspects of the Exodus story, the hardening of
Pharaoh's heart. We read in the Haggadah many times about the signs, wonders,
and miracles associated with the Exodus. We recite the names of the plagues one
by one and sing about the parting of the Red Sea in *Dayyenu*. Mysteriously, the
Haggadah omits even a single reference to the hardening of Pharaoh's heart,
though in Exodus it is mentioned in conjunction with every plague and elsewhere—twenty times in all.

Interestingly, the answer to the simple child's question includes only the passage above. Here's the verse that follows it in the Torah:

And it was when Pharaoh hardened [his heart] against sending us free, that YHWH killed every firstborn throughout the land of Egypt, from the firstborn of man to the firstborn of beast. . . .

—EXODUS 13:15[1]

One can easily imagine the debate among the Haggadah's compilers as they argued about whether or not to answer the simple child's question with a few more words. To do so would have been more faithful to the Exodus saga, as it would have brought the theme of God's hardening Pharaoh's heart into the Seder. But, given that motif's moral complexity, we can well understand the decision to avoid it by opting for a simple answer to a simple question!

THE BIBLE AND THE HARDENING OF PHARAOH'S HEART

The Bible's twenty references to the hardening of Pharaoh's heart (see pages 73–76) make for a fascinating discussion before you begin your Seder. It would be helpful to make a copy of these twenty verses from the Bible for each of your guests.

Read these questions aloud to your group before you begin reading the biblical passages that describe the hardening of Pharaoh's heart. Remind your guests that the Pharaoh of the hard heart is not the same one who earlier in Exodus ordered the killing of Jewish male infants. He is that Pharaoh's successor.

• Who appears to bear the responsibility for hardening Pharaoh's heart in each particular passage?

• Does this remain constant throughout?

• How do you feel about the notion of God hardening Pharaoh's heart? Was it justified? Was it necessary?

• What is the primary reason given in the text for hardening Pharaoh's heart?

• Why do you think the Haggadah omits this subject?

• What contemporary situations does the theme of a hard-hearted political leader conjure up for you?

You can use this material in different ways depending on the age and interests of your Seder guests. Take turns reading the biblical passages aloud.[2] Then either discuss the questions on page 72 or ask your group to divide into two groups, one defending God's hardening of Pharaoh's heart, the other opposing it.

If you have a group that enjoys text study, you might also spend some time checking out what the commentators have said, beginning on page 76.

1. After the burning bush, when Moses is about to return to Egypt. God says: "When you go to return to Egypt, see: All the portents that I have put in your hand, you are to do before Pharaoh, but I will make his heart strong-willed [*achazeik*], so that he will not send the people free" (Ex. 4:21).

2. After Moses returns to Egypt and just before he and Aaron speak to Pharaoh for the first time. God says: "But I will harden [*aksheh*] Pharaoh's heart, I will make my signs and my portents many in the land of Egypt: Pharaoh will not hearken to you, so I will set my hand against Egypt, and I will bring out my forces, my people, the Children of Israel, from the land of Egypt with great (acts of) judgment" (Ex. 7:3–4).

3. Moses' rod turns into a snake. Pharaoh's magicians perform the same trick, but Moses' snake swallows up their snakes: "Yet Pharaoh's heart remained strong-willed [*vayechezak*], and he did not hearken to them, as Adonai had spoken" (Ex. 7:13).

4. The next verse: "Adonai said to Moses, 'Pharaoh's heart is heavy-with-stubbornness [*kaveid*]—he refuses to send the people free'" (Ex. 7:14).

5. After the first plague, when the rivers turn to blood, Pharaoh's magicians also turned water to blood: "But the magicians of Egypt did thus with their occult-arts, and Pharaoh's heart remained strong-willed [*vayechezak*], and he did not hearken to them, as Adonai had spoken" (Ex. 7:22).

6. After the onset of the second plague, frogs, Pharaoh asks Moses to end the plague and says that he will let the Israelites conduct sacrifices in the desert as they had requested. The frogs return to the river at the appointed time: "But when Pharaoh saw that there was breathing-room, he made his heart heavy-with-stubbornness [*v'hakhbeid*], and did not hearken to them, as Adonai had spoken" (Ex. 8:11).

7. Following the onset of the third plague, lice, which Pharaoh's magicians were not able to duplicate: "The magicians said to Pharaoh: This is the finger of a god! But Pharaoh's heart remained strong-willed [*vayechezak*], and he did not hearken to them, as Adonai had spoken" (Ex. 8:15).

8. Pharaoh asks Moses to end the fourth plague, swarms of insects.[3] The plague ends and Pharaoh promises to let the people go so they can sacrifice to God in the desert: "But Pharaoh made his heart heavy-with-stubbornness [*vayakhbeid*] this time as well, and he did not send the people free" (Ex. 8:28).

9. Following the onset of the fifth plague, the death of cattle: "But Pharaoh's heart remained heavy-with-stubbornness [*vayikhbad*], and he did not send the people free" (Ex. 9:7).

10. Following the sixth plague, boils: "But Adonai made Pharaoh's heart strong-willed [*vayichazeik*], and he did not hearken to them, as Adonai had said to Moses" (Ex. 9:12).

11. After the onset of hail, the seventh plague, Pharaoh says, "This-time I have sinned! Adonai is the one-in-the-right, I and my people are the ones-in-the-wrong!" He pleads for the end of the plague: "But when Pharaoh saw that the rain and the hail and the thunder had stopped, he continued to sin: He made his heart heavy-with-stubbornness [*vayakhbeid*], his and his servants" (Ex. 9:34).

12. Next verse: "Pharaoh's heart remained strong-willed [*vayechezak*], and he did not send the Children of Israel free, as Adonai had spoken through Moses" (Ex. 9:35).

13. Next verse. Before the announcement of locusts, the eighth plague: "Adonai said to Moses: 'Come into Pharaoh! For I have made his heart and the heart of his servants heavy-with-stubbornness [*hikhbad'ti*], in order that I may put these my signs among them and in order that you may recount in the ears of your child and of your child's child how I have been capricious with Egypt, and my signs, which I have placed upon them—that you may know that I am Adonai'" (Ex. 10:1–2).

14. After the onset of the locusts, Pharaoh begs Moses to bring an end to the plague, saying that he has sinned against God and Moses. The plague

ends: "But Adonai made Pharaoh's heart strong-willed [*vayichazeik*], and he did not send the Children of Israel free" (Ex. 10:20).

15. After the onset of the ninth plague, darkness, Pharaoh is willing to let the Israelites and their children go to pray for three days in the desert as they had requested. Pharaoh insists that the Israelites leave their cattle behind. Moses says they need the cattle to make sacrifices in the desert: "But Adonai made Pharaoh's heart strong-willed [*vayichazeik*], so that he would not consent to send them free" (Ex. 10:27).

16. Moses announces the killing of the firstborn. The last plague will begin at midnight: "Adonai said to Moses: Pharaoh will not hearken to you, in order that my portents may be many in the land of Egypt. Now Moses and Aharon had done all the portents in Pharaoh's presence, but Adonai had made Pharaoh's heart strong-willed [*vayichazeik*], and he had not sent the Children of Israel free from his land" (Ex. 11:10).

17. After the Israelites leave Egypt the text includes a summary of the events and instructions about the laws of Passover: "It shall be when your child asks you on the morrow, saying: 'What is this?' You are to say to him: 'By strength of hand Adonai brought us out of Egypt, out of a house of serfs. And it was when Pharaoh hardened [*hikshah*] (his heart) against sending us free, that Adonai killed every firstborn throughout the land of Egypt, from the firstborn of man to the firstborn of beast'" (Ex. 13:14–15).

18. The Israelites are in the desert but have not yet reached the Red Sea. God says: "Now Pharaoh will say of the Children of Israel: 'They are confused in the land! The wilderness has closed them in!' I will make Pharaoh's heart strong-willed [*v'chizakti*], so that he pursues them, and I will be glorified through Pharaoh and his army, so that the Egyptians may know that I am Adonai" (Ex. 14:3–4).

19. A few verses later: "He had his chariot harnessed, his (fighting) people he took with him, and he took six hundred selected chariots and every (kind of) chariot in Egypt, teams-of-three upon them all. Now Adonai made the heart of Pharaoh king of Egypt strong-willed [*vayichazeik*], so that he pursued the Children of Israel" (Ex. 14:6–8).

20. God says to Moses He will part the sea: "But I, here, I will make Egypt's heart strong-willed [*m'chazeik*], so that they come in after them and I will be glorified through Pharaoh and all his army, his chariots and his riders; and the Egyptians shall know that I am Adonai, when I am glorified through Pharaoh, his chariots and his riders" (Ex. 14:17).

THE COMMENTATORS' STRUGGLE

Commentators have long labored to justify God's hardening of Pharaoh's heart.[4] Some have stressed the fact that initially Pharaoh seemed to harden his *own* heart. God only stepped in to strengthen the decision Pharaoh had freely made. Others see this as the exception that proves the rule that God does not interfere with human free will. But the volume of commentary on this theme points to its difficulty. Below you'll find six responses to the hardening of Pharaoh's heart. Choose one or two to read aloud and discuss.

> *For I have hardened his heart (Ex. 10:1)* . . . Rabbi Johanan said: "Does this not provide heretics with ground for arguing that he had no means of repenting, since it says, *'For I have hardened his heart?'*" To which Rabbi Simeon ben Lakish replied: "Let the mouths of the heretics be stopped up . . . When God warns a man once, twice, and even a third time and he still does not repent, then does God close his heart against repentance so He should exact vengeance from him for his sins." Thus it was for wicked Pharaoh.
>
> —EXODUS RABBAH (13:3), A COLLECTION OF ANCIENT MIDRASHIM COMPILED IN THE TENTH CENTURY

> *And I will harden (Ex. 7:3)* . . . Since he dealt wickedly and offered resistance against Me, and it is manifest before Me that there is no delight among the nations to set their whole heart to repentance, it is better that his heart be hardened in order to increase through him My signs, and you will recognize my might . . . Nevertheless, as regards the first five plagues it is not stated, *"And Adonai hardened the heart of Pharaoh,"* but *"And Pharaoh's heart was hardened."*
>
> —RASHI (1040–1105), FRANCE

There are some verses that lead people to fancy that God preordains and compels disobedience. This is false . . . Rather, whoever is bad is so by his own choice. If he wishes to be virtuous, he can be so; there is nothing preventing him . . . [God's] saying *"And I will harden Pharaoh's heart"*—and then punishing him and destroying him—contains a subject for discussion and a major principle stems from it . . . If Pharaoh and his followers had committed no other sin than not letting Israel go free, the matter would undoubtedly be problematic, for He had prevented them from setting Israel free . . . However, the matter is not like this, but rather Pharaoh and his followers disobeyed by choice, without force or compulsion. He oppressed the foreigners who were in their midst and treated them with sheer injustice . . . This action was due to their choice and to the evil character of their thought; there was nothing compelling them to do it. God punished them for it by preventing them from repenting so that the punishment which His justice required would befall them.

—MAIMONIDES (1135–1204), SPAIN[5]

Nowhere in the Bible is the fact of human freedom questioned, apart from the episode where God hardens Pharaoh's heart . . . But the Pharaoh episode is precisely the exception that proves the rule, for the biblical account assumes that under all normal conditions Pharaoh too would be free to release the Israelites. This is not a normal situation because God has a broader purpose to accomplish. That's why God has to intervene directly to limit Pharaoh's freedom. It takes a specific divine intervention to rob Pharaoh of his freedom—so much is freedom a natural part of the order of creation.

—NEIL GILLMAN (1933–) UNITED STATES[6]

The final decision always rests with man. At the beginning, however, man is free to choose any path of action he so desires. He is afforded equal opportunity to do good or evil. But as soon as he has made his first choice, then the opportunities are no longer so evenly balanced. The more he persists in the first path of his choosing, shall we say, the evil path, the harder will it become for him to revert to the good path, even though his essential freedom of choice is not affected. In other words, it is not the Almighty who has hampered his freedom and made the path of repentance difficult. He has, by his own choice and persistence in evil, placed obstacles in the way leading back to reformation.

—NEHAMA LEIBOWITZ (1905–1997), ISRAEL[7]

In Pharaoh's case, not listening becomes a fatal reflex, closing him to vulnerability and to growth. Nevertheless, it is based on a horror and a desire that are not alien to human experience. The process by which he moves from hardening his own heart to God's hardening his heart (in general terms, this happens after the first five plagues) is essentially a mysterious one. A stamina of endurance possesses Pharaoh: to the bystander, there is an unnatural, compulsive quality about his refusal that is . . . [as others have suggested] the idiomatic meaning of the formula: "God hardened Pharaoh's heart": where God is described as the cause of human emotional response, the effect is to suggest an *unaccountable* human reaction. On such a reading, Pharaoh increasingly strikes the reader with a kind of fascination as he compulsively resists the bombardment that should have defeated him. What demonic strength possesses him? "I shall strengthen his heart," "God made his heart impenetrable": These expressions only serve to underline the mystery of human self-destruction.

—AVIVA GOTTLIEB ZORNBERG (1944–), ISRAEL[8]

"I WILL SEND ALL MY PLAGUES INTO YOUR HEART . . ."

Read the following and lead a conversation based on the question on page 79.

The language of the seventh plague, hail, differs from all previous ones.

For this time I will send all My plagues upon your person [literally into your heart], and your courtiers, and your people, in order that you [sin-

78

gular] may know that there is none like Me in all the world . . . This time tomorrow I will rain down a very heavy hail, such as has not been seen in Egypt from the day it was founded until now. Therefore, order your livestock and everything you have in the open brought under shelter; every man and beast that is found outside, not having been brought in, shall perish when the hail comes down upon them!

—EXODUS 9:14, 18–19

Here's an interpretation by Arnold Ehrlich (1848–1919), a Bible scholar from Poland and Germany who moved to New York in 1876.

Know that when one strikes another, and it is clear that the whole purpose of the strike is the strike itself, and to cause suffering to the one stricken, the latter invariably hardens his heart and learns no moral from the suffering. If, however, the striker is able to convey that his purpose is to chasten rather than to cause pain, the one stricken may actually take it to heart. Occasionally, the experience may even improve him. Thus, when God saw that Pharaoh had not taken any of the first six plagues to heart, God tried a different strategy with the hail. He warned Pharaoh about it in a way that demonstrated care for Pharaoh's household, which God urged him to bring indoors. God had done no such thing in the first six plagues. With this, God demonstrated that the purpose was not Pharaoh's destruction, and the end of his nation, but rather the chastening of the Egyptians so that they would do God's will . . . This is why God said in this case, "This time I will send all of My plagues into your heart," that is, now the point of all the previous plagues will dawn upon you.[9]

• How might this interpretation be applied to the conflict between Israel and the Palestinians or the United States and its adversaries?

THE SOFTENING OF GOD'S HEART

Read this on your own or do so with your group after discussing the material above.

Your view of God's role in hardening Pharaoh's heart may depend on where you enter the story. If you focus just on the sequence of the plagues, it appears that Pharaoh hardens his own heart for the first five plagues, with God only stepping in for the last five. Commentators such as Maimonides and Leibowitz stress that Pharaoh's initial hard-hearted attitude foreclosed any subsequent softening. This view suggests that Pharaoh dug himself into such a hole that he *couldn't* change his mind, that he had been trapped by his own evil ways.

This interpretation tends to ignore that the first two announcements that *God* will harden Pharaoh's heart occur well before the plagues begin.

Clearly a cruel character, Pharaoh also appears to have been left with little chance for softening his position in response to the barrage of God's signs and wonders that bore down upon him. After the very first sign from God, when the snakes of Pharaoh's magicians are swallowed by those of Moses and Aaron, we read: "Yet Pharaoh's heart remained strong-willed and he did not hearken to them, *as Adonai had spoken* [emphasis mine]" (Ex. 7:13).

As Adonai had spoken? God never said anything about Pharaoh making his own heart "strong-willed." God spoke only of a divine role in making Pharaoh's heart "strong-willed." In four instances (plagues 3, 5, 6, and 7) when Pharaoh's heart becomes strong-willed or stubborn, but not explicitly on account of God, the verse ends with the same phrase *"as Adonai had spoken."* What on the surface appears to be Pharaoh's independent stubbornness upon closer inspection seems to reflect God's intervention, *"as Adonai had spoken."*

This conclusion plainly adds an uncomfortable measure of moral confusion to the Exodus story. No longer an autonomous agent of evil who brings God's wrath on his people, Pharaoh becomes a victim, a pawn in God's greater plan. The longer the story continues, the more painful the moral ambiguity becomes.

When the Egyptian army heads to the Red Sea in what will prove to be a suicidal mission of pursuit, God's strong hand and motivation both become painfully clear: "But I, here, I will make Egypt's heart strong-willed, so that they come in after them, and I will be glorified through Pharaoh and all his army, his chariots and his riders; and the Egyptians shall know that I am Adonai, when I am glorified through Pharaoh, his chariots and his riders" (Ex. 14:17). Lest there be any mistake about it, the dissonant note of divine glorification through the drowning of Pharaoh's troops strikes twice to ring down the curtain on this portion of the Exodus.

The Egyptian ruler's stubbornness and his inability to repent emerge as unmistakable props in the divine drama to teach the Egyptians that God is God and Pharaoh is not.

And we can now understand why the theme of God's hardening of Pharaoh's heart may have been excluded from the Haggadah. It paints a picture of humanity deprived of free will, and of God—not Pharaoh—as the one with a hard heart.

Add to this the fact that, as the Seder was evolving, Christianity was fast making inroads among gentiles and had reinterpreted the symbols of Passover to signify the sacrifice of Jesus. And Christians worshiped a face of God that seemed far more merciful than the God of the Exodus:

> Do you despise the riches of [God's] kindness and forbearance and
> patience? For do you not know that God's kindness is meant to lead
> you to repentance? But by your hard and impertinent heart you are
> storing up wrath for yourself on the day of wrath . . . ?
>
> —ROMANS 2:4–5

The God of the Exodus was plenty wrathful but allowed Pharaoh no real opportunity to repent.

We also know that during this era, the creators of what we now call Rabbinic Judaism were fearful that Jews would prove susceptible to what the Rabbis saw in Christianity—in their eyes, a religion centered on an individual rather than on God. This may be one of the reasons the Haggadah mentions Moses only once explicitly, in passing. If the Rabbis could virtually leave Moses out of the Passover story, all the easier it must have been to drop the disturbing theme of God's hardening Pharaoh's heart.

Having looked at some of the Bible's most difficult verses, let's now consider them in a broader context. The depiction of God in Genesis and Exodus differs considerably from that in later books of the Bible, particularly Prophets. In the flood, except for one family and a pair of each animal species, God destroys a morally corrupt world. No chance for repentance whatsoever! A few chapters later, God lays waste the evil cities of Sodom and Gomorrah. But the cataclysm is confined just to those two sites, and Abraham has a chance to argue for sparing the innocent. Lot and his daughters do escape. Still, the cities' residents have no opportunity to repent.

Pharaoh at least receives warnings and on the surface seems to have an opportunity to mend his ways. And the plagues are relatively contained. Only certain species of animals perish and the last plague targets the Egyptian firstborn—human and animal.

Later, after the Israelites build the Golden Calf, God threatens to wipe them out and to keep a new covenant through Moses. But God heeds Moses' plea for mercy and compassion. The Israelites repent and, in the process, mercy and compassion become central to our subsequent understanding of God.

The image of a compassionate God finds its most dramatic expression in the Book of Jonah, read on the afternoon of Yom Kippur. Here, God sends the reluctant prophet to warn the people of Nineveh of destruction unless they repent. God pleads for the innocent children and animals in "Nineveh, that great city in which there are more than 120,000 persons who cannot tell their right hand from their left hand; and also much cattle. . . ."[10] Much to the hard-hearted prophet's consternation, from the king down, the Ninevites repent.

With so many raw memories of suffering under Rome, the composers of the Haggadah surely wished to call down God's wrath upon this Egypt incarnate. The God of the Exodus appealed to them. But, they were hardly willing to give up the God who saved Nineveh.

You can reconcile these contrasting images of God with the notion that the Bible reveals how the human understanding of God has evolved. Or, as Jack Miles boldly argues in *God—A Biography,* you can study the Bible as the story of how God's character has evolved through interaction with humanity.[11] Or you use creative midrash, such as the eighth-century *Pirke de Rabbi Eliezer,* to do the same thing. This midrash describes Pharaoh's repentance at the Red Sea and puts a verse from the Israelites' Song of the Sea in Pharaoh's mouth: "Who is like You, O Lord . . . ?"

> The Holy One, blessed be He, delivered [resurrected Pharaoh] him from amongst the dead . . . He went and ruled in Nineveh . . . When God sent for Jonah to prophesy against the city's destruction, Pharaoh hearkened and arose from his throne, rent his garments and clothed himself in ashes . . . And God repented of the evil he said he would do to them and did not do it.[12]

7

The Festival of Spring:
Reconnecting Passover and Nature

יָכוֹל מֵרֹאשׁ חֹדֶשׁ, תַּלְמוּד לוֹמַר בַּיּוֹם הַהוּא...

It might have been thought that the telling should begin on the new moon [of Nisan]:
therefore the text teaches us "in that day." But since it says "in that day," we might
have thought that we should begin while it is day; therefore the Scripture also teaches
"because of this." You could not say "because of this," if it were not referring
to the time when unleavened bread and bitter herbs were lying before you.
—THE PASSOVER HAGGADAH, FROM THE MEKHILTA OF RABBI ISHMAEL,
A THIRD-CENTURY MIDRASH

O mitted from many modern Haggadot, this ancient passage takes pains to ensure that we recount the Exodus saga at the proper time: not on the new moon of Nisan, but on the date when the Israelites sacrificed the paschal offering in Egypt, the fifteenth of the month; and not during the day, but at night. This places the Seder at the most critical religious moment in the ancient Near East—the full moon after the vernal equinox![1]

The fact that Passover, *Chag HaAviv,* "the Festival of Spring," occurs when it does seems so natural that you may not have stopped to wonder why or what it means. Here we'll "unpack" the Passover-spring connection and consider what the holiday can teach us about the environment.

Why focus on spring and nature during Passover? Because humanity's survival now depends squarely on restoring our capacity to live in harmony with the environment. Jewish tradition can provide inspiration and strength for that task. Judaism evolved when humanity's dependence on the earth for sustenance was undeniable: The motif of famine runs through the Bible like a red thread. We can no longer afford to speak of *tikkun olam,* mending the world, in a metaphoric sense. We must begin repairing the earth—now. And to the extent that healing the earth brings us a little closer to nature, we'll also mend our souls.

There's not a better time for renewing our commitment to this work of *tikkun* than the Seder, when we celebrate our liberation and ponder the uses and misuses of freedom.

Sadly, our celebration of Passover gives virtually all the attention to the "what" of the Exodus and focuses very little on the "when." As a result, for many, the connections between Passover and the natural world have all but disappeared from the Seder. Those who observe the practice on the second Seder of beginning to count the *omer,* the forty-nine days from Passover to Shavuot, experience one link between Passover and the world of nature: That interval marked the period between the beginning of the barley harvest and the completion of the wheat harvest. But in Israel, where Seders are held only on the first night of Passover, even this connection fades. Those who attend synagogue on the first day of Passover will also be aware of another important link between the festival and nature. It rarely rains in Israel after Passover, so with the holiday comes a special prayer for dew, which plays an important role in sustaining crops during the hot, dry summer. In what follows, we'll try to root Passover a bit more firmly in its season and in the process develop a deeper appreciation for the festival as well as our responsibilities to the environment.

I also include a range of activities for your Seder to strengthen the Passover/spring connection and build environmental awareness. Along with readings, these include the opportunity to step outside and recite a number of appropriate and very beautiful blessings related to the unfolding spring season. You may want to raise the following questions with your guests during the Seder.

86

- It is often said that parsley on the Seder plate reminds us of spring. The Bible instructs us to observe Passover in the month of Aviv, the month of spring. What relationships do you see between springtime and the celebration of redemption?

- Without using these particular terms, the Bible sets Passover at the full moon near the vernal equinox. This means that on Passover the periods of daylight and darkness are about equal and that the moon rises just when the sun sets and sets just when the sun rises. After this equinox, the period of daylight becomes longer than that of darkness. How might the vernal equinox or its symbolism be related to Passover?

- If Passover is a celebration of freedom, how have we used our freedom in relation to the natural environment? What do you think Jewish tradition can contribute to the environmental movement? Do you think environmental issues are a high enough priority for the Jewish community?

ON SPRING AND TIME

Depending on your group, you might read this during the Seder or on your own.

Several verses from the Book of Exodus fix the time for celebrating Passover. Everett Fox's translation of the Bible captures the ancient relationship between the festival and its season:

> YHWH said to Moshe and to Aharon in the land of Egypt saying, "Let this New-Moon be for you the beginning of New-Moons . . . [The paschal lamb or goat] shall be for you in safekeeping, until the fourteenth day after this New-Moon, and they are to slay it—the entire assembly of the community of Israel—between the setting times [twilight] . . . In the first (month), on the fourteenth day after the New-Moon, at sunset, you are to eat *matzot* until the twenty-first day of the

month, at sunset" . . . Moshe said to the people, "Remember this day on which you went out from Egypt the house of serfs; for by strength of hand YHWH brought you out from here: no fermentation is to be eaten. Today you are going out, in the New-Moon of Ripe Grain [*chodesh Aviv*] . . . You are to keep this law at its appointed-time from year-day to year-day."

—EXODUS 12:1–2, 12:6, 12:18, 13:3–4, 13:10

Aviv refers to the first stage of grain's ripening, when its "ears" are well formed but still soft and green. The stalks stand fresh and verdant in the field.[2] Later it came to mean "spring." *Aviv* was also the name of the month when the vernal equinox fell. After the Babylonian Exile, the names of the months changed and Aviv became Nisan.

Because calendars in the ancient Near East marked the beginning of each month with the appearance of the new moon, the fifteenth corresponds to the full moon. The Bible carefully sets the first Passover at the full moon near the vernal equinox. Why tell us to "keep this law at its appointed-time"? Because otherwise Passover and all the other Jewish holidays would have fallen in their appointed months, but those months and their festivals would have wandered through the seasons, just as the Muslim festival of Ramadan does. The complexity of the Jewish calendar—which reckons months by the moon and years by the sun and adds an extra month to the calendar seven out of nineteen years—derives precisely from this specification: that Passover must come "at its appointed-time," at the full moon of the vernal equinox, when the barley has just begun to ripen.

Our ancestors understood that the Bible points to a vital relationship between the season *when* the Exodus occurred and *what* the Exodus means. It is no accident, in other words, that we celebrate the freedom and birth of our people in the period that marks the rebirth of the earth itself. As the earth passes from a darker to a brighter season and renews itself, so can we: Spring embodies the potential for growth on every plane. In many ancient Near Eastern cultures, the year began on the full moon of the vernal equinox. It was a moment of the greatest imaginable awareness of the natural world, a moment of both enormous potential for regeneration and grave danger—would the standing grain yield a bountiful harvest, or would excessive heat or rain produce a devastating blight?

Feeling nature's mighty rhythms unleashes the human capacity for renewal. Disconnecting ourselves from that flow deprives us of a critical source of energy to grow, to change, to free ourselves from the narrow places where we've gotten stuck. As Rabbi Irving Greenberg notes:

> Biblical language and symbol point to spring as the proper season for deliverance. The rebirth of earth after winter is nature's indication that life overcomes death: Spring is nature's analogue to redemption. Life blossoming, breaking winter's death grip, gives great credence to the human yearning for liberation. A correct reading of the spring season would hear its message of breaking out and life reborn at the biological level simultaneously with an Exodus message of good overcoming evil, of love overpowering death, of freedom and redemption. The Bible envisions a world in which moral and physical states coincide, when nature and history, in harmony, confirm the triumph of life. The Exodus paradigm suggests that the outcome of history will be an eternal spring. Read with a historical /theological hermeneutic, spring is Exodus.[3]

The conjunction of Passover with a critical point in the lunar-solar cycle exemplifies Judaism's concept of time. Most ancient civilizations emphasized the cyclical aspect of time. The ancients watched the stars travel predictably through the heavens, the Nile flood each spring, the seasons rotate in an orderly fashion. Year after year, time returned from where it had begun. The cyclicality of nature infused life with a welcome sense of stability. Ancient religious rites embodied these cycles. They provided worshipers with a way to re-create themselves by reliving the creation of the cosmos through celebrating the birth, death, and resurrection of their gods. History, as we know it, mattered little. "Everything begins over again at its commencement every instant. The past is but a prefiguration of the future, no event is irreversible and no transformation is final . . . [Through] the repetition of paradigmatic gestures and by means of periodic ceremonies, archaic man succeeded . . . in annulling time. . . ."[4]

Against this static background, the Israelite religion made an astonishing assertion: that time could also be conceptualized as an arrow, not just an eternal cycle.[5] In proclaiming that God actively directed the course of human history, humanity now encountered God in a new realm. History became the record of God's actions and humanity's response. That record was not circular, but began with creation, moved through deliverance and revelation, and would conclude with ultimate messianic redemption. The forward march of time sweeps us away from the ancient, timeless cycles, headlong into the inexorably unfolding drama of history. (This view of time and history now dominates the secular world, which, of course, removed God from the plot, leaving the stage to humanity alone.) Archaic man might shudder, charging that we've sundered humanity from its roots, that the history we've made is pure terror. Modern man responds that at least we have the freedom to create something new![6]

If the Israelites stressed "time's arrow," they certainly had no intention of burying "time's cycle." The best evidence comes from the bond between Passover and the full moon of the vernal equinox. The Exodus from Egypt represents "time's arrow" par excellence. The full moon of the vernal equinox is the paradigmatic symbol of "time's cycle." Judaism says that we need to reckon time both ways. The cyclical aspect of time roots and strengthens us as we tap into the power of the natural world's enduring rhythms. The directional aspect of time inspires us to use that strength to change the world, to push it, however slowly, from what it is today to what it can become tomorrow. Punctuated by the weekly Sabbath, Jewish time revolves around the annual cycle of holy days, which likewise restore our capacity to repair ourselves and the world.

As did the religions of other ancient peoples, the Passover Haggadah also commands us to return to our beginning—not to the creation of the world (we do that in the fall festivals), but to our birth as a nation. "In every generation, each individual should feel as though he or she had gone out of Egypt." But the same Haggadah that bids us to remember the Exodus, when *everything* changed, calls us to go back in time, as if *nothing* had changed.

As you feast with the full moon overhead, celebrate your freedom and remember a few words from Judaism's traditional blessing for the new moon, *Kiddush Levanah:* "He told the moon to renew its crown of glory over those [He] sustained from the womb, so that like the moon, in the future, they too, will be renewed."[7] Now remember how the ancients thought about that luminous, silvery disc that graces heaven's darkened dome:

Time as governed and measured by the phases of the moon might be called "living" time. It is bound up with the reality of life and nature, rain and the tides . . . the time of sowing, the menstrual cycle . . . "Becoming" is the lunar order of things . . . The moon "divides," "spins," and "measures" or "feeds," "makes fruitful," and "blesses" . . . "initiates and purifies"—because it is living, and therefore in a perpetual state of rhythmic becoming . . .[8] [If] archaic man succeeded . . . in annulling time, he nonetheless lived in harmony with the cosmic rhythms; we might even say that he entered into these rhythms (we need only remember how "real" night and day are to him, and the seasons, the cycles of the moon, the solstices).[9]

Every spring, Passover beckons us to become free, born anew. We can begin again every year, every moment—but only if we preserve the earth, the source of our sustenance, our partner in growth, change, and renewal. The ancients may not have had much interest in history and change, but they couldn't forget their dependence on the earth for a minute. As we'll now see, that dependence gave rise to festivals—including the original Passover—dedicated to ensuring the earth's continued bounty.

THE ORIGINS OF PASSOVER: TWO VIEWS

Depending on your group, you might read this during the Seder or on your own.

As one scholar wisely observed, "A holiday is always older than the interpretation which is given to it."[10] Here we'll take a brief look at two theories of the origins of Passover. Although they differ considerably, both views emphasize the underlying ancient connection between Passover and the natural world.[11]

One school of thought holds that Passover as we know it today evolved from the fusion of two ancient festivals.[12] The first involved the annual sacrifice of a young sheep or goat firstling from the nomadic Israelites' flocks. Families carried out the sacrifice at night, in the spring under a full moon. The ritual may have begun before or after the Israelites' sojourn in Egypt. In any case, what had once been a sacrifice to ensure a healthy flock eventually became associated with the

Exodus and the legend of God's striking the firstborn of the Egyptians and sparing those of the Israelites.

Because the purity of the sacrificial victim was critical, it was essential to avoid contaminating it with the potential rot to which leavened bread was susceptible. Thus, families ate unleavened cakes with the offering. Smearing the blood of the offering on the entrance to the Israelites' tents, originally thought to ward off disease or misfortune, later acquired a historical meaning, further linking the ritual with legends of the last plague. Some maintain that the Pesach offering was initially more widely practiced in Judah, the Southern Kingdom, where seminomadic animal husbandry was more prevalent than in Israel, the agriculturally richer Northern Kingdom.

The Northern Kingdom of Israel placed greater emphasis on a spring grain holiday, the seven-day Festival of Matzot that began at the full moon before the harvest. Just after the first cereal crop—barley—had begun to ripen, farmers held a sacred feast to ensure a bountiful wheat harvest, still some weeks away. Leaven, or sourdough, a sour-smelling culture of yeast and bacteria grown from the old crop, was removed to express hope for a healthy crop and to avoid contamination of the new crop by the old. The moldy rot that leavened bread can develop was similar to what farmers feared could devastate their crops. Excessive rain and heat could destroy a barley crop with a fungal disease now known as smut.[13] Celebrated with unleavened bread from the previous year's crop, the Festival of Matzot marked the time after which the community could begin to consume grains from the new crop. It may be that this holiday developed later than the Pesach sacrifice, when formerly nomadic shepherds made the transition to sedentary agriculturists. Similar festivals occurred throughout the ancient Near East.

Because they both occurred around the same time of year, eventually the two festivals were merged. Elements of the Festival of Matzot were reinterpreted to harmonize with the Pesach offering and its ancient association with the Exodus from Egypt. What had begun as family-based rituals became centralized under King Josiah. Josiah ruled the kingdom of Judah between 640 and 609 B.C.E. and also briefly reconquered the Northern Kingdom from Assyria. Thought to have been written not too long before Josiah's era, the Book of Deuteronomy created a national festival that combined traditions of the North and South. The single Passover ritual, including both the Festival of Matzot and the paschal offering, emerged.

Other scholars trace Passover's origin to the New Year's rituals common in the ancient Near East.[14] Rather than explicitly linking Passover to the harvest, the Bible ties it to the calendar—the full moon of the month in which the vernal equinox occurs, when many cultures in the ancient Near East observed the New Year. Indeed, the Bible specifies that the month of the Exodus shall henceforth be counted as the *first* month of the year. These ancient rituals involved feasting and offering sacrifices to propitiate the gods at a time when they were thought to make decisions concerning the fate of the community for the coming year. It was also a season when the evil spirits of the passing year were feared to be particularly dangerous. Smearing blood on their doors or bodies served to protect the faithful.

To ensure health and good fortune, it was essential to carry out New Year's rites in a state of extreme ritual purity. Leaven, associated not just with bread's rising but also more importantly with its rot and decay, had to be stringently avoided lest it contaminate the New Year's sacrificial offering and the ripening cereal crops. This underlies Passover's ban on leavened bread. (In later times, leaven was banned from the altar in the Temple.) Similarly, the biblical injunction (Ex. 12:10) to eat the offering in a single evening and to burn any remains reflects the fear of decay and ritual impurity. This theory maintains that the paschal offering and the subsequent Festival of Matzot were always elements of a single ritual.

At a season when so much hung in the balance, the fate of the firstborn aroused heightened concern. The firstborn son represented a new generation and as such was thought to be especially vulnerable at the turn of the year. Special rites of purification and dedication for the firstborn were common. The practice of sacrificing a firstborn male from the flock represented the means to ensure the firstborn son's salvation for the coming year.

Ancient New Year's rituals included several other practices that left their imprint on the development of Passover. These included the recitation of the community's version of the creation story, a tale that often involved the victory of one god over another. Passover's recounting of the creation of the Israelite people and God's triumph over Pharaoh reflects a variation on that motif. The ancient ritual also included a journey from the city to the desert in which participants dressed in costumes. This symbolized the desire to flee from the evil spirits and contamination that remained behind in the cities, as well as a wish to reestablish contact with the gods of vegetation. Although this ritual finds more

93

concrete expression in Sukkot, it survives in Passover as we recall the flight from Egypt to the desert. The Book of Exodus (12:11) describes the appropriate costume for the journey: "This is how you shall eat it: your loins girded, your sandals on your feet, and your staff in your hand. . . ."

HISTORY TRUMPS NATURE

Depending on your group, you might read this during the Seder or on your own.

Passover is widely referred to as *Z'man Cherueinu,* "the season of our liberation," and also as *Chag HaAviv,* "the festival of spring." Why do themes associated with nature get such short shrift during the Seder? The answer is complex, but the process that produced this outcome seems to have begun in ancient times.

Over time, worship became increasingly centralized in the Temple in Jerusalem. A city grew up around the Temple; its residents, including the king and priests, could hardly carry out the agricultural feasts as people had in former times. "The movement towards Jerusalem meant a striving for uniformity, but at the same time a withdrawal from nature. The festivals no longer signified the direct sanctification of nature. The people were now sanctified by [the festivals]" through rites performed by the priesthood.[15] Over time, what had begun as agricultural festivals became "historicized."

After all, Judaism's great theological innovation was not simply that God rules the world of nature, but, more important, that God ultimately determines the shape of human history.

Downplaying the significance of nature within the Passover festival may also have represented a bulwark against the age-old tendency to worship nature, the "heavenly hosts," rather than God, who created the natural world. Deuteronomy's warning (4:19–20) could not have been more plain: "And when you look up to the sky and behold the sun and the moon and the stars, and the whole heavenly host, you must not be lured into bowing down to them or serving them. These the Lord your God allotted to other peoples everywhere under heaven; but you the Lord took and brought out of Egypt, that iron blast furnace, to be His very own people. . . ." Indeed, Ezekiel (8:16) attributes the destruction of the First Temple to sun worship by Israelites in the Temple itself.[16]

Following the commentary of Rabbenu Chananel (990–1050), some widely available Haggadot state that, "in the beginning [prior to monotheism] our ancestors worshiped the stars."[17]

The result of this evolution has produced a Passover Seder heavy with symbols that amplify the themes of redemption—political and spiritual—but relatively light on those that speak to the seasonal aspect of the holiday or the implicit relationship between the birth of a people and the rebirth of the earth.

Passover's origins seem to reach back to ancient Near Eastern agricultural and New Year's celebrations. Later it became the festival at which the Israelites expressed their gratitude through the paschal offering for redemption from Egypt. After the Temple's destruction in 70 C.E., Passover was transformed into a set of rituals to preserve the Jewish people's faith that God, who had long ago delivered the Israelites from Egypt, would once again intervene to alleviate Jewish suffering. Over the ages, Passover has been adapted to address profound spiritual needs for renewal, salvation, and hope in the face of changing external challenges. Given the festival's deep resonance with the cycles of nature and the grave environmental crisis that besets us today, it's not only appropriate but also crucial to add emphasis to these concerns during our Passover Seders.

ACTIVITIES, BLESSINGS, AND READINGS

1. *An Art Mirdrash Project:* Ask your guests to participate in an art midrash project by creating a collage that expresses the relationships among Passover, freedom, and spring. (See Appendix III on page 326 for art midrash directions.)

2. *Grow one of the items eaten during the Seder:* The Seder requires us to eat bitter herbs (usually either horseradish or romaine lettuce) and to dip a green vegetable (usually parsley) in saltwater. If you have access to a small garden, horseradish could not be easier to grow. Buy a horseradish root in the grocery store. Cut off the top and place it in a shallow bowl of water for several days until you see leaves begin to sprout from the top and small roots from the bottom. Plant it where it will get some sun. It requires vir-

tually no care beyond occasional watering. Every spring, you'll notice dark green leaves laying flat on the soil. Dig up the root below, and you're all set. Chances are you'll find more than one plant, because horseradish tends to spread quickly.

I've been growing horseradish for years. I can tell you that it adds a special zing to the Seder, and watching for the first leaves break through the softening soil helps me keep tuned in to the coming of spring and Passover. Depending on where you live, you may also be able to winter over some parsley from the previous season. If not, you may be able to grow a bit of parsley or some romaine lettuce in a flowerpot indoors. Plant your seeds a few months before Passover. If you're more ambitious, consider planting some barley. In ancient times, Passover was associated with the ripening of the barley crop. If you plant barley seeds after Sukkot in the fall, your crop will be nearing maturity by Passover. I assure you that this is an absolutely amazing experience! I grew the plants in a few flowerpots in our greenhouse, but they will do just as well in any sunny window. A pot of barley looks great on the Seder table and will certainly prompt questions.[18] Be careful not to bring harvested barley stalks indoors during Passover because it is one of the five kinds of grain that can become *chametz*!

3. *Step outside:* Before your Seder begins, consider stepping outdoors for a few minutes. If the weather is clear, you should see a beautiful full moon overhead. Take a few deep breaths of the spring air and think about the fact that Jews have been celebrating Passover under the full moon for thousands of years.

4. *Bless the new moon:* If you have not already said the Blessing for the New Moon of Nisan, or if you've never recited the blessing, try it on the first Seder. The moon must be clearly visible. The blessing can be recited indoors or, preferably, outside. You can find the Blessing for the New Moon in Appendix IV (page 327). You may be able to read it by the light of the moon. Generally, the blessing can be recited through the fifteenth of any Hebrew month, which means it can usually be said on the first night of Passover.[19] Much of the blessing comes from the Talmud and is

at least fifteen hundred years old. Before you recite the blessing, read the following statement from the Talmud (Sanhedrin 42a): "Whoever pronounces the benediction over the new moon in its due time welcomes, as it were, the presence of the Shekhinah . . . In the school of Rabbi Ishmael it was taught: Had Israel inherited no other privilege than to greet the presence of their Heavenly Father once a month, it would have sufficed."

5. *Recite the Prayer for Dew at your second Seder:* On the first day of Passover, we begin reciting the daily Prayer for Dew and continue until the end of Sukkot, when we resume the Prayer for Rain. It rarely rains after Passover in Israel, but the quantity of dew plays an important role in the development of crops throughout the dry season. Jewish tradition, of course, imagined that God controlled the quantity of dew, which, in turn, depended on the community's worthiness in God's eyes. Whether or not you believe that in a literal sense, you may want to consider reading this excerpt from the Sephardic version of the Prayer for Dew during your second Seder.[20]

Our God, our ancestors' God:
With dewdrops of Ancient light, illuminate the earth.
With dewdrops of Blessing divine, please bless the earth.
With dewdrops of Gleeful rejoicing, give joy to the earth.
With dewdrops of Dancing exultation, enrich the earth.
With dewdrops of Heavenly splendor, give glory to the earth.
With dewdrops of Wise assembly, let the earth be gathered.
With dewdrops of Song and melody, make musk through the earth.
With dewdrops of Healing life, enable the earth to live.
With dewdrops of Timeless good, give goodness to the earth.
With dewdrops of Your saving help, redeem the earth.
With dewdrops of Care and nurturing, nourish the earth.

For you are The Abundant One, our God, who makes the wind to blow and brings down the dew.

For blessing, not for curse.
For living, not for death,
For plenty, not for dearth.

6. *Recite the Blessings for Witnessing the Wonders of Nature:* In Talmudic times, the sages sought to ensure that Jews would neither take nature's wonders for granted nor lapse into the worship of nature itself. Several of the sages, for example, spoke of the virtues of praying "with the red glow of the sun."[21] More important, they developed an extensive catalog of blessings, praises to God, to be recited upon witnessing various natural phenomena. Although most of these are not explicitly tied to a particular season, many involve witnessing one or another aspect of spring's wondrous unfolding.

Here are several blessings that you might consider reciting on the appropriate occasion. You could step outdoors to recite one with your guests before the Seder begins. Whatever views you hold about God, reciting blessings of this sort has a way of adding something special to the experience of nature. They can also heighten your awareness of the world around you by giving you a moment to appreciate the wonder before your eyes. You may also find that blessings like these induce a welcome sense of humility. If these blessings don't speak to you, compose your own. But don't let wonder pass you by without marking the moment.

On seeing fruit trees in flower for the first time in the year (recited in the month of Nisan only):
Blessed are You, Lord our God, King of the Universe, who has created a world without deficiency, and has placed within it goodly creatures and noble trees to be a delight to the children of humankind.

Upon seeing trees of striking beauty:
Blessed are You, Lord our God, King of the Universe, who has such beauty in His world.

Upon smelling the fragrance of herbs or plants:
Blessed are You, Lord our God, King of the Universe, who creates fragrant plants.

Upon smelling fragrant fruit:

Blessed are You, Lord our God, King of the Universe, who gives a pleasant fragrance to fruits.

On tasting fruit for the first time of the season recite the Shehechiyanu *(best said during the second Seder to honor traditional practice):*

Blessed are You, Lord our God, King of the Universe, who granted us life and sustenance and permitted us to reach this season.

On seeing the wonders of nature (including mountains, hills, and deserts; lightning; and sunrise):

Blessed are You, Lord our God, King of the Universe, Author of the work of creation.

On seeing a rainbow:

Blessed are You, Lord our God, King of the Universe, who remembers the covenant and keeps Your promise faithfully.

On hearing thunder or seeing a storm:

Blessed are You, Lord our God, King of the Universe, whose power and might fill the world.

Upon seeing the ocean:

Blessed are You, Lord our God, King of the Universe, who has made the great sea.

7. *Choose one or two of the texts below to read and discuss at your Seder. Some relate specifically to Passover; others speak to Judaism's understanding of our broader responsibility to the natural world.*

[Unleavened] bread . . . gives its name to the feast. This may be regarded from two points of view, one peculiar to the nation, referring to the migration [from Egypt] . . . the other universal, following the lead of nature, and in agreement with the general cosmic order . . . In the vernal equinox we have a kind of likeness and portraiture of that first epoch in which this world was created. The elements were then separated and placed in harmonious order with reference to themselves and each other. The heaven was donned with sun and moon and the rhythmical movements and circlings of the other stars, both fixed and planetary . . . So every year God reminds us of the creation of the world by setting before our eyes the spring when everything blooms and flowers. And therefore there is good reason for describing [Nisan] . . . as the first month because in a sense it is an image of the primal origin . . . [Food], when unleavened, is a gift of nature, when leavened is a work of art . . . [The] springtime feast . . . is a reminder of the creation of the world and its earliest inhabitants . . . [The ancients] wished every year to rekindle the embers of the serious and ascetic mode of faring [i.e., eating unleavened bread] and to employ the leisure of a festal assembly to confer admiration on the old-time life of frugality and economy, and as far as possible to assimilate our present-day life to that of the distant past.

—PHILO OF ALEXANDRIA (FIRST CENTURY B.C.E.), JEWISH PHILOSOPHER[22]

When God created the first human beings, God led them around the Garden of Eden and said: "Look at my works! See how beautiful they are—how excellent! For your sake I created them all. See to it that you do not spoil and destroy My world; For if you do, there will be no one else to repair it."

—ECCLESIASTES RABBAH 7:20
(NINTH-CENTURY-C.E. MIDRASH), LAND OF ISRAEL

How astonishing . . . is the growth of foods from seeds. A single grain that has been saved from mishaps produces a thousand grains and more. It has even been that out of one grain of wheat, as many as three hundred [stalks] will spring up, each containing over twenty grains. We also come across gigantic trees whose roots have sprung out of a single seed or a single shoot . . . Praised be the All-Wise and Gracious One who brings into existence such vast effects from causes so small and weak. . . .

—BACHYA BEN JOSEPH IBN PAQUDA
(ELEVENTH CENTURY), SPAIN, PHILOSOPHER OF MORALS[23]

This God, honored and revered, it is our duty to love and fear; as it is said, "You shall love the Lord your God" (Deut. 6:5), and it is further said, "You shall fear the Lord your God" (Ibid., 6:13). And what is the way that will lead to the love of Him and the fear of Him? When a person contemplates His great and wondrous works and creatures and from them obtains a glimpse of His wisdom, which is incomparable and infinite, he will straightaway love Him, praise Him, glorify Him, and long with an exceeding longing to know His great Name; even as David said, "My soul thirsts for God, for the living God" (Psalms 42:3). And when he ponders these matters, he will recoil frightened, and realize that he is a small creature, lowly and obscure, endowed with slight and slender intelligence, standing in the presence of Him who is perfect in knowledge. And so David said, "When I consider Your heavens, the work of Your fingers—what is man that You are mindful of him?" (Psalms 8:4–5) . . . [Our] sages have remarked in connection with the theme of the love of God, "Observe the universe and hence, you will realize Him who spoke and the world was."

—MAIMONIDES (1135–1204), SPAIN, EGYPT, PHILOSOPHER,
CODIFIER OF JEWISH LAW, AND PHYSICIAN, [24]

Every blade of grass sings poetry to God without ulterior motives or alien thoughts—without consideration of reward. How good and lovely it is, then, when one is able to hear this song of the grasses. It is therefore a precious thing to conduct oneself with piety when strolling among them.

—REBBE NACHMAN OF BRESLOV (1772–1810),
PODOLIA, UKRAINE, HASIDIC MASTER [25]

Human beings have indeed become primarily tool-making animals, and the world is now a gigantic toolbox for the satisfaction of their needs . . . Nature as a toolbox is a world that does not point beyond itself. It is when nature is sensed as mystery and grandeur that it calls upon us to look beyond it. The awareness of grandeur and the sublime is all but gone from the modern mind. The sense of the sublime—the sign of inward greatness of the human soul and something which is potentially given to all—is now

101

a rare gift. Yet without it, the world becomes flat and the soul a vacuum.

—RABBI ABRAHAM JOSHUA HESCHEL (1907–1972),
POLAND, GERMANY, THE UNITED STATES, THEOLOGIAN, SOCIAL ACTIVIST[26]

We must dare to reexamine our longstanding preference for history over nature. The celebration of "historical monotheism" . . . is a legacy of nineteenth-century Christian-Jewish polemics, a fierce attempt by Jewish thinkers to distance Judaism from the world of paganism. But the disclaimer has its downside by casting Judaism into an adversarial relationship with the natural world. Nature is faulted for the primitiveness and decadence of pagan religion, and the modern Jew is saddled with a reading of his tradition that is one-dimensional. Judaism has been made to dull our sensitivity to the awe-inspiring power of nature. Preoccupied with the ghosts of paganism, it appears indifferent and unresponsive to the supreme challenge of our age: humanity's degradation of the environment. Our planet is under siege and we as Jews are transfixed in silence.

—RABBI ISMAR SCHORSCH (1935–), UNITED STATES CHANCELLOR OF THE
JEWISH THEOLOGICAL SEMINARY OF AMERICA,
"TENDING OUR COSMIC OASIS"[27]

8

The Exodus as a Personal Spiritual Journey

מִתְּחִלָה עוֹבְדֵי עֲבוֹדָה זָרָה הָיוּ אֲבוֹתֵינוּ.
וְעַכְשָׁו קֵרְבָנוּ הַמָּקוֹם לַעֲבוֹדָתוֹ.

In the beginning our ancestors worshiped idols, but now the Omnipresent has brought us close to His service.
—THE PASSOVER HAGGADAH

If you take a close look, you'll notice something special about this passage. It brims with different kinds of imagery associated with the idea of a spiritual journey—from *the beginning to now*, from *our ancestors to us*, from distance to *closeness*, from *worshiping idols* to *service* in the name of religious truth. Even this particular name of God, *HaMakom*, literally, "the Place," evokes the image of God as "destination."

After a long, arduous journey, we have drawn close to *HaMakom*, the Place of truth and insight. And that certainly merits praise and celebration.

The passage is based on the words of Rav, one of the leading sages of the early Talmudic period (Pesachim 116a). He brought not only legal traditions from

Israel to Babylonia but mysticism as well.[1] (For more on Rav and the Seder, see chapter 3.)

The Haggadah tells us that "in every generation, each individual should feel as though he or she had gone out of Egypt." On one level, that means we should relive the journey from slavery to freedom so that we neither take our freedom for granted nor lose hope in our ongoing struggles against oppression. But beneath this—and this would be Rav's view—the Haggadah cautions us to remember our ancestors' spiritual missteps so that we can better direct our own journeys.

Our journeys mark the progress of our efforts to live lives of ultimate purpose and meaning. Each stage of life presents us with particular challenges, so what feels "ultimate" at one stage of life may feel trivial at another. Phases of the journey focus on different themes: personal identity, interpersonal relationships, love, work, vulnerability. And sometimes, the journey focuses on our search for closeness to the Great One of Being.

Here we consider the story of the Exodus as a metaphor for our own spiritual journeys. We'll look at some of the milestones along the journey and at the significance of the fact that the Bible attributes humanity's first song to the Israelites after they cross the Red Sea. We conclude with a note about the spiritual journey's ultimate goal.

This chapter differs from all other chapters in this book in that it is meant to be read and digested on your own.

Before you begin, consider the following questions:

- The Haggadah tells us that "in every generation, each individual should feel as though he or she had gone out of Egypt." If you think of the Exodus as a personal journey, where are you trying to leave and where do you want to go?

- The Bible says that the paschal sacrifice was to be eaten *b'chipazon*, "hurriedly," "in a rush" (Ex. 12:11) because that was the manner in which the Israelites left Egypt (Deut. 16:3). When is it good to rush? When is it bad to rush? In your life, where and why are you rushing?[2]

- Is your destination a state that you think you could ever reach? How do you know whether you are getting closer?

- How would you know whether you had arrived?

- Have you ever felt as if you had a glimpse of your destination or a taste of what it would feel like to be there?

- To what extent is your journey shared with others? Is there an element of your journey that you must experience alone?

EXODUS: THE SPIRITUAL JOURNEY

Isaiah Horowitz (c. 1565–1630), one of the great Kabbalists, began his commentary on the Haggadah with a statement that might strike you as odd: "All the aspects of freedom that we deal with during this night [of the Seder] refer to freedom of the soul. . . ."[3]

In Hebrew, *Mitzrayim,* "Egypt," can also be read *maytzarim,* "the narrows," the places of spiritual constriction or illusion. These are not only the ruts where our ancestors got stuck, but also the places where we find ourselves trapped. Read this way, the story becomes an allegory of the times when we are hopelessly mired in misery, when our lives seem to lack true purpose and we're not sure there's a way out.

Think about Moses as the part of us that struggles for positive change, for getting out of the mud.[4] Pharaoh is the aspect of ourselves that resists moving on, that finds one excuse after another for maintaining the status quo, despite its pain. God is the source of the conviction, however fleeting, that even seemingly hopeless situations *can* change for the better. Followers of the great Hasidic master Rebbe Nachman of Breslov (1772–1810) write:

"Pharaoh" is king of *"Mitzrayim"* [Egypt]. He rules over the *maytzarim* [the narrow places]—the constrictions of the Mind, the limitations of Awareness. It is his function to restrain and repress human awareness of the Divine . . . To this aim, the king of Egypt kept us perpetually busy, our minds incessantly preoccupied with worldly illusions (Ex. 5:4–9).

105

Even today "Pharaoh" allows us to toil assiduously in the intricacies of the Torah study and zealously exert ourselves in rigid stringencies of the Halakhah. He also keeps our minds troubled with the unanswerable paradoxes in Judaism . . . anything we ask for, he will grant us. With one exception. "Pharaoh" denies us the thing we need most: the time and composure to yearn for greater awareness of God. . . .[5]

We each have our own path. A student of the Seer of Lublin (Yaakov Yitzchak, d. 1815), one of the early Hasidic masters, once said, "Show me one general way to the service of God." His teacher replied, "It is impossible to tell men what way they should take. For one way to serve God is through the teachings, another through prayer, another through fasting, and still another through eating. Everyone should carefully observe what way his heart draws him to, and then choose this way with all his strength."[6]

But you can lose your way, whichever path you choose. What began as a means to a lofty end winds up becoming an end in itself. What may have been adaptive in the past now cripples you.

Arthur Green, one of our generation's great teachers, described two points of the journey this way: "Our own innermost liberation is our 'coming out of Egypt'; our own moment of truth is our 'standing before Sinai.'"[7]

MILESTONES ALONG THE ROAD

Now, let's explore some of the milestones along the road. We'll alternate among three dimensions: the Exodus story; its relevance to our personal spiritual journeys; and occasionally the way some of this finds expression in the Haggadah. That's why you'll notice a shifting focus as we survey the journey.

The journey from the mud of Egypt to the fiery revelation at Sinai, with all the doubts and backsliding along the way, represents the road that stretches forth before each of us. As we mark some of the journey's milestones, keep in mind the ancient elements of earth, water, air, and fire. The mystical tradition holds that each of these is associated with four ascending worlds of being.[8]

Mired in the brick pits of Egypt, the Israelites had lost any sense of a world beyond the muck. Pharaoh had become their God in the sense that he completely determined the scope of their consciousness. But the midwives who refused to obey Pharaoh's order to kill newborn Israelite males knew another reality. These women, who ushered new life into the world, knew something about the mysteries of creation and the miracle of birth. They could see beyond the realm that Pharaoh had built and "they feared God." They defied Pharaoh. So, too, did Moses' mother: Placing him by the water's edge, she trusted a power greater than a king of flesh and blood.

"A long time after that . . . the Israelites were groaning under the bondage and cried out; and their cry for help rose up to God" (Ex. 2:23). Sometimes it takes a long time to realize the depth of our own misery. But acknowledging our suffering and expressing it to another are the first steps in moving beyond it.

Years later, at the burning bush, Moses encountered God and learned the destination of his journey. Of course, Moses doubted his suitability for the job. How many of us ever feel fully equipped to take up the responsibilities and challenges life sets before us? Who initially assumes the mantle of leadership, at whatever level, without hesitation? Leadership means stepping out ahead with a vision, seemingly alone, with no assurance of how things will turn out. The journey from Egypt to the Promised Land would take a lot longer than Moses expected.

The power of his experience at the burning bush also convinced Moses that simply *telling* the Israelites of his encounter with God would not open their eyes to the possibilities he had envisioned. Even getting Moses' attention required a minor miracle. Remember, hundreds of years separate the narratives of Genesis and Exodus. In the stories of Genesis, the presence of God infused the lives of the patriarchs and matriarchs. Over the intervening centuries, memory of God's presence faded. So, at the burning bush, Moses asked God for signs to help rekindle the Israelites' bygone spiritual insights. There comes a point along the road when we realize that discovery is actually rediscovery.

Those signs, and later the plagues, slowly painted a picture of worlds far beyond the narrows of Egypt. Still, not all the Israelites were convinced. According to the tenth-century midrash Exodus Rabbah (14:3), even until the darkness of the ninth plague, many Israelites had no interest in leaving Egypt: "There were transgressors in Israel who had Egyptian patrons and lived in affluence and honor, and were unwilling to leave. . . ." Every Egypt offers its own seductions, its own incentives for staying put.

As the plagues unfolded, the Israelites may have increasingly sensed a power greater than Pharaoh. But nothing had been required of them. They were passive witnesses, not actors. That was about to change for those who saw, as it were, through the darkness. After the plague of darkness, the Israelites faced their first real tests of faith: the paschal sacrifice and circumcision. Both involved literally marking themselves, setting themselves apart from the Egyptians. In our lives, too, each of us must be willing to stand apart from the crowd as we further define ourselves. If we allow the fear of doing so to paralyze us, we remain in Egypt, our lives stagnant.

As the plagues approach their climax, the Israelites receive instructions about the paschal sacrifice. Earlier, Moses had asked Pharaoh to let the people go so they could sacrifice to their God in the wilderness for three days. Pharaoh offered to let them "sacrifice to your God *within* the land." But Moses refused: "If we sacrifice that which is untouchable [sacred] to the Egyptians before their very eyes, will they not stone us?" (Ex. 8:22). Facing that fear is just what God finally required. Our journeys inevitably demand overcoming our most deep-seated fears. Fear deepens the ruts that prevent us from moving on in our lives.

Participating in the paschal sacrifice constituted a test of another kind as well. The Israelites themselves revered Egyptian deities, including the sheep and goats they were ordered to slaughter. Their willingness to carry out this sacrifice would demonstrate whether or not they realized the emptiness of worshiping the gods of Egypt. As the midrash Exodus Rabbah (16:2) says:

> God then said to Moses: "As long as Israel worships Egyptian gods, they will not be redeemed; go and tell them to abandon their evil ways and to reject idolatry." This is what is meant by: "Draw out lambs for your families, and slaughter the Passover offering" (Ex. 12:21). Draw out and take you lambs. That is to say: Draw away your hands from idolatry and take for yourselves lambs, thereby slaying the gods of Egypt and preparing the Passover; only through this will the Lord pass over you.

The order for circumcision came soon after: "The whole community shall offer [the paschal sacrifice] . . . but no uncircumcised person may eat of it . . . and all the Israelites did so" (Ex. 12:47–50).

The midrash suggests that the Israelites had abandoned circumcision relatively soon after settling in Egypt. "When Joseph died, they abolished the covenant of circumcision, saying: 'Let us become like the Egyptians'" (Exodus Rabbah 1:8). When the order to reinstitute circumcision came, many Israelites balked. For the Kabbalists, circumcision in Egypt symbolized removing the coverings that had fallen upon the children of Israel and prevented them from sensing even the faintest glimmer of the world beyond Egypt. The same collection of midrashim (19:5) informs us that the holdouts were only persuaded when God ordered the four winds to mingle the aroma of the paschal offering with the breezes from the Garden of Eden![9]

Together, the paschal sacrifice and circumcision represent an irrevocable declaration of identity—in the most public and private realms. It's the point in the journey when we realize we are no longer trying our nascent convictions on for size.

Still, the ambivalence persisted. After the last plague, the Israelites were still not sure about leaving. In the end, "they had been *driven* out of Egypt and could not delay; nor had they prepared any provisions for themselves" (Ex. 12:39). Even when the external circumstances for change have fully ripened, the inner Pharaoh holds us back.

Moving forward requires leaving the inessentials behind. "So the people took their dough before it was leavened" (Ex. 12:34). Rabbi Yehudah Leib Alter of Ger, the nineteenth-century Hasidic master known as the Sefat Emet, described the significance of matzah:

> On every Passover a Jew becomes like a new person, like the newborn child each of us was as we came forth from Egypt. The point implanted by God within our hearts is renewed. That point is called *lechem oni* (poor people's bread), because it is totally without expansion. Matzah is just the dough itself, not having changed through fermentation. Every Jew has this inner place, the gift of God. Our task is really to expand that point, to draw all our deeds to follow it. This is our job throughout the year, for better or worse. But this holiday of matzot is the time when the point itself is renewed, purified from any defilement. Therefore, it has to be guarded from any "ferment" or change on this holiday.[10]

CROSSING THE SEA AND THE FIRST SONG

When people think back on the Seders of their childhood, they often remember with particular fondness singing the Haggadah's songs. Do you share that feeling? If so what made those that experiences so special?

All the obstacles the Israelites faced in leaving Egypt paled in comparison to what they experienced at the Red Sea. As Pharaoh's troops appear on the horizon, the children of Israel stand at the Red Sea. Now the cost of setting out on a journey to leave Egypt has risen to its ultimate price, as they realize that the journey has all been a terrible mistake, leading nowhere but the ultimate dead end.

Every journey begins with excitement, but there's also a voice that asks, "Why are you doing this? Are you crazy? It would have been so much easier to stay home." When trouble appears, the voice says, "I told you so!" Then we look for someone to blame.

At the Red Sea, the Israelites said to Moses, "What have you done to us, taking us out of Egypt? Is this not the very thing we told you in Egypt, saying, 'Let us be, and we will serve the Egyptians, for it is better for us to serve the Egyptians than to die in the wilderness'" (Ex. 14:11–12).

Miraculously, the Israelites found a way out, a way to overcome an insurmountable obstacle. Here's the scene at the Red Sea according to a third-century midrash: "When the Israelites stood at the sea, one said: 'I do not want to go down to the sea first,' and the other said: 'I do not want to go down to the sea first . . .' While they were standing there deliberating, Nachshon, the son of Amminadav, from the tribe of Judah, jumped up first and went down to the sea and fell into the waves. . . ."[11] Nachshon acted on faith. Others may have thought he was crazy or suicidal. Sometimes we know that there is a way from here to there, though we may be the only one to see it.

The Haggadah does not explicitly mention Nachshon. But according to the Talmud, the beginning of Psalm 114 (which we recite just before blessing the second cup of wine) alludes to his willingness to take the plunge. "When Israel went forth from Egypt, the house of Jacob from a people of strange speech, Judah [the fourth son of Jacob and the ancestor of King David] became His sanctuary, Israel His dominion. The sea saw them and fled . . ." (Psalms 114:1–3). Says the Talmud, "[Because of Nachshon of the tribe of Judah] Judah was worthy to be made the ruling power in Israel, as it is said: 'Judah became His sanctuary, Israel His dominion.' Why did Judah become His sanctuary and Israel His dominion? Because the sea saw [Nachshon] and fled."[12] With Nachshon in the lead, the Israelites took a few steps into a higher world as they passed through the waters of rebirth.

Sometimes the seemingly "impossible" happens right before our eyes. The world contains possibilities neither the ancient Israelites nor we could ever imagine. What makes moments like this feel miraculous is the conviction that part of the breakthrough feels somehow to have come from *beyond* ourselves. We know we could never have done it on our own.

Such moments of "abiding astonishment," as the philosopher and theologian Martin Buber described them, call forth a profound outpouring of emotion beyond ordinary speech.[13] And so it is after crossing the Red Sea, after passing through the waters of spiritual rebirth, that something startlingly new appears in the Bible: the first song.

In that awestruck moment at the Red Sea, the Israelites sang a song to God, and that song became the ancestor of all Judeo-Christian prayer. Says Exodus Rabbah (23:4), "From the day when God created the world until the Israelites stood near the sea, no one save Israel sang unto God."[14] Many had expressed their gratitude by building altars and offering sacrifices, but until then, apparently no one in the Bible felt moved to use song for this purpose.[15] As Heschel put it: "The way to faith leads through acts of wonder and radical amazement . . . [We] sing to Him before we are able to understand Him."[16]

In song we sense more deeply the air we breathe. The Hebrew words for "breathing," *neshimah,* and "soul," *neshamah,* come from the same root and could not be closer. "The Lord God formed man from the dust of the earth. He blew into [Adam's] nostrils the breath of life (*nishmat chayyim*), and man became a living being" (Gen. 2:7). In the Song at the Sea, we discovered how to use the very breath of life to praise the One from whom it came: breath for breath. (Later in the Seder, just after Psalm 136, we recite *Nishmat kol chai,* "The breath of every living thing shall bless Your name. . . ." The Talmud refers to *Nishmat kol chai* as the "Benediction of the Song," doubtless because of its poetry and many allusions to song: "Though our mouths were full of song like the sea . . . we could never thank You enough.")[17]

Although the path continues on to Sinai and then Israel, we'll end our brief exploration of the Exodus as a spiritual journey at this point with a few final thoughts.

Our journey began in the muddy Egyptian brick pits. In crossing the Red Sea we moved through waters of rebirth. Filled with wonder, we breathed the air of salvation and poured forth the first song to God. We celebrate our redemption, not the drowning of the Egyptians. The fire of Sinai lies further down the road.

The Haggadah helps us to reenact our ancestors' journeys and in the process to become more conscious of our own. We taste the bitterness of the low point from which we began—the salty tears, the bitter herbs, and the muddy *charoset*. We eat matzah, the wayfarer's bread. It may not have had time to rise, but it certainly won't rot along the journey.

And we sing many, many songs of praise.

Let us sing as if we had just discovered song! Let us breathe new life into our Seder songs. Sing with the intention and fervor that we breathed into our first song on the other side of the Red Sea.

This is not easy. The followers of Rebbe Nachman of Breslov said: "Sometimes our voices are trapped. No words. No calling out. Everything caught in *maytzar hagaron,* the straits [narrows] of the throat. The voice of holiness is suppressed. We feel hampered in expressing ourselves before God. Stuck! It may be social norms or personal inhibitions. Either way, it is *Mitzrayim*. We are in 'exile.'"[18]

But don't be deterred. Ask people what they remember most fondly about the Seders of their childhood and many will tell you something about the songs. They once took us to another place; they can now, too.

It's worth noting that even though the songs most familiar to us in the Haggadah were added to the Seder during the Middle Ages, the Haggadah's emphasis on song is far older. According to the Mishnah (Pesachim 5:7), in Temple times the Levites sang the Hallel—Psalms 113–118—to accompany the paschal sacrifice. We chant those psalms during the Seder, two before and four after the meal. (Just before beginning the Hallel, Ashkenazic Haggadot read: "Let us then recite before Him a new song: Hallelujah.")

THE JOURNEY'S ULTIMATE PURPOSE

In a culture that celebrates the individual, a caution is in order, lest you conclude that from a Jewish perspective personal enlightenment constitutes the spiritual journey's ultimate goal.

Liberating the children of Israel from Egypt was an essential step in preparing the Israelites to join with God in the work of repairing the world. The midrash even asserts that the dreadful state of human affairs has forced God into exile. Heschel wrote:

> Man was the first to hide himself from God, after having eaten of the forbidden fruit, and is still hiding. The will of God is to be here, manifest and near; but when the doors of this world are slammed on Him, His truth betrayed, His will defied, He withdraws, leaving man to himself. God did not depart of His own volition; He was expelled. *God is in exile.*[19]

A world that resembled what God had intended would actually bring redemption for God and humanity alike.

From this perspective, the second sentence of the Maggid section of the Haggadah demands our attention: "*All* who are hungry, come and eat. All who are in need, come join in celebrating the festival of Passover." From the beginning, the Haggadah challenges us to take up the work of *tikkun,* "repair." Imagine if we took those words seriously. Could we ensure that on the night of Passover no one, anywhere, would be hungry? Would that be possible? Who knows? But would it bring the world one step closer to repair? Definitely. First we must do what we can to fix the world by lifting up the down and out. Then we can interpret the Haggadah metaphorically and make sure that our door remains open to those seeking spiritual nourishment.

Paradoxically, as we celebrate our liberation during Passover, we sharpen our awareness of the enslavement that reigns within and around us. At the moment we taste freedom, we remember the hungry. From a point of great light we peer through the darkness. From the heights of deliverance, we survey a shattered world crying out for healing.

You might ask, "I know I'm supposed to feed the hungry and welcome the stranger, but what is God's role in fixing the world?"

What is the source of the staggeringly audacious conviction that the present, the status quo, cannot be the end of the road? *That's* where God comes in. God speaks in a small voice within each of us, saying, "Never forget that yours is not a 'normal,' but a broken world, one that we can surely help fix." At the Seder, that voice calls a bit more audibly because with Passover we confront the reality of our freedom and how we have used it, for good or ill.

God contributes something else too. *Mitzvah goreret mitzvah.* Keeping one commandment leads to keeping another. Goodness begets goodness and unleashes a cycle of incalculable, unanticipated positive outcomes. The sum of our collective efforts to repair the world far exceeds that of our individual actions. As we take up the work of *tikkun* more earnestly, uncovering light within the darkness, God contributes all the unimaginable synergies that result from our collective efforts. God delivers as soon as we choose to treat the troubles of this earth as if they were our own leaky roof, not that of some distant stranger.

9

Enslaved in Egypt: Why?

בָּרוּךְ שׁוֹמֵר הַבְטָחָתוֹ לְיִשְׂרָאֵל. בָּרוּךְ הוּא.
שֶׁהַקָּדוֹשׁ בָּרוּךְ הוּא חִשֵּׁב אֶת־הַקֵּץ...

Blessed be He who keeps His promise to Israel. Blessed be He.
For the Holy One, blessed be He, determined the end of the bondage, thus doing that
which He said to Abraham our father in the Covenant between the Pieces.
As it is said, "He said unto Abram: Know well that your offspring shall be
strangers in a land not theirs, and they shall be enslaved and oppressed for four hundred
years; but I will execute judgment on the nation they shall serve, and in the end they
shall go out with great wealth" (GEN. 5:13–14).
—THE PASSOVER HAGGADAH

Before we look more closely at this passage, it's worth noting that commentators have long struggled to reconcile conflicts within the Bible about the duration of Israel's enslavement in Egypt. A reckoning based on Bible's genealogical accounts does not jibe with the figure of four hundred years, and Exodus itself (12:41) states that Israel left Egypt after four hundred thirty years. Traditional commentators hold that the four hundred years refers to the span from Isaac's birth to the Exodus, while four hundred thirty years marks the time from God's announcement to Abraham that his "offspring shall be strangers in a land not theirs." The period in Egypt itself amounted to 210 years: Isaac was 60 years old when Jacob was born (Gen. 25:26) and Jacob says (Gen. 47:9) that he was 130 when he arrived in Egypt (400–[60+130]=210). A fifth- or sixth-century rabbinic text analyzing the Bible's internal chronology concludes that the actual enslavement lasted between 86 and 116 years.[1]

But rather than concern ourselves with debates over the length of the enslavement, in this chapter we'll explore a far more fundamental question. Why were the Israelites enslaved at all?

THE COVENANT OF THE PIECES

Read the passage from the Haggadah on page 115 and the paragraphs that follow. Then lead a discussion based on the questions below.

Soon after the Haggadah's parable of the Four Children, we arrive at the above passage. It includes several verses from the Book of Genesis, often referred to as the "Covenant of the Pieces."

The Seder's account of our redemption from Egypt begins with remembering God's fateful promise to Abram (his name had yet to become Abraham). The Haggadah highlights this passage not only because it foretells Israel's suffering and salvation, but also because, according to ancient midrashic tradition, the Covenant of the Pieces occurred on the fifteenth of Nisan, the first night of Passover.[2]

How did God come to make this particular promise?

God had already told Abram that he would inherit the land, and, more important, that he would sire many descendents who would become a great nation. Still childless and well into his eighties, Abram had his doubts. So far, God had given instructions and made promises. Abram had faithfully listened and obeyed. But Abram had *said* nothing to God. The more God promised, the more Abram wondered. And those doubts gave rise to the very first words he addressed to God—a question: "O Lord God, what can You give me, seeing that I shall die childless . . . ?" (Gen. 15:2). God responded with yet another pledge of fruitfulness and reassurance that Abram would surely possess the land. Still unconvinced,

Abram spoke a second time. Another question. "O Lord God, how shall I know that I am to possess it?" (Gen. 15:8).

God answered by directing Abram to gather a number of animals and cut them in half. The sun began to set, Abram fell into a deep sleep, "and a great dark dread descended on him" (Gen. 15:12). That's when God told Abram that his descendents would be enslaved for four hundred years. And God added that Abram's descendents would not return for many years, "for the iniquity of the Amorites is not yet complete" (Gen. 15:16). The Amorites who inhabited Canaan had yet to become sufficiently sinful to warrant losing control of the land.

"When the sun set and it was very dark, there appeared a smoking oven, and a flaming torch that passed between those pieces [of the animals]. On that day the Lord made a covenant with Abram saying, 'To your offspring I assign this land . . .'" (Gen. 15:17–18).

Mysterious as this ritual sounds, this kind of covenant was common in the ancient Near East. When a king would make a grant of land and a house to a loyal subject, he would take a flaming torch or a portable stove and touch it to the blood of a sacrificed animal. The gesture sealed the king's promise as if to say, "He who breaks this covenant shall suffer the fate of this slaughtered animal."[3]

This Covenant of the Pieces represents God's eternally binding promise that Abram's descendents would return to inherit the land. And sure enough, according to the Haggadah, it all comes to pass just as God foretold. God remembers the promise of redemption, and after centuries of bitter suffering, the Exodus unfolds.

The Exodus is about more than liberation from Egypt. It's a tale of promise and fulfillment. God's promise in the passage from Genesis on page 115 includes three critical experiences the Israelites must undergo before God will redeem them: being strangers (*gerut*), being enslaved (*avdut*), and being afflicted (*inui*). We encounter the same terms again in the Haggadah's core text, which describes the ultimate fulfillment of that promise: "My father was a wandering Aramean. He went down to Egypt and 'sojourned there' (*gerut*) . . . the Egyptians 'afflicted' us (*inui*) . . . and 'they imposed heavy labor upon us' (*avdut*) . . . And the Lord brought us out of Egypt with a strong hand . . ." (Deut. 26: 5–8).

Avdut and *inui* occur repeatedly in Exodus 1:10, 11, and 13, which the Haggadah uses in its elaboration on the passage from Deuteronomy. In the book of Exodus (2:22), *ger* first appears when Moses names his son Gershom because

117

"I have been a stranger (*ger*) in a foreign land." Having undergone the three experiences described in the Covenant of the Pieces, God begins to honor the promise of redeeming Abraham's descendents. As we read in the Haggadah, "And their cry for help from the bondage rose up to God. God heard their moaning, and God remembered His covenant with Abraham . . ." (Ex. 2:23–24).[4]

- How do you understand what God tells Abram about the future? Is it merely a picture of what's to come or the outline of God's intentional plan that will first bring Israel to the depths of misery and then to freedom?

- How does God's statement that "the iniquity of the Amorites is not yet complete" contribute to your interpretation of God's vision of Israel's future?

ISRAEL ENSLAVED: MANY QUESTIONS, MANY ANSWERS

Read the paragraph below and lead a discussion on the questions that follow.

The Bible tersely depicts the ostensible reason for Israel's servitude in Egypt:

A new king arose over Egypt who did not know Joseph. And he said to his people, "Look, the Israelite people are much too numerous for us. Let us deal shrewdly with them, so that they may not increase; otherwise in the event of war they may join our enemies in fighting against us." So they set taskmasters over them to oppress them.
—EXODUS 1:8–11

- What might Pharaoh's fears of the dangers of a sizable Israelite minority suggest about his underlying attitude toward the Israelites or about their status in Egypt?

- If you were going to advise Pharaoh about how to prevent the Israelites from becoming a disloyal minority, what would you propose?

- What lessons might American society learn from this story about how to treat its minorities? What lessons might Israel learn about how to treat its 20-percent minority of Arab citizens?

- Did the Israelites' enslavement in Egypt serve some kind of purpose? If so, what?

- Are you more inclined to think of Israel's suffering in Egypt as a form of punishment, as a painful method of teaching an important lesson, or as a story that demonstrates that the children of Israel are somehow destined to suffer? Explain your position.

- Was the enslavement somehow necessary or could it have been avoided?

- The Talmud suggests that the new king who arose and "did not know Joseph" was in fact not a new king, but had simply begun to act as if "he did not know Joseph."[5] Is the tale of the new regime that "forgets" the contributions Jews have made to a particular society, and then turns against them, paradigmatic of the Jewish experience in Diaspora? Is aliyah, moving to Israel, the only solution, as some Zionist voices have argued?[6]

> Below you'll find a wide range of explanations for Israel's enslavement.
> Read through them and choose a few for discussion during your Seder.
> Ask your guests to discuss their reactions to these texts and to assess
> the strengths and weaknesses of each approach.

Jewish tradition has struggled for a long time to explain Israel's enslavement in Egypt.

The question has prompted so many responses because, at least on the surface, the Bible does not offer a clear answer as to why the Israelites suffered such an excruciating ordeal. These explanations fall into five categories:[7]

1. The enslavement resulted from the Egyptians' fear or wickedness.

The Bible clearly places primary culpability for Israel's enslavement upon Pharaoh. He feared that the Israelites had grown too numerous and would side with Egypt's enemies in case of war.

> 2. The enslavement punished the Israelites for a variety of sins: Abraham's lack of faith; Abraham and Sarah's mistreatment of Hagar; the Israelites' assimilationist tendencies; or their idol worship in Egypt.

In his first words addressed to God, Abraham expresses his doubts that God will deliver on the divine promise that Abraham will sire children and inherit the land (Gen. 15:2–9). The Babylonian Talmud (Nedarim 32a) suggests that Abraham's lack of trust constituted a grave sin. Rabbinic thought held that the lives of Judaism's founding ancestors were so critical in shaping the Jewish people's identity that their merits accrued to the future generations, as did guilt for their sins.

Nachmanides (1195–1270), the great Spanish philosopher and Bible scholar, believed that Abraham and Sarah's cruel treatment of Hagar helped set the stage for Israel's affliction in Egypt. Unable to conceive, Sarai—her name had yet to become Sarah—told Abraham to have a child with her handmaid, Hagar, whom the midrash says was none other than Pharaoh's daughter (generations before the time of Moses).[8] When Hagar became pregnant, Sarai became jealous. "And Sarai afflicted her and she ran away from her" (Gen. 16:7). An angel of the Lord then spoke to Hagar, saying that she will bear a son, and his "hand will be against everyone" (Gen. 16:12). Nachmanides concludes:

"Our mother transgressed by this affliction, and Abraham also by his permitting her to do so. And so, God heard [Hagar's affliction] and gave her a son . . . to afflict the seed of Abraham and Sarah with all kinds of affliction."[9]

Sarah "afflicted" Hagar. Later the Egyptians "afflicted" the Israelite strangers. (Ger, the Hebrew word for "stranger," is linked to the name Hagar.) Likewise, Hagar's fertility led to her persecution just as the Israelites' fecundity bent Pharaoh on their destruction. Bondage in Egypt is the punishment for Sarah's cruelty to Hagar.[10]

Exodus Rabbah (1:8), a tenth-century midrash, interprets the enslavement as God's punishment for the assimilationist behavior of the wayward Israelites in

Egypt. After Joseph died, the Israelites abandoned circumcision and said, "Let us become like the Egyptians . . . God converted the love with which the Egyptians loved them into hatred."

Echoing themes of the Haggadah, Ovadia Sforno (1470–1550), a great Italian Bible commentator, believed that the Israelites' ordeal in Egypt resulted from the fact that they had adopted idol worship: "'Then I [God] resolved to pour out My wrath (*lishpokh chamati*) upon them, to vent all My anger upon them there, in the land of Egypt' (Ezekiel 20:8). Thus they were enslaved with hard labor until a small number repented, prayed to God and a messenger did save them."[11]

3. The enslavement was a prerequisite for accepting the Torah.

Other commentators have looked at the experience in Egypt as an essential prerequisite for accepting the Torah at Sinai. Yitzchak Arama (1420–1494, Spain) concluded, "Only this experience would make [the Israelites] see the yoke of Heaven as a relatively easy burden to bear, and they could be induced to shoulder it voluntarily, enthusiastically."[12] Others focused on Egypt as an excruciating but necessary purification. Such views often elaborate on Deuteronomy (4:20): "The Lord took you and brought you out of Egypt, that iron blast furnace, to be His very own people. . . ."

4. The enslavement embodied a difficult, but essential, educational experience.

Nehama Leibowitz (1905–1997, Russia and Israel), a great modern Bible teacher, held that the bitterness of Egypt served to teach the Israelites what *not* to do to "strangers" in the society that they would build in the Promised Land. Many of the Torah's injunctions on proper treatment of the vulnerable members of society end with a coda invoking the memory of suffering in Egypt. One of numerous examples demonstrates the point: "Six days shall you labor and do all your work, but the seventh day is a Sabbath of the Lord your God; you shall not do any work—you, your son or your daughter, your male or female slave . . . or the stranger in your settlements, so that your male and female slave may rest as you do. Remember that you were a slave in the land of Egypt . . ." (Deut. 5:13–15).[13]

5. The enslavement arose as a consequence of Joseph's agrarian policies.

The Book of Genesis describes seven years of famine, during which Joseph provided the Egyptians with food and in the process enslaved them to Pharaoh. Traditional sources generally idealize Joseph, referring to him as *Yosef Hatzadik,* Joseph the Righteous.[14] Still, one can find traces of ambivalence. For example, noting that Joseph died before any of his brothers, the Babylonian Talmud (Berachot 55a) asks, "Why did Joseph die before his brethren? Because he assumed airs of authority [i.e., haughtiness]."[15] Chaim Ibn Attar (1696–1743, Morocco) offers an unusually frank analysis of Joseph's actions. He explains that initially Joseph only accepted payment in cash for food during the famine, and he refused to accept payment in kind (livestock) until he had drained each farmer of his money. This forced the farmers not only to buy food for themselves, but for their livestock as well, further accelerating their impoverishment. Ibn Attar uses the same verb to describe Joseph's shrewd planning (*nitchakam*) as the Bible uses to describe Pharaoh's subsequent call to deal shrewdly (*nitchakmah*) with the Israelites who had become dangerously numerous.[16]

JOSEPH AND THE ENSLAVEMENT?

Before you begin this activity, ask your guests the following question:
What is the first story in the Bible in which an entire people becomes enslaved to Pharaoh? You can read aloud this story about Joseph before or during your Seder.
Lead a discussion based on the questions that follow.

Joseph was a dreamer. As a boy he dreamed that his brothers' sheaves of wheat bowed down to him. He dreamed that the sun and the moon and eleven stars bowed down to him. When Joseph told this dream to his father and eleven brothers, his father said angrily, "What! Are we all to bow down to you?" But Joseph was his father's favorite son. That made his brothers so jealous that they threw Joseph into a pit. Slave traders found him and sold him in Egypt.

Thirteen years later, after a series of successes and setbacks, Joseph was called upon to interpret Pharaoh's troubling dreams. He dreamt that seven lean cows swallowed seven fat cows. He dreamt of seven healthy stalks of corn. Then came seven sickly stalks of corn. Joseph said the dreams meant there would be seven years of plenty followed by seven years of famine. Joseph also suggested a plan for Egypt to survive the famine. Pharaoh was impressed and appointed the thirty-year-old Joseph to be his second in command. Pharaoh gave Joseph the job of carrying out the plan to save Egypt.

Joseph naturally received all the goodies that came with his new position—the finest Egyptian linen clothing, chariots, a gold chain around his neck, Pharaoh's special ring, and of course, a beautiful Egyptian wife. "Pharaoh said to Joseph, 'I am Pharaoh; yet without you, no one shall lift up hand or foot in all the land of Egypt'" (Gen. 41:44).

During the seven years of plenty, Joseph began storing up food for the famine.

Just as Joseph predicted, seven years later, the famine began. It spread so wide that even Joseph's brothers in Canaan came down to Egypt in search of food. Eventually Joseph and his brothers were reunited. Joseph brought the whole family down to Egypt, including Jacob, his aged father. Joseph introduced them to Pharaoh.

Pharaoh told Joseph to settle them in "the best part of the land; let them stay in the region of Goshen. And if you know any capable men among them, put them in charge of my livestock" (Gen. 47:6).

As the famine grew worse, "Joseph gathered in all the money that was to be found in the land of Egypt and in the land of Canaan, as payment for the rations that were being procured, and Joseph brought the money into Pharaoh's palace. And when the money gave out in the land of Egypt and in the land of Canaan, all the Egyptians came to Joseph and said, 'Give us bread, [or we will] . . . die before your very eyes; for the money is gone!' And Joseph said, 'Bring your livestock, and I will sell to you [bread in exchange] . . . for your livestock, if the money is gone.' So they brought their livestock to Joseph, and Joseph gave them bread in exchange for the horses, for the stocks of sheep and cattle . . ." (Gen. 47:14–17).

Finally they had nothing else left to sell for food. They came to Joseph and said, "Let us not perish before your eyes, both we and our land. Take us and our land in exchange for bread, and we with our land will be slaves to Pharaoh . . . So Joseph gained possession of all the farmland of Egypt for Pharaoh, every Egyptian having sold his field because the famine was too much for them; thus the land passed over to Pharaoh. And he removed the population town by town, from one end of Egypt's border to the other" (Gen. 47:19–21).

> Then Joseph said to the people, "Whereas I have this day acquired you and your land for Pharaoh, here is seed for you to sow the land. And when harvest comes, you shall give one-fifth to Pharaoh, and four-fifths shall be yours as seed for the fields and as food for you and those in your households, and as nourishment for your children." And they said, "You have saved our lives! We are grateful to my Lord, and we shall be slaves to Pharaoh" (v'hayinu avadim l'pharaoh).[17] And Joseph made it into a land law in Egypt, which is still valid . . . Thus Israel settled in the country of Egypt, in the region of Goshen; and they acquired holdings in it, and were fertile and multiplied.
>
> —GENESIS 47:23–27

The Egyptians sold themselves into slavery. But the Israelites prospered under Joseph's protection.

- Would you say Joseph's plan to save the Egyptians was fair, or did he take advantage of their situation? If you think Joseph was unfair, how would you explain his motives?

- Was it necessary for Joseph to *sell* grain to the Egyptians? Could he simply have given it to them?

- Faced with starvation or enslavement, the Egyptians twice said, "We shall be slaves to Pharaoh" (v'hayinu avadim l'pharaoh). Those words should sound familiar because they are so similar to the Haggadah's opening response to the Four Questions, "avadim hayinu l'pharaoh," "We were slaves to Pharaoh." The Haggadah quotes this passage from Deuteronomy (6:21): "We were slaves to Pharaoh in Egypt and the Lord took us out from Egypt with a mighty hand." What do you make of the fact that the Bible uses virtually identical words to describe the situation of the Israelites under Pharaoh and the Egyptians under Joseph?[18]

- *Etz Hayim,* the Conservative Movement's new commentary on the

Five Books of Moses, offers the following note on the Egyptians' declaration, "We shall be slaves to Pharaoh" (Gen. 47:25): "A generation later, the Egyptians would take their revenge on Joseph for having reduced them to slavery, by enslaving his people."[19] This interpretation implies that the enslavement of the Israelites may have been a measure-for-measure punishment (*midah k'neged midah*) for Joseph's enslavement of the Egyptians. Do you agree? If so, what lesson might the Bible be trying to teach in its depiction of Joseph, the famine, and Israel's subsequent enslavement? How does the story of Joseph and the famine color your understanding of the meaning of Passover?

THE SELF-CRITICAL VOICE—BENEFITS AND DANGERS

Read aloud the section that follows and discuss it before your Seder.

The fact that commentators have offered such a huge number of explanations for Israel's enslavement reflects one thing: They are unwilling to accept the Bible's explanation at face value.

In part, commentators have probed beneath the surface of the biblical account from a deeply held conviction that God, and not a king of flesh and blood, ultimately directs history. Hence the many interpretations of Israel's suffering in Egypt as divinely wrought—be it punishment, purification, or preparation. But what about views that explain Israel's suffering in Egypt as flowing from the natural consequences of human rather than divine action? For example, the Talmud chides Jacob for favoring Joseph and concludes that "on account of two ounces of wool that Jacob gave Joseph [for a special coat] . . . Joseph's brothers became jealous of him, which eventually resulted in our ancestors' descent into Egypt."[20] What about the assertions that Abraham and Sarah's harsh treatment of Hagar, or Joseph's enslavement of the Egyptians, may have helped set the stage for the misery into which the Israelites would eventually fall?

These interpretations begin to blur the comfortable distinction between Israelite victim and Egyptian perpetrator. Remembering that Pharaoh's oppression of Israel included a genocidal dimension beyond mere enslavement restores that distinction. Still, reckoning Joseph's exploitation of the Egyptians among the factors contributing to Israel's oppression definitely leads to a more nuanced understanding of the Exodus story. And it certainly casts new light on Deuteronomy's injunction (23:8): "You shall not abhor an Egyptian, for you were a stranger in his land."

This line of interpretation rests on the assumption that "in the field of human destiny we reap what we sow," especially when our deeds inflict pain on others.

Two texts make this point with stunning power. First let's consider the Babylonian Talmud's (Sanhedrin 99b) astounding comment on the genealogy of Amalek, Israel's prototypical enemy, whose descendents viciously attacked the Israelites in the desert. The genealogy appears simple enough: "And Timna was the concubine of Esau's son Eliphaz; she bore Amalek to Eliphaz" (Gen. 36:12). The Talmud elaborates:

> Timna wanted to convert. She came before to Abraham, Isaac and Jacob, but they did not accept her. So she went and became a concubine to Eliphaz the son of Esau. She said, "It is better to be a maidservant of this nation [i.e., the nation of Esau], and not to be a noblewoman of another nation [i.e., Israel]." Amalek issued from her, who vexed Israel. What is the reason? They should not have put her off.[21]

Here, the Talmud argues that the patriarchs' unwillingness to embrace a would-be convert literally sowed the seeds for the birth of Israel's archenemy, later personified by Haman, of Purim infamy, a descendent of Amalek.

Now let's look at the Zohar's elaboration on the fact that when Pharaoh's daughter opened the basket containing Moses she saw it was "a boy crying. She took pity on it . . ." (Ex. 2:6):

> Rabbi Isaac said: "The redemption of Israel depends only on weeping: When the effect of the tears of Esau ['And Esau wept aloud,' Gen. 27:38] which he shed before his father on account of the [stolen blessing] shall have been exhausted, redemption will begin for Israel." Said Rabbi Yossi: "Esau's weeping brought Israel into captivity, and when their force is exhausted, Israel, through their tears, shall be delivered from him."[22]

The Zohar implies that the deceit of Jacob brought about a fundamental rupture in the fabric of human relations, a rupture that clearly awaits repair. Esau's tears have only partially been quenched through the tears shed by the infant Moses.

Unbound by normal constraints of linear time, the midrash freely describes the Passover celebration of the patriarchs centuries before the Exodus from Egypt. The eighth-century midrash, *Pirke de Rabbi Eliezer,* supplies a fateful connection between Esau's stolen blessing and Passover. "The nightfall of the festival day of Passover came, and Isaac called unto Esau his elder son, and said, 'O my son! Tonight the heavenly ones utter songs, on this night the treasuries of dew are opened; on this day the blessing of the dews [is bestowed]. Make me savory meat whilst I am still alive, and I will bless thee. . . .'" (For more on the relationship between Passover and dew, see page 97–98.) Rebecca intervened and instructed her favored son, Jacob, to bring two goats quickly. One goat, the midrash concludes, served as the paschal offering. The other she cooked for Isaac in deceit.[23]

- What are the strengths and weaknesses of these kinds of interpretations?

- To what kinds of situations would or wouldn't you feel comfortable applying this self-critical approach?

- Sometimes the deeds of evil people may express certain realistic grievances. But evil enters the picture when the reaction to a "normal" grievance assumes vast and murderous proportions. For example, Pharaoh may have had an understandable fear of the Israelite demographic explosion. But that did not justify genocide. Do the above approaches adequately address this concern?

- What are the implications of connecting Passover with the incident of Jacob stealing the blessing from his brother Esau?

- What do you think about the difficulties placed before would-be converts by the Rabbinate in Israel in view of the Talmud's story about Timna?

10

"Strangers in a Land Not Theirs": Remembering
to Treat the Strangers among Us Justly

וַיֹּאמֶר לְאַבְרָם יָדֹעַ תֵּדַע
כִּי־גֵר יִהְיֶה זַרְעֲךָ בְּאֶרֶץ לֹא לָהֶם...

He said unto Abram: "Know well that your offspring
shall be strangers in a land not theirs . . ." (GEN. 15:13).
—THE PASSOVER HAGGADAH

Although the Haggadah enjoins each of us to feel as if we had personally
gone out of Egypt, it does not explicitly call on us to remember our suffering in Egypt in order to avoid imposing on others. In the Bible, the injunction
to treat the "stranger" justly recurs dozens of times, more often in fact than any
other positive commandment.[1] On this theme, the Haggadah remains silent, dis-
concertingly so to my ear. Here we'll sample the Bible's repeated exhortations
that our memory of slavery in Egypt should serve as the basis for humane treatment of minorities and the weaker members of society over whom we have power.
The chapter includes a blessing on this theme, which I've composed to be recited at
the Seder. We'll follow that with a look at a difficult subject—the status of Israel's 20
percent minority of Arab citizens. Questions for discussion are included throughout.

When you arrive at the passage in the Haggadah that appears on page 129—not long after the Four Children—read it aloud slowly and ask each of your guests to respond to the question that follows.

- What do you think is the most important lesson we should learn from reexperiencing our redemption from slavery in Egypt?

KNOWING THE HEART OF THE STRANGER

Read the paragraphs below and then the twelve biblical passages about the stranger.

Over the long centuries of the Haggadah's evolution, Jewish weakness, vulnerability, and exile fueled a powerful yearning for divine redemption. Oppression in Egypt became paradigmatic of later painful experiences at the hands of the Persians, Greeks, Romans, Christians, and others. The Haggadah proclaimed hope to a powerless people: "In every generation they rise up to destroy us, but the Holy One, praised be He, saves us from their hands." Understandably, the compilers of the Haggadah worried more about preserving hope for the downtrodden than about how a *strong* Jewish people would wield power.

While we certainly have our enemies, and Israel has not yet achieved peace, today the Jewish people have been blessed with a different reality than that which produced the Haggadah. Despite real setbacks in recent years, Jews throughout the world still probably enjoy greater security than at any other time in our history.

Now we must attend to another theme of the Exodus: Tonight we remember our suffering as strangers in Egypt to help us avoid imposing it on others and to renew our capacity for empathy.

Easier said than done. Once empowered, long-persecuted Christians lost no time in turning upon vulnerable Jews. Ruthless kings and colonial oppressors have been overthrown by insurgents who all too often create even more brutal, despotic regimes. We need to remember Hillel's seemingly simple words: "What is hateful to you, do not do to your neighbor. That is the meaning of the whole Torah. All the rest is commentary. Now go and study."[2]

The Haggadah speaks plainly: "In every generation, each individual should feel as though he or she had gone out of Egypt." Therefore, tonight we remember that we were strangers in the land of Egypt. Tonight we study the Bible's teachings about how we should relate to the *ger*, the stranger in our midst—the other, whom we have the power to oppress or uplift, to shun or welcome, to insult or honor, to neglect or protect. The Bible contains so many reminders to treat the stranger fairly because the experience of suffering more often leaves a thirst for vengeance rather than compassion for others: "The earth shudders . . . [when] a slave becomes king" (Proverbs 30:21–22).

Copy the passages below and the blessing that follows for each of your guests. Take turns reading the passages aloud. These are only some of the many variations on this theme.

1. [Moses' wife Zipporah] bore a son whom he named Gershom; for he said, "I was a stranger in a foreign land."
   —EXODUS 2:22; *GER:* STRANGER, AND *SHOM:* THERE

2. There shall be one law for the citizen and for the stranger who dwells among you.
   —EXODUS 12:49

3. You shall not wrong a stranger or oppress him, for you were strangers in the land of Egypt. You shall not ill-treat any widow or orphan. If you do mistreat them, I will heed their outcry as soon as they cry out to Me, and My anger shall blaze forth and I will put you to the sword, and your own wives shall become widows and your children orphans.
   —EXODUS 22:20–23[3]

4. And you shall not oppress a stranger, for you know the feelings of the stranger, having yourselves been strangers in the land of Egypt.
   —EXODUS 23:9

5. Six days you may do your work, but on the seventh day you shall cease from labor, in order that your ox and your ass may rest, and that your bondman and the stranger may be refreshed.
   —EXODUS 23:12

6. When a stranger resides with you in your land, you shall not wrong him. The stranger who resides with you shall be to you as one of your citizens; you shall love him as yourself, for you were strangers in the land of Egypt: I, the Lord, am your God.

—LEVITICUS 19:33–34

7. But the land must not be sold beyond reclaim, for the land is Mine; you are but strangers resident with Me.

—LEVITICUS 25:23

8. When you gather the grapes of your vineyard, do not pick it over again; that shall go to the stranger, the fatherless, and the widow. Always remember that you were a slave in the land of Egypt; therefore do I enjoin you to observe this commandment.

—DEUTERONOMY 24:17–22

9. If you really mend your ways and your actions; if you execute justice between one man and another, if you do not oppress the stranger, the orphan, and the widow; if you do not shed the blood of the innocent in this place; if you do not follow other gods, to your own hurt—then only will I let you dwell in this place, in the land that I gave to your fathers for all time.

—JEREMIAH 7:5–7

10. And the people of the land have practiced fraud and committed robbery; they have wronged the poor and needy, have defrauded the stranger without redress. And I sought a man among them to repair the wall or stand in the breach before Me in behalf of this land, that I might not destroy it, but I have found none.

—EZEKIEL 22:29–30

11. This land you shall divide for yourselves among the tribes of Israel. You shall allot it as a heritage for yourselves and for the strangers who reside among you, who have begotten children among you. You shall treat

them as Israelite citizens; they shall receive allotments along with you among the tribes of Israel. You shall give the stranger an allotment within the tribe where he resides—declares the Lord God.

—EZEKIEL 47:21–23

12. Hear my prayer, O Lord, and give ear to my cry; do not disregard my tears; for like all my forebears I am a stranger resident with You.

—PSALMS 39:13

- How do these biblical verses make you feel?

- Which passages evoke the strongest reactions?

- Who are the strangers among us today and how might you, or we as a people, act more justly toward these individuals or groups?

- Why do you think the Haggadah does not explicitly take up the theme of our relations to the stranger?

A BLESSING: TREATING STRANGERS JUSTLY

The following original blessing expresses some of Judaism's core principles.[4] You can recite it when you engage in social justice activities that advance the status of groups that suffer neglect or discrimination. Recite it after your discussion of the questions above. You can also include it regularly near the beginning of the Seder just after *Ha lachma anya*, "This is the bread of affliction," when we invite the hungry and needy to join our Passover celebration.

Blessed are You, Lord our God, Sovereign of the universe, who sanctifies us by Your commandments and commands us to remember that we were strangers and slaves in Egypt, and are thus obligated to treat with justice the stranger who resides among us.

בָּרוּךְ אַתָּה יְיָ אֱלֹהֵינוּ מֶלֶךְ הָעוֹלָם

אֲשֶׁר קִדְּשָׁנוּ בְּמִצְוֹתָיו

וְצִוָּנוּ לִזְכּוֹר כִּי גֵרִים וַעֲבָדִים הָיִינוּ בְּמִצְרַיִם

וְעַל כֵּן חוֹבָה עָלֵינוּ לַעֲשׂוֹת צֶדֶק

עִם הַגֵּר הַגָּר בְּתוֹכֵנוּ.

Barukh Atah Adonai Eloheinu melekh ha-olam asher kid'shanu b'mitzvotav v'tzivanu lizkor ki gerim va'avadim hayinu b'Mitzrayim v'al ken chovah aleinu la'asot tzedek im ha-ger ha-gar b'tocheinu.

ISRAEL AND ITS MINORITY OF ARAB CITIZENS

Read the following section aloud and discuss it during your Seder

Now let's take a brief look at a complex—some would say controversial—question, one that might be tempting to save for more tranquil times. But in light of our obligation to treat the stranger among us fairly, let's consider the case of Israel's 20 percent minority of Arab citizens. These are the descendents of Arabs who remained in Israel after the War of Independence and became citizens of the state. They live within the formal borders of Israel, not in the West Bank or Gaza Strip and despite a history of tension, in general their relationship with the State has been peaceful.

In 1947 Chaim Weizmann, who would soon become the first president of the Jewish State, wrote: "There must not be one law for the Jew and another for the Arabs. We must stand firm by the ancient principle enunciated in our Torah: 'There shall be one law for the native and for the stranger who resides in your midst.' . . . I am certain that the world will judge the Jewish State by what it will do with the Arabs, just as the Jewish people at large will be judged by what we do or fail to do in this State where we have been given such a wonderful opportunity after thousands of years of wandering and suffering."[5]

With statehood, Israel's Declaration of Independence promised "full social and political equality" to all its citizens, Jewish and Arab, and "to develop the country for the benefit of all its inhabitants."

Notwithstanding much progress, as in any democracy, gaps remain between promise and practice. A few examples paint the picture. A recent study by an Israeli nongovernmental organization, Sikkuy: The Association for the Advancement of Civic Equality in Israel, found that the Ministry of Construction and Housing and the Ministry of Science, Culture, and Sport both devote about three percent of their budgets to the Arab sector.[6] According to government figures, the infant mortality rate among Arabs is twice as high as that among Jews. And Arabs represent only about 3 percent of those enrolled in university graduate programs.[7]

As the second *intifada* erupted in the fall of 2000, Israeli Arabs launched a series of demonstrations that turned increasingly violent when police fired live ammunition into crowds. Twelve Israeli Arabs died. One Jew died in his car when Arabs stoned it. Three years later, the government commission charged with investigating the events faulted a number of police commanders and the Minister of Public Security and former Prime Minister Ehud Barak for failing to prevent the inappropriate use of deadly force against Arab citizens. The investigation also condemned the inflammatory rhetoric of several Israeli Arab Knesset members. In addition, the commission pointed repeatedly to Israel's "neglectful and discriminatory" treatment of its Arab citizens and the need "to wipe out the stain of discrimination . . . ,"[8] but it remains to be seen if these recommendations will be taken to heart.

A survey conducted in 2001 found that only forty percent of Israeli Jews fully support equal rights for the Arab minority. Another nine percent agree somewhat. Of note, immigrants from the former Soviet Union, a group that had certainly experienced its share of difficulties in the Former Soviet Union, evinced the least support for equal treatment of Israel's Arab community. Only seventeen percent of these Israelis gave unqualified endorsement to the concept of equality for the Arab minority.[9]

In 1993, David Grossman, one of Israel's most prominent authors, concluded his book on relations between Israel's Jewish and Arab citizens with this chilling observation:

How long can a relatively large minority be assumed by the majority to be an enemy without in the end actually turning into one? How long can the state exist as a stable political framework if this is how it treats [a fifth] of its citizens? Slowly and steadily, as if slumbering, Israel is missing its chance to rescue itself from a horrible mistake. It is creating for itself the enemy it will run up against after its other enemies have made their peace with it. And war (as the Serbs and Croats teach us . . .) means war.[10]

- Do you agree with Grossman's assessment?

- What is your vision for future relations between Israel's Jewish and Arab citizens?

- Is this an issue with which American Jews should become more involved? Why or why not?

Vladimir Jabotinsky (1880–1940) led the Revisionist Movement in Zionism, a group that among other things opposed the partition of Palestine to create both a Jewish and an Arab state. Jabotinsky's ideology has played an important role in Israel's right-wing political movements. The following is an excerpt from his 1910 article, "Man is a Wolf to Man":

Sometimes we base too many rosy hopes on the fallacy that a certain people has itself suffered much and will therefore feel the agony of another people and understand it and its conscience will not allow it to inflict on the weaker people what had been earlier inflicted upon it. But in reality it appears that these are mere pretty phrases . . . Only the Bible says, "And you shall not oppress a stranger, for you know the feelings of the stranger, having yourselves been strangers in the land of Egypt." Contemporary morality has no place for such childish humanitarianism.[11]

- What is your reaction to Jabotinsky's statement?

- Does this voice emerge in the Haggadah?

11

"In Every Generation"? God's Role in History
and the Jewish People's History among the Nations

וְהִיא שֶׁעָמְדָה לַאֲבוֹתֵינוּ וְלָנוּ.
שֶׁלֹּא אֶחָד בִּלְבָד עָמַד עָלֵינוּ לְכַלּוֹתֵנוּ.
אֶלָּא שֶׁבְּכָל דּוֹר וָדוֹר עוֹמְדִים עָלֵינוּ לְכַלּוֹתֵנוּ.
וְהַקָּדוֹשׁ בָּרוּךְ הוּא מַצִּילֵנוּ מִיָּדָם.

*It is this [promise] that has sustained our ancestors and us, for not just one has
arisen to destroy us; rather in every generation there are those who seek our destruction,
but the Holy One, praised be He, saves us from their hands.*[1]
—THE PASSOVER HAGGADAH

With this passage, we arrive at a clear statement of one of the Haggadah's views on God's role in history and the Jewish people's history among the nations. The nations perennially seek our destruction, but God saves us. These words are often sung with such a stirring tune that you may not have paid much attention to the song's meaning. Suffice it to say, this passage raises more than a few difficult issues, discussion of which will make for an important pre-Seder activity. Let's focus on the paragraph below in bold. It gains meaning from its particular context within the Haggadah.

> Blessed be He who keeps His promise to Israel. Blessed be He. For the Holy One, blessed be He, determined the end of the bondage, thus doing that which He said to Abraham our father in the Covenant between the Pieces. As it is said, "He said to Abram, 'Know well that your offspring shall be strangers in a land not theirs, and they shall be enslaved and oppressed for four hundred years; but I will execute judgment on the nation they shall serve, and in the end they shall go out with great wealth'" (Genesis 15:13–14).
>
> *The participants lift their cups of wine and say:*
>
> **It is this [promise] that has sustained our ancestors and us, for not just one has arisen to destroy us; rather in every generation there are those who seek our destruction, but the Holy One, praised be He, saves us from their hands.**
>
> *The cups are put back on the table.*
>
> Go out and learn what Laban the Aramean sought to do to Jacob, our father. While Pharaoh decreed death only for the male children, Laban sought to uproot all.
>
> —THE PASSOVER HAGGADAH

This passage expresses one of the Haggadah's central ideas: that salvation from the oppression of Egypt was not the one-time event God referred to in the preceding paragraph. Rather, Egypt becomes a motif that characterizes Jewish life in every generation. Just as that motif defined Jacob's experience in the house of Laban, generations before the enslavement in Egypt, so too will it shape Jewish life in our era, millennia after the Exodus.[2]

• What emotions does this passage express? What feeling do you have when you recite these words?

• What is your reaction to the image portrayed here of God's role in the world?

- A fragment of an ancient Haggadah discovered in the Cairo Geniza, a repository for Jewish documents over many centuries, reads: "It is this that has sustained our ancestors and us, for not just one enemy has arisen to destroy us; but the Holy One, praised be He, saves us from their hands."[3] The Geniza text omits the phrase "rather in every generation there are those who seek our destruction." How does adding or deleting that phrase change the tone of the passage?

- There's another passage in the Haggadah that contains the phrase "in every generation," *b'khol dor vador:* "In every generation, each individual should feel as though he or she had gone out of Egypt." How would you compare these two passages? Do they both convey the same view of Jewish history? If not, how do they differ? How does the role of God seem to differ in these passages?

- How do you feel about the image of the Jewish people reflected in the passages above?

- What do you make of the fact that the passage gives all-powerful God the credit for saving the Jewish people, but ascribes our suffering to the work of our enemies?

- The Jewish people has known political helplessness for centuries. We don't have much experience wielding political power. What are the challenges facing a people that has known the Holocaust and yet now possesses the power of the State of Israel and the American Jewish community? How well have we met these challenges?

GOD: THE ELEPHANT, AS IT WERE, AT THE SEDER

Read the following aloud and discuss it along with the questions on the next page.

God is the Haggadah's central character, an active God who rescues the innocent Israelites and punishes the wicked Egyptians. Over the ages, many have struggled to reconcile that view of God with experiences that seem to challenge it. How do we maintain faith in the God of the Exodus during the darkest times when a just, all-powerful, all-knowing God seems absent? Perhaps the interchange in the Haggadah between Rabbi Elazar ben Azariah and Ben Zoma about whether to include a reference to the Exodus in the evening prayers—times of metaphorical darkness—points to the same struggle.

According to one survey, fewer than 20 percent of American Jews believe that God intervenes in the course of human events.[4] But it is precisely an interventionist God that we encounter in the Haggadah and throughout Jewish liturgy in general. The typical gap between one's beliefs about God and the representations of God in liturgy generates dissonance. And that dissonance can easily interfere with engagement in the Passover Seder and other aspects of Jewish life where liturgy plays a central role. The words on the page are hard to take literally, and yet how else should we take them?

Maybe you didn't come to the Seder to contend with God. Maybe, you came because you value the idea of celebrating freedom and talking about what that means with the people closest to you. But God is what you get—in almost every line of the Haggadah. Yet in most Seders no one talks about God. That makes God the Seder's "elephant" as it were, a big enough one to create plenty of discomfort. Rather than ignore God at the Seder, let's talk about God.

For many, the God of the Exodus is tough to accept. God saves the Israelites from a terrible ordeal, but not without virtually destroying Egypt—hardening Pharaoh's heart so he cannot let the Israelites go; raining down plagues that wipe out plants, animals, and much human life; and finally drowning a huge number of Egyptians in the Red Sea in a frightful display of divine might. What kind of God is this?

But that's not the only problem. The God of the Exodus may have been tough. But at least that God was *there,* and sooner or later everyone knew it. Our experience of God is very different, especially if we're looking for a God like the one in the Haggadah. And yet that probably *is* the God all of us carried around in our heads as children. The Seder represents a complicated, bittersweet encounter with an image of God that, on one hand, no longer seems quite realistic but, on the other, feels familiar, like an old childhood neighborhood that's no longer home. As distant as the Haggadah's God may have become, that God evokes a certain yearning.

Ana-Maria Rizzuto, a psychoanalyst, wrote a book called *The Birth of the Living God* in which she studied the development of people's concepts of God. Many individuals she interviewed began by saying that they didn't believe in God. "Tell me," she then asked, "about the God you don't believe in." Invariably they would tell her about a god who didn't measure up to the image of an ideal god they had developed in early childhood. God now seemed too strict, punished the innocent, failed to provide comfort, appeared uninvolved, and so on.[5]

Most of us experience similar disappointment with our parents. We learn to accept their limitations and love them nonetheless. But that's a lot harder to do with God because God's not supposed to have any limitations. For many, it's easier to reject completely the idea of God than it is to develop a concept of God that can coexist with the reality of such a profoundly imperfect world and the absence of an Exodus-like, interventionist God.

And that brings us face to face with a problem that has vexed theologians and philosophers for a long time. It's a problem with a fancy name—theodicy: the attempt to reconcile God's attributes with the reality of evil and unjustified suffering. St. Augustine (354–430) is credited with its earliest and most stark formulations: "Either God cannot abolish evil or He will not. If He cannot then He is not all-powerful. If He will not then He is not all-good."[6] Joseph Albo, the fifteenth-century Jewish philosopher from Spain, offered one of the most succinct responses to the problem: "If I knew Him, I would be Him."[7]

Six hundred years and a Holocaust later, with suicide bombings now commonplace and a war on terrorism raging, the enigma still haunts us. In our age, what do we mean when we sing, "the Holy One, praised be He, saves us from their hands"?

Elliot Dorff, a contemporary Conservative theologian, formulated the dilemma as follows:

> If one believes that (1) God is one, (2) God acts in human history, (3) God is all-knowing (omniscient), (4) God is all-powerful (omnipotent), (5) God is good, and (6) there is unjustified evil in the world, then one is involved in a self-contradiction. An all-knowing, all-powerful God, who is also good, after all, could never allow unjustified evil to exist and would never need to.[8]

Dorff's conclusion deserves pondering—as much for its honesty as for its ultimate *inconclusiveness:*

> Our distress will not be alleviated for long by pretending that we understand unjustified evil in our world or by divorcing God from it; denial can be beneficial for a brief time . . . but ultimately it is not healthy either psychologically or philosophically. We must instead face the ultimate ambiguity of our existence with the commitment to truth, the faith, the strength and the good sense of Jews over the ages.[9]

Here are some questions to discuss before or duing your Seder.
You can discuss them after reading the passage above or independent of it.
Remember, the Seder should be a gathering where all
questions can safely be put on the table.

- Elliot Dorff, a contemporary Conservative theologian, highlights six assumptions about the nature of God and evil. He believes that you can't hold all of these assumptions without one or more being contradicted by the others: (1) God is one, (2) God acts in human history, (3) God is all-knowing (omniscient), (4) God is all-powerful (omnipotent), (5) God is good, and (6) there is unjustified evil [or unjustified suffering] in the world. Do you agree with Dorff? Does the notion that God gave human beings free will—which implies the capacity to do good or evil—allow you to hold on to all six assumptions? How do different kinds of natural disasters challenge these assumptions about God? Which of these assumptions about God are the easiest for you to accept? Which are the most difficult?

- How do you understand the following challenging verse from Isaiah (45:6–7): "I am the Lord, and there is no one else. I form the light, and create darkness; I make peace, and create evil; I the Lord do all these things." The Rabbis of the Talmud (Berachot 11b) found this verse so disturbing that they authorized a modification for its use in the morning prayers: "I form the light, and create darkness; I make peace, and create *all things*."

- What are the kinds of events that raise questions for you about God? What are the kinds of experiences that make you feel the presence or existence of God?

- Can you imagine an event or experience that would convince you that God definitely does or does not exist? From the nature of this hypothetical event or experience what can you learn about your concept of God?

ARGUING WITH GOD

Read the paragraphs below on your own or during your Seder
and then read a few of the illustrations of arguing with God.
Then discuss one or both of the questions that follow.

People have problems "believing in God" for many reasons. Many are angry with God for having "hidden His face." Others blame belief in God for many of the world's troubles. Others are disappointed when the ways of God seem so different from what they were taught to expect when they were younger. What are we to do with these feelings? Where do we express them? The matter becomes even more complicated because many also think that these very feelings put them "beyond the pale" when it comes to believing in God. The result? "I don't believe in God." The choice seems to be either being grateful to God and faithfully accepting what God sends our way or walking away from "the God proposition" entirely.

You may think that Judaism's great heroes chose the path of unending gratitude to God and faithful acceptance of their fate. But that's only on the surface. Jewish tradition contains a third approach. When God's ways appear unfair, we can argue and struggle with God.

Take a lesson from great characters such as Abraham, Jacob, Moses, Jeremiah, and Job.

God tells Abraham that God plans to destroy Sodom and Gomorrah. Abraham shoots back: "Will you sweep away the innocent with the guilty? . . .

Far be it from you! Shall not the Judge of all the earth deal justly?" (Gen. 18:23, 25). God responds through a bargaining process and agrees to spare the city if it contains ten righteous people.

After wrestling a blessing out of an angel, Jacob's name is changed to Israel, meaning "he wrestled with God."

After the sin of the Golden Calf, God wants to destroy the Israelites and make a new covenant with Moses and his descendents. Moses refuses the bargain: "Alas, this people is guilty of a great sin in making for themselves a god of gold. Now, if You will forgive their sin [well and good]; but if not erase me from the record which You have written" (Ex. 32:31–32).

Jeremiah lived during the destruction of the First Temple in 587 C.E. and called God to court! Scholars have diagrammed the prophet's ancient arguments with God and found them to conform to the proceedings of the ancient law courts. They include an address, an argument, a petition, and a response:[10]

> [*Address:*] You will win, O Lord, if I make claim against You, yet I shall present charges against You.
>
> [*Argument:*] Why does the way of the wicked prosper? Why are the workers of treachery at ease? You have planted them and they have taken root, they spread, they even bear fruit. You are present in their mouths, but far from their thoughts.
>
> [*Petition:*] Yet, You, Lord, have noted and observed me; You have tested my heart, and found it with you. Drive them out like sheep to the slaughter, prepare them for the day of slaying!
>
> [*Response:*] If you race with the foot-runners and they exhaust you, how then can you compare with horses? [God seems to say, "Jeremiah, you must be stronger. And wait, the contest is not yet over."]
>
> —JEREMIAH 12:1–5

The Bible tells us that Job "was blameless and upright; he feared God and shunned evil" (Job 1:1). Unbeknownst to Job, Satan has engaged God in a little wager: that after a dose of suffering Job would curse God. So God gives Satan the right to afflict Job, kill his family, and deprive Job of every shred of comfort. Job refuses to curse God. Nor will he accept his "friends'" suggestion that somehow he must deserve his suffering. Instead, Job calls God to account:

Who can say to Him, What are You doing?
God does not restrain His anger . . .
The earth is handed over to the wicked one.
He covers the eyes of its judges.
If it is not He, then who? . . .
I insist on arguing with God.

—JOB 9:12–13, 24; 13:3

Many of the psalms also preserve the challenges to God's justice. For example, during the Seder we recite Psalm 115—the third psalm of the Hallel—which calls God to restore Israel's fortunes: "Let the nations not say, 'Where, now, is their God?' . . . The dead cannot praise the Lord. . . ."

In the spirit of their biblical forebears, the sages of the Talmud sometimes expressed their frustration with God's ways through their personal prayers. These kinds of prayers are now known as "law court prayers," because they demand justice from God, the judge. But there was a proper time and a place for these prayers. Here's how one scholar put it: "According to the vast majority of the Talmudic Sages, the 'forceful' prayer which 'hurls accusations at heaven' and demands the rights of the petitioner is definitely considered to be out of place in the statutory public prayer. This pattern is strictly reserved for emergencies only, when all other means of petition have not availed, and is most appropriately used by pious men who are interceding for the community."[11] Honi the Circle Drawer represents the classic example. When rain had not fallen he drew a circle around himself and told God he would not move from it until God showed mercy "upon his children" by ending the drought. It worked![12]

- How do you feel about the concept of arguing with God?

- If you were going to argue with God, what kinds of things would you say? Try to answer this question whatever your beliefs about God.

THE SAGES ON INNOCENT SUFFERING

Below you'll find six examples of how the sages of ancient times
struggled with the question of why "bad things happen to good people."
Before your Seder begins (perhaps in your living room) explain that
you'll be having a conversation on this issue based on a number of views
held by the Rabbis of ancient times. Depending on your group, you might
read all six responses and take a few minutes of discussion after each.

Begin by reading aloud the paragraph below.

The Rabbis of ancient times felt free to argue with God when they felt God's actions were unjust. But this did not exhaust their struggle to justify their belief in an all-just, all-powerful God in the face of the undeserved suffering they witnessed at every turn. Here are six classic rabbinic approaches to the question of why "bad things happen to good people." The fact that many of these explanations are followed by rebuttals (not included here) demonstrates how unwilling the sages were to accept simple answers to difficult questions.[13] The Rabbis offered so many solutions to the problem because in the end none was truly satisfying. Despite, or perhaps because of, their questions, the Rabbis instituted a blessing upon receiving bad news: "Blessed is the true Judge."[14] The Rabbis concluded that faith must be affirmed at the very moment it is most likely to waver.

1. *Innocent on the outside, guilty within:* "There is no suffering without sin" (Babylonian Talmud, Shabbat 55a).

2. *Suffering is a sign of God's love:* Afflictions should lead to introspection and in turn to more virtuous behavior. "If the Holy One, blessed be He, is pleased with a man, he crushes him with painful sufferings . . . Rabbi Hiyya bar Abba fell ill and Rabbi Yochanan went in to visit him. He said to him: 'Are your sufferings welcome to you?' He replied: 'Neither they nor their reward'" (Babylonian Talmud, Berachot 5a-b).

3. *Wait for the world to come:* Only in the world to come will the righteous receive their just desserts. "Rabbi Akiva said: 'He deals

strictly with the righteous, calling them to account for the few wrongs which they commit in this world, in order to lavish bliss upon and give them a goodly reward in the world to come'" (Genesis Rabbah 33:1).

4. *Human beings possess free will, for good or ill:* God endowed humanity with both a good and an evil inclination (*yetzer ha-tov* and *yetzer ha-ra*). God also provided the Torah as an "antidote" to the evil inclination. Straying from its teachings allows evil to invade the world. "The sword comes to the world from the delay of justice, from the perversion of justice, and from interpreting the Torah in opposition to Jewish law" (Mishnah, Avot 5:11).

5. *God's ways are simply inscrutable:* Once, God granted Moses the privilege of looking into the future and seeing that Rabbi Akiva taught the same Torah that had been revealed to Moses. "Then said Moses, 'Lord of the Universe, You have shown me his Torah, now show me his reward.' 'Turn around,' said He; and Moses turned round and saw them weighing out Akiva's flesh at the market-stalls [after his martyrdom in 135 C.E.]. 'Lord of the Universe,' cried Moses, 'such Torah, and such a reward!' He replied, 'Be silent, for such is My decree'" (Babylonian Talmud, Menachot 29b).

6. *God suffers along with us:* We may not know why we suffer, but we don't suffer alone. "God said to Moses: 'Do you not realize that I live in trouble just as Israel lives in trouble? Know from the place whence I speak unto you—from a thorn-bush—that I am, as it were, a partner in their trouble'" (Exodus Rabbah 2:5). When the Temple was destroyed, God "wept and said, 'Woe is Me for My house! My children, where are you? My priests, where are you? My lovers, where are you?'" (Lamentations Rabbah, Prologue 24).

7. Which, if any, of these positions, expresses a view that you can accept? Which is most problematic?

MODERN VOICES

Choose one or more of these passages to read aloud and discuss before
or during your Seder. If you do so during the Seder, relate the conversation
to the passage from the Haggadah at the beginning of this chapter. Argue with
these readings! But don't forget that in the end, Judaism worries more about
our actions than those of God's. As you'll see, a number of these selections
refer to God's hidden face, an image that recurs frequently in the Bible.

Whenever Rabbi Levi Yitzhak came to that passage in the Haggadah of
Passover which deals with the four sons, and in it read about the fourth
son, about him who "knows not how to ask," he said: "'The one who
knows not how to ask,' that is myself, Levi Yitzhak of Berditchev. I do
not know how to ask you, Lord of the world, and even if I did know, I
could not bear to do it. How could I venture to ask you why everything
happens as it does, why we are driven from one exile into another, why
our foes are allowed to torment us so. But in the Haggadah, the father
of him 'who does knows not how to ask,' is told: 'It is for you to disclose
it to him.' And the Haggadah refers to the Scriptures in which it is
written: 'And you shall tell your son.' And, Lord of the world, am I not
your son? I do not beg you to reveal to me the secret of your ways—I
could not bear it! But show me one thing; show it to me more clearly
and more deeply: show me what this, which is happening at this very
moment means to me, what it demands of me, what You, Lord of the
world, are telling me by way of it. Ah, it is not why I suffer, that I wish
to know, but only whether I suffer for your sake."[15]

—LEVI YITZHAK OF BERDITCHEV (1740–1810),
POLAND AND RUSSIA, HASIDIC MASTER

If God lived on earth, people would break the windows in God's house.

—YIDDISH PROVERB[16]

On the road that leads to the one and only God, there is a way station
without God. True monotheism must frame answers to the legitimate
demands of atheism. An adult person's God reveals himself precisely in

148

the emptiness of the child's heaven . . . But only the person who recognized the veiled God can demand his revelation.

—EMMANUEL LEVINAS (1905–1995), LITHUANIA AND FRANCE,
JEWISH EXISTENTIALIST PHILOSOPHER[17]

Does not history look like a stage for the dance of might and evil—
with man's wits too feeble to separate the two and God either directing
the play or indifferent to it? The major folly of this view seems to lie
in its shifting the responsibility for man's plight from man to God . . .
God was thought of as a watchman hired to prevent us from using our
loaded guns. Having failed us in this, He is now thought of as the ultimate Scapegoat.

—ABRAHAM JOSHUA HESCHEL (1907–1972), POLAND, GERMANY,
AND THE UNITED STATES, THEOLOGIAN[18]

When I say we live in the time of the death of God, I mean that the
thread uniting God and man, heaven and earth, has been broken. We
stand in a cold, silent, unfeeling cosmos, unaided by any purposeful
power beyond our own resources. After Auschwitz what else can a Jew
say about God? . . . The time of the death of God does not mean the
end of all gods. It means the demise of the God who was the ultimate
actor in history . . . In a world devoid of God we need Torah, tradition,
and the religious community far more than in a world where God's
presence was meaningfully experienced.

—RICHARD RUBENSTEIN (1924–),
THE UNITED STATES, THEOLOGIAN[19]

When the sound of the closing of the door, after the first child was
shoved into the crematorium, reached heaven, Michael, the most
beneficent of angels, could not contain himself and angrily approached
God. Michael asked, "Do You now pour out Your wrath upon children? In the past, children were indirectly caught up in the slaughter.
This time they are the chief target of destruction. Have pity on the
little ones, O Lord." God, piqued by Michael's insolence, shouted back

at him, "I am the Lord of the Universe. If you are displeased with the way I conduct the world, I will return it to void and null." Hearing these words, Michael knew that there was to be no reversal. He had heard these words once before in connection with the Ten Martyrs. He knew their effect. He went back to his place, ashen and dejected, but could not resist looking back sheepishly at God and saw a huge tear rolling down His face, destined for the legendary cup which collects tears and which, when full, will bring the redemption of the world. Alas to Michael's horror, instead of entering the cup the tear hit its rim, most of it spilling on the ground—and the fire of the crematorium continued to burn.

—DAVID WEISS HALIVNI (1927–), ROMANIA AND THE UNITED STATES, SCHOLAR OF RABBINIC THOUGHT AND LITERATURE, HOLOCAUST SURVIVOR[20]

Evil, which can neither be explained nor comprehended, does exist. Only if man could grasp the world as a whole would he be able to gain a perspective on the essential nature of evil. However, as long as man's apprehension is limited and distorted, as long as he perceives only isolated fragments of the cosmic drama and the mighty epic of history, he remains unable to penetrate into the secret lair of suffering and evil. To what may the matter be compared? To a person gazing at a beautiful rug, a true work of art, one into which an exquisite design has been woven—but looking at it from its reverse side. Can such a viewing give rise to a sublime aesthetic experience? We, alas, view the world from its reverse side. We are, therefore, unable to grasp the all-encompassing framework of being. And it is only within that framework that it is possible to discern the divine plan, the essential nature of the divine actions.

—JOSEPH B. SOLOVEITCHIK (1903–1992) RUSSIA AND THE UNITED STATES, CENTRIST ORTHODOX SCHOLAR AND LEADER[21]

An engine bolt breaks on flight 205 instead of on flight 209, inflicting tragedy on one random group of families rather than another. There is no message in all of that. There is no reason for those particular people to be afflicted rather than others. These events do not reflect God's choices. They happen at random, and randomness is another name for chaos, in those corners of the universe where God's creative light has not yet penetrated.

—HAROLD S. KUSHNER (1935–), THE UNITED STATES, CONSERVATIVE RABBI AND BEST-SELLING AUTHOR[22]

Examining the world scene, a Jew can see nowhere the presence of God in the history of the nations or religions—unless it be in the history of Israel and only through it also in the history of man . . . Only the reality of Israel resists explanation on the level of man-made history alone. Because of Israel the Jew knows that history is messianism, that God's guidance—however impenetrably wrapped in mystery—is never absent from the life of the nations.

—ELIEZER BERKOVITZ (1908–1992), THE UNITED STATES, ORTHODOX THEOLOGIAN[23]

[God] is the liberator of men and their societies. God is the Power working within individuals that will not permit them to acquiesce in servitude, their own or that of others. He is the spark that kindles them into rebellion and the iron that makes them stubborn for freedom's sake. And simultaneously He hardens the heart of tyrants, until, lost to reason, incapable of either learning or forgetting, they destroy themselves.

—MILTON STEINBERG (1903–1950), THE UNITED STATES, CONSERVATIVE RABBI[24]

If a person who cynically refused to believe in God could observe everything a congregation said and did whenever its members gathered for prayer, study, and communal meetings, by the end of a year or two he would know a lot about what God does, even if God never showed up. For, while God does not have hands, we do. Our hands are God's. And when people behave as if their hands were the hands of God, then God "acts" in history.

—LAWRENCE KUSHNER, (1943–), THE UNITED STATES, REFORM RABBI AND AUTHOR[25]

From biblical times to the present day, the Jews have wandered the uncertain terrain between power and powerlessness, never quite achieving the power necessary to guarantee long-term security, but equally avoiding, with a number of disastrous exceptions, the abyss of absolute impotence. They developed the consummate political art of living with uncertainty and insecurity; their long survival owes much to this extraordinary achievement. Jews today must struggle to come to terms with this history in light of their present power, to see both past and present through a realistic lens, neither inflating their power nor exaggerating their powerlessness.

—DAVID BIALE (1949–), THE UNITED STATES,
PROFESSOR OF JEWISH HISTORY[26]

12

"Go Out and Learn . . .": How the Haggadah
Tells the Story of the Exodus

צֵא וּלְמַד,
מַה בִּקֵּשׁ לָבָן הָאֲרַמִּי לַעֲשׂוֹת לְיַעֲקֹב אָבִינוּ.
שֶׁפַּרְעֹה לֹא גָזַר אֶלָּא עַל הַזְּכָרִים
וְלָבָן בִּקֵּשׁ לַעֲקֹר אֶת־הַכֹּל
שֶׁנֶּאֱמַר: אֲרַמִּי אֹבֵד אָבִי,
וַיֵּרֶד מִצְרַיְמָה, וַיָּגָר שָׁם בִּמְתֵי מְעָט.
וַיְהִי שָׁם לְגוֹי גָּדוֹל, עָצוּם וָרָב:

*Go out and learn what Laban the Aramean planned to do to Jacob,
our father. While Pharaoh decreed death only for the male children,
Laban sought to uproot all. As it is said: "An Aramean sought to destroy
my father. He went down to Egypt with few in numbers and sojourned there;
but there he became a great and very populous nation . . ." (Deut. 26:5).*
—THE PASSOVER HAGGADAH

You'll find this passage in your Haggadah in the Maggid section, just after *v'hi she-amdah la-avoteinu,* "And it is this that has stood by our ancestors and us. . . ."

Every year many people come to the Seder expecting to hear the story of the Exodus. They leave with a certain frustration: "I sort of heard the story, but it was confusing and all broken up!" Here we'll look at one of the central ways that the Haggadah "tells" the story—midrash—and why it chose that approach. We'll also explore the biblical passage on which the Haggadah bases its midrash. As we'll see, the Haggadah later gave that passage a special introduction that describes Laban the Aramean and then interpreted *arami oved avi* to mean "an Aramean sought to destroy my father."

HOW THE HAGGADAH TELLS THE STORY

This will make a good pre-Seder activity. Read aloud what follows.

About eighteen hundred years ago, the Mishnah's instructions for the Seder said we should "begin with disgrace and conclude with praise and . . . expound upon *arami oved avi,* 'My father was a wandering Aramean' . . . until [finishing] the whole section" (Pesachim 10:4). The Mishnah refers to a passage from the twenty-sixth chapter of the Book of Deuteronomy known as the Pilgrims' Prayer. Farmers would recite it when they brought their first ripe fruits to the Temple beginning in the early summer and continuing through the fall. Originally, the prayer was not connected with Passover, but with the festival of Shavuot, also known as *Yom Habikurim,* "the day of first fruits." Later, when the Rabbis reinterpreted the ancient agricultural festivals in historical terms, Shavuot came to commemorate receiving the Torah at Sinai. Some scholars believe that the Pilgrims' Prayer was also recited as part of the Passover celebration during the time of the Second Temple until it was destroyed in 70 C.E.[1] The Mishnah indicates that this was one of relatively few prayers that had to be recited in Hebrew. Since many pilgrims spoke dialects of Aramaic, priests prompted those who couldn't manage the Hebrew. Gradually, embarrassed non-Hebrew speakers stopped bringing offerings to the Temple. So a new custom evolved: *Everyone* recited the prayer phrase by phrase following a priest.[2]

A little background on the Book of Deuteronomy sheds a good deal of light on the Pilgrims' Prayer. Most scholars agree that the Book of Deuteronomy was composed either shortly before of during the reign of King Josiah, ruler of the kingdom of Judah between 640 and 609 B.C.E. Josiah introduced far-reaching religious reforms to strengthen monotheism against inroads of idol worship, including the centralization of sacrifice at the Temple in Jerusalem. In the process, Passover evolved into a national festival. Josiah also briefly succeeded in wresting the Northern Kingdom of Israel from Assyrian domination. Jeremiah, who lived during Josiah's reign, evoked powerful imagery of the redemption from Egypt to fortify support for the king's military campaigns: "'In that day,' declares the Lord of Hosts, 'I will break the yoke from off your neck and I will rip off your bonds. Strangers shall no longer make slaves of them; instead they shall serve the Lord their God . . .'" (Jeremiah 30:8–9).

The Pilgrims' Prayer represents one of only three examples of a prescribed prayer in the Five Books of Moses, all of them found in Deuteronomy.[3] Given Josiah's interest in ridding his nation of alien religious practices, the development of fixed prayers makes perfect sense.

> Following the instructions below, you'll find the passage from Deuteronomy upon which the Haggadah builds its midrash. The nonitalicized verses provide important context for understanding the Pilgrims' Prayer, Deuteronomy 26:3–10. (The Haggadah includes only the italicized verses.) Read the entire passage aloud. Then try either of these activities.

- Discuss the questions below.

- Read the passage from Deuteronomy through once aloud. Then ask your guests to take turns reading a phrase or two of the italicized verses and adding a few sentences of elaboration, including details, their own interpretations, comments about contemporary parallels, etc. Use these few verses as a framework around which to weave the tale of Israel's sojourn and departure from Egypt. Make your own midrash!

When you enter the land that the Lord your God is giving you as a heritage, and you possess it and settle in it, you shall take some of every first fruit of the soil, which you harvest from the land that the Lord your God is giving you, put it in a basket and go to the place where the Lord your God will choose to establish His name. You shall go to the priest in charge at that time and say to him, "I acknowledge (*higad'ti*) this day before the Lord your God that I have entered the land that the Lord swore to our fathers to assign us." The priest shall take the basket from your hand and set it down in front of the altar of the Lord your God. You shall then recite as follows before the Lord your God:

"My father was a wandering Aramean. He went down to Egypt few in numbers and sojourned there; but there he became a great and very populous nation. The Egyptians dealt harshly with us and oppressed us; they imposed heavy labor upon us. We cried to the Lord, the God of our fathers, and the Lord heard our plea and saw our plight, our misery, and our oppression. The Lord took us out from Egypt by a mighty hand, by an outstretched arm and awesome power, and by signs and portents.

He brought us to this place and gave us this land, a land flowing with milk and honey. Wherefore I have now brought the first fruits of the soil which You, O Lord, have given me.

—DEUTERONOMY 26:1–10

- Why do you think the Mishnah wants us to tell the story by elaborating on these italicized verses, rather than giving us a number of verses to read from the Book of Exodus, which tell the story in a more direct way?

- What makes this passage particularly suitable for telling the Passover story? What seems to be missing from this brief review of Israelite history? What might account for this?

- Why do you think the Rabbis who compiled the Mishnah, about 130 years after the Temple's destruction, would have chosen a declaration so strongly associated with the Temple for the Haggadah's central text?

- Does this passage place more emphasis on God as author of history or ruler of the natural world? Why might the passage have taken this position?

- The Haggadah mentions Moses' name just once. How would you explain that? Are you comfortable with the Haggadah's minimization of Moses?

THE PILGRIMS' PRAYER AND THE HAGGADAH

Read this on your own, or depending on your group,
do so following the discussion above.

Now let's look at why the compilers of the Haggadah may have chosen this passage as a basis for telling the story of the Exodus and how it functions within the Haggadah. First, remember that Deuteronomy prescribed the recitation of this passage when farmers brought their offerings of first fruits to the Temple. As such, for centuries it would have been one of the most familiar of all biblical texts. Beyond this, it's important to consider four additional aspects of this passage.

The language of family history: The Book of Exodus enjoins us to tell the Passover story to our children as we would the history of our family. With that tone in mind, our passage begins "My *father* was a wandering Aramean." Most of the narration that follows occurs in the first person plural. *We, us,* and *our* are the operative pronouns, and their presence helps erase the long years that separate the pilgrim from his ancestors who suffered and escaped from Egypt. "The Egyptians dealt harshly with *us* and oppressed *us;* they imposed heavy labor upon *us. We* cried out to the Lord, the God of *our* fathers, and the Lord heard *our* plea and saw *our* plight, *our* misery, and *our* oppression. The Lord took *us* out . . ." For the Jew, this is *our* story, *our* family history—not a tale about other people who lived long ago or far away. If the pilgrim bringing his first fruits to the Temple centuries after the Exodus could find meaning in the story of redemption from Egypt, so can we today.

The language of promise and fulfillment: Within the sequence of the Haggadah, the story of the "wandering Aramean" occupies a critical place. Shortly before we come to our passage, we bless God, "who keeps His promise to Israel." Then we read several verses from Genesis (15:13–14) in which God foretells Abraham of his descendents' enslavement and redemption from Egypt. Then we recite, *v'hi she-amdah la-avoteinu,* "and it is this [usually thought to mean 'this promise'] that has stood by our ancestors and us." Now we come to the story of the "wandering Aramean."

157

Structurally, the passage serves to demonstrate that God kept the promise to Abraham. God redeemed Abraham's ancestors and brought them to the Promised Land. But more than that, our passage from Deuteronomy repeats the precise terms of God's covenantal promise to Abraham. God tells Abraham that his descendents must experience three things before they will be redeemed: being strangers (*gerut*), being enslaved (*avdut*), and being oppressed (or afflicted, *inui*). We find all three terms (the roots of each word) in two verses from our passage: "My father was a wandering Aramean. He went down to Egypt with few in number and sojourned there (*gerut*); but there he became a great and very populous nation. The Egyptians dealt harshly with us and oppressed us (*inui*); they imposed heavy labor (*avdut*) upon us." These three terms occur in close proximity only twice in the Five Books of Moses, and the Haggadah includes them both: first in God's promise to Abraham in Genesis (15:13–14) and again in our passage from Deuteronomy![4]

"Not by the hands of a messenger . . .": There's another factor that renders the Pilgrims' Prayer particularly suitable for the Haggadah. The Haggadah wants us to understand that God participated directly in the redemption from Egypt. In its elaboration on the Pilgrims' Prayer, the Haggadah repeats the point: "'And the Lord took us out from Egypt' (Deut. 26:8): not by the hands of an angel, and not by the hands of a seraph, and not by the hands of a messenger, but the Holy One . . . Himself."

You can only appreciate this aspect of Deuteronomy's version of the Exodus if you compare it to other examples in the Bible. Deuteronomy omits the intermediary found in the Book of Exodus (12:23): "The Lord will pass over the door and not let the Destroyer enter and smite your home." The Book of Numbers (20:16) uses similar language: "We cried to the Lord and He heard our plea, and He sent a messenger [angel, *malach*] who took us out from Egypt." According to Rashi, this messenger was Moses.

The fact that the Pilgrims' Prayer leaves Moses out of the story may have further added to its suitability for the Haggadah. At a time when nascent Christianity was constructing a religion that revolved around Jesus as the redeeming intermediary—in the Gospel of John (14:6), Jesus says, "No one comes to the Father but through Me"—Judaism emphasized redemption through an unmediated relationship between God and humanity.[5] But the absence of Moses in this passage may also point to an even older concern. The Book of Deuteronomy tells us that the great leader's burial place remains unknown "to this day" (Deut. 34:6). Why the secret? As the philosopher Gersonides (1288–1344) put it, "So that generations to come should not go astray and worship him as a deity."[6] This was precisely one of the issues of debate in the ancient but long-simmering conflict with the Samaritans, a sect that not only revered Moses as God's only true prophet but also elevated him to an almost Christ-like position: Moses served as humanity's intercessor before God, and in the future he would return to bring the final redemption. Of note, the midrash preserves ancient Jewish notions about Moses that were remarkably similar.[7] Some scholars believe that the Haggadah's virtual omission of Moses may reflect both an anti-Christian and an anti-Samaritan polemic, as well as a dismissal of Jews who were inclined to deify Moses.[8]

The meaning of making midrash: With all these explanations in mind, a question still remains. Why does the Mishnah (Pesachim 10:4) say "he expounds" on a passage from Deuteronomy rather than simply recounting the Passover story as it unfolds in the Book of Exodus?

"He expounds," *hu doreish,* means "he makes midrash," "draws out meaning," "studies." Indeed, the Haggadah prefaces its midrash with these words: "Go out and learn. . . ." The injunction to "expound" or "go out and learn" constitutes a theme that runs throughout the Haggadah. The Seder table includes objects and rituals designed to prompt the Four Questions. After a short answer to those questions, the Haggadah says, "Whoever elaborates on the story of the Exodus is praiseworthy." Then five sages discuss the Exodus all through the night. Then the Four Children present additional questions. Then we "expound" on "my father was a wandering Aramean." After recounting the plagues, three sages again expound on the location and number of the plagues. Rabbi Akiva "proves" there were not ten, but three hundred plagues!

All of this points to the Haggadah's conviction that the Seder should embody *expounding, learning,* and *teaching* about the meaning of the Exodus. A dry, mechanical reading of the same text year in and year out is the antithesis of what a Seder should be.

We can fully appreciate the significance of this instruction to "expound" and make meaning, and to "go out and learn," only when we remember what had been Passover's central rite when the Temple stood: sacrifice. The loss of the Temple, and with it the central ritual of Passover, posed an enormous challenge to Judaism's future and demanded a far-reaching reinterpretation of Passover, the very holiday associated with the Jewish people's birth.[9] At the same time, the Temple's destruction rendered Passover's celebration of redemption all the more crucial. In a move both radical and adaptive, the Rabbis of the post-Temple era resolved that sacrifice would be replaced by acts of kindness, prayer, and observing the commandments, and particularly by study. In fact, the seeds for such a development had begun to sprout among the Pharisees while the Temple stood, but they only came into full flower after the Temple had fallen. In the words of the Talmud, "whoever occupies himself with the study of the Torah needs neither burnt-offering, nor meal-offering, nor sin-offering, nor guilt-offering."[10]

In one sense, the instruction to "expound" on the Pilgrims' Prayer embodied the rabbinic ideal of combining the written Torah with the beloved oral tradition (all the legends and lore passed down through the generations).[11] It also expressed the daring freedom to midrashically re-create what had previously been a hallowed, but frozen, declaration.

For the Israelites in Egypt, slavery was about submission, not creativity. The Rabbis resolved to encounter God, to join God in the creative process through the medium of midrash, drawing out meaning from what they knew to be God's words and discovering new connections among them. It's not just that the mode of "expounding" breathed new life into an old text. At its best, the midrashic method actually gives birth to new texts—the Haggadah, for example—an act of creation and freedom that for the Rabbis epitomized the meaning of redemption from Egypt, if not godliness itself.

JACOB IN THE HOUSE OF LABAN

Depending on your audience, you may want to read aloud this brief overview from Genesis (chapters 29–31) of the relationship between Jacob and Laban, Jacob's maternal uncle.

Isaac, the son of Abraham and Sarah, marries Rebecca. They have twin sons: Esau, the elder, and Jacob, the younger. Their rivalry seems to begin in the womb. As boys, Jacob persuades Esau to sell him his birthright. Later in life, when Isaac approaches death, Rebecca advises Jacob to trick his dim-sighted father into giving him the special covenantal blessing that Esau was due to receive. The plan works. When Esau discovers what has happened, he wants to kill Jacob. Rebecca urges Jacob to flee to her brother, Laban the Aramean. Jacob immediately falls in love with Rachel, Laban's youngest daughter. But Laban insists that Jacob must work for him for seven years before he can marry Rachel.

Seven years later, the wedding takes place. After consummating the marriage, Jacob lifts his bride's veil only to find Leah, Rachel's older sister. He has been tricked by Laban. Jacob works another seven years to marry Rachel. Jacob becomes a prosperous shepherd. He wants to leave his uncle, but Laban wants him to stay longer. Jacob tricks Laban into making a deal that provides Jacob with the healthy additions to the flock while the weaker ones go to Laban. Laban's sons are furious at Jacob. By now Jacob has eleven sons and one daughter from his two wives and two additional concubines. (Rachel will die giving birth to Benjamin, his last child.) God appears to Jacob in a dream and tells him to leave "and return to your native land."

Fearing his uncle's opposition, Jacob sneaks off with his family and flocks while Laban is off sheering sheep. Before she leaves, Rachel steals one of Laban's idols. As Laban sets off in pursuit, God tells him to "beware of attempting anything with Jacob, good or bad." Laban catches up to Jacob and they exchange angry words. Laban complains that he didn't have a chance to kiss his daughters good-bye or to give Jacob a proper sendoff. Jacob complains that he has labored for twenty years and Laban has cut his wages time and again. The discussion leads to a pact of peace between them. Sometime later, before meeting his brother Esau, Jacob wrestles with a figure (an angel, a man, himself?) who says that henceforth Jacob's name will be Israel, "for you have striven with beings divine and human and have prevailed."

Note that the Haggadah's comparison between Laban and Pharaoh rests in part on the fact that the Bible uses a number of the same words to tell both stories. Here's Laban's pursuit of Jacob (Gen. 31:22–23): "On the third day, Laban was told (*vayugad*) that Jacob fled (*ki barach*). So he took (*vayikach*) his kinsmen with him and pursued him (*vayirdof*). . . ." Now here's Pharaoh's pursuit of Jacob's descendents, "the children of Israel" (Ex. 14:5, 7–8): "When the king of Egypt was told (*vayugad*) that the people had fled (*ki barach*) . . . He ordered his chariot and took (*vayikach*) his men . . . and he pursued (*vayirdof*) the Israelites . . ." The story of Jacob's travails in the house of Laban also employs the three terms—*avdut, inui,* and *gerut*—of God's covenantal promise to Abraham that we read about earlier in the Haggadah. As we've seen, these three terms appear prominently in the Exodus story as well as in the Pilgrims' Prayer we've discussed here.[12]

- In what ways are the stories of Jacob in the house of Laban and that of the Israelites in Egypt similar? How are they different?

- How does the Haggadah's brief allusion to the story of Jacob and Laban compare with the Bible's version? In what sense can we say that Laban has tried to destroy Jacob?

A MUCH-INTERPRETED PHRASE

Read the following indented paragraph aloud and discuss the questions below with your guests.

The Mishnah's instructions for the Seder tell us to "expound" on the passage from Deuteronomy that begins with the Hebrew phrase *Arami oved avi*. The Haggadah also gives the passage the following introduction:

Go out and learn what Laban the Aramean planned to do to Jacob, our father. While Pharaoh decreed death only for the male children, Laban sought to uproot all. As it is said: *Arami oved avi,* "An Aramean sought to destroy my father. . . ."

Most translations of the Bible render *Arami oved avi* as "My father was a wandering Aramean." Interpreters such as Rashi and others have claimed that the phrase's grammatical structure supports a very different reading: "An Aramean sought to destroy my father." Suffice it say, despite centuries of debate, the latter became standard for all traditional renderings of the Haggadah.[13] The preference to identify the Aramean as Laban also rests on the fact that the Torah uses the designation "Aramean" exclusively in reference to Laban, or Bethuel, his father.

- What are the major differences between the two readings of *Arami oved avi:* "My father was a wandering Aramean" versus "the

Aramean sought to destroy my father"? Which reading do you prefer and why? Why do you think the Haggadah wanted to suggest that Laban, the Aramean, was a greater threat to the Jewish future than Pharaoh?

• In ancient times, before Haggadot were standardized, different versions of it used either of these readings of the text. By medieval times, the latter became traditional for Ashkenazic, Sephardic, and Yemenite Haggadot.[14] Today we seem to have returned to an approach more typical of ancient times: Once again, Haggadot display no uniformity in how they interpret *Arami oved avi*. Why do you think that some modern Haggadot are more comfortable with "My father was a wandering Aramean" than "The Aramean sought to destroy my father?"

> Following are four interpretations of *Arami oved avi*.
> Choose one or two to compare and discuss at your Seder.

An Aramean destroyed my father. Laban sought to uproot all when he pursued Jacob. [And because he contemplated doing so] the Omnipresent charges him as though he had done it; for [as regards] the heathen peoples, the Holy One, blessed be He considers . . . a thought to be the equivalent of a deed.

—RASHI (RABBI SHLOMO BEN YITZHAK), 1040–1105, FRANCE,
THE MOST FAMOUS BIBLE AND TALMUD COMMENTATOR

"Go and learn what Laban the Aramean planned to do to Jacob, our father." [The Haggadah begins] to recount from the first of the evildoers who plotted against us to destroy us [*aleinu l'khaloteinu*, as in the foregoing passage in the Haggadah, "In every generation they rise up to destroy us . . ."]. And this is Laban. In order to continue this recounting, those who bring the first fruits also recall the going out of Egypt. And we expound on these verses in the Passover Haggadah, as the Mishnah says, "from *Arami oved avi* to the end of the portion."

—RASHBETZ (RABBI SHIMON BEN TZEMACH DURAN), 1361–1444, SPAIN AND
NORTH AFRICA, RABBINIC AUTHORITY, PHILOSOPHER, AND SCIENTIST[15]

Arami, that is the evil inclination [*yetzer ha-ra*] because it is a great deceiver [*ramai*, a play on *Arami*]. This is the meaning of "Now the serpent was the shrewdest [*arum*] of all . . ." (Gen. 3:1). He deceived the creatures [Adam and Eve] in order to destroy them. That is the meaning of "destroyed my father" (*oved avi*). It means the first human being [Adam]. This is the meaning of "Your earliest ancestor sinned" (Isaiah 43:27). And [the serpent, the evil inclination] destroyed him and brought death to him and to the generations coming after him. And he implanted in every soul a part of that evil.

> —RABBI CHAYIM BEN MOSHE ATTAR (1696–1743), MOROCCO AND ISRAEL,
> TORAH COMMENTATOR, ALSO KNOWN AS *OHR HACHAYIM*, THE TITLE
> OF HIS MAJOR COMMENTARY, KABBALIST, AND LEADER OF
> THE EARLY MOROCCAN COMMUNITY IN ISRAEL[16]

[The claim that Laban was worse than Pharaoh] is trying to show us two things about Pharaoh [and the Egyptians] that deserve praise . . . First . . . that we ate their food for a long time, as it says, "We remember the fish that we used to eat free in Egypt, the cucumbers, the melons, the leeks, the onions, and the garlic" (Num. 11:5). And we also know that Jacob went down to Egypt with seventy people and [hundreds of thousands] left with great wealth. From this we must clearly recognize the goodness of the Egyptians, hence "You shall not abhor an Egyptian, for you were a stranger in his land" (Deut. 23:8). Second, the Torah does not suggest that Pharaoh forced the Israelites to worship idols and caused them to sin. He just afflicted them with physical labor. By contrast, Laban wanted Jacob to assimilate . . . And this is what the compilers of the Haggadah wanted . . . to stress on the night of Passover—that we have faced evildoers worse than Pharaoh, evildoers who wanted us to assimilate and thereby uproot and eradicate the people of Israel . . . And evildoers of this kind are sometimes more dangerous to us than those like Pharaoh.

> —MENACHEM KASHER (1895–1983), POLAND AND ISRAEL,
> RABBI AND HALAKHIST, DISTINGUISHED FOR
> HIS RESEARCH IN RABBINIC LITERATURE[17]

Dating from the early decades of the fourteenth century, the Sarajevo Haggadah is thought to have been created in Spain. It is the most celebrated and perhaps the oldest surviving illuminated manuscript of a Haggadah. This page includes the verse in Exodus (14:31) "and when Israel saw the great hand which the Lord had wielded against the Egyptians, the people feared the Lord; they had faith in the Lord and in Moses His servant." The last word on the left above the illumination is *u'v'moshe*, "and in Moses." Traditional Haggadot still include this single mention of Moses' name as well as an allusion to Moses' rod (Ex. 4:17).

MOSES IN THE HAGGADAH

Read the following passage aloud during your Seder.

We've seen that the Pilgrims' Prayer, the Haggadah's central text on the Exodus, omits any reference to Moses. But contrary to what is often said, Moses is not *entirely* missing from the traditional Haggadah. It includes two references to Moses—one explicit, the other implicit.

Moses' name appears in Rabbi Yossi the Galilean's third-century midrashic elaboration on the number of plagues the Egyptians suffered at the Red Sea.[18] Rabbi Yossi's midrash refers to the following passage: "And when Israel saw the great hand which the Lord had wielded against the Egyptians, the people feared the Lord; they had faith in the Lord and in His servant Moses" (Ex. 14:31). As is often the case in rabbinic literature, this midrash quotes only the beginning of the verse from Exodus and therefore excludes the name of Moses. Many early Haggadot that include this midrash did so with its partial quotation from Exodus. By the fourteenth century, Haggadot routinely included the full verse from Exodus, and with it, Moses' name.[19] Today, all "standard" traditional renderings of the Haggadah include this single mention of Moses' name.

This reference involves a particular phrase that occurs just once in the entire Bible: "And in his servant Moses" (*u-v'moshe avdo*). Despite its rarity, almost everyone who has had a bar or bat mitzvah knows this phrase. It occurs in the blessings before reading the haftarah!

Maimonides omitted the elaboration on the plagues from his Haggadah because he believed the Seder should focus exclusively on the events that occurred on the night of Passover rather than including what later befell the Egyptians at the Red Sea. But he hardly intended to exclude Moses from the Seder. To the contrary, Maimonides wrote that during the Seder parents should inform their children about "what happened to us in Egypt and the miracles wrought for us by Moses, our teacher. . . ."[20] Since a few modern Haggadot have dropped the passage about the plagues at the Red Sea—perhaps following Maimonides' lead—some will find that Moses' name *has* completely disappeared from the story.

Since at least the ninth century, Haggadot have also included an important *implicit* reference to Moses. It appears in the midrashic elaboration on the following verse from the Pilgrims' Prayer: "'The Lord freed us from Egypt by a mighty hand, by an outstretched arm and awesome power, and by signs and portents' (Deut. 26:8) . . . 'And by signs:' This is the rod, as it is said, '. . . And take with you this rod, with which you shall perform the signs' (Ex. 4:17)." The Haggadah quotes the conclusion of God's instructions to Moses at the burning bush. Indeed many contemporary translations read, "This is the rod *of Moses,*" adding his name although it does not appear in the Hebrew.

Given his prominence in the biblical Exodus, the Haggadah's minimization of Moses is certainly striking. But there's a difference between minimizing and erasing Moses. The claim of Moses' "complete absence" from the Haggadah is generally used to prove the point that the Haggadah wants to paint a picture of God as Israel's ultimate redeemer. Although obviously true, this is not the Haggadah's only message. For example, the Haggadah also wants us to understand redemption in covenantal terms, as a fulfillment of God's covenantal promise to Abraham. Of Abraham, God says, "I have singled him out, that he may instruct his children and his posterity to keep the way of the Lord by doing what is just and right, in order that the Lord may bring about for Abraham what He has promised him" (Gen. 18:19). Abraham keeps his part of the bargain and God keeps God's promise.

The midrashic traditions asserting that the Israelites merited redemption because they did not assimilate, for example, or because of the righteousness of the women of that generation, stress the covenantal dimension to the redemption from Egypt. In other words, the actions of the Israelites *also* contributed to the process of redemption. The notion of the "completely absent Moses" blinds us to this message in the Haggadah. It also helps us overlook the numerous other human characters who appear in the Haggadah, many of whom also play key roles in the redemptive process. Worse, it may cause us to gloss over our responsibility for helping to redeem the world today. Whatever miraculous properties Moses' rod may have possessed, it did not walk into Pharaoh's palace by itself. God chose a human being to bring it there. God and Moses—God and humanity, in a broader sense—work together to bring about redemption. The presence of Moses' rod in the Haggadah reminds us of that part of the redemptive process that we hold in *our* hands.

DEUTERONOMY'S ISRAELITE HISTORY WITHOUT SINAI

Read the following passage aloud during your Seder.

Deuteronomy's understanding of God and revelation helps explain a glaring omission from the Pilgrims' Prayer—the absence of any reference to receiving the law at Sinai. Deuteronomy depicts God in far more abstract terms than does Exodus. In Deuteronomy's brief account of the revelation (4:36), the people hear God's voice from heaven amidst divine fire. In Exodus (19), God actually descends upon Sinai, and the people need to keep their distance lest they *see* God and die. In Deuteronomy, revelation is almost cerebral; in Exodus, it's physical—frighteningly so.[21] In fact, Deuteronomy envisions an understanding of God's will that transcends the need for a Sinai-like revelation. Not long before his death, Moses speaks pointedly of the contrast. "Surely this Instruction which I enjoin upon you this day is not too baffling for you, nor is it beyond reach. It is not in the heavens, that you should say, 'Who among us can go up to the heavens and get it for us and impart it to us, that we may observe it?' . . . No, the thing is very close to you, in your mouth and in your heart, to observe it" (Deut. 30:12–14).[22]

In addition, for the Deuteronomist, Sinai represented only one version of the covenant: "These are the terms of the covenant which the Lord commanded Moses to conclude with the Israelites in the land of Moab, in addition to the covenant which He had made with them at Horeb [Sinai]" (Deut. 28:69). A reference to both covenants would have complicated an otherwise simple declaration; the exclusion of either would have offended those closer to one tradition or the other.

The absence of any reference to received law in the Pilgrims' Prayer allows the declaration to speak fully in terms of reciprocity rather than commandment. Instead of bringing his first fruits because the law commands it (which, of course, it does), the pilgrim's actual declaration states that I brought (*heiveiti*) this offering to God because God "brought us" (*vayivi'einu*) to the land of Israel. This roots ritual in personal experience, not abstract legal obligation. Moses told the Israelites that the Torah was in their mouths and hearts, not in heaven. The absence of any reference to revelation in the Pilgrims' Prayer affirms that point.

Our celebration of Passover should likewise feel as if it comes from our heart rather than from imposed laws.

13

Women of the Exodus: Redeemed
by Their Righteousness

גָּדוֹל עָצוּם, כְּמָה שֶׁנֶּאֱמַר:
וּבְנֵי יִשְׂרָאֵל פָּרוּ וַיִּשְׁרְצוּ וַיִּרְבּוּ
וַיַּעַצְמוּ בִּמְאֹד מְאֹד
וַתִּמָּלֵא הָאָרֶץ אֹתָם...
וַיַּרְא אֶת־עָנְיֵנוּ, זוֹ פְּרִישׁוּת דֶּרֶךְ אֶרֶץ...

"... Great and very populous ..." (Deut. 26:5): "But the Israelites were fertile and
prolific; they multiplied and increased very greatly, so that the land
was filled with them" (Ex. 1:7).

"And [God] saw our affliction ..." (Deut. 26:7):
that is the enforced separation of husband and wife. ...
—THE PASSOVER HAGGADAH

Much of the Haggadah can be read as an extended midrash on the biblical Exodus. But the Haggadah's rendering curiously differs from that
of the Bible and the midrash in its virtual omission of women. In fact, the
Haggadah mentions only one woman by name—in a song toward the end of the

Seder. This becomes all the more striking in light of a teaching by Rabbi Akiva from the Talmud: "The Israelites were delivered from Egypt as a reward for the righteous women who lived in that generation."[1] The Haggadah alludes to Pharaoh's plan to destroy the Israelites by preventing them from procreating—"the enforced separation of husband and wife." Akiva credits women with thwarting Pharaoh's scheme by defiantly meeting their weary husbands in the fields under the apple trees, feeding them warm food, anointing them with oil, seducing them, and later stealing off to deliver their children. Akiva's allusion to the apple tree finds its way onto the Seder plate. The Talmud explains that *charoset*—in many traditions made with apples—must be thick as a reminder of the clay from which the Israelites made bricks. But it must also be "tart to commemorate the apple trees" and the events that transpired beneath them.[2] For Akiva, women's unwillingness to forsake love and sensuality in the midst of degradation was the critical ingredient that human beings contributed to their redemption from Egypt. Women brought life into a world where Pharaoh had decreed death. But as we'll see, even this hardly gives full credence to the many roles women played in the Exodus.

In this chapter, we'll explore the contributions of women to the Exodus through readings and rituals you can include in your Seder.

Before you begin your Seder, ask your guests to try to list the names of as many of the biblical and rabbinic figures mentioned in the Haggadah as they can. A reference of any significance in any part of the Haggadah counts. But we're not counting God.

What do you notice about this list? Unless your group is unusual, you probably won't get them all. The traditional Ashkenazic Haggadah includes more than twenty such figures. When you begin your Seder, ask your guests to let you know whenever a name appears. With a little imagination, you can easily make this into a game.

PASSOVER IN AN UPSIDE-DOWN WORLD

Read the following passage aloud during your Seder.

In these trying times, what can we learn from the story of the Exodus about how to repair our world? According to the Passover Haggadah, God is the main character in the drama of the Exodus. Alone, God's strong arm and outstretched hand brings us from sorrow to joy. To drive that lesson home, traditional Haggadot mention Moses' name only once, in passing.

This message does not help at a time when the world so desperately needs fixing. It leads both to passivity and alienation as a result of God's seeming absence precisely when evil struts so brazenly about.

Alas, while the Haggadah provides a deep reservoir of hope, it may not be the best guide to fixing the world. Today, we also need a powerful reminder that righting our upside-down world depends on *human* action.

We don't have to look far for this lesson. The beginning of the Book of Exodus contains the inspiring, but often overlooked, story of five women whose actions ultimately play a decisive role in the Exodus. Pharaoh has turned the Israelites' world upside down. He decrees that birth shall not mean life, but death. Pharaoh speaks to Shiphrah and Puah, two midwives of the Hebrews, and orders them to kill all newborn Hebrew males. "The midwives, fearing God, did not do as the king had told them; they let the boys live" (Ex. 1:17). Yocheved, Moses' mother, hides the baby for three months as Egyptians scour the country for newborn Hebrew boys to drown. Unable to hide her son any longer, Yocheved cooks up a risky plan. She builds a miniature ark to float the baby to safety. Pharaoh's daughter brashly defies her father's call for the murder of Hebrew male infants. Hearing Moses' cry from the basket along the banks of the Nile, "She took pity on it and said, 'This must be a Hebrew child'" (Ex. 2:6). Miriam, Moses' sister, the spy in the tale, then steps in and arranges for Moses' mother to nurse him. Raised in Pharaoh's palace, Moses grows up as both an insider and an outsider—the essential experience for a leader who must shepherd his people from one world to another, from slavery to freedom.

The heroic deeds of these five women should speak volumes to us about what it takes to fix our world. They display the courage for decisive action, but they act in concert with others. They take risks because they know there are never guarantees. They don't wait for signs and miracles. They also demonstrate the capacity for maintaining concern about the welfare of others in circumstances when it might seem smarter to save your own skin.

Through these women's actions, Moses becomes the leader God chooses to confront Pharaoh. The rest, so to speak, is history. God plays a role in the story, but only well after human beings have acted decisively to transform their world.[3]

WOMEN AND THE HAGGADAH: MISSING IN ACTION

Depending on your group, read this on your own or aloud.

Over the past generation, we've seen many additions to the Seder highlighting the role of women, particularly Miriam, in the story of the Exodus. Some have opposed this development on the grounds that it violates a central theme of the Haggadah: God's exclusive responsibility for the Exodus from Egypt. That's why the Haggadah "stars" God, not Moses. Leaving aside the question of God's ultimate authorship of history, let's explore other reasons why it makes sense to weave female Jewish figures into the Seder's ritual.

First, the Haggadah tells us that "whoever elaborates on the story of the Exodus deserves praise." As a result, even the "traditional" Haggadah represents a liturgy that has evolved over more than a thousand years. The beloved Ashkenazic ritual of Elijah's Cup seems to have first appeared in Seders in the Middle Ages. If a cup for Elijah could be added to the Seder, why not one for Miriam?

The Haggadah's vision of history doesn't exclude human actors—only women. Although it certainly considers God the director of history, it also features a huge cast of exclusively male characters, with the single exception of Hadassah (Esther), who is mentioned in a song for the second Seder.[4] The cast includes ten rabbinic sages (not uncoincidentally the traditional number for a prayer *minyan*), Abraham, his brother Nahor, and their father Terah; Isaac, Jacob, his brother Esau, and their uncle, Laban; Aaron, Pharaoh, David, and his father Jesse; Elijah; Haman; Daniel; Moses; and a few more depending on which songs you include. (The explicit reference to Moses—from Exodus 14:31—appears in Rabbi Yossi the Galilean's elaboration of the number of plagues the Egyptians suffered at the Red Sea and is included in all traditional versions of the Haggadah. Many modern Haggadot omit these paragraphs.)

The Haggadah clearly envisions a place for human actors on the stage of Jewish history because, like the Bible, it understands that God acts through human beings—men *and* women. That's why there is no good theological reason why the Haggadah's human actors should exclude females. Rather, women's absence from the Haggadah reflects the particular cultural milieu of its compilers.

In recent times, scholars have studied the declining public role of women from the biblical era through the Second Temple era (538 B.C.E.–70 C.E.) and into rabbinic times. One view holds that in their earlier, more revolutionary days, the Pharisees were more open to public roles for women. When they became the "rabbinic establishment," they adopted the more "misogynistic" views reflected in the Mishnah.[5] The absence of women in the Haggadah may also reflect the inexorable influence of the Hellenistic world in which women were clearly consigned to the private rather than the public domain.[6]

The Passover Seder serves as a perfect illustration of the profound Hellenistic influence on developing Jewish practice. The Seder was modeled after the Greek symposium, a banquet, to which a learned man would invite a few of his colleagues for a meal followed by a stylized intellectual discussion over successive glasses of wine. If women were present, they remained "socially invisible."[7]

The traditional Haggadah provides unhappy confirmation of Judith Plaskow's penetrating observation: "The need for a feminist Judaism begins with hearing silence. It begins with noting the absence of women's history and experiences as shaping forces in the Jewish tradition."[8] The Seder ought not perpetuate that silence.

THE WOMEN OF THE EXODUS IN MIDRASH

Although the Haggadah represents a wonderful specimen of rabbinic midrash, it overlooks the enormous role of women in the Exodus. Yet other midrashim hardly remain silent on this matter. Below you'll find a collection of biblical and midrashic texts recounting the early events of the Exodus story. Passages in italics indicate verses from the Bible. Selections from various midrashim and Talmudic *aggadah* (i.e., stories from the Talmud) have occasionally been reworked to make them more accessible.

Read the story below and discuss the questions that follow. You might consider using the story to supplement a portion of the Maggid section of the Haggadah.[9]

The midwives, fearing God, did not do as the king of Egypt had told them; they let the boys live . . . And God dealt well with the midwives; and the people multiplied and increased (Ex. 1:17 and 20). The midwives modeled their conduct after Abraham, of whom God said, *"For now I know that you fear God"* (Gen. 22:12). They said: "Abraham, our ancestor, peace be upon him, opened an inn where he fed travelers belonging to many different religions. As for us, not only have we nothing to feed the babies we deliver, but we have even been ordered to slay them! No, we will keep them alive." But the midwives went further than this. They performed deeds of kindness. When poor women came to them, the midwives would go to the houses of the rich to collect water and food and give them to the poor and thus keep alive their children.

Then Pharaoh charged all his people, saying, "Every boy that is born you shall throw into the Nile, but let every girl live" (Ex. 1:22). "Amram was the greatest man of his generation; when he saw that the wicked Pharaoh had decreed, '*Every boy that is born you shall throw into the Nile,*' he said: 'We labor in vain. Why should we continue to have children?' He arose and divorced his wife. So all [the Israelites] divorced their wives. His daughter, Miriam, said to him, 'Father, your decree is more severe than Pharaoh's. Pharaoh decreed only against the males whereas you have decreed against the males and females . . . In the case of the wicked Pharaoh there is a doubt whether his decree will be fulfilled or not, but in your case, you are righteous. It is certain that your decree will be fulfilled . . .' He arose and took his wife back; and they all took their wives back."

Yocheved became pregnant. Miriam, the prophetess, said, "My mother will bear a son who will be the savior of Israel." When Moses was born, the whole house was filled with light. Her father arose and kissed her upon her head, saying, "My daughter, your prophecy has been fulfilled."

[Yocheved, Moses' mother, hid him for three months.] When she could hide him no longer, she got a wicker basket for him and caulked it with bitumen and pitch. She put the child into it and placed it among the reeds by the bank of the Nile (Ex. 2:2–4). When they cast Moses into the river, Miriam's father arose and smacked her upon her head, saying: "Where is your prophecy now?" . . . But she still believed her prophecy. And that is why we read *"And his sister stationed herself at a distance, to learn what would befall Moses"* (Ex. 2:4).

The daughter of Pharaoh came down to bathe in the Nile, while her maidens walked along the Nile. She spied the basket among the reeds and sent her slave girl to fetch it. When she opened it, she saw that it was a child, a boy crying. She took pity on it and said, "This must be a Hebrew child." . . . *She named him Moses, explaining, "I drew him out of the water"* (Ex. 2:5–10).

Why did Pharaoh's daughter, known in the midrash as Bitya, go down to the Nile? The midrash says it was to cleanse herself of her father's idols. "When [the maidens] saw that she wished to rescue Moses, they said to her, 'Mistress, it is the custom of the world that when a human king makes a decree, though everybody else does not obey it, at least his children and the members of his household obey it; but you transgress your father's decree!' The angel Gabriel came and beat them to the ground."

Pharaoh's daughter called him Moses, because she had "drawn" him out of the water, and because he would "draw" the children of Israel out of the land of Egypt in a day to come. From this you can learn how great the reward is for those who perform kind acts. Although Moses had many names, the name by which he is known throughout the Torah is the one that Bitya, the daughter of Pharaoh, called him, and even God called him by no other name.

God said to Bitya, the daughter of Pharaoh: "Moses was not your son, yet you called him your son. You, too, are not My daughter, yet I will call you My daughter, Bat-Ya, the daughter of God."

Bitya enjoyed an unusual life. Because of her special relationship with Moses, she was the only firstborn Egyptian that God spared during the last terrible plague. Bitya left Egypt with the Israelites and later married Caleb, an Israelite. Along with Joshua, Caleb was one of the two spies who gave truthful reports about what he saw in the land of Israel.

Why, of all people, did Bitya marry Caleb? Because they were both rebels: He rebelled against the counsel of the spies and she rebelled against her father's decree to kill newborn Israelite boys. Some say that they were well suited because Caleb helped prevent Israel, the sheep, from wandering back to Egypt and Bitya helped deliver Moses, their shepherd.

According to legend, Bitya never died. She joined a small and celebrated group who ascended to heaven while still alive.

- What do you make of the fact that the Bible identifies the midwives by name, but not Pharaoh?

- The Bible is ambiguous about whether the midwives are actually Hebrew or not. Pharaoh addresses *"la-meyaldot ha-ivriyot,"* a phrase that can imply either the "Hebrew midwives" or the "midwives of the Hebrews." The midrash resolves this ambiguity in identifying the midwives as Yocheved and Miriam. What difference does it make if the midwives are Egyptian or Israelite?

- Suzanne Scholz, a feminist Bible scholar, offers the following assessment of the roles occupied by the women of the Exodus. Do you agree with this critique?

  "Many feminists have cherished [Exodus] 1:22–2:10 as a proto-type story because it teaches women to live in solidarity with each other. Overcoming ethnic, religious, and social differences, mother, sister and pharaoh's daughter care for the infant who eventually escapes the cruel order of the king. However, the characterization of these women as heroines is problematic. The women stay within traditional gender boundaries that are never challenged or subverted by the narrative."[10]

- In these midrashim, women accomplish their aims without force. In contrast, Amram hits his daughter and Gabriel strikes down Pharaoh's handmaidens. What might these stories be suggesting about a male and female approach to bringing about redemption? Remember, of course, that Moses' first act involves striking and killing an Egyptian taskmaster and that God accomplishes the redemption through ten blows against the Egyptians. The Bible certainly does not describe women as universally nonviolent. Witness Yael's killing of the enemy general Sisera (Judges 4:21) or Jezebel's slaying of God's prophets (I Kings 18:13). Might the Bible be offering the women of the Exodus as a model of nonviolence, albeit one that neither men nor women always manage to follow?

EDEN AND EGYPT: TWO TALES OF EXODUS

Read this on your own or aloud at your Seder.

You'll understand the role that women play in the Exodus better—and the story of the Exodus itself—if you take a look back at the beginning of the Book of Genesis.

Just as children must outgrow childhood, Eve understood that human destiny could not be fulfilled in Eden, a comfortable, but limiting, garden. Nachmanides (1195–1270), the great Spanish Bible commentator, offers an astounding interpretation of life in Eden, comparing human behavior to the predetermined motion of the moon:

> Man's original nature was that he did whatever was proper for him to do naturally, just as the heavens and all their hosts do, "faithful workers whose work is truth, and who do not change from their prescribed course" [a phrase from the Talmud's blessing for the new moon] and in whose deeds there is no love or hatred . . . But after he ate of the tree of knowledge, he possessed the power of choice; he could now do evil or good to himself or to others.
>
> —NACHMANIDES' COMMENTARY ON GENESIS 2:9[11]

Without knowledge of good and evil, precisely what God denied Adam and Eve, humanity's moral development would have been stillborn. As Buber wrote, "The curse [of expulsion] conceals a blessing."[12] So Eve, *Chavah* ("mother of all the living," according to Genesis 3:20), defied the masculine God's decree, and in humanity's first test of free will, she ate from the tree of knowledge of good and evil. God sent Adam and Eve out to begin their journey.

As the Book of Exodus begins, women receive another decree from a different male authority figure. Armed with the knowledge of good and evil, they defy Pharaoh. Eventually, he too sends the people out.

Eden and Egypt (*Mitzrayim*) both ultimately represent narrow places (*maytzarim*). The Bible points to a connection between the two. When Abraham's nephew, Lot, surveys the land, he looks over a well-watered plain "like the garden of the Lord [i.e., Eden], like the land of Egypt" (Gen. 13:10). The midrash explains that as a reward for Egypt's honorable treatment of Joseph and Jacob, God said, "I will call [Egypt] by the name of the Garden of Eden." God knows that just as humanity had to leave the Garden, so Israel must eventually leave Egypt.[13]

Although not often reflected in translation, the operative verbs describing the departures from Eden and Egypt are the same. Everett Fox's translation captures the similarity. "So YHWH, God, sent (*vayeshalcheihu*) him away from the Garden of Eden . . . He drove (*vayegaresh*) the human out . . ." (Gen. 3:23–24).

"YHWH said to Moshe: I will cause one more blow to come upon Pharaoh . . . When he sends (*k'sholcho*) you free, it is finished—he will drive, yes drive (*yigaresh*) you out from here" (Ex. 11:1). What awaits humanity upon leaving Eden is "to work (*la'avod*) the soil" (Gen. 3:23). What awaits Israel after the Exodus is "to serve (*la'avod*) YHWH our God" (Ex. 10:26).[14]

Eden and Egypt: each an Exodus. To fulfill its destiny, humanity must leave the first. Israel's destiny requires going forth from the second. That women should be central in pushing humanity and then Israel through those narrows should come as no great shock. It's what giving birth is all about.[15]

SERAKH BAT ASHER AND THE EXODUS

Read the following story about the amazing Serakh and discuss the questions that follow. Consider substituting this for a portion of the Maggid section of the Haggadah.

A word of background: The Bible includes three genealogies listing Serakh. Genesis 46:17 mentions her among those who went down into Egypt. Numbers 26:46 counts her among those who departed. I Chronicles 7:30 enumerates her as one of Jacob's descendants. In all three cases she is the only granddaughter of Jacob mentioned. That she is listed among those who went into Egypt and those who left, a period of several hundred years, suggests unusual longevity. (Moses lived to 120.) Other than her tantalizing presence in these genealogies, Serakh is nowhere else mentioned in the Bible. Midrash filled the void, and then some.[16]

In the Bible, Shiphrah and Puah, two midwives, refused to obey Pharaoh's command to kill all the Israelite boys they delivered. Yocheved, Moses' mother, saved her son by floating him down the Nile River in a basket. Miriam watched out for her brother as he drifted to the spot where Pharaoh's daughter, Bitya, bathed. Bitya took pity on the baby and pulled him from the water. Miriam offered to find a Hebrew nurse for Moses—his mother. As a result of her goodness, Bitya was the only Egyptian who did not suffer from the plagues. According to legend, she never died, but was taken up to heaven while she was still alive. (The same happened to Elijah the Prophet, for whom we will open our doors near the end of the Seder.)

But there is one story that may top even these, the legend of Serakh bat Asher, the adopted daughter of Asher, the eighth son of Jacob.

Joseph's brothers were jealous because their father, Jacob, favored him. They hated Joseph and decided to throw him into a pit in the desert to die. They told their father that a wild beast had killed Joseph, and Jacob never stopped mourning for his lost son.

But Joseph survived. Traders pulled Joseph from the pit and sold him. He became a slave in Egypt. Many years later, when his brothers went down to Egypt to buy food during a famine, they discovered that Joseph had risen to become Pharaoh's top advisor. When Jacob's sons returned from Egypt to tell their father the good news about Joseph, they were afraid that the depressed and fragile old man would die from shock. Rather than tell him directly, they found Serakh, who was wise and skilled at playing the harp, and she played a song for Jacob over and over again with these words: "Joseph is in Egypt. There have been born on his knees Menashe and Ephraim." (In Hebrew the phrases rhyme: *Yosef b'Mitzrayim/yuldo lo al birkayim/Menashe v'Ephrayim.*) Gradually the words began to penetrate, and Jacob's heart filled with joy. "My daughter," he said to Serakh, "May death never have power over you, for you revived my spirit." As a result of Jacob's wish, Serakh lived a long life and instead of dying she became one of the few people taken up to heaven while she was still alive. Because she never really died, Serakh returned over the ages to help her people at critical moments when they needed her.

Serakh went down to Egypt with Jacob's family. Eventually, a new Pharaoh arose who did not know Joseph. He enslaved the Israelites. Hundreds of years later, Moses came to liberate them, but the Israelites did not believe that God had really chosen him to lead them out of Egypt. At the burning bush, God told Moses what to tell the Israelites in order to convince them. God said to tell them, "I have surely remembered you, *pakod pakadti. . . .*" The people heard these words and saw the special signs God had given Moses. But they still refused to believe him. Only Serakh could convince the Israelites that Moses was indeed God's chosen leader.

Long before, God had told Jacob that when the redeemer of Israel came to Egypt he would utter special words. Jacob handed down this secret to Joseph, who later told his brothers. Asher, one of Joseph's older brothers, handed down the secret to his daughter Serakh. When Moses called on the people to leave Egypt, Serakh was the only person still alive who had heard the secret words. Serakh recognized them. *Pakod pakadti,* "I have surely remembered. . . ." She told the Israelites that Moses had truly been sent by God.

179

Finally, when the Israelites were about to leave Egypt, Moses realized that they could not depart until they honored a request that Joseph had made generations earlier, just before he died. Joseph made the children of Israel promise to take his bones with them when they left Egypt for the land God had sworn to Abraham, Isaac, and Jacob. He wanted to be buried in Israel.

But only Serakh remembered where Joseph had been laid to rest in Egypt. She told Moses, "The Egyptians made a metal coffin for [Joseph] which they put in the river Nile so that its waters would be blessed." Moses went and stood on the bank of the Nile and cried, "Joseph, Joseph! The time of God's promise to redeem you has arrived. If you appear we'll take you with us. If you don't, we are free of our promise to you." Joseph's coffin immediately floated to the surface of the Nile.

Serakh's people needed her again, many years later, during the reign of King David. An evil man tried to start a rebellion against the king. David's general rushed off to destroy the entire city where the man lived. He had already begun to batter down the walls when he heard a woman shouting to him. "Listen! Listen," she cried, "there's another way." Serakh persuaded him to wait and then convinced the townspeople to turn over the evil fellow. The city was saved. Serakh taught everyone an important lesson. "Wisdom is more valuable than weapons of war" (Eccl. 9:18).[17]

More than a thousand years later, in the first century C.E., Yochanan ben Zakkai, one of the most famous rabbis of the time, was teaching his students about the Israelites crossing the Red Sea. "When the sea parted," he said, "the wall of water was like a lattice." A woman in the back of the class disagreed. "I was there and it was only like a window opened for illumination." It was Serakh.

Tonight, we remember Serakh. Without her help, we might still be in Egypt!

- How would you compare the roles of the women of the Exodus in the beginning of the story (Shiphrah and Puah, the two midwives; Miriam, Moses' sister; Yocheved, his mother; and Bitya, Pharaoh's daughter) with those played by Serakh?

- Why was it so important to take Joseph's bones out of Egypt? What does the story about Joseph and Serakh have to tell us about the importance of memory?

• Serakh taught her people that "wisdom is more valuable than the weapons of war." What can we learn from that today?

• What meanings might there be in the difference between the way Rabbi Yochanan ben Zakkai and Serakh described what the Israelites saw when they crossed the Red Sea: a lattice as opposed to a window opened for illumination?

THE LEGEND OF MIRIAM'S WELL

Here we explore the legend of Miriam's Well and her complex relationship with Moses, her brother. You may want to read this yourself or read it aloud during your Seder in connection with Miriam's Cup. Questions for discussion follow.

The legend of Miriam's Well developed from the juxtaposition of two biblical verses. The first mentions Miriam's death; the next, a sudden absence of water, a problem that had not occurred since the Israelites' early days in the desert. "The Israelites arrived in a body at the wilderness of Zin on the first new moon [of the fortieth year] and the people stayed at Kadesh. Miriam died there and was buried there. The community was without water . . ." (Num. 20:1–2).

Phyllis Trible offers a moving interpretation of this passage. "Nature's response to Miriam's death is immediate and severe. It mourns, and the community suffers. Miriam, protector of her brother at the river's bank and leader in the victory at the sea, symbolized life. How appropriate, then, that waters of life should reverence her death."[18]

The midrash describes the well as a "rock, shaped like a kind of beehive, and wherever they journeyed it rolled along and came with them. When the standards [under which the tribes journeyed] halted and the tabernacle was set up, that same rock would come and settle down in the court of the Tent of Meeting and the princes would come and stand upon it and say, 'Spring up, O well' (Num. 21:17), and it would rise" (Numbers Rabbah 1:2). Another midrash holds that from the well came "most of the Israelites' enjoyments . . . The well used to produce for them various kinds of herbs, vegetables, and trees. The proof of this is that when Miriam died and the well ceased to give its waters to them they said, 'Why did you make us leave Egypt to bring us to this wretched place, a place with no grain or figs or vines or pomegranates? There is not even water to drink!'" (Num. 20:5; Song of Songs Rabbah 4:27).

The imagery of water is also crucial in the complex relationship between Miriam and Moses, binding them together throughout their lives. Miriam's name may mean "bitter sea" (*mar:* bitter, and *yam:* sea). The midrash attributes the link with bitterness to the fact that her birth occurred when Pharaoh's oppression of the Israelites began.

Later, Miriam watched over her infant brother as he floated down the Nile in a basket. When Pharaoh's daughter took him from the river, she named him Moshe, meaning, "I drew him from the water." After crossing the Red Sea, Moses led the people in song. When his song was finished, "Then Miriam the prophetess, Aaron's sister, took a timbrel in her hand, and all the women went out after her in dance with timbrels" (Ex. 15:20). Two years later, "Miriam and Aaron spoke against Moses because of the Cushite [Ethiopian] woman he had married . . . They said, 'Has the Lord spoken [prophesied] only through Moses? Has he not spoken through us as well?' The Lord heard it" (Num. 12:1–2).

As punishment for their challenge to Moses, God afflicted Miriam—only Miriam—with leprosy. Moses successfully prayed for her healing. Miriam is not mentioned again until her death, thirty-eight years later, not long before the Israelites entered the Promised Land. Just after Moses lost his sister, a figure so deeply linked with water and all it represented, he lost his temper when God told him to "order the rock to yield its water. Thus you shall produce water for them from the rock . . ." (Num. 20:8). Instead, Moses angrily struck the miraculous, water-bearing rock (a rock that is reminiscent of the above description of Miriam's Well itself). After that lapse, God barred Moses from entering the Promised Land.

- For Moses, Miriam represented both protection and nurturing despite her one-time challenge to his authority. To what extent do you think Moses' wrath toward the water-giving rock may have expressed his anger and anxiety over the loss of his older sister?

• If the complexities of his relationship with Miriam ultimately prevented Moses from entering the Promised Land, what may the Bible be suggesting about family relationships?

THE RITUAL OF MIRIAM'S CUP

The ritual of Miriam's Cup that has developed over the past twenty-five years represents a wonderful example of the Seder's continuing evolution. It evokes not only Miriam's critical role in the story of the Exodus but also that of the Israelite women in general. As Rabbi Akiva taught, "The Israelites were delivered from Egypt as a reward for the righteous women who lived in that generation."

When you set the table, place a large, empty glass goblet or wine glass beside the Cup of Elijah. This will serve as Miriam's Cup. After reciting the blessing for candlelighting, read the following paragraphs aloud. If everyone has a copy of this material, follow the directions as to who reads what. If not, pass the book around and ask several guests to read a few paragraphs each. Tell your guests that you will be returning to Miriam's Cup toward the conclusion of the Seder.

The following excerpt from *The 1997 Ma'yan Passover Haggadah: The Journey Continues* can be used at your Seder to help integrate the women of the Exodus into your celebration.

All: Miriam's Cup. Legend tells of a mysterious well filled with *mayim chayim,* living waters that followed the Israelites though their wandering in the desert while Miriam was alive.

Reader: Miriam's Well was said to hold divine power to heal and renew. Its fresh waters sustained our people as we were transformed from a generation shaped by slavery into a free nation. Throughout our subsequent journeys, we have sought to rediscover these living waters.

[When the Seder falls on a Saturday night, add the following: In the sixteenth century, this is what Moses Isserles, one of the greatest rabbis of his era, said about Miriam's Well: "Some make it a practice to draw fresh water after the Sabbath. They say that every Saturday night Miriam's Well encircles all the wells of the world and those who are ill and drink of these waters will be healed."[19]]

All: Tonight at our Seder, let us remember that we are still on the journey. Just as the Holy One delivered Miriam and her people, just as they were sustained in the desert and transformed into a new people, so may we be delivered, sustained and transformed on our journey to a stronger sense of ourselves, both as individuals and as one people. May the Cup of Miriam refresh and inspire us as we embark on our journey through the Haggadah.

Miriam's Cup is now filled. Each individual pours water from her or his own water glass into Miriam's Cup. Return Miriam's Cup beside the Cup of Elijah. You will drink from it later.

זֹאת כּוֹס מִרְיָם, כּוֹס מַיִם חַיִּים.
זֵכֶר לִיצִיאַת מִצְרָיִם.

All: Zot Kos Miryam, kos mayim chayim. Zeicher l'ytzi-at Mitzrayim.

Reader: This is the Cup of Miriam, the cup of living waters. Let us remember the Exodus from Egypt. These are the living waters, God's gift to Miriam, which gave new life to Israel as we struggled in the wilderness.

All: Blessed are You, God, Who brings us from the narrows into the wilderness, sustains us with endless possibilities, and enables us to reach a new place.

When it is time to open the door for Elijah the Prophet, return to this section and continue reading.

Reader: At this point in the Seder, Jewish communities, beset by persecution during the Crusades, opened their doors and recited the angry plea, *"Sh'fokh chamat'kha . . ."* ("Pour out Your wrath upon the nations who do not know You").

All: In other communities during the same period, the hope for redemption was so intense that they sang to invoke the Prophet Elijah, who, according to legend, would herald an era of messianic peace, justice, and healing.

Reader: We open our doors now with the need to act on both impulses. The crimes of humanity that we continue to see—the rape and torture of innocents, ethnic cleansing, the destruction of entire cities and cultures—cry out for just retribution beyond our limited capacity. And our longing for peace, for healing of earth, body, and spirit, still brings the hope-drenched melody of *"Eliyahu Hanavi"* to our lips.

All: Elijah the Prophet, come to us soon, for you herald messianic days. Miriam the Prophet, strength and song are in her hand. Miriam will dance with us to strengthen the world's song. Miriam will dance with us to heal the world. Soon, and in our time, she will lead us to the waters of salvation.

All sing the familiar tune of *"Eliyahu Hanavi,"* adding the verses about Miriam.

אֵלִיָּהוּ הַנָּבִיא, אֵלִיָּהוּ הַתִּשְׁבִּי, אֵלִיָּהוּ הַגִּלְעָדִי

בִּמְהֵרָה בְיָמֵינוּ, יָבוֹא אֵלֵינוּ עִם מָשִׁיחַ בֶּן דָּוִד.

מִרְיָם הַנְּבִיאָה, עֹז וְזִמְרָה בְּיָדָהּ.

מִרְיָם תִּרְקוֹד אִתָּנוּ, לְהַגְדִּיל זִמְרַת עוֹלָם.

מִרְיָם תִּרְקוֹד אִתָּנוּ, לְתַקֵּן אֶת הָעוֹלָם.

בִּמְהֵרָה בְיָמֵנוּ הִיא תְּבִיאֵנוּ,

אֶל מֵי הַיְשׁוּעָה, אֶל מֵי הַיְשׁוּעָה.

Eliyahu ha-navi, Eliyahu ha-tishbi,
Eliyahu ha-giladi.
Bimheirah v'yameinu, yavo eileinu,
im Mashiach ben David.
Miryam ha-nevi'ah, oz v'zimrah b'yadah.
Miryam tirkod itanu,
l'hagdil zimrat olam.
Miryam tirkod itanu, l'takein et ha-olam.
Bimheirah v'yameinu, hi t'vi-einu.
El mei ha-yeshu'ah, el mei ha-yeshu'ah.[20]

Now each person takes a sip from the Cup of Miriam and all continue with the Seder.

REDEEMED THROUGH BLOOD AND WATER:
BALANCING ELIJAH'S CUP WITH MIRIAM'S CUP

Here we explore water and blood as mediums for redemption. You can read this yourself or read it aloud during your Seder in connection with Miriam's Cup.
Questions for discussion follow.

According to the Mishnah (Avot 5:8), Miriam's well was one of ten things God fashioned on the eve of the Sabbath just before completing the work of creation. Deuteronomy Rabbah (3:8), a collection of midrashim compiled between 450 and 800 C.E., recounts six miraculous instances in the story of the Exodus when salvation came through water. Each comes with its own biblical "prooftext."

> The Rabbis say: Come and see how all the miracles that God wrought for Israel He wrought only through water. How? While they were still in Egypt, He wrought miracles for them through the river. Rabbi Isaac said: The Egyptians and the Israelites went to drink from the river; the Egyptians drank blood, but the Israelites drank water. And when Israel came out of Egypt He wrought miracles for them only through water. How so? For it is said, "The sea saw it, and fled" (Psalms 114:3). What did it see? Rabbi Nehorai said: It saw the name of God engraved upon [Moses'] staff and it parted . . . After the Israelites crossed through the Red Sea they arrived at Marah where the waters were bitter, and He wrought for them miracles. How so? For it is said, [Moses threw a branch] "into the water and the water became sweet" (Ex. 15:25). At the Rock he wrought miracles for them through water. How so? For it is said, "Order the rock to yield its water. Thus you shall produce water for them from the rock . . ." (Num. 20:8). At the well He wrought miracles for them and they sang a song, as it is said, "Then Israel sang this song" (Num. 21:17). Moses said to Israel: "Know that all the miracles which God wrought for you, He wrought only through water. And also when you pass over the Jordan to take possession of the land God will also work miracles for you through the waters of the Jordan."

Beyond honoring the role of women in the Exodus, Miriam's Cup restores to the Seder an element of the Jewish tradition's appreciation of water as a symbolic source of salvation, as the above midrash amply demonstrates. By contrast, the Haggadah gives that role to blood alone. After the ninth plague, the Israelites received two essential commandments, both involving blood. The Passover sacrifice should forever commemorate that God saw the blood of the lamb smeared on the Israelites' doorposts, passed over their homes, and spared their firstborn. And for men, in ancient times, eating the paschal offering would require circumcision, a covenant, as it were, of blood.

A common addition to many Sephardic and Ashkenazic Haggadot evokes these commandments in a quotation from Ezekiel 16:6, a passage that also figures prominently in the ritual of circumcision: "Then I passed you and saw you wallowing in your blood [literally, 'bloods']. I said to you, 'In your [two] bloods you shall live'; and I said to you, 'In your [two] bloods shall you live.'"[21] The Seder's invocation of Elijah the Prophet further reinforces the theme of redemption through blood. Elijah not only heralds the Messiah, but, according to tradition, he also witnesses every circumcision!

Against this backdrop, the water of Miriam's Cup adds an important balance to the wine/blood of Elijah's. The Jewish ritual for conversion reflects a similar balance: immersion in "living waters" for both men and women, and circumcision for men.[22]

- What do you think blood and water might symbolize?

- How do you feel about adding Miriam's Cup to the Seder ritual?

- Women have gradually found their voice in Western society. What are other groups that remain silenced?

14

The Ten Plagues: Who Suffered and Why?

אֵלוּ עֶשֶׂר מַכּוֹת שֶׁהֵבִיא הַקָּדוֹשׁ בָּרוּךְ הוּא
עַל־הַמִּצְרִים בְּמִצְרַיִם, וְאֵלוּ הֵן:
דָּם. צְפַרְדֵּעַ. כִּנִּים. עָרוֹב. דֶּבֶר. שְׁחִין.
בָּרָד. אַרְבֶּה. חֹשֶׁךְ. מַכַּת בְּכוֹרוֹת:

These are the ten plagues which the Holy One, blessed be He,
brought upon the Egyptians: blood, frogs, lice, insects, cattle blight, boils,
hail, locusts, darkness, the slaying of the firstborn.
—THE PASSOVER HAGGADAH

Near the conclusion of the Haggadah's lengthy account of the Israelites' suffering in Egypt, we arrive at the point in the Seder when we recount the ten plagues.[1] We do so briefly, first reciting "blood and fire and pillars of smoke," a passage from the prophet Joel (3:3), then naming each plague, and concluding with Rabbi Yehuda's ten-letter acronym, *"Detzakh, Adash, B'achav."*[2] With each word, we spill a drop of wine from our cups. Traditional texts of the Haggadah follow this with a much longer elaboration of the number of plagues the Egyptians suffered in Egypt and at the Red Sea. Of note, this extended midrashic treatment of the plagues includes different methods of enumerating the plagues, but it does not actually mention what a single one of these plagues involved. And many modern Haggadot omit this elaboration entirely.

What's interesting about this is that in the Book of Exodus, the plague narrative occupies the bulk of the story, extending through more than five chapters, while details of the Israelites' suffering in Egypt involves relatively few verses. The Haggadah reverses this, expounding on suffering and skimming over the plagues. Why? Because the Haggadah's purpose is to renew our faith in redemption, not to whet our appetite for our enemy's defeat. But as we'll see, the plagues raise a number of uncomfortable issues, of which the compilers of the Haggadah were doubtless aware. The tendency to consign the ten plagues to a supporting rather than starring role in the Haggadah may reflect those discomforts as well.

- If you had the same amount of power that God displayed through the plagues, how might you have tried to bring about the Exodus?

- Why did God's plan to redeem the Israelites require such a lengthy series of plagues? And why these kinds of plagues? Why didn't God just have Moses announce to Pharaoh that unless Pharaoh let the Israelites go, God would side with an invading army from some other country that would defeat Pharaoh and let the Israelites go?

- Toward the end of the Book of Deuteronomy (28:49), Moses tells the people of Israel that if they defy God's will, "The Lord will bring a nation against you from afar, from the end of the earth, which will swoop down like the eagle" to punish the wayward Israelites. Why didn't God do the same with the Egyptians?

- Whom do the plagues seek to influence and to what end?

PLAGUES AGAINST THE ISRAELITES?

Read the following paragraphs and discuss the question on the next page.

A plain reading of the Bible suggests something surprising: that the Israelites themselves suffered through the first three plagues—blood, frogs, and lice. God expressly

190

spares the Israelites and afflicts the Egyptians in five of the remaining plagues—insects (4), cattle blight (5), hail (7), darkness (9), and slaying of the firstborn (10). While less clear-cut, the language of the sixth (boils) and eighth (locusts) plagues also can be taken to mean that only the Egyptians were targeted.

Two great medieval Spanish commentators differed on whether the first three plagues struck the Egyptians alone.

Ibn Ezra (1089–1164) argues that the first three plagues struck both the Israelites and the Egyptians. "Many say that the water near the Egyptians turned red like blood, but in the hands of the Israelites it became clear. If so, why wasn't this sign (*ot*) written in the Torah? And according to my opinion, the plagues of blood, frogs and lice included the Egyptians and the Hebrews, because we must follow what is written in the Torah. These three plagues did but little damage. Only starting with the plague of insects, which was severe, did God distinguish between the Egyptians and Israel."[3]

Nachmanides (1195–1270) asserts that none of the plagues fell upon the Israelites. "Due to the fact that the first [three] plagues were not migratory in nature, [there was no need for the Bible to mention that] that they were confined to the land of Egypt and were not to be in the land of Goshen [Israel's habitation]. But this [the fourth plague, swarms of insects] was a migratory plague . . . Therefore it was necessary for God to say, 'I will set apart the region of Goshen.'"[4]

- What difference does it make to your understanding of the story if the Israelites were completely spared the plagues or suffered the first three? Why do you think God may have visited the first three plagues on the Israelites as well as the Egyptians? Or, alternatively, why would one want to argue that Israel escaped all the plagues?

WHY SPILL WINE FROM OUR CUPS?

Read aloud and discuss the following section.

Traditional Haggadot prescribe spilling a total of sixteen drops of wine from our cups: one for each of the three wonders mentioned by the prophet Joel (3:3), "blood and fire and pillars of smoke"; one for each of the ten plagues; and one for each of the three terms of Rabbi Yehuda's acronym—*Detzakh, Adash, B'achav.* Why sixteen drops? Some say because there are sixteen individuals called to the Torah each week and the Torah is a "tree of life" (*etz chayim hi*). The numerical value for the last word in this expression (in Hebrew spelled *hey, yod, alef*) is sixteen.

But why spill any wine from our cups in connection with the plagues? Following are two explanations. Discuss which explanation you prefer and why.

> It is as if to say we were saved from all this [i.e., the plagues]. And it will be brought upon those who hate us. These very cups [now symbolically purged of ill fortune] represent the success of Israel.[5]
>
> —JACOB BEN MOSES MOELLIN (CIRCA 1360–1427), GERMANY

> A drop of wine is spilled from each cup at the mention of each plague to indicate that the joy of our redemption is not complete. Even though the plagues were deserved, our redemption was brought about through the suffering meted out to the Egyptians. "When your enemy falls, do not exult" (Proverbs 24:17).[6]
>
> —WIDELY (BUT QUESTIONABLY) ATTRIBUTED TO ISAAC ABARBANEL
> (1437–1508), PORTUGAL AND ITALY

WHEN OUR ENEMIES FALL

Read the following section aloud or on your own.

The aversion to celebrating the suffering of our enemies is hardly new to Jewish ethical sensibilities.

The Talmud (Megillah 10b) asks, "What is the meaning of the verse, 'And one came not near the other all the night?' (Ex. 14:20). The ministering angels wanted to chant their hymns, but the Holy One, blessed be He, said, 'The work of my hands is being drowned in the sea, and you are chanting hymns?'"

An eleventh-century midrash elaborates, imagining a dialogue between God and various angels, including Uzza, the angel of the Egyptians. Uzza finally persuades God to deal "with [the Egyptians] according to Your attribute of mercy, and take pity upon the work of your hands . . . The Lord had almost yielded to Uzza's entreaties, when [the angel] Michael gave a sign to Gabriel that made him fly to Egypt swiftly and fetch thence a brick for which a Hebrew child had been used as mortar. Holding this incriminating object in his hand, Gabriel stepped into the presence of God, and said: 'O Lord of the world! Will You have compassion upon the accursed nation that has slaughtered Your children cruelly?' Then the Lord turned Himself away from His attribute of mercy, and seating Himself upon His throne of justice He resolved to drown the Egyptians in the sea."[7]

An early-fourteenth-century midrash, *Yalkut Shimoni,* observes that, with reference to Sukkot, the Bible instructs us to rejoice—in three passages. We find no such command with respect to Passover. Why does Scripture give not even one command to rejoice on Passover? "Because the Egyptians died during the Passover. Therefore you find that, though we read the entire Hallel on each of the seven days of Sukkot, on Passover we read the entire Hallel only on the first day and the night preceding it. Why not on the other days of the festival? 'If your enemy falls, do not exult; if he trips, let not your heart rejoice'" (Prov. 24:17).[8]

In the end, we must recognize that, as wonderful as it was, the redemption from Egypt was not, as it were, complete or ideal. To use Franz Rosenzweig's distinction, the Exodus may be better understood as a temporary deliverance rather than an ultimate redemption.[9] The human cost of our deliverance was enormous, and deliverance from Egypt did not inoculate the children of Israel from subsequent oppression. We can only pray that if an ultimate redemption awaits us, it will be brought about through peace, not suffering.

THE PLAGUES AND KNOWING GOD

Read aloud the passage below and discuss the questions that follow.

We can understand the story of the plagues from many points of view—as a punishment to Pharaoh and the Egyptians, as a demonstration of God's superiority over the gods of Egypt, or as a difficult but important opportunity for the Israelites and the Egyptians to come to know God in a new way. Here we'll concentrate on the last approach.[10]

Nehama Leibowitz (1905–1997), one of our generation's great Bible teachers, notes the significance of Pharaoh's opening response in what will prove a lengthy dialogue with Moses.[11]

> Afterward Moses and Aaron went and said to Pharaoh, "Thus says the Lord, God of Israel: Let my people go that they may celebrate a festival for Me in the wilderness." But Pharaoh said, "Who is the Lord that I should heed Him and let Israel go? I do not know the Lord, nor will I let Israel go."
>
> EXODUS 5:1–2

Leibowitz notes that the theme of "knowing God" recurs ten times during the plague narrative and the events at the Red Sea. Consistent with her view, the Book of Exodus generally refers to the plagues as "signs" (*otot*) and "wonders" (*moftim*). Only three times does the narrative refer to these afflictions as a form of punishment or judgment (*sh'fatim*) against the Egyptians (Ex. 6:6, 7:4, and 12:12).

It's worth noting what the Bible seems to want the Israelites and the Egyptians to "know" about God.

After Moses and Aaron's first meeting with Pharaoh, the king orders the Israelites to gather their own straw to make bricks:

> [God instructs Moses to tell the Israelites] I am the Lord . . . I will redeem you with an outstretched arm and through extraordinary chastisements. And I will take you to be My people, and I will be your God. And you shall *know* that I, the Lord, am your God who freed you from the labors of the Egyptians.
>
> —EXODUS 6:6–7[12]

Before the first plague, God announces that "the Egyptians shall *know* that I am the Lord when I stretch My hand over Egypt and bring out the Israelites from their midst" (Ex. 7:5). After this simple statement, we find a gradual elaboration of what God wants the Egyptians to know: "that there is none like the Lord our God," "that I the Lord am in the midst of the land," "that there is none like Me in all the world," "that the earth is the Lord's."[13]

- Do you tend to think of the plagues more in terms of punishing the Egyptians or of teaching them something about God?

- If you think of the plagues as an educational strategy, is it successful? Who learns what?

SIGNS, WONDERS, AND FAITH: OR DID THE PLAGUES FAIL?

Read the following section on your own or aloud,
perhaps as a conclusion to your discussion above.

And you [the Israelites] shall *know* that I, the Lord, am your God who freed you from the labors of the Egyptians . . . But when Moses told this to the Israelites, they would not listen to Moses, their spirits crushed by cruel bondage.

EXODUS 6:7–9

Do the Israelites come to "know God" through the plagues? Before the cycle of signs and wonders, the Israelites seem a sullen bunch. Since Moses' first visit to Pharaoh, the Israelites' plight has only grown more desperate. The foremen of the Israelites angrily confront Moses. "May the Lord look upon you and punish you for making us loathsome to Pharaoh and his courtiers—putting a sword in their hands to slay us" (Ex. 5:21).

Throughout the plagues, the Israelites remain mute. They neither complain when the first three plagues strike them along with the Egyptians nor rejoice when the subsequent afflictions spare them. All we hear of them is that by the time the last blow falls upon the Egyptians they've begun to follow orders. Moses tells the Israelites how they should sacrifice the paschal offering: "The people then bowed low in homage. And the Israelites went and did so, just as the Lord had commanded Moses and Aaron, so they did" (Ex. 12:27–28).

Their faithful posture doesn't last long. With the Egyptians in hot pursuit, the Israelites speak at the Red Sea for the first time since the plagues began. "And they said to Moses, 'Was it for want of graves in Egypt that you brought us to die in the wilderness?'" (Ex. 14:11).

195

After the sea parts, the children of Israel seem to have changed their tune. They sing: "The Lord is my strength and might; He is become my deliverance" (Ex. 15:2). But how enduring is their faith now?

Soon enough—three days later—they are grumbling about a lack of water and whining about the food. Manna from heaven was not sufficient. Three months later they worshiped the Golden Calf. Despite the mighty signs and wonders they witnessed, the Israelites do not come to "know God" in a lasting way.

We can explain this in several ways. Perhaps their spirits had been destroyed to the point that "knowing God" in any enduring way was impossible. Or maybe awesome signs and wonders didn't make quite the impression that God imagined they would.

Sensational acts of this sort actually represent an innovation in God's modus operandi. Prior to the Exodus, God's communication with the characters of Genesis was far more intimate. Even Moses' encounter with the miraculous burning bush involved a comparatively "low-key" manifestation of divine power. Maybe God thought that a crowd demanded an earthshaking display. If so, it would seem that God miscalculated.

Or maybe God was really more interested in punishing the Egyptians and humiliating their gods than in using the plagues to teach anyone anything. Maybe the goal was simply to instill fear. Perhaps God equated fear with faith. Another miscalculation.

Strange as it sounds, the Bible is full of such divine "miscalculations." God "regrets" creating the world and destroys it in a flood. Having redeemed the Israelites from Egypt, God nearly destroys them when they worship the Golden Calf. God then turns to plan B—to establish a new covenant with Moses, a deal that Moses flatly refuses. And the idea of sending forth spies to reconnoiter the Promised Land also comes from God. It too backfires: "And the Lord said to Moses, 'How long will this people spurn Me, and how long will they have no faith in Me despite all the signs that I have performed in their midst?'" (Num. 14:11).

Here God painfully acknowledges the limits of trying to build a relationship based on signs and wonders. Eventually God will discover, as it were, that human faith arises not from impressing us with awesome gestures, but from touching us during quiet, intimate moments of openness. And even after countless fleeting glimpses and whispering intuitions—often overlooked, forgotten, or misunderstood—the sense of God's presence consolidates only slowly.

Like the Israelites of the Exodus, how often do we find ourselves blind to the very insights that yesterday seemed so compelling? In the end, God discovers a cornerstone of rabbinic thought: "Everything is in the hand of heaven except the fear of heaven."[14]

MEASURE FOR MEASURE

Read aloud what follows and discuss the questions below.

Most of us probably think of the plagues as God's punishment of the Egyptians. Indeed, toward the beginning of the Haggadah (just before the section about the wandering Aramean) we read a passage from Genesis that raises this theme. God says to Abram (his name has not yet been changed to Abraham): "Know well that your offspring shall be strangers in a land not theirs, and they shall be enslaved and oppressed for four hundred years; but I will execute judgment on the nation they shall serve, and in the end they shall go out with great wealth" (Gen. 15:14).

Although the Book of Exodus does not stress this interpretation of the plagues, it refers to judgments (*sh'fatim*) against the Egyptians on three occasions, twice before the plagues begin and once in connection with the slaying of the firstborn. The midrash elaborates on the theme of punishment, measure for measure, and attempts to link each blow against Egypt with a particular aspect of its oppression of the Israelites. The tenth-century midrash Exodus Rabbah (3:8) justifies the drowning of Pharaoh and his armies at the Red Sea: "[God] would drown [the Egyptians] in the sea, to exact from them measure for measure, because the [Egyptians] had said: 'Every boy that is born you shall throw into the Nile . . .'" (Ex. 1:22).

The problem is that the Pharaoh who had ordered the drowning of all newborn Israelite males had long since died when the plagues begin to unfold. The Pharaoh of the plagues is not the Pharaoh whose orders nearly resulted in the murder of Moses in his infancy and of so many other Jewish male infants. Before Moses returns from Midian with God's charge to lead the Israelites out of Egypt, the Bible tells us that "the king of Egypt died" (Ex. 2:23).

The last plague, the slaying of the Egyptian firstborn, becomes even more morally dubious in light of the fact that it seems to have included the firstborn of Egyptians in prison. "In the middle of the night the Lord struck down all the firstborn in the land of Egypt, from the firstborn of Pharaoh who sat on the throne to the firstborn of the captive who was in the dungeon, and all the first-born of the cattle" (Ex. 12:29).

Exodus Rabbah (18:10) offers the following explanation:

> God made a day of rejoicing for Israel when He redeemed them and He proclaimed: "All who love My sons may come and rejoice with them." The virtuous among the Egyptians came, celebrated the Passover with Israel, and went up with them, for it says: "And a mixed multitude went up with them" (Ex. 12:38), but those who did not desire the redemption of the Israelites died with the firstborn. . . .

- This midrash illustrates a measure of moral discomfort with the plagues. Does this explanation satisfy you? Why or why not?

- One of the questions the plague narrative raises is whether the entire Egyptian population deserves the suffering that befalls it. Pharaoh makes all the decisions. But the entire Egyptian people, the land, the plants, and the animals all suffer as a result of a mighty king who refuses to accept limitations on his power. Are the Egyptian people also guilty? Should they be punished for the policies of their despotic ruler, a ruler whom they probably had little chance to influence or oppose? What contemporary issues does this story raise?

REVEALING THE CREATOR THROUGH ANTI-CREATION

Read this on your own.

If, through the plagues, God wished to become known to the Israelites, the Egyptians, and indeed the whole world, what were they to learn about God? God is all-powerful; even a casual reader of Exodus could not miss that. Some scholars believe that the story contains a related, but more pointed, lesson—that God is not only powerful but also the creator of all.

If you read the tale of the plagues carefully, you find a surprising number of allusions to the creation story. This makes sense, because Exodus marks the creation or birth of a people. It also makes sense because, as we've seen, the festival of Passover shares many attributes of other ancient Near Eastern spring New Year's celebrations, a major feature of which included recounting myths of the creation. Recitation of the myth brought renewal of the year and with it revival of nature and fertility. During their spring festival, the Israelites recounted the story of their creation as a people, while the fall festivals related the story of the world's creation.

In the ancient Near East, creation myths revolved around the transition from watery chaos to order. Kings were expected to perpetuate the fundamental order of creation. Whether the king violated or maintained the created order determined whether his land would be blessed with plenty or afflicted with famine, drought, disease, and so forth. In this view, "law, nature, and politics are only aspects of one comprehensive order of creation."[15] In Israelite culture, the ruler and populace shared the responsibilities of maintaining the rules of God's created order. But the consequences remained:

> Now if you obey the Lord your God, to observe faithfully all His commandments . . . Blessed shall be the issue of your womb, the produce of your soil, the offspring of your cattle, the calving of your herd and the lambing of your flock . . . The Lord will open for you His bounteous store, the heavens, to provide rain for your land in season and to bless all your undertakings . . . But if you do not obey the Lord your God to observe faithfully all His commandments and laws . . . The Lord will make the rain of your land dust, and sand shall drop on you from the sky . . . The Lord will inflict extraordinary plagues upon you and your offspring, strange and lasting plagues, malignant and chronic diseases. He will bring back up all the sickness of Egypt that you dreaded so . . . You shall be left a scant few, after having been as numerous as the stars in the skies, because you did not heed the command of the Lord your God.
>
> —DEUTERONOMY 28:1, 4, 12, 15, 24, 59–62

The Talmud (Shabbat 88a) made the point more succinctly: "The Holy One, blessed be He, stipulated with the works of creation and said to them, 'If Israel accepts the Torah, you shall exist; but if not, I will turn you back into *emptiness and formlessness*'" (Gen. 1:1).

Pharaoh's treatment of the Israelites flouted the very concept of God as the ultimate creator and ruler of all.

God promised Abraham that his descendents would be "as numerous as the stars of heaven and the sands on the seashore" (Gen. 22:17). That promise reached fulfillment in Egypt. "The Israelites were fertile and prolific; they multiplied and increased very greatly, so that the land was filled with them" (Ex. 1:7). God also promised that "all the families of the earth shall bless themselves by you" (Gen. 12:3). But instead of Pharaoh feeling blessed by Abraham's descendents, he feels cursed by them and seeks their destruction. God creates life, and Pharaoh destroys it. In response, God strikes back, selectively undoing the general order of the natural world. In Pharaoh's Egypt, nature loses one of its chief characteristics: predictability.[16]

The prophet Ezekiel (29:3) captures this aspect of the conflict between God and Pharaoh. "Thus said the Lord God: I am going to deal with you, O Pharaoh king of Egypt, mighty monster, sprawling in your channels, who said, 'My Nile is my own: I made if for myself.'" (This reading from Ezekiel serves as the haftarah for the portion in Exodus that describes the plagues.)

The general theme of "de-creation" becomes obvious as soon as you look at the parallel between God's destruction of the world through the flood and the significance of water in God's battle with Pharaoh. Water, a source of life, but also the prime symbol of primordial chaos, frames the contest. The first plague turns the Nile to blood. The last blow falls at the Red Sea with the drowning of Pharaoh and his army.

The events at the Red Sea evoke dramatic symbols of creation and de-creation. Ancient Near Eastern creation stories regularly began with a god subduing a watery, chaotic void and establishing a dry home for humanity. When humanity sinned against the gods, the world returned to watery formlessness. The Egyptian Book of the Dead (1550–1350 B.C.E.) describes a threat by the enraged god Atun. "I shall destroy all that I have made, and this land will return unto Nun, into the floodwaters, as [in] its first state."[17] God's splitting the Red Sea so the Israelites could walk on dry land, then allowing the "waters to turn back" upon the Egyptians, recapitulates creation and the flood.

The midrash, of course, notes the parallel:

Let us [say the Egyptians] deal cunningly with Israel and plan such a serfdom for them that their God will not be able to punish us in the same coin. For if we persecute them with the sword, He can visit us with the sword, and if with fire, He can bring fire upon us. We know that He swore that He would no longer bring a flood on the world, let us, therefore, persecute them with water, which He cannot bring upon us. God then said to them: "Wretches! True I have sworn that I will not bring a flood into the world, but I will do this to you; I will drag each one of you to his own flood."[18]

Some have also pointed to a relationship between the ten plagues and the ten utterances, through which the Mishnah states that God created the world: "With ten [divine] pronouncements was the world created. Now what is this meant to teach us? . . . It is but to [make clear that God will] exact punishment from the wicked who destroy the world that was created by ten pronouncements."[19]

Beyond these general parallels, the creation and plague narratives share a number of common expressions that serve to link the themes of creation and anti-creation. Following are three of many other examples:[20]

- *Blood:* In delivering this plague, God tells Moses that Aaron should hold his rod over the waters of Egypt, literally, "over the gathering of its waters" (*v'al kol mikveih meimeihem,* Ex. 7:19). On the third day, God separates the waters. "God called the dry land Earth, and the gathering of waters He called Seas" (*u'l'mikveih ha'mayim;* Gen. 1:10).

- *Frogs:* "The Nile shall swarm (*v'sharatz*) with frogs" (Ex. 7:28). On the fifth day, God creates "the living creatures of every kind that creep which the waters brought forth in swarms . . ." (*shartzu,* Gen. 1:21). In Egypt, the frogs come up and cover the land. In Genesis, God tells the creatures of the waters to fill the sea, to be fruitful and multiply. In Egypt, the frogs exceed the boundaries of creation. The creator seems to have rewritten the rules. (On the fifth day, God also creates the great sea monsters, *ha-taninim ha-gedolim*. When Aaron casts down the rod before Pharaoh it becomes a serpent, *tanin*. In Ezekiel 29:3, when Pharaoh says he has created the Nile, God calls Pharaoh the great sea monster, *ha-tanim ha-gadol*. Not infrequently, the Bible depicts God's battle against Israel's enemies as a clash with sea monsters, which are symbolic of the uncontrollable and, hence, of evil.)[21]

• *Darkness:* "People could not see one another, and for three days no one could get up from where he was; but all the Israelites enjoyed light in their dwellings" (Ex. 10:23). On the first day of creation, "God saw that the light was good, and God separated the light from the darkness" (Gen. 1:4). On the fourth day. God creates "lights in the expanse of the sky to separate day from night . . ." (Gen. 1:14). In Egypt, light and darkness have been separated geographically and the cycle of day and night has come to a halt.

So what does this mean? Why bother to link the plagues and creation?

Exodus offers us two paradigms of faith. The first represents the relationship between a people and their liberator, a relationship that with time may cool. Besides, human beings can also bring about liberation. The second represents the connection between humanity and its creator, a more fundamental relationship that may well enjoy greater durability. Creation, on the cosmic scale at least, still remains beyond human reach. Hence the redactors of the Exodus story may have been reluctant to leave the stage solely to God as liberator.

The justifications for the Sabbath given in the Torah's two versions of the Ten Commandments illustrate both paradigms. The fourth commandment of Exodus (20:11) instructs us to remember the Sabbath because "in six days the Lord made the heaven and earth and sea, and all that is in them, and He rested on the seventh day." Deuteronomy's fourth commandment (5:15) tells us to keep the Sabbath in remembrance of the fact that "you were a slave in the land of Egypt and the Lord your God freed you from there with a mighty hand and an outstretched arm. . . ."

As reflected in the daily liturgy, Jewish tradition has clearly chosen to harmonize both paradigms. Certain prayers speak to God as creator, while others give greater weight to God as liberator. The Kiddush for Shabbat may represent the perfect balance: "You have graciously given us Your holy Sabbath as a heritage in remembrance of the creation. The Sabbath is the first among the holy festivals which recall the Exodus from Egypt."

15

Rabban Gamaliel: An Embattled Leader

רַבָּן גַּמְלִיאֵל הָיָה אוֹמֵר:

כָּל שֶׁלֹּא אָמַר שְׁלֹשָׁה דְבָרִים אֵלּוּ בַּפֶּסַח

לֹא יָצָא יְדֵי חוֹבָתוֹ, וְאֵלּוּ הֵן:

פֶּסַח, מַצָּה, וּמָרוֹר:

Rabban Gamaliel used to say, "Whoever does not explain these three things
on Passover does not discharge his duty, and they are: the Passover offering,
unleavened bread, and bitter herbs [pesach, matzah, and maror]."
—THE PASSOVER HAGGADAH, QUOTING MISHNAH PESACHIM 10:5 (CIRCA 200 C.E.)

Although the Haggadah evolved over many centuries, it explicitly attributes one of its core elements—the injunction to explain the significance of the Passover offering, matzah, and bitter herbs—to Rabban Gamaliel II, who lived during the first and early second centuries C.E. The Haggadah gradually elaborated on Gamaliel's statement from the Mishnah. Biblical verses were added to explain the meaning of each element. During the Middle Ages, Haggadot began to frame these explanations as simple questions and answers. For example, "This matzah we eat, what is the reason for it . . . [*al shoom mah?*] The reason is . . . [*al shoom*]. . . ." Because the language of this exchange occurs nowhere else in rabbinic literature, some scholars believe that it reflects a folk custom that spread and eventually found its way into the traditional Haggadah.[1]

This chapter explores Gamaliel's career and his stormy relations with many of the other sages mentioned in the Haggadah. We include a story about Gamaliel's life and times that focuses on a dramatic clash with his peers.[2] The story sheds light on an important period in Judaism's development and on several of the leaders who shaped it. Although these conflicts are illuminating in their own right, what makes them interesting to us here is that they may also have left subtle traces in the Haggadah.

> This story was designed to be read either for general enrichment or for discussion prior to sitting down at the table. In our home, we've found that dividing our participants into smaller groups for discussions before beginning the Seder works very well. If you try this, allow at least half an hour for this material and ask group members to take turns reading aloud. After singing *Dayyenu*, when you come to the part of the Haggadah that mentions Rabban Gamaliel, ask someone to summarize the key points of his or her conversation about this sage and his travails.

WHO WAS GAMALIEL?

Read aloud the following section.

Gamaliel belonged to a rabbinic dynasty that led Israel from the days of Hillel, beginning in about 20 B.C.E., and with a few interruptions, until 425 C.E. According to tradition, the family traced its lineage back to King David, from whom the Messiah would descend. The title "rabban" means "our master" or "our teacher" and was used to refer only to rabbis who served as the Nasi of the Sanhedrin, the head of the highest court in the land. Those holding the position also required at least tacit endorsement from Rome.

Rabban Gamaliel II served as the religious and political leader of the Jewish community in Israel between the fateful years of 80 and 110 C.E. Just ten years before he came to power, the Romans had crushed an ill-conceived Jewish revolt and burned the Second Temple. Many questions faced the Rabbis. Would the Temple be rebuilt quickly as it had been after it was destroyed the first time in 586 B.C.E.? How could Judaism survive without the Temple at its center? What and who would hold the community together? Rabban Yochanan ben Zakkai, the foremost sage during the time of the revolt, taught that prayer, study, acts of loving-kindness toward others, and living a life based on Jewish law could replace the Temple and its sacrifices. To train the next generation of leaders and teachers, ben Zakkai founded an academy at Yavne (now a small town not far from Tel Aviv).

Gamaliel worked hard to implement ben Zakkai's vision. He argued that prayer should be more uniform and defined eighteen benedictions to be included in the Amidah or *Shmoneh Esrei,* which still form the core of Jewish worship. He generally ensured that the rulings of the more lenient school of Hillel became law rather than those of the stricter school of Shammai. In an age of much suffering and loss, Gamaliel believed that the observance of Passover, with its promise of hope for better times, was especially important. In fact, more of his rulings dealt with the laws of Passover than with any other single subject. Rabban Gamaliel formalized many of the Seder's still evolving traditions.

To this day, the Seder bears his stamp. In demanding that we explain the meaning of the paschal offering, matzah, and bitter herbs, Gamaliel took an unusual step because in rabbinic literature the fulfillment of a religious obligation—in this case, the commandment to celebrate Passover—generally need not be accompanied by explanation. His requirement to define these symbols may have given voice to the biblical injunction that parents should tell their children about the meaning of Passover. At the same time, some scholars believe that Gamaliel sought to sharpen the boundaries between Judaism and Jesus' followers, who radically reinterpreted the same symbols.[3]

DEPOSED AND REINSTATED

Read aloud and discuss the following section.

Despite his many accomplishments, Rabban Gamaliel sometimes failed to be an effective leader. He often acted arrogantly and resented having to share power with his colleagues. Gamaliel often found himself at odds with other sages, particularly Rabbi Joshua, whom he publicly humiliated several times.

The Babylonian Talmud (Berachot 27b–28a, compiled between 200 and 500 C.E.) recounts their most serious conflict and apparent reconciliation. Scholars still debate which aspects of this story are historically accurate. Most agree that Rabban Gamaliel's autocratic tendencies precipitated a revolt against him by two powerful factions in the early post-Temple era. A humble blacksmith by trade, Rabbi Joshua was also a brilliant mathematician and led a faction of Yochanan ben Zakkai's disciples. Rabbi Elazar ben Azariah, a brilliant eighteen-year-old, represented a group of priests who had formerly controlled the Temple. (Note: Brackets indicate material that has been paraphrased for clarification.)

[Rabban Gamaliel and Rabbi Joshua once had a dispute. Gamaliel argued that the evening prayer was mandatory. Joshua claimed it was optional.] For the sake of peace, Joshua [accepted Gamaliel's position in front of a large gathering of scholars. Still not satisfied, Gamaliel told Joshua to stand up while he delivered a long lecture about why Joshua was wrong.]

Rabbi Joshua remained standing, until all the people there began to shout "Stop!" And he stopped. They then said, "How long is Rabban Gamaliel to go on insulting [Rabbi Joshua]? [Twice before he humiliated him] and now he insults him again! Come, let us depose him! Whom shall we appoint instead? We can hardly appoint Rabbi Joshua, because he is one of the parties involved. We can hardly appoint Rabbi Akiva because perhaps Rabban Gamaliel will bring a curse on him because he has no ancestral merit. Let us then appoint Rabbi Elazar ben Azariah, who is wise and rich and the tenth in descent from Ezra [and a member of the priestly tribe with] ancestral merit so Rabban Gamaliel cannot bring a curse on him."

They went and said to Elazar ben Azariah, "Will your honor consent to become head of the Academy?" He replied, "I will go and consult the members of my family." His wife said, "Perhaps they will depose *you* later on." [Besides, she said,] "You have no white hair." He was eighteen years old that day and a miracle was wrought for him.

Eighteen rows of hair [on his beard] turned white. That is why Rabbi Elazar ben Azariah said [as we read in the Haggadah], "Behold, I am *like* a man seventy years old" and he did not say simply, "[I am] seventy years old." . . .

On that day the doorkeeper from the house of study was removed and permission was given to [many new students] to enter. For Rabban Gamaliel had issued a proclamation [that]: "No disciple whose [inner] character does not correspond to his exterior [piety] may enter the house of study." On that day [hundreds of new] benches were added [for new students] . . . And whenever the expression "on that day" is used, it refers to that day [when Gamaliel was deposed].

But Rabban Gamaliel did not absent himself from the house of study a single hour . . . When Gamaliel realized that Joshua was so highly respected [he decided it was time to apologize]. When he reached Joshua's house he saw that the walls were black. Gamaliel said to him, "From the walls of your house it is apparent that you are a blacksmith." Joshua replied, "Alas for the generation of which you are the leader, seeing that you know nothing of the troubles of the scholars and their struggles to support and sustain themselves!" Gamaliel said to him, "I apologize. Forgive me." Joshua paid no attention to him. "Accept my apology," said Gamaliel, "out of respect for my father" [and the House of Hillel]. Joshua then [forgave him] . . .

[Rabbi Joshua explained to the Rabbis who ousted Gamaliel that they should reinstate him because he was a descendent of Hillel, the first Nasi, and according to tradition a descendent of King David as well. Besides, deposing a leader recognized by Rome would have further strained the already difficult relations with the Empire.] . . . Rabbi Akiva said to Joshua . . . "Tomorrow morning you and I will [tell Elazar ben Azariah]." They said, "What shall we do? Shall we depose Rabbi Elazar ben Azariah? We have a rule that we may raise an object to a higher grade of sanctity but must not degrade it to a lower grade. If we let one Master preach on one Sabbath and one on the next, this will cause jealousy. Let therefore Rabban Gamaliel preach three Sabbaths and Rabbi Elazar ben Azariah one."

So ends the only recorded case of a Nasi's even brief removal from office.

• What seem to be the major disagreements and tensions between Rabban Gamaliel and Rabbi Joshua? How do they relate to the disagreements among Jews today?

• What do you make of Gamaliel's proclamation: "No disciple whose [inner] character does not correspond to his exterior [piety] may enter the house of study."

• What lessons about leadership might this story teach, and how would you apply them to events in America or Israel?

• How do you explain the reconciliation between Gamaliel and Joshua? What do you think about the power-sharing arrangement between Rabban Gamaliel and Elazar ben Azariah?

FINGERPRINTS ON THE HAGGADAH

Read this section aloud or on your own.

Gamaliel's brief fall from office was a virtual coup d'etat, and it reverberated throughout rabbinic literature and the Jewish collective memory. Although the Haggadah does not include a direct reference to the story, it comes pretty close: "Rabbi Elazar ben Azariah said: *Behold! I am like a man of seventy,* yet I have never been worthy [to find a reason] why the Exodus should be mentioned at night, until Ben Zoma explained it . . ." (Mishnah, Berachot 1:5). The seating arrangement at the Seder of the five sages in B'nei B'rak is also revealing: Eliezer, Joshua, Elazar ben Azariah, Akiva, and Tarfon. The Talmud (Berachot 46b) indicates that the individual with the highest-ranking position in the community sits in the middle. Elazar ben Azariah's position in the center hints at his brief stint as the replacement for Rabban Gamaliel as Nasi.[4]

• Ben Zoma's explanation about why one should include a reference to the Exodus in the evening prayers seems to have taken place on the day that Elazar ben Azariah replaced Rabban Gamaliel and became head of the Court. The redactors of the Haggadah had a choice among several other versions of Ben Zoma's explanation found in rabbinic literature, none of which mentions Elazar ben Azariah.[5] Why might they have preferred the only version that includes this veiled reference to Gamaliel's unseating, an act tantamount to revolution?

In addition to the Seder of the five sages mentioned in the Haggadah, ancient rabbinic literature includes a somewhat similar story involving Rabban Gamaliel. Make a copy of both for your guests and discuss the questions that follow.

It once happened on the first night of Passover that Rabban Gamaliel and the sages were reclining in the house of Boethus ben Zeno [a pious merchant] in Lod, and they were discussing the laws of Passover the entire night until the cock crowed. Then each pushed aside his table, stretched, and went along to the house of study.

—TOSEFTA, PISCHA 10:12 (THIRD CENTURY C.E.)

It once happened that Rabbi Eliezer, Rabbi Joshua, Rabbi Elazar ben Azariah, Rabbi Akiva, and Rabbi Tarfon were reclining in B'nei B'rak. They were discussing the Exodus from Egypt the entire night, until their students came and said to them: Our teachers, the time has arrived for reading the morning *Sh'ma*.

—THE PASSOVER HAGGADAH

• What are the differences between these two descriptions?

• Why may the composers of the Seder have rejected the first?

In portraying the Seder of the sages, the redactors of the Haggadah seem to have preferred assembling a group of Gamaliel's opponents rather than selecting the text from the Tosefta in which Gamaliel alone occupies center stage. On the feast of freedom, perhaps the Haggadah sought to remind future leaders that treating one's colleagues with less than respect carries serious consequences. Perhaps they also had the following Talmudic dictum in mind:

> Our Rabbis taught: Over three the Holy One, blessed be He, weeps every day: over him who is able to occupy himself with [the study of] the Torah and does not; and over him who is unable to occupy himself with [the study of] the Torah and does; and over a leader who domineers over the community.[6]

16

Reliving the Exodus:
The Story of the Last Night in Egypt

זֶבַח פֶּסַח הוּא לַיהוָה

אֲשֶׁר פָּסַח עַל בָּתֵּי בְנֵי יִשְׂרָאֵל בְּמִצְרַיִם,

בְּנָגְפּוֹ אֶת־מִצְרַיִם וְאֶת־בָּתֵּינוּ הִצִּיל...

*It is the Passover sacrifice to the Lord because He passed over the houses of the Israelites
in Egypt when He struck the Egyptians, but saved our houses . . . (Ex. 12:27).*
—THE PASSOVER HAGGADAH

Ever since the compilation of the Mishnah eighteen hundred years ago, the
Seder has required us to *explain* the meaning of three of Passover's central
symbols—the ancient paschal offering, matzah, and bitter herbs. The passage
above serves as the Haggadah's explanation of the ancient paschal sacrifice. But
the Haggadah challenges us to go further than mere explanation. It calls us to
reexperience the pain of slavery and the joy of freedom, reliving the journey from
one state to the other: "In every generation, each individual should feel as though
he or she had gone out of Egypt." How can we achieve this? The Haggadah contains the answer in a simple phrase: "Moreover, whoever elaborates upon the story

of the Exodus deserves praise." In that spirit, here is a set of pre-Seder activities designed to bring the saga of the Exodus to life. As you'll see, this chapter involves a number of "reenactments" of the Exodus that will prove particularly engaging when children and adults participate together.

These activities have been designed to take place before your Seder actually begins (unless you intend to begin early), so you may want to ask guests to arrive earlier than usual. If you are adding a number of pre-Seder activities, you may want to keep this in mind when planning your formal Seder.

We begin with a review of what you'll need to prepare before your guests arrive and continue with suggestions for how to present the activities included. *The Last Night in Egypt,* the story of the Exodus, has been written for reading aloud with children.

SETTING THE STAGE

What you'll need:

- A small, wrapped sandwich of horseradish and matzah and a backpack, shopping bag, or small suitcase for each Seder participant

- Several yards of red ribbon or several sheets of red construction paper, cut or torn into shapes resembling blood smeared on a doorpost

- Several yards of blue ribbon or blue construction paper, torn, cut or folded to resemble the parted Red Sea

- Scotch tape

- Copies of the Wayfarer's Prayer (see page 223) for each of your guests

Before your guests arrive, take a few pieces of red ribbon, fabric, or construction paper and fashion them to represent the lamb's blood smeared upon the Israelites' doorposts on their last night in Egypt. Tape these around the doorway of the room where you will conduct the activities that follow. (You can also ask younger participants to help with this.) This room will represent Egypt. Later, you can explain to the group that this blood served as a sign for God to pass over the houses of the Israelites as he slew the Egyptian firstborn (Ex. 12:21–23). This will help set the mood for getting back to Egypt. Prepare strips of blue ribbon, fabric, or construction paper to represent the Red Sea. Have these ready so you can later place them at the exit of this room when you head out of Egypt.

Place a small piece of matzah and a slice of horseradish in aluminum foil, plastic wrap, or a waxed paper bag. If you are using chopped horseradish, make a sandwich. Make enough packages for each Seder participant. Bring these along with the backpacks, etc. into your "Egypt" room.

When your guests arrive, if possible, gather them together in a room other than the room where you will be eating the Passover meal. This will enhance the feeling of departure from Egypt and arrival in the Promised Land. (In our house, we sit in the living room.)

Now you are ready to begin.

Explain that you will be engaging in a variety of activities designed to help achieve the goal of the Haggadah: "In every generation, each individual should feel as though he or she had gone out of Egypt."

If you haven't already done so, explain the meaning of the red ribbon construction paper on the doorpost. Tell your guests that you'll be reading a story about the Exodus from Egypt, *The Last Night in Egypt,* and then taking up one or two questions it raises:

- Should the Israelites let Egyptians who are seeking to escape from God's final plague into their homes?

- Should the Israelites risk leaving Egypt for an unknown destination?

Following the story below, you'll find suggestions for using these questions as the basis of a short bibliodrama that your Seder participants will be sure to remember. If you prefer, you can simply discuss these questions after you read the story and skip the bibliodrama. As a third option, you might include an activity based on the Wayfarer's Prayer, described on pages 222–23.

THE LAST NIGHT IN EGYPT

Read *The Last Night in Egypt* aloud. Depending on your group, you might ask one
individual to read the entire story or let everyone read a few paragraphs.
This works best if you have a copy for everyone. The story sets the stage for addressing
the two questions described earlier, but you can also use it on its own.
Italics indicate quotations from the Book of Exodus.

Once, more than three thousand springtimes ago, near the very beginning of the
Jewish people's history, there lived a very rich and mighty Egyptian king. He was
also super stubborn. Everyone called the king "Pharaoh." Many kinds of people
lived in his kingdom—Egyptians, Africans, and many Israelites (that's what they
called Jews in the olden days).

Kings who are very mighty sometimes get scared that someone else will try
to take away some of their power. That happened to Pharaoh. He always worried
that someone would rise up against him. He was afraid his enemies would attack
him. He was even afraid his friends would attack him. He was so afraid that he
became meaner and meaner.

The Israelites had come to Egypt several hundred years before. They had
grown from about seventy people to more than a million. Pharaoh began to fear
that maybe the Israelites would side with his enemies. That made him really scared
and even meaner than usual. Pharaoh enslaved the Israelites. He also gave orders
to the midwives who delivered the Israelite babies to kill all the boys. That would
be the end of them! But the midwives feared God and disobeyed Pharaoh's order.

So Pharaoh gave an order to the Egyptian people saying, *"Every [Hebrew] boy
that is born you shall throw into the Nile, but let every girl live"* (Ex. 1:22).

One mother named Yocheved decided to help her baby son escape. She
lined a wicker basket with waterproof tar, put her son inside, and placed it in the
reeds along the riverbank. She kissed him. "Good-bye, my sweet little boy," she
called sadly. "I pray that an Egyptian mother will see your cradle and save you."
Miriam, the baby's sister, hid nearby to see what would happen to her brother.

Soon, Pharaoh's daughter came down to bathe in the Nile. Guess what she
found! *She spied the basket among the reeds and sent her slave to get it. When she opened
it, she saw it was a child, a boy crying. She took pity on it and said, "This must be a
Hebrew child"* (Ex. 2:5–6).

She wondered how her own father could be so mean.

Just then Miriam popped out of the bushes. Moses' sister *said to Pharaoh's daughter, "Shall I get you a Hebrew woman to nurse the child for you?"*

And Pharaoh's daughter answered, "Yes."

So the girl went and called the child's mother.

And Pharaoh's daughter said to her, "Take this child and nurse it for me, and I will pay your wages."

So the woman took the child and nursed it. When the child grew up, she brought him to Pharaoh's daughter, who made him her son. She named him Moses, explaining, "I drew him out of the water" (Ex. 2:7–10).

Only a few people knew that Moses was an Israelite, and they kept it a big secret from Pharaoh.

But Pharaoh was still afraid and mean. He forced the Israelites to become his slaves. They built huge buildings. They built whole cities. The weather in Egypt was boiling hot, especially in the summer. Hotter than 100 degrees. But Pharaoh hardly gave them any water. They weren't even allowed to ask any questions. When his slaves complained or sat down in the shade, his soldiers beat them with whips.

Meanwhile, Prince Moses grew up in Pharaoh's palace. One day, he took a walk to watch a new city being built. That was very exciting. Huge blocks of stone that weighed tons were being rolled along on round logs. Using long ropes, Israelite slaves dragged these stones for miles. As Moses came closer, he saw some soldiers whipping a Hebrew slave.

"Why is he doing that?" Moses wondered. "That slave is so weak, he couldn't hurt anyone."

"I may be a prince of Egypt," Moses said to himself, "but these are still my people." Moses looked this way and that way. He saw no one. He punched the soldier so hard that the soldier died. Moses buried him in the sand.

When Moses came back the next day, the Israelite slaves were afraid of him. One said, *"Do you mean to kill us like you killed the Egyptian?"* (Ex. 2:14). Moses knew he had to leave Egypt. Soon Pharaoh would hear what Moses had done. Pharaoh would finally learn that he had been deceived. Soon he would know that Moses was not really an Egyptian, but an Israelite.

So Moses set off into the desert to escape from his adopted father. He came to the land of Midian, where he became a shepherd. He got married and had two sons. Many years went by. The old Pharaoh died, but a new one took his place who was just as mean, and even more stubborn.

One day, while tending his flocks, Moses saw a strange light in the mountains. It was a bush on fire. Instead of burning up, it kept on burning and burning. Moses wondered, *"Why doesn't the bush burn up?"* (Ex. 3:3).

Suddenly Moses heard a voice. *"Do not come closer. Remove your sandals from your feet, for the place where you stand is holy ground. I am,"* He said, *"the God of your father, the God of Abraham, the God of Isaac, and the God of Jacob."* And Moses hid his face for he was afraid to look at God (Ex. 3:5–6).

Moses had heard about this God from his mother. She told him that the God of the Israelites was invisible and even stronger than Pharaoh. God knew everything, even exactly what was going to happen in the future. The voice told Moses that God knew about how mean Pharaoh had been to his Israelite slaves. God heard their cries of pain and wanted to take them out of Egypt and set them free.

"But Moses, you must be their leader," said God. "Go tell Pharaoh to let my people go. I know that mean Pharaoh won't want to let the Israelites go. I will harden his heart so I, the mighty and awesome God, will show him who is boss. I'll send ten plagues to Egypt and then Pharaoh will let my people go."

Moses heard all this and grew more and more afraid. "What if no one believes you?" Moses asked God. "And why should the Israelites listen to me. I have a lisp and can't even speak clearly. And forget about Pharaoh! He doesn't listen to anybody anyway!"

"Your brother Aaron will help you," said God. And God gave Moses special signs to convince the Israelites and the Egyptians that God meant business. God gave Moses three mysterious signs to show when he got back to Egypt—turning a rod into a snake, making the skin on his hand change from very smooth to very rough, and making water turn red like blood. God gave Moses a special rod to help create these signs.

Moses was right! No one listened. Pharaoh just made his Israelite slaves work even harder! He even took away the straw they needed to make bricks. That made their work so hard it was almost impossible.

So God told Moses to warn Pharaoh about the plagues, one at a time. First the rivers all turned to blood. But Pharaoh didn't care. Then frogs started jumping out of the river until the whole country smelled of frogs. Pharaoh pleaded with Moses to make the frogs go away. But when they did, he still wouldn't let the children of Israel leave Egypt.

Then lice came and made everyone itch. Then insects covered everything. Then all the cattle that belonged to the Egyptians started to get sick. Then all the Egyptians started to get big sores all over their bodies. Then huge hailstones fell all over Egypt. The hailstones were so big they made holes in the roof. Then swarms of crickets came and ate all the plants. Then the sun didn't come out for three whole days. And the darkness was so thick you could touch it.

Each time a plague came Pharaoh agreed to let the Israelites go. But as soon as the plague ended he changed his mind. Pharaoh's heart grew harder and harder. So God sent another plague. Pharaoh told Moses never to come back. But he still wouldn't let the Israelites go.

God told Moses to get ready for the last and worst plague of all. This one would finally convince Pharaoh to let the Israelites go free. God was going to kill all the firstborn Egyptian males—people and even animals. God spoke to Moses, saying, "Tell the Israelites to paint their doorposts with the blood of a lamb as a sign so I will *pass over* their homes. They should roast the lamb and eat it with bitter herbs and matzah. And tell them to stay inside their homes."

God also told Moses this: "Tell the Israelites that every spring they should have a holiday to remember what happened on this last night in Egypt. For seven days they should eat matzah but no bread. When your children ask what this holiday is all about you shall tell them, *'It is the Passover sacrifice to the Lord because God passed over the houses of the Israelites in Egypt when God struck the Egyptians, but saved our houses'"* (Ex. 12:27).

That was a long, scary, and very sad night for everyone in Egypt. Many Egyptians died. The Israelites were safe. But Egyptian mothers trying to save their children kept knocking on the doors of Israelite homes. And the Israelites did not know what to do.

Should they let these Egyptians in or not?

That was one thing the Israelites were thinking about that night. But they were also wondering about leaving Egypt the next morning. Life was bad in

Egypt, but it was still home. And where would they go? Out into the desert, following orders that Moses got from the mighty and invisible God? And what would they take with them? And what would they eat and drink in the desert? Maybe it would be better to stay in Egypt?

But by the time morning came, stubborn Pharaoh had finally decided to send the Israelites out of Egypt. And the children of Israel had finally decided it was time to leave Egypt. It was time to learn how to be a free people. "Maybe," they thought, "we can make a country that is a better place for people to live than Egypt." And that is what we, the Jewish people, are still trying to do.

> B'khol dor vador chayav adam lirot et atzmo k'ilu hu yatza mimitzrayim.
> In every generation, each individual should feel as though he or she had gone out of Egypt.

BIBLIODRAMA: KNOCKING IN THE NIGHT

In the middle of the last plague, Egyptian mothers seeking to save their firstborn sons knock frantically on the doors of the Israelites' homes. Should the Israelites let them in?

This works very well as a simple drama. Choose someone to be a door. He or she simply stands in the middle of the room with arms outstretched parallel to the floor. Ask a few people to stand on one side of the door and play the part of Egyptians trying to seek refuge. Ask a few other people to be on the other side of the door and play the role of Israelites. Some should argue for letting in the Egyptians and others should oppose this. If you have many people at your Seder, you can either let people participate in the drama from the "audience" or ask people who have something to say to join the drama on one side of the door or the other. Feel free to allow questions about the morality of this last plague.

After the "drama" has reached an end, share the following midrash (Exodus Rabbah 18:2) with the group. It was written down about a thousand years ago, but it is probably based on a more ancient source:

When the Egyptians heard that God would strike down their firstborn, some were afraid and some were not. Those who were afraid brought

220

their firstborn to an Israelite and said: "Do please allow him to pass with you this night." When midnight struck, God smote all the first-born. As for those who took asylum in the houses of the Israelites, God passed between the Israelites and the Egyptians, killing the Egyptians and leaving the Israelites alive. When the Jews awoke at midnight, they found the Egyptians dead among their surviving firstborn.

Now ask the group to reflect on what contemporary situations the "drama" and midrash evoke for them. The theme of rescue, from the Holocaust to September 11, should be fairly close to the surface.

- Have we acted as our "brothers' keepers"?

- The Seder begins with an invitation to the hungry and poor to join us. Should we invite a homeless person to our Seders? Why or why not?

- Have we stood "idly by the blood" of our neighbors (Lev. 19:16)?

- Have we remembered to "know the heart of the stranger because [we] were strangers in Egypt" (Ex. 23:9)?

- Have we used our memories of suffering and persecution—in Egypt and elsewhere—to nurture vengeance or to affirm our responsibility to create a better world?

BIBLIODRAMA: TO STAY OR TO LEAVE?

Should the Israelites risk leaving Egypt for promises of a better life in their own land?

Set the stage by giving your guests the following background:

Life in Egypt was difficult, but maybe heading out into the unknown desert would be even worse. The text in Exodus tells us that God was not very trusting of the Israelites' loyalty to their new destination:

Now when Pharaoh let the people go, God did not lead them by way of the land of the Philistines, although it was nearer; for God said, "The people may have a change of heart when they see war and return to Egypt" (Ex. 13:17).

A bit later, Pharaoh changes his mind and sets out for the Red Sea to capture his fleeing slaves. The Israelites too have a change of heart.

Greatly frightened, the Israelites cried out to the Lord. And they said to Moses, "Was it for want of graves in Egypt that you brought us to die in the wilderness? What have you done to us, taking us out of Egypt? Is this not the very thing we told you in Egypt, saying, 'Let us be, and we will serve the Egyptians, for it is better for us to serve the Egyptians than to die in the wilderness'?" (Ex. 14:10–12).

Ask some members of your group to defend leaving and others to defend staying. After arguing the pros and cons of leaving Egypt, you may want to try broadening the discussion to include contemporary events or personal situations that involve the plight of refugees. The road to freedom always requires risks. The responsibility for building a just society is daunting because it never ends.

As individuals and a community, here and in Israel, how well have we done this year? What are the habits or the empty values that keep us enslaved and prevent us from moving on in our lives?

A PRAYER FOR THE JOURNEY

The Exodus from Egypt represents one of *the* paradigmatic journeys of all time. Before you prepare to set off for the Promised Land, ask your group this question:

> If you were setting out on a journey as momentous as the Israelites'
> departure from Egypt, and you wanted to offer a prayer before you
> left, what would be the main ideas you'd include in your prayer?

Briefly summarize the themes that emerge in your guests' answers. When you've finished this, hand out a copy of the Wayfarer's Prayer to each guest. Read it aloud and ask for a few very brief comments on the differences and similarities between the themes included in this prayer and those raised by your guests.[1]

With only a few modifications, the Wayfarer's Prayer—*Tefilat Ha-derekh*—comes from the Babylonian Talmud (Berachot 29b), which was completed in about the year 500.

In the Talmud, the prayer is in the singular, while the traditional version recited today is always in the plural, even if the journey involves only a single individual. One who sets out on a journey should recite the following prayer upon leaving the city limits:

The Wayfarer's Prayer
May it be Your will, our God, and God of our ancestors, that You lead us toward peace, cause us to take steps toward peace, and guide us toward peace. And bring us to our desired destination—life, joy, and peace. Save us from the hand of every enemy or ambush on the road and from every kind of disaster that could ever threaten the world. May You bless the work of our hands and grant us grace, kindness, and mercy—in Your eyes and in the eyes of all who see us. Hear the voice of our supplication, because You are a God who hears prayer and supplication. Blessed are You, God, who hears prayer.

MARCHING FROM EGYPT TO THE PROMISED LAND

Now you are ready to begin the march from Egypt, through the Red Sea, to the Promised Land—the Seder table. Jews from some Islamic countries still practice the custom of symbolically re-creating the Exodus by walking around the Seder table while carrying matzah wrapped in napkins slung over their back. We conclude with a variation on that wonderful tradition. Give everyone a plastic bag with a piece of matzah and a slice of horseradish (or a sandwich of chopped horseradish). Everyone should take his or her bag of bitterness and load it into a backpack, suitcase, or shopping bag. We must never forget our oppression in Egypt even when we Jews are a free people, and especially when we have power. Before you leave Egypt don't forget to lay down the blue fabric or construction paper that represents the Red Sea.

When everyone is ready, form a line, with children at the head, and wind your way from Egypt, where you've been, across the Red Sea, through the desert to the Promised Land. Remember that the journey from Egypt to the Promised Land took a long time and the route was circuitous. Walk in circles, up and down stairs, etc., until you reach the Seder table!

Just before you start your journey, read the following ancient midrash:[2]

The only edibles the Israelites took were the remains of the unleavened bread and the bitter herbs, and these not to satisfy their hunger, but because they were unwilling to separate themselves from what they had prepared lovingly at the command of God. These possessions were so dear to them that they would not entrust them to their beasts of burden; they carried them on their own shoulders.

On your journey, sing *Let My People Go* with gusto!

When Israel was in Egypt's land
Let my people go
Oppressed so hard they could not stand
Let my people go
Go down, Moses, way down in Egypt land
Tell ole Pharaoh
To let my people go

Unpack your suitcases and save your sandwich of matzah and bitter herbs for the appropriate point in the Seder.

17

Israel and the Haggadah

וְאוֹתָנוּ הוֹצִיא מִשָּׁם לְמַעַן הָבִיא אֹתָנוּ
לָתֶת לָנוּ אֶת־הָאָרֶץ אֲשֶׁר נִשְׁבַּע לַאֲבֹתֵינוּ.

And us He took out from there, that He might bring us and give us the
land that He promised on oath to our ancestors (Deut. 6:23).
—THE PASSOVER HAGGADAH

Based on many of the biblical passages quoted in the Haggadah, you might expect references to the land of Israel to appear throughout the Seder. But, as we'll see, that's hardly the case. In this chapter, we'll consider how the Haggadah relates to Israel as well as some broader questions concerning the relationship between Passover and the State of Israel.

As you make your way through your Seder, ask your guests to let you know every time they notice a reference to the land of Israel, Zion, Jerusalem, the Temple, and the land of Canaan. See whether you notice any parts of the Seder where these references occur more or less often. Ask your guests to discuss why this might be the case.

THE FRUITS OF ISRAEL AND EGYPT: A PUZZLE

This activity requires a trip to the grocery store. Pick up a head of garlic, a cucumber, a leek, an onion, a melon, grapes, figs, and a pomegranate (if you can't find a pomegranate, make one out of red paper). Put the garlic, cucumber, leek, onion, and melon in one basket (or bowl) and the remaining items in another.

Before your Seder begins, gather your guests and show them both baskets. Explain that you'll be solving a puzzle based on two passages in the Bible in which these groups of fruits and vegetables appear. Read the paragraphs below and the question that comes after. After you've concluded your discussion, you may want to read one or both of the "solutions" that follow.

Following the Exodus from Egypt, the Israelites camped near Mount Sinai for almost a year. After having received the Torah and dedicated the Mishkan (the portable sanctuary for the Ark of the Covenant), they finally began their march to the Promised Land, a distance of only several months' (or maybe less) travel. Three days into the journey, they complained bitterly, longing to return to Egypt:

> The riffraff in their midst felt a gluttonous craving; and then the Israelites wept and said, "If only we had meat to eat! We remember the fish that we used to eat free in Egypt, the cucumbers, the melons, the leeks, the onions, and the garlic. Now our gullets are shriveled. There is nothing at all! Nothing but this manna to look to."
>
> —NUMBERS 11:4–6

A few chapters later, twelve spies are sent to scout out the land of Canaan. All except Joshua and Caleb spread evil reports about the land in order to persuade the Israelites to return to Egypt. After the ensuing rebellion against Moses and Aaron, God condemns the people to thirty-nine more years in the desert. What did the spies bring back from Canaan?

> They reached wadi Eshcol, and there they cut down a branch with a single cluster of grapes—it had to be borne on a carrying frame by two of them—and some pomegranates and figs.
>
> —NUMBERS 13:23

• Why do you think garlic, cucumbers, leeks, onions, and melons are associated with Egypt, while grapes, figs, and pomegranates are connected with Israel? There is more than one satisfying answer to this puzzle! Deuteronomy 8:8 notes the seven choice species of the land of Israel—wheat, barley, grapes, figs, pomegranates, olives, and honey. Here we are just concerned with those mentioned in Numbers 13:23.

Following are two solutions to the puzzle that you might share with your group.

From the Depths to the Heights: Garlic, onions, leeks, melons, and cucumbers mature under or upon the soil. When harvested, they bear the signs of their habitat: they are fully or partially covered with dirt. These crops shared their earthen realm with the Israelites, who were so long mired in the muddy clay of Egypt's brick pits. Grapes, figs, and pomegranates grow on trees or vines, which elevate them above the ground. This difference represents the journey from degradation to redemption on both the physical and the spiritual plane.

Israel's descent begins with Jacob's journey down to Egypt. As we read in the Haggadah, "My father was a wandering Aramean. He went down few in numbers to sojourn there . . ." (Deut. 26:5).

The Egyptians ruthlessly imposed upon the Israelites the various labors that they made them perform. Ruthlessly they made life bitter for them with harsh labor at mortar and bricks and with all sorts of tasks in the field.

—EXODUS 1:13

Redeeming the Israelites first meant literally lifting them out of the mud, then bringing them to Sinai, and later up to Israel, as in Psalms 40:3–4: "He lifted me out of the miry pit, the slimy clay, and set my feet on a rock, steadied my legs. He put a new song into my mouth, a song of praise to our God." The produce of Egypt represents the lowly state to which Israel had fallen and to which they had sadly grown accustomed. The fruits of Israel embody the promise of ascent. "And God spoke to Israel in the visions of the night . . . I myself will go down with you to Egypt; and I will also surely bring you up again" (Gen. 46: 2–4).

The yearning for the crops of *Mitzrayim* suggests that it is easier to take the slaves out of Egypt than to take Egypt out of the slaves.

Roots and Responsibilities: Cucumbers, leeks, garlic, onions, and melons are all annuals—they have to be replanted each year. Grapes, figs and pomegranates are perennials—plant them once and they produce for many, many years. They also take several years before they mature and bear fruit. Now, although the Israelites stayed in Egypt for several hundred years, it was never truly their home. When God promises the land to Abraham, God also says this to Abraham: "Know well that your offspring shall be strangers in a land not theirs . . ." (Gen. 15:13).

The land of Egypt does not belong to the Israelites, despite how long they have resided in it. Later, when Joseph brings his father Jacob to meet Pharaoh, Jacob says he has come to "sojourn in this land." The stay may be long, but it is ultimately temporary. So the Israelites put down shallow roots in Egypt, like the plants for which they yearn. For the Israelites, the Promised Land is their ultimate destination, home in the deepest sense. And that is where one really puts down roots. That is where one is sure to be long enough to justify plantings that will take time to bear fruit.

The issue of roots—shallow or deep—also relates to the type of care required by these different kinds of plants. The plants associated with Egypt need people to water them, and fairly frequently. That takes work. These particular fruits of Israel draw their own water from the soil's depths. But that water only comes if the Israelites obey the laws they have received in the desert after leaving Egypt. That too takes work, but of a different kind:

> For the land that you are about to enter and possess is not like the land
> of Egypt from which you have come. There the grain you sowed had
> to be watered by your own labors, like a vegetable garden; but the land
> you are about to cross into and possess, a land of hills and valleys, soaks
> up its water from the rains of heaven. It is a land which the Lord your
> God looks after, on which the Lord your God always keeps His eye,
> from year's beginning to year's end. If, then, you obey the command-
> ments that I enjoin upon you this day, loving the Lord your God and
> serving Him with all your heart and soul, I will grant the rain for your
> land in season, the early rain and the late.
>
> —DEUTERONOMY 11:10–14

When given the choice between serving Pharaoh and God, between the familiar land of Egypt and the strange land of promise, the Israelites who had come of age in *Mitzrayim* preferred Pharaoh and Egypt. As a result, they wandered for forty years in the desert and never made it to the Promised Land.

ISRAEL'S ABSENCE FROM THE HEART OF THE HAGGADAH

Take turns reading the following paragraphs aloud and then lead
a discussion on any or all of the questions at the end of this section.

Where were the Israelites headed after leaving Egypt? Doesn't the Haggadah lead us on a journey from slavery to redemption, from Egypt to Israel, albeit an Israel from which we were exiled for so many long centuries? Reading only the beginning and the conclusion of the Haggadah, that would seem to be the case.

Near the beginning of the Haggadah we read:

This is the bread of affliction that our ancestors ate in the land of Egypt. Whoever is hungry, let him come and eat; whoever is in need let him come join in celebrating the Pesach festival. This year we are here, next year may it be in the land of Israel! This year, slaves; next year, free people!

At the Haggadah's conclusion we read:

The order of the Pesach service is now completed in accordance with all its laws, its ordinances and statutes. Just as we were found worthy to perform it, so may we be worthy to do it in the future. O Pure One who dwells on high, raise up the congregation which is without number! Soon, and with rejoicing, lead the offshoots of the stock that you have planted redeemed to Zion.
L'shanah ha-ba'ah birushalayim!
Next year in Jerusalem!

So far, so good. But now let's look more closely at some of the Haggadah's core texts, where Israel literally drops off the page.[1]

The Haggadah answers the Four Questions with the following quotation from Deuteronomy 6:21: "*Avadim hayinu . . .* We were Pharaoh's slaves in Egypt; and the Lord took us out of Egypt with a mighty hand. . . ."

But the next verses from Deuteronomy read: "The Lord wrought before our eyes marvelous and destructive signs and portents in Egypt, against Pharaoh and all his household; and us he took out from there that He might bring us and give us the land that He had promised on oath to our ancestors" (Deut. 6:22–23).

A bit later, the Haggadah describes God's covenant with Abraham:

Blessed be He who keeps His promise to Israel. Blessed be He. For the Holy One, blessed be He, determined the end of the bondage, thus doing that which He said to Abraham our father in the Covenant between the Pieces. As it is said, "He said unto Abram: 'Know well that your offspring shall be strangers in a land not theirs, and they shall be enslaved and oppressed for four hundred years; but I will execute judgment on the nation they shall serve, and in the end they shall go out with great wealth'" (Gen. 15:13–14).

God's promise to Abram went further, but the Haggadah omits the rest of it: "And they shall return here . . . To your offspring I assign this land . . ." (Gen. 15:16, 18).

Eighteen hundred years ago, the Mishnah described many of the Seder's essentials, instructing us to read the following passage from the Book of Deuteronomy *"until [we] complete the whole section"*:

My father was a wandering Aramean. He went down to Egypt few in numbers and sojourned there; but there he became a great and very populous nation. The Egyptians dealt harshly with us and oppressed us; they imposed heavy labor upon us. We cried to the Lord, the God of our fathers, and the Lord heard our plea and saw our plight, our misery, and our oppression. The Lord took us out from Egypt by a mighty hand, by an outstretched arm and awesome power, and by signs and portents.

—DEUTERONOMY 26:5–8

Despite the Mishnah's clear instructions to complete the section, the Haggadah stops short and omits the next verse: "And he has brought us to this place and has given us this land, a land flowing with milk and honey" (Deut. 26:9).

Let's consider one more example of Israel's diminished presence in the Haggadah. According to the most common explanation, the Seder's four cups of wine each correspond to an aspect of God's fourfold redemptive promise:

> Say, therefore, to the Israelite people: I am the Lord. I will [1] take you out from the labors of the Egyptians and [2] deliver you from their bondage. I will [3] redeem you with an outstretched arm and through extraordinary chastisements. And I will [4] take you to be My people and I will be your God. . . .
>
> —EXODUS 6:6–7

But the next verse includes a fifth promise: "I will [5] bring you into the land which I swore to give to Abraham, Isaac, and Jacob, and I will give it to you for a possession, I the Lord" (Ex. 6:8).

The fifth aspect of redemption relates to Israel.

So shouldn't we drink five cups of wine instead of four? Some used to. Today, standard versions of the Talmud (Pesachim 118a) read: "Over the fourth cup one recites the Hallel and the Great Hallel (Psalm 136)." But other manuscripts of the Talmud read: "Over the *fifth* cup one completes the Hallel and the Great Hallel. These are the words of Rabbi Tarfon." Rashi preferred the text that specified only four cups and, for most, his view held sway.[2]

- Why do you think the compilers of the Haggadah downplayed the presence of Israel?

- If you were writing a Haggadah today, what role would you assign Israel?

- How do you feel when you say, "Next year in Jerusalem"? What do you mean when you say it?

- Do you think a people can be truly free without a connection to a particular land? Can the Jewish people be free without Israel?

WHITHER ISRAEL?

You may want to read this on your own or, depending on your group,
after discussing the issues in the previous section.

Had not Bar Kochba's disastrous rebellion (132–135 C.E.) led to the exile of most Jews from Israel, Jewish history and Judaism itself would surely have evolved differently. Rabbinic Judaism developed after the Second Temple's destruction, and its task was to create a portable Judaism, independent of both the Temple and the land of Israel. Building on earlier examples in the Bible, Rabbinic Judaism consolidated the transformation of the Exodus from Egypt into a symbol of hope in God's future redemption of the Jewish people. The Jew would encounter God in the world of sacred time and commandments instead of sacred space and sacrifice.

At Passover, the celebration of faith in God's ultimate redemption of Israel, a people in exile, could hardly give repeated emphasis to passages promising that Abraham's descendents would inherit the land. Of course, the hope of restoration to Israel remained. But exile must have imposed its own reading upon the Haggadah's injunction: "In every generation, each individual should feel as though he or she had gone out of Egypt." Gone *out* of Egypt; not necessarily *into* the Promised Land. That's another story and one that required a good many years to complete.

The sages, of course, continued to extol the beauties of Zion. But it didn't take long for the idea of a heavenly Jerusalem to take root, a city whose mythic radiance far outshone that of the earthly city.[3] Likewise, they also lauded the virtues of living in Israel, while at the same time putting the brakes on any messianic impulse to retake the land. Thus, Rabbi Helbo, a sage active in Israel during the early fourth century C.E. interpreted a verse from the Song of Songs (8:4)—"Do not wake or rouse love until it please"—as God's warning to the Jewish people "that they should not attempt to go up from the Diaspora by force."[4] The Jewish people should not force God's redemptive hand.

The references to Israel in the beginning and at the end of the Seder (as well as in its various psalms and songs) were not necessarily to the Israel of this world, but to the Israel of an idealized, messianic future. As Benjamin Segal writes:

If one's eyes were set Zionward, they were also primarily set toward the future. The "city of the kings, the royal city" was such in *potential,* but in the present she could only be called on . . . to "arise, come forth from the rubble." On the Sabbath in particular, but in all other prayer cycles as well, the "Israel" of note is a future, ideal, rebuilt, perfected Zion—in short, messianic Jerusalem.[5]

Although there were many differences of opinion about the significance of living in Israel, rabbinic Judaism succeeded so well that Maimonides no longer counted returning to Israel among his enumeration of the 613 *mitzvot,* or commandments.[6]

Remember, too, that between the third and tenth centuries, when much was added to the Haggadah's Mishnaic core, the community in Babylonia increasingly became the intellectual center of the Jewish world. In 922, rivalry between the communities of Israel and Babylonia turned bitter over whose calendar would determine the date of Passover. Unable to resolve the dispute, each community followed its own calendar for a year. Ultimately, Saadiah Gaon, the chief Babylonian protagonist, proved victorious. It's probably not accidental that Saadiah's Haggadah omitted the following passage included in the Haggadot of his predecessors and those of today:[7] "And us He took out from there, that He might bring us and give us the land that He had promised on oath to our ancestors" (Deut. 6:23). Even before Saadiah, the Babylonian drive for dominance over Israel may have left its fingerprints on the Haggadah in Israel's rather muted presence.

The compilers of the Haggadah may also have downplayed Israel because they did not want it to overshadow what they felt to be the ultimate purpose of the redemption from Egypt, namely the revelation at Sinai with the gift of Torah. In fact, at the end of the second Seder we begin counting the *omer,* marking the forty-nine days between Passover and Shavuot when, according to tradition, we received the Torah. Joseph B. Soloveitchik explained it this way:

[A]lthough the Jewish people did enter into the Land of Israel subsequent to the Exodus from Egypt this was not the primary goal of *Yitziat Mitzrayim* [the Exodus from Egypt]. It was their destination but not their destiny. The direct goal of *Yitziat Mitzrayim* was the revelation at Sinai. The goal was the transformation of a subjugated people into "a kingdom of priests and a holy nation" [Exodus 19:6]. It was not just to grant them political and economic freedom, but also to create a sacred people.[8]

There's one more factor that may contribute to the way compilers of the Haggadah treated Israel. First, it's important to note that the elimination of allusions to "the land" occurs in the part of the Haggadah that addresses the enslavement in Egypt. To bring Israel into the Seder at that point would be to undermine one of the Haggadah's central injunctions: to reexperience not just the suffering but also the hopelessness that our ancestors endured in Egypt. The notion of a homeland in which the children of Israel would one day enjoy sovereignty could not have been further from the consciousness of those mercilessly enslaved for generations in Egypt. Reminders of Israel in this part of the Haggadah would undercut the intended dramatic tension, giving away, as it were, the story's ending.

That's why Israel begins to appear after the Haggadah's treatment of the plagues, with the singing of *Dayyenu,* which concludes: "Had He taken us to the land of Israel without building the Temple for us—it would have sufficed."

We noted earlier that the passage from Deuteronomy (6:21) that provides the answer to the Four Questions (*Avadim hayinu . . .* We were slaves) continued with a reference to God's promise of the land to Abraham's forebears. That reference was omitted at the beginning of the Seder. It appears after *Dayyenu,* just before we recite the first two psalms of the Hallel (literally, "praise"): "And us He took out from there, that He might bring us and give us the land that He had promised on oath to our ancestors."

THE FIFTH CUP

Read the following paragraphs aloud. Then either discuss with your
Seder participants whether or not they would like to celebrate the fifth cup
or explain why you've decided to do so. You can decide where it would be
most appropriate to insert the fifth cup. Some have suggested doing so after *Dayyenu,*
because its conclusion refers to Israel. A somewhat more traditional view

234

would suggest inserting an extra cup after completing the *Yehalelukha* passage that follows the conclusion of the Hallel. According to this tradition, the fourth cup would be drunk without a blessing. The fifth and final cup would then be drunk with a blessing as described for the former fourth cup. To accompany the fifth cup, you may wish to read one of the selections that follow this reading.[9]

Say, therefore, to the Israelite people: I am the Lord. I will [1] take you out from the labors of the Egyptians and [2] deliver you from their bondage. I will [3] redeem you with an outstretched arm and through extraordinary chastisements. And I will [4] take you to be My people and I will be your God . . . I will [5] bring you into the land which I swore to give to Abraham, Isaac, and Jacob, and I will give it to you for a possession, I the Lord.

—EXODUS 6:6–8

If the cups of wine we drink at the Seder correspond to the number of God's redemptive promises, we should enjoy five cups of wine. Indeed, by the twelfth century, commentators noted interpretations that linked a fifth cup to the fifth promise of redemption.[10] A long list of Judaism's greatest sages—Rashi, Maimonides, the Maharal of Prague, and many others—added a fifth cup to their Seders. They all recognized that the Haggadah required only four cups, but they deemed a fifth cup to be "an excellent work of piety."[11] Still, the fifth cup has remained a debated question of Jewish law.[12] In the eighteenth century, the Vilna Gaon offered what has become a well-known response to the question: Because we are unable to answer this question with certainty, we shall leave the fifth cup for Elijah and await his return to settle the matter.

With the establishment of the State of Israel, the rationale for a fifth cup corresponding to the fifth redemptive promise becomes even more compelling. In our era, the Seder *should* be a time for marking Israel's rebirth and expressing our hopes for the country and its citizens. From the early days of Zionism, the dreams for a Jewish state resonated with the ancient themes of the Passover Seder. In a passage from *Altneuland* ("Old-New Land"), Theodore Herzl's 1902 novel about life in the Jewish state, we read:

235

It was one of the happy moments when one realizes the progress of civilization. For a time we even considered doing business by wire, quite a marvel. And so it was. At that time we had not got the power from the Dead Sea Canal. Today we no longer need English coal for ploughing the soil of Palestine. Even the locomotive standing at the edge of the field has become outmoded in our eyes. We now have the cables bringing power to our fields from the falls of the Jordan, from the Dead Sea Canal, and the brooks of the Hermon and Lebanon. Instead of coal we have water . . . It was a new version of *Chad Gadya* ["one lamb"] . . . [It] is the story of the plough which is first dragged by man, then by oxen, then by a locomotive driven by coal, then by a petrol-motor, then by power taken from water . . . And above it all is God—down to the one lamb, the one lamb.[13]

Not long after the State of Israel's establishment, Rabbi Menachem Kasher, one of the last century's greatest scholars of rabbinic literature, approached the Rabbinate in Israel to request that they institute the fifth cup. They refused. Nonetheless, the custom has begun to catch on.[14]

READINGS FOR THE FIFTH CUP

Soon after the birth of the State of Israel in 1948, the Rabbinate of Israel and S.Y. Agnon, the Israeli writer and scholar who won the Nobel Prize for Literature in 1966, composed this prayer for Israel. It is included in most prayer books.

A Prayer for the State of Israel

Our Father in heaven [*avinu she-bashamayim*], Rock and Redeemer of the people Israel: Bless the State of Israel, the first flowering of our redemption. Shield it with Your love; spread over it the shelter of Your peace. Guide its leaders and advisers with Your light and Your truth. Help them with Your good counsel. Strengthen the hands of those who defend our Holy Land. Deliver them; crown their efforts with triumph. Bless the land with peace, and its inhabitants with lasting joy. And let us say: Amen.

Rabbi Shlomo Riskin notes that the additional cup is traditionally drunk after the words *Ki mei'olam v'ad olam atah Eil,* "For from eternity to eternity You are God." This endows it with universal redemptive significance that extends beyond the matter of the Jewish people and their land.[15] In that spirit, the reading below focuses on world peace.

A Prayer for Peace

May we see the day when war and bloodshed cease, when a great peace will embrace the whole world. Then nation will not threaten nation, and mankind will not again know war. For all who live on earth shall realize we have not come into being to hate or to destroy. We have come into being to praise, to labor, and to love. Compassionate God, bless the leaders of all nations with the power of compassion. Fulfill the promise conveyed in Scripture: I will bring peace to the land, and you shall lie down and no one shall terrify you. I will rid the land of vicious beasts and it shall not be ravaged by war. Let love and justice flow like a mighty stream. Let peace fill the earth as the waters fill the sea. And let us say: Amen.[16]

Rabbi Menachem Kasher (1895–1983) composed this not long after Israel's birth.

The Fifth Cup: We Are Commanded to Give Thanks for a Miracle

Now, in our time . . . we have been privileged to behold the mercies of the Holy Name . . . and His salvation over us in the establishment of the State of Israel, which is the beginning of redemption and salvation from . . . exile . . . Even as it is written, *"And I shall bring you into the land, the same which I have lifted my hand to give unto Abraham, unto Isaac, and unto Jacob, and I have given it unto you as an inheritance. I am the Eternal"*—it is fitting and proper that we observe this pious act, the drinking of the fifth cup, as a form of thanksgiving . . .

Just as we have been privileged to see the first realization of "And I shall bring them," so may we be worthy of witnessing the perfect and complete redemption, the coming of the Messiah. May we witness fulfillment of the vision of the prophets, that "evil shall disappear as smoke in the wind, and that all the earth shall be filled with the knowledge of God."[17]

PASSOVER, MESSIANISM, AND ISRAEL

This is a reading for discussion before or during your Seder. Tragically, Israel has known little peace in its short life. While the country has perpetually struggled to contend with dangers from without, it has also faced threats from within. A fervent strain of messianism has flourished in Israel that has exacerbated the conflicts between Israel and its Arab neighbors.

Read the short essay below. Depending on your group, you may wish to discuss how serious a danger Jewish messianism poses to Israel and the Jewish people today.

Shortly before his death, Theodore Herzl (1860–1904) told a close friend about a dream he had in his twelfth year. The "King Messiah" appeared to Herzl and took him "on the wings of heaven" on an ascent where he met Moses:

> The Messiah called out to Moses, "For this child I have prayed." To me he said, "Go and announce to the Jews that I shall soon come and perform great and wondrous deeds for my people and for all mankind!"[18]

After the Holocaust and two homeless millennia of reciting a liturgy laden with a longing for Zion, the redemptive significance of statehood loomed large. In 1946, David Ben-Gurion testified before the Anglo-American Committee of Inquiry, one of the numerous postwar commissions charged with deliberating Palestine's fate:

> [M]ore than 3,300 years ago the Jews left Egypt. It was more than 3,000 years before the *Mayflower,* and every Jew in the world knows exactly the date when we left. It was on the 15th of Nisan. The bread they ate was matzot. Up till today all the Jews throughout the world

. . . on the 15th of Nisan eat the same matzot, and tell the story of the exile to Egypt; they tell what happened, all the sufferings that happened to the Jews since they went into exile. They [begin] with these two sentences: "This year we are slaves; next year we shall be free. This year we are here; next year we shall be in the Land of Israel." Jews are like that.[19]

Yet the Haggadah dreams not only of returning to Israel but of rebuilding the Temple as well. The blessing over the second cup of wine, the core of which the Mishnah attributes to Rabbi Akiva, gives voice to that yearning.[20] And Akiva was not merely imagining a Temple in the "heavenly Jerusalem." In 132 C.E., he threw his support behind the Bar Kochba rebellion, convinced that its leader was the Messiah himself.

Blessed are You . . . who has redeemed us and our ancestors from Egypt and enabled us to reach this night that we may eat *matzah* and *maror* . . . Enable us to celebrate in peace other holy days and festivals, joyful in the rebuilding of Your city and joyful in Your [Temple] service; and there we shall partake of the sacrifice and Pesach offerings, whose blood will reach the walls of Your altar with favor . . . Then we shall sing a new song for our redemption and for the deliverance of our souls. Blessed are You, O Lord, who has redeemed Israel.

The exile and devastation that followed Bar Kochba's failed rebellion went a long way to dampening the messianic strivings that have nonetheless erupted at different times and places throughout Jewish history.

Israel's birth gave concrete expression to messianic yearnings that had long lain dormant.

Soon after 1948, Israel's Rabbinate composed a prayer for the new state, celebrating its birth as "the first flowering of our redemption." Israel's stunning victory in 1967 unleashed a powerful movement to hasten the coming of the Messiah and rebuilding of the Temple.

Masquerading as Swiss tourists, Rabbi Moshe Levinger and friends booked rooms in Hebron's Park Hotel one day before the first Seder in 1968. After the Seder, they refused to leave. Thus began the first attempt to redeem Israel and bring the Messiah by settling the territories conquered during the Six-Day War. The Jewish settlement in Kiryat Arba, just outside of Hebron, was the child of Levinger's Seder.

In 1984, Israeli police arrested a group of Jewish terrorists planning to blow up the Dome of the Rock in Jerusalem, an act that would almost certainly have precipitated a devastating Arab response. The abortive plot hardly extinguished hopes to rebuild the Temple. An organization called the Temple Mount Faithful regularly engages in provocative deeds, including repeated efforts to lay a cornerstone for the Third Temple. Posters depicting the Third Temple in place of the Dome of the Rock are widely available in Israel. In 2003, one group proudly announced in the *New York Times* that it had built a replica of the Temple's altar and awaits a sufficiently chaotic moment to sneak it onto the Temple Mount and resume animal sacrifice.[21]

What can we learn from this?

First, that Jewish messianism taps deep into the core of Judaism's commitment to hope, not in itself a bad thing. The capacity to produce messianic offshoots attests to a religion's vitality. But those offshoots are not always benign. The ancient notion "of the birth pangs of the Messiah"—that things must get worse before they get better—coupled with the messianist's proclivity to disregard the law, create an explosive mixture.

One may, of course, ask, "Why worry about internal dangers of this kind at a moment when the Jewish people find themselves beset with so many real external enemies?" Alas, history suggests that messianic movements often arise precisely at such moments of vulnerability. We dangerously flatter ourselves if we imagine that we are immune from producing messianic zealots similar to those bred by other religious traditions.

18

The Restoration of Wonder:
The Miracles of Egypt and Our Day

לְפִיכָךְ אֲנַחְנוּ חַיָּבִים לְהוֹדוֹת...
לְמִי שֶׁעָשָׂה לַאֲבוֹתֵינוּ וְלָנוּ אֶת־כָּל־הַנִּסִּים הָאֵלוּ.

Therefore it is our duty to thank . . . the One who performed
all these miracles for our ancestors and for us.
—THE PASSOVER HAGGADAH, QUOTING THE MISHNAH, PESACHIM 10:5 (CIRCA 200 C.E.)

It's hard to read the Haggadah without feeling that it is trying to convince you to believe in miracles. The question is, "What's a miracle?"

The passage above from the Haggadah is followed by this statement: "He has brought us forth from slavery to freedom, from sorrow to joy, from mourning to festivity, from darkness to great light and from bondage to redemption. Let us then recite before Him a new song; Hallelujah." In one sense, these are the Haggadah's miracles—once we were idol-worshiping slaves and now we are free to worship the true God.

But of course, the Haggadah points to wonders of another kind as well. After recounting the suffering of the Israelites, the Haggadah turns to the Book of Deuteronomy (26:8) to describe God's mighty deeds of redemption. The words are among the Seder's most memorable. "The Lord took us out from Egypt by a mighty hand, by an outstretched arm and awesome power, and by signs and wonders (*b'otot u-v'moftim*)."[1] After elaborating on this passage, the Haggadah cites another from Deuteronomy (4:34) that seeks to remove any lingering doubts: "Has any god ventured to go and take for himself one nation from the midst of another by prodigious acts, by signs and wonders, by war, by a mighty hand and an outstretched arm and awesome power (*mora'im gedolim*), as the Lord your God did for you in Egypt before your very eyes?"

These are just a few of the Haggadah's references to the miraculous.

> As you proceed through the Haggadah, ask your guests to interrupt
> and let you know whenever they notice a reference to miracles.

In this chapter, we'll consider "the miraculous," a subject that leaps out from the Haggadah, but one that you may never have discussed at your Seder.

THE BIBLE AND THE DICTIONARY

Read the following section aloud or on your own.

The Bible uses many different terms to describe what we might call miraculous phenomena: *mora'im gedolim* (great deeds), *nifla'ot* (wondrous deeds), *pele* (from the same root as *nifla'ot*), *ot* ("sign"; plural, *otot*), *mofeit* ("wonder" or "portent"; plural, *moftim*), and many more. The last two appear frequently in passages the Haggadah quotes from Deuteronomy.

The final verses of Deuteronomy (34:10–12) provide a beautiful illustration of how the Bible uses many of these terms:

> Never again did there arise in Israel a prophet like Moses—whom the Lord singled out, face to face for the various signs and wonders (*ha-otot v'hamoftim*) that the Lord sent him to display in the land of Egypt, against Pharaoh and all his courtiers and his whole country, and for all the great might and awesome power (*ha-mora ha-gadol*) that Moses displayed before all Israel.[2]

Sometimes these expressions appear in surprising contexts. For example, *ot,* "sign," refers both to the sign of a rainbow (Gen. 9: 12, 17) and to the sign of circumcision (Gen. 17:11).[3]

The most familiar term in modern Hebrew for "miracle," *nes* (as in the dreidel's *nes gadol hayah sham,* a great miracle—*nes*—happened there), appears only once in the Bible in the context of a wondrous sign. In the Book of Numbers (26:10), the followers of Korach who rebelled against Moses were swallowed up by the earth and "became an example" [or a "sign," *l'nes*]. As a term for miracle, *nes* only became common in rabbinic parlance.

In the Bible, *nes* generally means a banner, ensign, or pole used to communicate a particular message. The copper serpent that Moses makes to cure snake bites (Num. 21:8–9) is mounted on a standard or pole, a *nes.* As one scholar notes, "In certain scriptures, the pole serves as a symbol of freedom, its function being to inform captives, exiles and imprisoned people of their 'liberation' and return to their homes . . . Indeed, the primary purpose of 'freedom' [in ancient Near Eastern cultures] is the restoration of the individual to his home and to his inheritance."[4] For example, in the haftarah for the eighth day of Passover we read: "He will hold up a signal (*nes*) to the nations and assemble the banished of Israel, and gather the dispersed of Judah from the four corners of the earth" (Isaiah 11:12).

In many translations of the Bible you won't even find the word "miracle." That's because the Torah speaks about "signs," "wonders," or "portents" rather than outright miracles. These phenomena refer to events that point beyond themselves to something greater, to the creator of nature and the author of human destiny. The Bible's miracles are meant to inculcate faith.

The crossing of the Red Sea and the sight of drowned Egyptians on the shore provide a perfect example: "And when Israel saw the wondrous power [literally, the "great hand"] that the Lord had wielded against the Egyptians, the people feared the Lord; they had faith in the Lord and in His servant Moses" (Ex. 14:31). Note that this is the traditional Haggadah's only explicit reference to Moses.

The Bible does describe some great wonders that would seem to lie *beyond* the laws of nature. For instance, the sun stands still to provide extra daylight to facilitate Joshua's victory over the Amorites (Jos. 10:13). But even here, later commentators disagreed about whether this meant the battle went so quickly that the sun seemed not to move or the sun actually stood still.[5] Generally, the Bible's wonders involve events that are highly unlikely or unexpected rather than impossible. For example, the earth swallows Korach and his followers, who have rebelled against Moses (Num. 26:10).

Most often, however, the Bible finds the wondrous *within* nature: "When I behold Your heavens, the work of Your fingers, the moon and stars that You set in place . . ." (Psalms 8:4). "Let abundant grain be in the land, to the tops of the mountains . . . and let men sprout up in towns like country grass . . . Blessed is the Lord God, God of Israel, who alone does wondrous things [*nifla'ot*]" (Psalms 72:16, 18). Even in parting the Red Sea, God works through nature: "The Lord drove back the sea with a *strong east wind* all that night, and turned the sea into dry ground" (Ex. 14:21).

Still, if hearing about miracles makes us feel uncomfortable, part of that discomfort may derive from how we define them.

Most likely, we have embraced the definition of miracles developed by the British philosopher David Hume (1711–1776). Hume wrote, "A miracle is a violation of nature. A miracle may be accurately defined as a transgression of a law of nature by a particular volition of the Deity, or by the interposition of some invisible agent."[6] Indeed, Hume's definition comes very close to the first one listed in the dictionary: "An effect or extraordinary event in the physical world that surpasses all known or natural powers and is ascribed to a supernatural cause."[7]

The dictionary includes another definition. "A wonder, a marvel." Here we find the ancient Latin root of the word: *mirari,* "to wonder," *mirus,* "wonderful." And this definition brings us a lot closer to what the Bible had in mind. Skepticism about miracles *beyond* nature blinds us to the truly miraculous *within* nature.

THE SAGES ON MIRACLES

Read the paragraphs that follow. Then choose one or more of the
three selections from ancient rabbinic literature to read aloud and discuss.
Questions follow each selection.

What did the sages who lived in the era of the Haggadah's early development think about miracles? Of course, they held different opinions. They accepted the notion of God's infinite power and the possibility of miracles, but they were generally reluctant to rely on them. For example, Rabbi Yannai (active in Palestine between 220 and 250 C.E.) said, "A man should never stand in a place of danger and say that a miracle will be wrought for him, lest it is not."[8] Many of the sages believed that the miraculous was best evidenced in God's creation of the natural world, hence the dictum, "The day of rain is greater than that of the resurrection of the dead."[9] At the same time, the Mishnah prescribes a special blessing to be recited if a person sees "a place where miracles had been wrought for Israel . . . : Blessed is He that wrought miracles for our ancestors in this place."[10]

Since ancient times, the daily liturgy (*Modim anachnu lakh*) has expressed thanks "for Your miracles which are daily with us." The sages also included references to miracles in other prayers. Still, the concept of miracles aroused a certain ambivalence, because it implied that God's original creation may have been less than perfect. Why would a "violation of nature" be required if God's creation had been perfect in the beginning? Hence, the sages taught that God fashioned the conditions or instruments for the Bible's miracles during creation. (In this, the Rabbis expressed greater comfort with the notion of miracles within rather than beyond nature.)

The sages knew well that most of us remain oblivious to the wonders around us. Rabbi Eliezer, one of the rabbis we encounter in the Haggadah, taught that "even the person for whom a miracle is performed is unaware of the miracle."[11]

And, of course, the Rabbis understood that occasionally even the Torah's claims could not be taken literally. Sometimes, says the Talmud, "the Torah spoke in exaggerated terms."[12]

Choose one or two of the following selections to read aloud and discuss during your Seder.

Rabbi Johanan [late second century C.E.] said: The Holy One, blessed be He, made a stipulation with the sea that it should divide before Israel; thus it is written, "And the sea returned to its strength" (*l'eitano*, Ex. 14:27): that is, in accordance with its agreement (*l'tenao*, a wordplay on *l'eitano*). Rabbi Jeremiah ben Eliezer [early fourth century C.E.] said: Not with the sea alone did God make a stipulation, but with everything which was created in the six days of creation, as it is written, "My own hands stretched out the heavens, and I marshaled all their host . . ." (Isaiah 45:12). "I commanded the sea to divide. . . ."

—GENESIS RABBAH 5:5, FIFTH-CENTURY-C.E. MIDRASH

• Which is easier to believe—that God might simply contravene a law of nature or that at creation God had anticipated all the historical circumstances that might require "miraculous" intervention? What about human free will in determining historical events?

Said Rav Papa to Abaye [active 278–338 C.E.]: How is it that for the former generations miracles were performed and for us miracles are not performed?

—BABYLONIAN TALMUD, BERACHOT 20A

• How might you respond to this question?

The Rabbis were inclined to find "miracles" in the seemingly common-place. The following midrash picks up on Psalm 136, which we read toward the end of the Seder. The Psalm includes these verses: "Who alone works great marvels" and "Who split apart [sundered] the Red Sea."

Many miracles and wonders do You perform for us every day and no man knows. Then who does know? You, O Lord. Rabbi Eliezer ben Pedat [active 290–320 C.E.] said: See what is written: Who alone works great wonders. He alone knows. And what is written thereafter? "Who split apart the Red Sea"—the piece of bread [literally, "the divided bread," i.e., livelihood] is equal in importance to the sea which was divided in two. Just as the world cannot do without the piece of bread, so it is not possible for the world to do without miracles and wonders. How are we to envisage this? A man is lying on a bed, and a serpent is on the ground before him. When he seeks to rise, the serpent becomes aware of him. When he is about to put his feet on it, the serpent flees from him. And the man does not know what wonders the Holy One, blessed be He, performs for him. . . .

—MIDRASH ON THE PSALMS, COMPILED
BETWEEN THE THIRD AND THIRTEENTH CENTURIES C.E.[13]

- Are there particular times when you've felt as though you've witnessed a miracle or have had a strong sense of the miraculous? In the grind of "earning bread" what can you do to retain awareness of the wonders around you?

THE RESTORATION OF WONDER

Read this on your own or aloud at your Seder.

It's hard to ignore miracles in the Haggadah. The Haggadah takes us through the Red Sea three times.

- "Had He torn the sea apart for us, but not brought us through on dry land" (*Dayyenu*).

- "The sea saw them [the Israelites] and fled . . . What alarmed you, O sea, that you fled . . . ?" (Psalms 114:3, 5).

- "Praise the Lord . . . Who split the Red Sea . . ." (Psalms 136:1, 13).

How are we to understand these allusions to the miraculous? The plagues and miracles of the Exodus were supposed to provide the Israelites with firsthand experience of God. But the experience didn't last very long:

They did not keep God's covenant; they refused to follow His instruction; they forgot His deeds and the wonders that He showed them. He performed marvels in the sight of their fathers, in the land of Egypt . . . He split the sea and took them through it; He made the waters stand still like a wall.

—PSALMS 78:11–13

Maybe the wonders and miracles were aiming at something more modest: the restoration of the capacity for wonder. Maybe the wonders of Egypt just helped the children of Israel open their eyes. To be aware of God, you must first open your eyes.

Think of Egypt as the paradigmatic experience that destroys the ability to experience wonder. You keep your nose so close to the grindstone that all else begins to fade. The tedium of work and the fear of the taskmaster's lash cripple your curiosity. Nothing can surprise you. One day is exactly like the next. The months blur together. The seasons slide by unnoticed. Beauty becomes imperceptible. Nothing shimmers or sparkles. Egypt, "the narrow place," blunts the acuity of your senses: Your eyes don't see, your ears don't hear.

During the Seder, we read the psalmist's description of idols. It applies just as well to the Israelites enslaved in Egypt: "They have mouths but cannot speak, eyes but cannot see; they have ears, but cannot hear, noses but cannot smell. . . ." (Psalms 115:5). Oppression deadens awareness, and with it, the capacity for wonder. Without wonder, life becomes routine, dull, joyless. The spirit has become enslaved. Hasidic master Rabbi Chanokh said, "The real exile of Israel in Egypt was that they had learned to endure it."[14]

The Haggadah's recounting of the miracles of Egypt reminds us that we, like our ancestors, may have lost the ability to glimpse the extraordinary that breathes behind the commonplace. We remain slaves, trapped in a monotonous, gray existence where everything seems oppressively ordinary. References to color in the Book of Exodus only begin to appear with the plagues and the disintegration of routine life in Egypt. The Nile turns to blood and the locusts leave not a green thing uneaten. Color appears more vividly with the building of the Mishkan, in which blue, purple, and scarlet dominate the decor. In Genesis, the sign—ot—of God's covenant with Noah is the rainbow.

God sends mighty wonders precisely because the Israelites have become trapped in a colorless, wonderless world. Suddenly, nothing can be taken for granted. The miraculous takes center stage in both the Exodus story and the Haggadah because both understand the relationship between "knowing God" and wonder. Heschel said it best: "Awareness of the divine begins with wonder."[15]

"Why is this night different from all other nights?" asks the Haggadah. Because the Seder seeks to arouse our dormant sense of curiosity. The Talmud says that Rabbi Akiva used to "distribute parched ears of corn and nuts to children on the eve of Passover, so that they might not fall asleep but ask [the 'questions']."[16]

The children at the table may literally close their eyes. But the rest of us may be even more asleep to the Seder's call to rekindle our sense of wonder.

JEWISH VOICES ON MIRACLES

Here you'll find a sampling of Jewish thought on miracles
over the past thousand years. Choose one or more to read aloud
and discuss the questions that follow each.

How great is the blindness of ignorance and how harmful. If you told a man . . . that God sends an angel who enters the womb of a woman and forms a fetus there, he would be pleased with this assertion and would accept it and should regard it as a manifestation of greatness and power on the part of the deity, and also of His wisdom . . . Nevertheless he would also believe at the same time that the angel is a body formed of burning fire and that his size is equal to that of a third part of the whole world. He would regard all this as possible with respect to God. But if you tell him that God has placed in the sperm a formative force shaping the limbs and giving them their configuration and that this force is the angel . . . he would shrink from this opinion. For he does not understand the notion of the true greatness and power that consists in the bringing into existence of forces active in a thing, forces that cannot be apprehended by any sense.

—MAIMONIDES (1135–1204), *THE GUIDE OF THE PERPLEXED*[17]

- Because Maimonides acknowledged God's creation of the cosmos, he admitted the possibility of miracles that *seem* to contravene natural law, but he preferred to explain such events in terms of natural causes. He also had a deep appreciation for the "miraculous" within nature. Do you tend to think of life itself as a miracle? Is there anything more miraculous?

It follows that the great signs and wonders constitute faithful witnesses to the truth of the belief in the existence of the Creator and the truth of the whole Torah. And because the Holy One, blessed be He, will not make signs and wonders in every generation for the eyes of some wicked man or heretic, He therefore commanded us that we should always make a memorial or a sign of that which we have seen with our eyes, and that we should transmit the matter to our children, and their children, to the generations to come . . . Through the great open miracles, one comes to admit the hidden miracles. . . .

—NACHMANIDES (1195–1270), SPANISH BIBLE
COMMENTATOR AND PHILOSOPHER[18]

• Nachmanides is alluding to the Passover Seder, an important occasion for transmitting the story of the Exodus to our children. How do you explain "miraculous" stories, such as the parting of the Red Sea, to children? Ask some of the children seated around the Seder table to share their ideas about the story of the Red Sea. (Please urge all to listen with great respect.) What might the difference be between open and hidden miracles?

By a similar Divine mandate the sea opened a way for the Jews, namely by an east wind which blew strongly all night . . . Although the circumstances attending miracles are not related always in full detail, yet a miracle was never performed without them. This is confirmed in Exodus 14:27, where it is simply stated that "Moses stretched forth his hand, and that waters of the sea returned to their strength in the morning," no mention being made of a wind; but in the Song of Moses (Ex. 15:10) we read, "You made Your wind (i.e., with a very strong wind) blow, the sea covered them." Thus the attendant circumstance is omitted in the history and the miracle is thereby enhanced.

—BARUCH SPINOZA, DUTCH PHILOSOPHER (1632–1677)[19]

The Amsterdam rabbinical authorities excommunicated Baruch Spinoza in 1656 in part because he concluded that God and nature were essentially indistinguishable. With reference to miracles, he argued that because natural laws are divine decrees, to think that God would act contrary to God's own laws would be absurd. Spinoza therefore sought natural explanations for all miracles.

• Imagine that you saw Moses stretch out his rod and witnessed the sea split exactly as the Bible describes. What effect would it have on your belief in God? How long do you think that effect would last? If you told others who had not seen what you did, how do you think they would react?

The following phenomenon is a common occurrence in the region of the Suez: at high tide, the waters of the Red Sea penetrate that sand from under the surface, and suddenly that water begins to ooze up out of the sand, which had hitherto been dry; within a short time the sand turns to mud, but the water continues to rise and ultimately a deep layer of water is formed above the sand, the whole area becoming flooded . . . This sometimes happens when the Red Sea is at low tide; the water covering the sand gradually diminishes and finally disappears, and in the part that, several hours earlier, was covered by water suddenly dry land appears . . . I have no wish whatsoever to rationalize the biblical story . . . The miracle consisted in the fact that at the very moment when it was necessary, in just the manner conducive to the achievement of the desired goal, and on a scale that was abnormal, there occurred, in accordance with the Lord's will, phenomena that brought about Israel's salvation.

—UMBERTO CASSUTO (1883–1951), ITALIAN BIBLE SCHOLAR WHO BECAME
CHAIR OF BIBLE STUDIES AT HEBREW UNIVERSITY IN 1939[20]

• Does Cassuto's attempt to explain the miracle in natural terms work for you? From this point of view, what is the relationship between a miracle and good luck? Is the Torah's intent supported by such explanations or undermined by them?

A scientific theory, once it is announced and accepted does not have to be repeated twice a day. The insights of wonder must be constantly kept alive, since there is a need for daily wonder, there is a need for daily worship. This is one of the goals of the Jewish way of living: to experience commonplace deeds as spiritual adventures, to feel the hidden love and wisdom in all things. In the Song of the Sea [when the Israelites celebrate having crossed the Red Sea] we read:

Who is like Thee, O Lord, among the gods?
Who is like Thee, majestic in holiness,
Sublime in glorious deeds, doing wonders.

—EXODUS 15:11

The Rabbis remarked: It is not written here: *Who did wonders,* but *Who does wonders . . .* He did and still does wonders for us in every generation. . . .

—ABRAHAM JOSHUA HESCHEL (1907–1972), SCHOLAR, THEOLOGIAN, AND SOCIAL ACTIVIST[21]

• What are the principal wonders that you experience? What enhances your sense of wonder? Is your sense of wonder enhanced by prayer? What is the relationship between wonder and the story of the Exodus?

You find it strange that I consider the comprehensibility of the world . . . as a miracle or an eternal mystery. Well, *a priori* one should expect a chaotic world which cannot be grasped by the mind in any way. One could (yes *one should*) expect the world to be subjected to law only to the extent that we order it through our intelligence. Ordering of this kind would be like the alphabetical ordering of the words of a language. By contrast, the kind of order created by Newton's theory of gravitation, for instance, is wholly different. Even if the axioms of the theory are proposed by man, the success of such a project presupposes a high degree of ordering of the objective world, and this could not be expected *a priori.* That is the "miracle" which is being constantly reinforced as our knowledge expands.

—ALBERT EINSTEIN (1879–1955), FROM A 1952 LETTER TO A FRIEND[22]

• Does the underlying order of which Einstein speaks stir your sense of wonder? Does it affect your opinion of this viewpoint to know that these are Einstein's words rather than those of a religious figure?

The Egyptians, who were situated in strongly fortified positions, shot everything they had at the Israeli [amphibious landing craft] crossing the canal. You could see tracer bullets and the tails of rockets flashing over the canal. We could not really see the boats, and were slightly puzzled why the Egyptians were wasting such firepower. But, when the boats landed, the Egyptians fled their positions. The next day a pontoon bridge was built and Israeli soldiers crossed the canal on this bridge relatively safe from the enemy fire. My unit made its way to Fuad, an Egyptian air base. We arrived *erev* Shabbat and took over a building for sleeping quarters and set up for Shabbat. In the building next to us were the [boat] drivers and their vehicles. They were still totally exhausted and were resting under the vehicles. It was from them that I heard the story of their crossing of the Canal. One of them said, "I saw God's hand push the missiles away from my [boat]." All of the others nodded in agreement, indicating that they too had seen it. I asked him what he meant by that. He said simply, "I saw a hand, like a big hand, the palm of a hand, and as the shell approached my boat this hand pushed it aside." . . . That night at Kabbalat Shabbat, as we sang *Lekha Dodi,* when we came to the verse which says, "Those who despoil you shall become a spoil, and all who would devour you shall be far away," I myself felt the presence of a giant hand in the room, the same hand I am sure that had removed those who wanted to swallow us up. At dinner others recounted having the same feeling; it was as if we also had been protected by the hand.

—RABBI MICHAEL GRAETZ, WHOSE ISRAEL DEFENSE FORCES
UNIT OVERLOOKED THE SUEZ CANAL,
A PASSAGE BETWEEN THE MEDITERRANEAN
AND RED SEAS, DURING THE 1973 WAR[23]

- How do you react to this story? Have you ever had a similar feeling? How do you relate to this story in light of the following observation by Abraham Joshua Heschel: "The God of Israel is also the God of her enemies. . . ."[24]

When the people of Israel crossed through the Red Sea, they witnessed a great miracle. Some say it was the greatest miracle that ever happened. On that day they saw a sight more awesome than all the visions of the prophets combined. The sea split and the waters stood like great walls, while Israel escaped to freedom on the distant shore. Awesome. But not for everyone.

Two people, Reuven and Shimon, hurried along among the crowd crossing through the sea. They never once looked up. They noticed only that the ground under their feet was still a little muddy—like a beach at low tide.

"Yucch!" said Reuven, "there's mud all over this place!"

"Blecch!" said Shimon, "I have mud all over my feet!"

"This is terrible," answered Reuven. "When we were slaves in Egypt, we had to make our bricks out of mud, just like this!"

"Yeah," said Shimon. "There's no difference between being a slave in Egypt and being free here."

And so it went, Reuven and Shimon whining and complaining all the way to freedom. For them there was no miracle. Only mud. Their eyes were closed. They might as well have been asleep (Exodus Rabbah 24:1).

People see only what they understand, not necessarily what lies in front of them. For example, if you saw a television set, you would know what it was and how to operate it. But imagine someone who had never seen a television. To such a person it would be just a strange and useless box. Imagine being in a video store, filled with movies and stories and music, and not even knowing it. How sad when something is right before your eyes, but you are asleep to it. It is like that with our own world too.

—RABBI LAWRENCE KUSHNER (1943–), AUTHOR OF

A DOZEN BOOKS ON JEWISH SPIRITUALITY AND MYSTICISM[25]

• What might you pay more attention to so you can better appreciate the wonders that surround you? What makes it hard for Reuven and Shimon to open their eyes? What makes it hard for you to open yours?

AT THE RED SEA: TWO MIDRASHIM

In the following section we explore two intriguing passages from the midrash about events at the Red Sea. One describes dissension among the Israelites before the sea parted; the other imagines God's judgment of the Egyptian horses and drivers who pursued them. If you decide to divide into small discussion groups before the Seder, you can assign one of these selections and the accompanying questions to one or more groups. Or you can take a few minutes before the singing of *Dayyenu* (which mentions the parting of the Red Sea) to read and discuss either of these midrashim with your entire group. Depending on your group, you may want to read aloud Appendix II, "What Is Midrash?"

The selections on the following pages come from a large, ancient collection known as the *Mekhilta of Rabbi Ishmael. Mekhilta* is an Aramaic word that means a "measure," as in a collection of legal or, in this case, midrashic material. A student of Rabbi Joshua, Rabbi Ishmael was one of the most influential sages of his time. As opposed to those who attributed hidden significance to every letter in the Torah, Rabbi Ishmael said, "The Torah used human language." He lived during the latter part of the first century C.E. and probably died before 132 C.E. The *Mekhilta* was most likely assembled in the third century C.E. and was attributed to Rabbi Ishmael because his name appears in its opening paragraph.

BETWEEN PHARAOH AND THE RED SEA

The scene is as follows: Soon after the last plague and the Exodus from Egypt, Pharaoh has a change of heart (according to the text, God hardens his heart) and his army sets out to capture the errant slaves.

As Pharaoh drew near, the Israelites caught sight of the Egyptians advancing upon them. Greatly frightened, the Israelites cried out (*vayitzaku*) to the Lord. And they said to Moses, "Was it for want of graves in Egypt that you brought us to die in the wilderness? What have you done to us, taking us out of Egypt? Is this not the very thing we told you in Egypt, saying, 'Let us be, and we will serve the Egyptians, for it is better for us to serve the Egyptians than to die in the wilderness'?" But Moses said to the people, "Have no fear! Stand by, and witness the deliverance which the Lord will work for you today; for the Egyptians whom you see today you will never see again. The Lord will battle for you; hold your peace!"

—EXODUS 14:10–14

The midrash elaborates:

The Israelites at the Red Sea were divided into four groups. One group said, "Let us throw ourselves into the sea." One said, "Let us return to Egypt." One said, "Let us fight against them." And one said, "Let us scream out against them." The group that said, "Let us throw ourselves into the sea," was told, "Stand by, and witness the deliverance that the Lord will work for you today." The one that said, "Let us return to Egypt," was told, "For the Egyptians whom you see today you will never see again." The one that said, "Let us fight them," was told, "The Lord will do battle for you." The one that said, "Let us scream out (*nitzavei'ach*) against them," was told, "And you shall hold your peace."

—MEKHILTA OF RABBI ISHMAEL, BESHALACH 3:128–136[26]

- Which group would you have joined and why? (Note: Exodus 13:19 states that "The Israelites went up armed out of the land of Egypt." This midrash and the passage from the Book of Exodus above it use different Hebrew words for *cry out* versus *scream out*.)

- What does this midrash suggest about the issue of Jewish unity?

- What do you think about the answers each group receives?

THE HORSE AND DRIVER

The scene is as follows: The Red Sea has miraculously parted and the Israelites have safely passed through. "The waters turned back and covered the chariots and the horseman—Pharaoh's entire army that followed them into the sea; not one of them remained . . . Then Moses and the Israelites sang this song to the Lord. They said: 'I will sing to the Lord, for He has triumphed gloriously; Horse and driver He has hurled into the sea . . .'" (Ex. 14:28; 15:1).

The midrash expounds:

> The Holy One, blessed be He, would bring the horse and his driver and make them stand trial. He would say to the horse, "Why did you run after My children?" The horse would answer, "The Egyptian drove me against my will, as it is said: 'And the Egyptians pursued . . .'" (Ex. 14:9). God would then say to the Egyptian, "Why did you pursue My children?" And he would answer, "It was the horse that ran away with me against my will, as it is said, 'For the horses of Pharaoh went in . . .'" (Ex. 15:19). What would God do? He would make the man ride upon the horse and thus judge them together. As it is said, "The horse and driver He has hurled into the sea" (Ex. 15:1).
>
> —MEKHILTA OF RABBI ISHMAEL, SHIRATA 2:120–127[27]

- What contemporary situations does this midrash make you think about?

- What might the midrash be saying about human nature?

- Earlier in the Book of Exodus, God says, "And I will stiffen the hearts of the Egyptians so that they go in after them; and I will gain glory through Pharaoh and all his warriors, his chariots and his horsemen" (Ex. 14:17). With this in mind, what is your reaction to the midrash?

19

"From Darkness to Great Light":
What Do These Words Mean to Us Today?

הוֹצִיאָנוּ מֵעַבְדוּת לְחֵרוּת, מִיָּגוֹן לְשִׂמְחָה,
מֵאֵבֶל לְיוֹם טוֹב, וּמֵאֲפֵלָה לְאוֹר גָּדוֹל,
וּמִשִּׁעְבּוּד לִגְאֻלָּה.
וְנֹאמַר לְפָנָיו שִׁירָה חֲדָשָׁה.
הַלְלוּיָהּ:

The participants lift their cups, recite nine expressions of praise, and continue . . .
He has brought us forth from slavery to freedom, from sorrow to joy, from mourning
to festivity, from darkness to great light, and from bondage to redemption.
Let us then recite before Him a new song; Hallelujah.
—THE PASSOVER HAGGADAH

In this chapter, we'll explore the development and meaning of one of the Haggadah's most poetic passages. We begin with some general questions for a discussion about this passage that you could lead before or during your Seder:

• What does this passage mean to you today?

• Does it strike you differently at this period in our history than it might have in others?

• How do you interpret the relationship among the phrases within this passage?

• Which one is not quite like the others?

AN ART MIDRASH PROJECT

(See Appendix III on page 326 for general directions.)

Read the passage on page 259 and ask everyone to spend about twenty minutes making a collage that expresses something about one or more of these five transitions: *from slavery to freedom, from sorrow to joy, from mourning to festivity, from darkness to great light, and from bondage to redemption.*

VARIATIONS ON A THEME

Distribute a copy of the table below to each of your guests.
Then read aloud what follows and discuss the questions below.

We arrive at this evocative passage just before reciting Psalms 113 and 114, the first two psalms of the Hallel.

Some scholars believe that the text's five pairs of terms may have evolved from a single original phrase: *from slavery to freedom.* Indeed, the oldest manuscripts of the Mishnah include this solitary phrase. Saadiah Gaon's (882–942) Haggadah includes this phrase alone. But there are also ancient Genizah fragments that are completely different. One, for example, thanks God for taking us "from slavery to freedom, from hardship to freedom (*chofesh*), from pressure to rest, from the narrow to the expansive."[1] The development of this passage exemplifies the spirit of the Haggadah: "Whoever elaborates on the story of the Exodus deserve praise."[2]

A beautiful illustration of creative pluralism, there are at least three different traditional texts of the Haggadah—Ashkenazic, Sephardic, and Yemenite—each with its own version of this particular sentence.[3]

- What is the major difference between the Ashkenazic text and the others?

- How does altering the order of these phrases change what the text says about the nature and trajectory of Jewish history?

- In what order would you arrange this passage's five phrases? Why?

THREE VARIATIONS ON A THEME

Ashkenazic *(from Amram Gaon's Haggadah, ninth century C.E.)*	Sephardic *(from Spanish Haggadot, such as the Sarajevo Haggadah, fourteenth century C.E.)*	Yemenite *(from Netronai Gaon's Haggadah, ninth century C.E.)*
Slavery to freedom	Slavery to freedom	Slavery to freedom
Sorrow to joy	Sorrow to joy	Bondage to redemption
Mourning to festivity	Mourning to festivity	Sorrow to joy
Darkness to great light	Darkness to great light	Mourning to festivity
Bondage to redemption		Darkness to great light

FOUR INTERPRETATIONS OF FIVE PHRASES

Explore on your own or, depending on your group, distribute a copy of the table on pages 262–263 and discuss the questions that follow.

Commentators have offered many interpretations of our passage. Some have related the five redemptive images to God's five promises in Exodus 6:6–7: "I will free you . . . I will deliver you . . . I will redeem you . . . I will take you to be My people . . . I will bring you into the land. . . ." Others have related the five phrases to a tradition of drinking the five cups of wine during the Seder, which again hearkens back to God's five promises of redemption. Another view connects the

five terms of this passage to a verse from Deuteronomy (26:8) that figures prominently in the Haggadah and that also contains five noteworthy phrases: "The Lord
took us out from Egypt by [1] a mighty hand, by [2] an outstretched arm and [3]
awesome power, and by [4] signs and [5] portents."

In the table that follows you'll find a summary of how four commentators
have interpreted this passage.[4]

	Isaac Abarbanel 1437–1508, Spain	Judah Loew ben Bezalel (the Maharal of Prague) 1525–1609, Prague
Scope of interpretation	Redemption from Egypt	Redemption from Egypt
Slavery to Freedom	The end of subordination to the will of others	The end of harsh labor
Sorrow to Joy	The end of slavery, which was degrading and unnatural to a noble people	The end of the harsh labor that had broken the Israelites' spirit transforms sorrow into joy
Mourning to Festivity	From incessant work to freedom to celebrate Passover	The Israelites' ability to observe the festival of Passover brought them from embittered mourning to festivity
Darkness to Great Light	From lack of faith to faith in God	In Egypt, it was as if the Israelites had yet to be spiritually born. Their deliverance brought them from darkness to great light.
Bondage to Redemption	No longer subject to rigorous labor	In the Exodus the Israelites were redeemed from bondage, a state to which they have never since returned

- What are the primary differences among them?

- Which interpretation do you prefer and why?

- Which one of these interpretations seems most relevant to our own times?

Elijah ben Solomon Zalman (the Vilna Gaon), 1720–1797, Lithuania	Jacob ben Jacob Moses of Lisa, d. 1832, Germany
From Egypt through the reign of David and Solomon	From Egypt to future final redemption
Exodus from Egypt	Redemption from Egypt
Rescue of Israel at the Red Sea	Destruction of the First Temple and rebuilding of the Second Temple
Aftermath of Golden Calf: the emotions associated with God's withdrawal from the Israelites and subsequent return	From near destruction by Haman in Persia to triumph
From darkness in the wilderness to great light in the land of Israel	From darkness under the Greeks to the Maccabees rekindling the great light of Torah
Bondage to foreign nations in the era of the Judges to redemption under David and Solomon	From the current situation of seemingly endless bondage to ultimate, final redemption

A DEEPER LOOK AT A MEMORABLE PASSAGE

The origins of this passage are intriguing. Some of its phrases reach back to the Bible; the passage also reflects a clear literary affinity with the broader cultural milieu of the rabbinic period. In any case, as we'll see, the sages who composed this passage selected their words with great care. Indeed, the words they favored (and those they rejected) provide a subtle but fascinating glimpse into the midrashic process and the sages' understanding of the meaning of freedom. Here we'll consider the sources of our passage, phrase by phrase.

Choose one or two to read aloud during your Seder.

FROM SLAVERY TO FREEDOM

Given its mighty ring, you may expect *"from slavery to freedom"* to appear in the Book of Exodus, maybe alongside one of its nine repetitions of "Let my people go!" It appears nowhere in the Bible. In fact, neither of these particular words—slavery (*avdut*) nor freedom (*cherut*)—is found in the Bible at all. The phrase does, however, appear in the Ashkenazic prayer for announcing the new month on the Sabbath before the new month actually begins. The prayer may refer to the redemption from Egypt because the first commandment associated with the Exodus (12:2) was to reckon Nisan as the first of the months.

> May the One who wrought miracles for our ancestors, redeeming them *from slavery to freedom,* redeem us soon and gather our dispersed from the four corners of the earth in the fellowship of the entire people Israel.

FROM SORROW TO JOY, FROM MOURNING TO FESTIVITY

The phrase *"from sorrow to joy, from mourning to festivity"* occurs near the very end of the Book of Esther (9:22) in connection with the institution of the festival of Purim. The Jews have just been saved from Haman's genocidal plan, and Mordecai sends out instructions to observe Purim annually on "the same days on which the Jews enjoyed relief from their foes and the same month which had been transformed for them from one of *sorrow to joy and from mourning to festivity*

264

(*yom tov*)." (From the point of view of Jewish law, it's worth noting that a festival cancels many of the rites of mourning.)

Why bring Purim into the Seder? Because Passover and Purim share striking thematic parallels and yet differ in important respects. Both holidays celebrate redemption from a tyrant's maniacal plan. As the Haggadah warns, "In every generation they rise up to destroy us." But there's more. The climax of the Purim story actually takes place during Passover! The Book of Esther never mentions Passover, but it supplies precise dates for critical events in the story. Haman sent out his letters alerting the population of his plan to annihilate the Jews on the thirteenth of Nisan (Esther 3:12), two days before Passover. Queen Esther immediately ordered the Jewish community to fast for three days. The midrash recounts Mordecai's reaction: "He sent back word to her: 'But these include the first day of Passover?' She replied: 'Elder of Israel, why is there a Passover?' [i.e., what good is Passover if all the Jews are killed?] Mordecai thereupon acceded to her request. . . ."[5] On the fifteenth of Nisan, the first night of Passover, she arranged a "wine feast" for the king and approached him for a fateful audience. She requested his permission for a second wine feast the next night, at which she intended to engineer Haman's downfall. Esther's plan succeeded, and the king executed Haman on the sixteenth of Nisan, the second day of Passover.

A song traditionally sung at the second Seder, "And You Shall Say: It is the Sacrifice of Passover," includes the verse: "Hadassah [Esther's Hebrew name] called an assembly to a three-day fast. You hanged the head of the wicked house [Haman] on a fifty-cubit tree."

As a result of the Purim/Passover connection, Esther became the only woman mentioned by name in the Haggadah.

Our passage's reference to Purim is significant for an even more important reason. In the Jewish calendar, Passover is the first holiday, Purim the last. God's active presence defines the Exodus. The midrash compares the children of Israel in Egypt with a fetus that God must ultimately deliver.[6] The Purim story draws the starkest contrast: Human beings redeem the Jews of Shushan; the Book of Esther does not even mention God. The cycle of the Jewish year traces the course of God's decreasing intervention on the one hand and humanity's maturing responsibility on the other. Passover demonstrates the potentiality of redemption and of God's role as redeemer. Purim reminds us that in a world where God's hand remains hidden, redemption lies in our hands.[7] In placing an allusion to Purim at the heart of the Seder, the compilers of the Haggadah are calling us, albeit subtly, to remember humanity's responsibility for the work of redemption at the very moment when we celebrate God's role in the process.

FROM DARKNESS TO GREAT LIGHT

The Bible never employs the expression *"from darkness* [afelah] *to great light* [or gadol]*"* either, though it does use both terms separately. This particular word for darkness first appears in reference to the ninth plague (*choshekh-afelah*), usually translated as "thick" or "gloomy" darkness, though both words are roughly synonymous. As thick darkness overcame the Egyptians, "the Israelites enjoyed light in their dwellings" (Ex. 10:23). (*Choshekh* is the term for darkness associated with creation, when God separates light from dark. It appears in the Bible more than a hundred times, while *afelah* occurs in only eight instances.) "Great light" (*or gadol*) occurs just once, in a powerful messianic passage from Isaiah (9:1): "The people who walked in darkness (*choshekh*) have seen a great light (*or gadol*). . . ."[8] Isaiah uses *choshekh,* not *afelah.*

Even though the phrase *from darkness to great light* does not occur in the Bible, the authors of this passage could have chosen language for light and dark from a wide variety of biblical verses that contain both images. Instead, they paired one expression that occurs comparatively infrequently in the Bible, "darkness" (*afelah*), with one that occurs only once, "great light" (*or gadol*).

What were the sages trying to tell us by their choice? First, that just as the blackness of the ninth plague in Egypt was different than ordinary darkness, so the great light of ultimate salvation will be extraordinary as well. As God wrought that "unnatural" darkness, so God will bring the great light of the messianic era.

Second, in reconstructing this simple phrase, *from darkness to great light,* the sages are also demonstrating the freedom to create, so central to what it means to leave Egypt. As human beings fashioned in the image of a freely creating God, we express our godliness when we create new worlds of meaning through new texts created in the image of the Bible.

FROM BONDAGE TO REDEMPTION

The Bible does not utilize this particular term for *bondage* (sh'ibud), though it appears quite frequently in the Talmud. There, *bondage* refers to Israel's plight under the various kingdoms that oppressed it or to the pledge of one's land or even one's person to satisfy a debt. The biblical context of *redemption,* the second term in this phrase, clarifies the meaning of *bondage.*[9] This precise form of the word for *redemption (ge'ulah)* occurs only five times in the Bible—thrice in Leviticus 25 and twice in Jeremiah (32:8). In Leviticus, the term applies to the redemption of a relative whose dire straits have forced him into bondage to a foreigner. It also refers to the obligation to redeem land through the repurchase of a relative's property when he has been compelled by poverty to sell his property, and it refers to redemption of the land through the fifty-year Jubilee cycle. "But the land must not be sold beyond reclaim, for the land is Mine; you are but strangers resident with Me. Throughout the land you hold you must provide for the redemption *(ge'ulah)* of the land" (Lev. 25:23–24). In Jeremiah, God instructs the prophet to redeem a parcel of land that had belonged to Jeremiah's cousin. This occurs against the background of Jerusalem's imminent fall and the exile to Babylonia, transforming the story into a symbolic affirmation: God will redeem the people and land of Israel as Jeremiah has redeemed his relative's land. (Of note, the reading for Jeremiah serves as the haftarah for the above chapters from Leviticus.)

Elsewhere, of course, the Bible speaks directly of God as the redeemer of Israel, *go'ayl Yisrael.* In fact, we recite similar words *(ga'al Yisrael)* during the Seder in the blessing over the second cup of wine. Again, the particular biblical context of the term *ge'ulah* sheds light on its meaning here. Although *redemption* surely evokes overtones of messianic or divine intervention and restoration to the land of Israel, its use here also highlights the importance of two ideas. First, when humanity forgets its place in the scheme of things—"the land is Mine"—we bring grave danger upon ourselves.[10] Second, in an echo of the Haggadah's earlier allusion to Purim, we can understand *from bondage to redemption* as a reminder that, while we may yearn for God to redeem us, we have responsibilities here and now to redeem one another.

This helps explain why in the Ashkenazic text the phrase *from darkness to great light* precedes *from bondage to redemption.* The sequence says this: "Yes, we all yearn for the ultimate messianic 'great light,' but leave that to God. And while the pursuit of spiritual enlightenment is noble, don't divorce it from reality. Come down to earth. Come back to *this* world—tend it, fix it. Start by caring for those

267

closest to you, as you would wish God to care for you. Who knows? Maybe if we'd all do that, the messiah *would* come!"

THE CULTURAL MILIEU

Read this section on your own or aloud during your Seder.

Light/dark imagery was clearly in vogue at the beginning of the Common Era. For example, one of the Dead Sea Scrolls is called the "War of the Sons of Light Against the Sons of Darkness." The phrase *darkness to light* or variations on it also appear a number of times in the New Testament.[11] Some scholars believe that elements of this passage may have been inspired by what has been called an early "Christian Haggadah" composed by Melito, Bishop of Sardis, between 160 and 170 C.E.[12] Christians used texts of this sort to celebrate Easter, then still observed by many on the first night of Passover:

> This [Jesus] is the one who delivered us from *slavery to freedom, from darkness into light,* from death into life, from tyranny into an eternal Kingdom, and made us a new priesthood, and a people everlasting for himself.[13]

Another ancient text, *Joseph and Aseneth* (generally believed to date from the first or second century C.E.), also includes some of the same imagery. Joseph speaks the following words to Aseneth, the daughter of an Egyptian priest, whom, according to the Bible, he eventually marries (Gen. 41:45). Through her love for Joseph, Aseneth realizes the emptiness of idol worship and converts to Judaism:

> O Lord, the God of my father Israel, the Most High, the Mighty One,
> Who didst quicken all things, and didst call them *from darkness into light.*
> And from error into truth, and from death into life;
> Do thou, O Lord, thyself quicken and bless this virgin,
> And renew her by thy spirit, and remold her by thy secret hand,
> And quicken her with thy life.
> And may she eat the bread of thy life,

And may she drink the cup of thy blessing,
She whom thou didst choose before she was begotten,
And may she enter into thy rest, which thou has prepared for thine elect.[14]

Whether or not these ancient documents definitively influenced our passage, they certainly remind us that rabbinic texts such as the Haggadah did not develop in a cultural vacuum. We've seen that the Seder's structure owes much to the Greek symposium. Perhaps our passage bears witness yet again to the once comfortable, even seamless, rabbinic integration of biblical traditions with elements of the wider contemporary culture.

20

"Blessed Are You . . . Who Redeemed Us": The Seder of Redemption

בָּרוּךְ אַתָּה יְיָ אֱלֹהֵינוּ מֶלֶךְ הָעוֹלָם,
אֲשֶׁר גְּאָלָנוּ וְגָאַל אֶת־אֲבוֹתֵינוּ מִמִּצְרַיִם
וְהִגִּיעָנוּ לַלַּיְלָה הַזֶּה,
לֶאֱכָל־בּוֹ מַצָּה וּמָרוֹר.

*Blessed are You, Lord our God, King of the Universe, who has redeemed us
and our ancestors from Egypt and enabled us to reach this
night that we may eat matzah and maror.*
—FROM THE HAGGADAH'S BLESSING OVER THE SECOND CUP OF WINE

When you sit down for your Passover Seder, remember that you are doing so at what was and probably remains one of Judaism's most fertile moments for redemption.

Ever since the Exodus from Egypt, the month of Nisan, with its festival of Passover, has shimmered with the alluring promise of redemption. As the Talmud (Rosh Hashanah 11a) taught, "In Nisan they *were* redeemed and in Nisan they *will be* redeemed in the time to come." Unable to bear constraint, redemptive yearnings

271

have periodically erupted—sometimes in connection with the season of Passover. It's no accident that the climax of Jesus' ministry unfolded during Passover.

More than a millennium later, Maimonides railed against an early-twelfth-century messianist in Yemen who preached that the Messiah would reveal himself on Passover.[1] Amidst the fervor surrounding the brief messianic career of Shabbetai Zevi (1626–1676), the resonance with Passover continued. The Jews of Yemen had concluded that for them the Messiah would arrive on Passover: Their only question was whether it would be in 1666 or 1667.[2] Marvelous tales also spread about Shabbetai Zevi's "innovations" in Jewish law. For example, on the evening of Passover in 1666 he sacrificed a lamb and roasted it with its fat—both major transgressions. He accompanied the deed with the following blessing: "Blessed art Thou, O God, who permits that which is forbidden."[3]

According to legend, the Baal Shem Tov (1700–1760), founder of Hasidism, set out during Passover on an abortive journey to Israel "to prepare for the hour of deliverance."[4] When World War II broke out in 1939 (5699 in the Hebrew calendar), large numbers of religious Jews in Europe were convinced that the war would be short-lived. Numerous arcane sources predicted the Messiah's arrival in 5700. One popular speculation was based on "deciphering" a verse from the Song of the Sea, sung by the Israelites after they crossed the Red Sea. The "decoded" verse contained this message: "On the day after the festival in the month of Nisan [i.e., Passover] in the year 5700, the Jews will be redeemed."[5]

This chapter explores the concept of redemption, undoubtedly the Haggadah's primary theme.

THE SEDER OF HOPE: TUNING IN TO THEMES OF REDEMPTION

Before you begin your Seder, perhaps in the living room,
read the following paragraphs aloud. Discuss the questions that follow.

A single word captures the concern of the entire Passover Haggadah: redemption.

The story of the Exodus recounts Israel's redemption from Egypt and we relive it every Passover. "In Nisan they were redeemed," the Talmud teaches, "and in Nisan they will be redeemed in the time to come." So whatever darkness this Nisan may hold, the next one promises to dispel it with great light.

Symbols of salvation permeate the Seder. Matzah may be called the bread of affliction, but it's equally the bread of liberation. As the Seder begins, we uncover the matzah, invite the poor to join us, and declare, "Now we are here; next year may we be in the land of Israel. Now we are slaves; next year we will be free."

The four cups of wine (as we saw earlier) are traditionally associated with God's fourfold promise of redemption in the Book of Exodus. Some believe we should drink a fifth cup of wine corresponding to the fulfillment of a fifth redemptive promise, "I will bring you into the land [of Israel]." And a special cup belongs to the Prophet Elijah, herald of the Messiah, for whom we open our door near the Seder's conclusion.

The text of the Haggadah refers to many different dimensions of redemption, for example:

- (*Prior to the Four Children*): The sages define the requirement to "remember the day you left Egypt all the days of your life." "The days of your life" means the present world, and "all the days" includes the messianic era.

- (*After the Four Children*): "At first our forefathers worshiped idols, but now the Omnipresent has brought us near to His service. . . ."

- (*Traditionally recited before the Seder's concluding songs, but placed at the Seder's conclusion in some Haggadot*): "Soon, and with rejoicing, lead the offshoots of the stock that You have planted, redeemed to Zion. Next year in Jerusalem."

- (*The last verse of* Chad Gadya, *the final words of most traditional Haggadot*): "The Holy One, blessed be He, came and slew the angel of death. . . ."

The *Encyclopedia Judaica* defines *redemption* as "salvation from the states or circumstances that destroy the value of human existence or human existence itself."[6]

Redemption can apply both to individuals and to groups, to the body and to the soul. Redemption from physical forms of oppression may be easier to understand. But human beings who seem to be relatively free often wind up living empty lives, trapped by the pursuit of goals that they themselves find relatively unimportant. Some see redemption as an evolving process of change or progress, the result of human efforts to repair the world. Others see it in more messianic terms, as a radically new era ushered in by God or by the bold actions of particular individuals.

Before you begin the Seder, ask your guests to let you know every time they come across something in the Haggadah that relates to the theme of redemption. Also ask your group to pay close attention to biblical and rabbinic figures as they are mentioned in the Haggadah. Invite your guests to comment about what role these figures play in the redemptive drama. Then discuss the following questions.

- What does redemption mean to you in terms of your own life? Do you believe that humanity's lot will change for the better? Do you believe that anti-Semitism will someday end? Do you believe that eventually Israel will live in peace with its neighbors?

- What is the relationship between the Haggadah's treatment of redemption and the question of hope?

- Is the yearning for redemption a response to the bitterness of Jewish history? If so, is it an adequate response?

- How might the Jewish people be different today had our commitment to the concept of redemption been weaker or had it been replaced by something else? What might have replaced it?

- Do you think the Haggadah represents Judaism as a fundamentally optimistic religion? If so, in your experience, does today's Jewish community reflect that optimism?

REDEMPTION IN THE BIBLE AND THE ANCIENT NEAR EAST

You may want to read this aloud at your Seder, asking participants to share their reactions to each passage. This would be suitable for a short conversation before or after one of the four cups of wine.

The theme of redemption lies at the heart of the Haggadah. But it is a concept that many find confusing or maybe even alienating. In part, that's because the idea is so multifaceted.

In the Bible it is God who redeems the Israelites from Egypt. But in other contexts, the Bible places the responsibility for redemption squarely upon human shoulders: "And you must redeem every firstborn male among your children" (Ex. 13:13). If desperation leads an individual to become a slave, "one of his kinsman shall redeem him" (Lev. 25:48). "If your kinsman is in [dire] straits and has to sell part of his holding, his nearest redeemer [kinsman] shall come and redeem what his kinsman has sold" (Lev. 25:25). A murderer was to be killed by the victim's next of kin, literally known as a "blood redeemer" (Num. 35:19).

But the biblical view of redemption extends far beyond this. "Zion shall be redeemed in judgment and its inhabitants with righteousness" (Isaiah 1:27). God "will redeem Israel from all their iniquities" (Psalms 130:8). "In famine He will redeem you from death, in war from the sword" (Job 5:20). "I [God] will save them, redeem them from very Death" (Hosea 13:14). The list goes on and on.

In the context of the ancient Near East, redemption figures prominently in "proclamations of freedom" from virtually all ancient civilizations in the region. Ramses IV issued the following freedom proclamation when he became pharaoh of Egypt in 1154 B.C.E.:

> It is a good day. Heaven and earth rejoice, because you are the great lord of Egypt. Fugitives have returned to their cities, those in hiding have come out. The hungry are sated and rejoice, the thirsty are satisfied, the naked are clothed with good linen clothing . . . the chained are released, those who are bound now rejoice. The houses of the widows have been opened, the exiles return. . . .[7]

Another common kind of proclamation freed forced laborers from a particular area and assigned them to serve in the local temple. A Mesopotamian king from the twenty-second century B.C.E. issued the following order:

> [The god] opened up for the path of justice . . . thirty-eight cities were liberated for Shamash (the god), indeed, I sought no forced labor from

them, I drafted them not into military service. They shall serve (Shamash) in the temple alone.[8]

Although the terms of these royal proclamations differed, they included a number of common elements. Prisoners and slaves were permitted to return home, and various special signs announcing their impending freedom accompanied their release. In Mesopotamia, for instance, it was customary to raise a torch signifying the liberation. Ancient texts compare the torch to a light that illuminates the country or to the sun. In other civilizations, it was common to raise a special pole or banner for the occasion. Often the king issued such proclamations to inculcate loyalty among his people, but another motive also came into play— the notion that enslaving the servants of a god could bring destruction upon the oppressor's kingdom.[9]

Although brief, even this small bit of background sheds enormous light on the cultural milieu of the Exodus story. In the role of liberator, God takes the Israelites from captivity, enabling and fully expecting them to serve God instead of Pharaoh. The biblical laws (Lev. 25:42–43) forbidding the permanent enslavement of one Israelite by another sharpen the point. "For they are my servants [*avadai,* "my servants" or "my slaves"], whom I freed from the land of Egypt; they may not give themselves over into servitude. You shall not rule over them ruthlessly [*b'farekh,* the same word that appears in Exodus to describe Pharaoh's oppression of the Israelites]. As one scholar observed, the events of the Exodus conform to an ancient Near Eastern practice, when a slave undergoes "a change of master."[10] Pharaoh's refusal to "let My people go to worship Me," the refrain that runs throughout the plague narrative, brings ruin upon his country.

When the Israelites finally do leave, the Egyptians give them silver and gold, and also clothing (Ex. 12:36), as one might expect in light of Ramses IV's freedom proclamation. The Bible connects political and economic aspects of redemption.

The various signs that precede the Exodus go further than mere poles and banners, though Isaiah (11:11–12) uses the same imagery. "In that day, My Lord will apply His hand again to redeeming the other part of His people from Assyria—as also from Egypt . . . He will hold up a signal [*nes*] to the nations and assemble the banished of Israel." The word *nes* also means "miracle," though this word is not used in the Book of Exodus. The pillar of fire that gives the departing Israelites light by night is reminiscent of the Mesopotamian sunlike torch that heralds the dawn of freedom.

There is, of course, one enormous difference between ancient Near Eastern freedom proclamations and the biblical account of Israel's redemption from Egypt. The beneficiaries of royal freedom proclamations owed loyalty to the king, not to any superior god. And if liberation led to temple service, it was service of the body, not the soul. When God freed the Israelites from Pharaoh, they owed *spiritual* service and loyalty to God alone.[11]

AN AGE-OLD QUESTION: WHY DID GOD REDEEM THE ISRAELITES FROM EGYPT?

This question echoes throughout the Midrash, that vast body of literature that seeks answers to the deepest questions raised by our ancient texts. Some say that the children of Israel merited redemption because of their own virtues or those of their ancestors. Others claim that Israel was essentially undeserving and only merited redemption after accepting the Torah at Sinai. A third view holds that prior to the Exodus, God gave the Israelites two specific commandments to follow; the Passover sacrifice and circumcision. Only observance of these commandments rendered them worthy of leaving Egypt.

> Copy one or both of the following texts and distribute them
> to your guests. This will make for an interesting discussion for small groups
> before the Seder. Ask each group to focus on one of these midrashim.
> During the Seder, ask each group to report briefly on its discussion.
> Each text is accompanied by a few questions, but don't let them limit
> the discussion. Depending on your group, you may want to
> introduce this with Appendix II, "What Is Midrash?"

Rabbi Eliezer ha-Kappar [active in Israel between 170 and 200 C.E.] says: Did not Israel possess four virtues more worthy than anything else in the whole world? They were above suspicion in regard to their sexual behavior [i.e., they refrained from sexual relations with those whom they could not marry, presumably Egyptians] and tale bearing [gossiping, *lashon ha-ra*]. They did not change their names and they did not change their language.

—THE MEKHILTA OF RABBI ISHMAEL, A COLLECTION OF MIDRASHIM
COMPILED IN THE THIRD CENTURY C.E.[12]

• Must a slave possess particular merits to deserve redemption? Which of these four virtues is the most surprising to you? What is the relationship among these qualities, and what role might they have played in the Exodus from Egypt? What other virtues might you have expected to be included in this list? How do these factors strike you in terms of current concerns about the Jewish future?

"These are the records of the Tabernacle . . ." (Ex. 38:21). When Israel toiled under harsh labor in Egypt, it was decreed that the men could not return at night to sleep in their homes. Rabbi Shimon bar Chalafta [active in Israel c. 200 C.E.] said: What would the daughters of Israel do? They went down to draw water from the Nile and the Holy One, blessed be He, filled their jugs with small fish. Some they sold to buy wine. Some they cooked and brought with the wine to their husbands in the fields. As it says, *"with all sorts of tasks in the field"* (Ex. 1:14). When they had eaten and drunk they would take [copper] mirrors and look into them with their husbands. She said, "I am more fair than you." And he said, "I am more fair than you." And this led to arousing their appetite for each other and they were fruitful and multiplied. And the Holy One, blessed be He, took note of them immediately. [They bore many children . . .] and all this resulted from the mirrors. As it says, *"The land was filled with them"* (Ex. 1:7). *"And the more they were afflicted the more they multiplied"* (Ex. 1:12). From the merit of those mirrors that they would show to their husbands and which would arouse them, they raised up all the hosts, as it says, *"All the hosts of the Lord departed from the land of Egypt . . . and the Lord brought the Israelites from the land troop by troop"* (literally in their "hosts," Ex. 12:41, 51).

When the Holy One, blessed be He, told Moses to build the Mishkan (the Tabernacle in the desert) all Israel donated. He who had silver or gold or copper . . . or other treasures, brought it all immediately. Said the women, "What have we to donate?" They stood up and brought the mirrors to Moses. When Moses saw them, he flew into a rage. He said to the men of Israel, "Take rods and break their thighs. These mirrors! Why are they necessary?" The Holy One, blessed be He, said to Moses, "Moses, these you despise? These mirrors raised up these hosts in Egypt. Take them and make a copper basin with a copper stand for the priests to sanctify themselves. As it says, *'He made the basin of copper and its stand of copper, from the mirrors of the women who performed tasks at the entrance of the Tent of Meeting'"* [or midrashically, *"from the mirrors of the women who created hosts"*] (Ex. 38:8).

—MIDRASH TANCHUMA, COMPILED BETWEEN
THE FIFTH AND NINTH CENTURIES C.E.[13]

• What is the relationship between the actions of women and of God in this midrash? What is the significance of the fact that procreation in the face of oppression is associated with redemption? How would you relate the women's actions to the concept in Genesis (1:27) that human beings, "male and female," are created in God's image? What do you make of the fact that Moses shows so little understanding of the significance of the women's mirrors?

THE FOUR CUPS OF REDEMPTION

The Mishnah (Pesachim 10:1) takes the drinking of wine on the night of Passover seriously: You must drink not less than four cups even if you have to borrow from the "pauper's dish" to buy the wine. On Shabbat you can substitute other drinks for wine, but not on Passover. The Babylonian Talmud (Pesachim 117b) explains: "Our Rabbis instituted four cups as symbolizing freedom." But why four cups? For that we must turn to the Jerusalem Talmud, compiled in the land of Israel between 200 and 400 C.E. Below are several of the Jerusalem Talmud's explanations.

Read the first interpretation and discuss the questions that follow. You may want
to contrast this with the text that follows the questions.

Whence four cups? Rabbi Yochanan said in the name of Rabbi Benaiah: [They] correspond to the four redemptions [or acts of redemption, mentioned in reference to Egypt]: "Say, therefore, to the Israelite people; 'I am the Lord. I will take you out [*v'hotzeiti*] from under the suffering of the Egyptians and deliver you [*v'hitzalti*] from their bondage. I will redeem you [*v'ga'alti*] with an outstretched arm and through extraordinary chastisements [i.e., judgments against the Egyptians]. And I will take you [*v'lakachti*] to be My people . . .'" (Ex. 6:6–7).[14]

—JERUSALEM TALMUD, PESACHIM 10:1

- Jacob Neusner, one of the great authorities on rabbinic literature, suggests that these four elements of redemption involve: "God's redeeming Israel from (1) Egyptian oppression; (2) subjugation to others; (3) a psychological slave mentality—by openly vanquishing their oppressor—and (4) their old identity, giving Israel a new identity as God's people." How would you explain the relationship among these four promises, or aspects, of redemption?

- What respective roles do you think God and human beings play in redemption?

- The same text in Exodus includes a fifth promise: "I will bring you [*v'heveiti*] into the land that I swore to give Abraham, Isaac, and Jacob, and I will give it to you for a possession, I the Lord" (Ex. 6:8). This has prompted some to argue for drinking a fifth cup of wine at the Seder. The ancient link between redemption and return to the land of Israel took on renewed meaning with the advent of Zionism. Now recited in many synagogues on the Sabbath, the Prayer for the State of Israel refers to Israel as *reishit tzemichat ge'ulateinu*, "the first flowering of our redemption." In your understanding of redemption, what role does or should the State of Israel play?

The Jerusalem Talmud also includes several less familiar explanations of the four cups. The tone of the interpretation below may remind you of the passage

"Pour out Your wrath," which appears in traditional Haggadot and is read prior to completing the Hallel.

> And Rabbis say, [They] correspond to the four cups of retribution that the Holy One Praised be He, will give the nations of the world to drink: For thus said the Lord, the God of Israel to me: "Take from My hand this cup of wine—of wrath—[and make all the nations to whom I send you drink of it]" (Jer. 25:15); "[Flee from the midst of Babylon. . . . For this is a time of vengeance for the Lord, He will deal retribution to her]. Babylon was a golden cup in the Lord's hand, it makes the whole earth drunk" (Jer. 51:6-7); "For in the Lord's hand there is a cup [with foaming wine fully mixed in; from this He pours; all the wicked of the earth drink, draining it to the very dregs]" (Psalms 75:9); "He will rain down upon the wicked blazing coals and sulfur, a scorching wind shall be the portion of their cup" (Psalms 11:6).
>
> —JERUSALEM TALMUD, PESACHIM 10:1

• How would you contrast this interpretation with the one above? What are the potential dangers of such texts? How do Jewish texts of this kind make you feel?

A QUARTET OF TWENTIETH-CENTURY JEWISH VOICES ON REDEMPTION

Even more than Judaism remembers the past redemption from Egypt, it finds evidence of redemption in the present and yearns for more to come in the future. Here are four twentieth-century voices on redemption. Choose one or two to read aloud and discuss the questions that follow. Or you may want to read a selection to accompany each of the four cups of wine.

• Which of these statements speaks most powerfully to you and why?

• Do you think you would have responded similarly five or ten years ago? Why?

• Do you agree that redemption of the individual and society are inextricably linked?

The salvation that modern man seeks in this world, like that which his fathers sought in the world to come, has both a personal and a social significance. In its personal aspect it represents the faith in the possibility of achieving an integrated personality . . . In its social aspect, salvation means the ultimate achievement of a social order in which all men shall collaborate in the pursuit of common ends in a manner which shall afford each the maximum opportunity for creative self expression. There can be no personal salvation so long as injustice and strife exist in the social order; there can be no social salvation so long as the greed for gain and the lust for dominance are permitted to inhibit the hunger for human fellowship and sympathy in the hearts of men . . . The God of salvation . . . is the Power that makes for the fulfillment of all valid ideas.

—MORDECAI M. KAPLAN (1881–1983)[15]

Mordecai Kaplan was born in Lithuania. His family moved to the United States in 1890. Kaplan was a rabbi, teacher, theologian, and spiritual father of the Reconstructionist Movement. He rejected most supernatural ideas in Judaism and defined God as the power that made possible the pursuit of fundamental values, such as freedom and improving the world.

The lived moment leads directly to knowledge of revelation, and thinking about birth leads indirectly to the knowledge of creation. But in his personal life probably not one of us will taste the essence of redemption before his last hour. And yet here, too, there is an approach. It is dark and silent and cannot be indicated by any means, save by my asking you to recall your own dark and silent hours. I mean those hours in the lowest depths when our soul hovers over the frail trap door which, at the very next instant, may send us down into destruction, madness, and suicide at our own verdict. Indeed, we are astonished that it has not opened up until now. But suddenly we feel the touch of a hand. It reaches down to us, it wishes to be grasped—and yet what incredible courage is needed to take that hand, to let it draw us up out of the darkness! This is redemption. We must realize the true nature of the experience proffered us: It is that "our redeemer lives" (Job 19:25), that He wishes to redeem us—but only by our own acceptance of His redemption with the turning of our whole being.

—MARTIN BUBER (1878–1965)[16]

Martin Buber was born in Vienna and immigrated to Palestine in 1938. A philosopher, Zionist leader, and scholar of biblical and Hasidic literature, Buber thought of God as an "Eternal Thou," always available to be experienced by those fully willing to open themselves to the encounter.

The destiny of man is to be a partner of God and a mitzvah is an act in which man is present, an act of participation; while sin is an act in which God is alone; an act of alienation. Such acts of man's revelations of the divine are acts of redemption. The meaning of redemption is to reveal the holy that is concealed, to disclose the divine that is suppressed. Every man is called upon to be a redeemer, and redemption takes place every moment, every day. . . . The world is in need of redemption, but the redemption must not be expected to happen as an act of sheer grace. Man's task is to make the world worthy of redemption. His faith and his works are preparations for *ultimate redemption*.

—ABRAHAM JOSHUA HESCHEL (1907–1972)[17]

Abraham Joshua Heschel, a descendent of great Hasidic masters on both sides of his family, was born in Warsaw and lived in Poland and Germany. He immigrated to the United States in 1940. A theologian and philosopher, Heschel was a professor of mystics and ethics and a social activist who marched with Martin Luther King Jr. during the civil rights era.

The hope for Redemption is the force that sustains Judaism in the Diaspora; the Judaism of Israel is the very Redemption . . . Redemption is continuous. The Redemption from Egypt and the Final Redemption are part of the same process, "of the mighty hand and outstretched arm," which began in Egypt and is evident in all of history. Moses and Elijah belong to the same redemptive act; one represents its beginning and the other its culmination, so that together they fulfill its purpose. The spirit of Israel is attuned to the hum of the redemptive process, to the sound waves of its labors which will end only with the coming of the days of the Messiah.

—RABBI ABRAHAM ISAAC KOOK (1865–1935)[18]

Rabbi Abraham Isaac Kook was an early religious Zionist leader. Deeply steeped in mysticism, Rav Kook immigrated to Israel in 1904 and from 1921 until his death he served as Chief Ashkenazic Rabbi of Palestine under the British Mandate. He revived the ancient notion that the ultimate Messiah would be preceded by the Messiah ben Joseph, a figure who would die in battle and lay the groundwork for the final redemption. In fact, when Kook eulogized Theodore Herzl in 1904, he likened the Zionist leader to Messiah ben Joseph. Kook believed that even secular Jews played a critical role in the redemptive process, and he built strong relationships among Jews from all religious backgrounds. Rav Kook's thinking has become central to Israel's settler movement.

ON FAITH IN REDEMPTION

Read the following passage aloud during your Seder.[19]

A single word captures the concern of the entire Passover Haggadah: redemption. The *Encyclopedia Judaica* defines redemption as "salvation from the states or circumstances that destroy the value of human existence or human existence itself."

At its core lies a relatively simple idea: that the future will be better than the present. Not just a little brighter—eventually it will be more like the difference between night and day. Maimonides put it simply: "In that era there will be neither famine nor war, neither jealousy nor strife."[20]

Redemption is about the potential for positive change, ultimately dramatic change, even if it comes about slowly.

"Now we are slaves. Next year we will be free." Whether you interpret that statement in terms of political oppression or spiritual enslavement to false gods, how can you say those words if you don't believe in the possibility of change?

Maybe that's what the Haggadah's "wicked" child represents: a cynical voice calling Passover a charade, arguing that *nothing* really changes. Why study all the laws and customs of Passover? They're all about making Passover different from the rest of the year. Why bother to make one night different from all others if the fundamental reality points to an eternal status quo rather than a world we can improve, however slowly? During the Seder we recline like kings and queens. We ask questions, as free people are wont to do. The Seder promises that we *can* make one night different, and that's a start.

The fact that Jews held Seders in concentration camps provides an infinitely poignant illustration of Judaism's unshakable faith in redemption. For some inexplicable reason, the Germans permitted Jews in Bergen-Belsen to bake matzah one Passover. Rabbi Israel Spira of Bluzhov (1881–1981) led the Seder. In the midst of unspeakable degradation (metaphorically in the word *avadim*, Hebrew for "slaves"), Rabbi Spira searched and found hope. Here's part of what he said:

> Tonight we have only matzah, we have no moments of relief, not a moment of respite for our humiliated spirits . . . But do not despair, my young friends . . . For this is also the beginning of our redemption. We are slaves who served Pharaoh in Egypt. Slaves in Hebrew are *avadim*; the Hebrew letters of the word *avadim* [ayin, bet, dalet, yod, mem] form an acronym for the Hebrew phrase: David, the son of Jesse, your servant, your Messiah [*David: dalet; ben: bet; Yishai: yod; avdekha: ayin; meshichekha: mem*— a phrase that appears in the morning liturgy for the Sabbath and festivals as well as in the Haggadah]. Thus, even in our state of slavery we find intimations of our eventual freedom through the coming of the Messiah. We who are witnessing the darkest night in history, the lowest moment of civilization, will also witness the great light of redemption. . . .

Perhaps faith in redemption would not have become such a prominent feature in the Jewish psyche had our history been less traumatic.

And that's the rub.

The very experiences that nurture faith in redemption can also spawn unbridled hopelessness. It's not hard to look back and agree that "in every generation they rise up to destroy us," to quote the Haggadah's powerful, but uncharacteristically embittered take on Jewish history. The good news is that "the Holy One, blessed be He, saves us from their hands." But that's hardly an end to the oppression and persecution that have stalked our people over the ages.

On the whole, however, the Haggadah wants us to choose hope over despair. The last verse of *Chad Gadya,* in many traditions the Seder's conclusion, leaves us with a glimmer of the ultimate hope—the triumph of life over death: "Then came the Holy One, blessed be He, and slew the angel of death."

We cannot know when our travails will end. We can only *know*—or have faith, if you prefer—that the future need not be as bleak as the past. To believe otherwise is to reject the promise of hope that animates the entire story of the Exodus and the Haggadah. To choose despair and cynicism is to endorse *Mitzrayim* as the end of the road, the ultimate truth. To have faith in redemption is to believe that suffering, exile, and oppression will end—someday. However distant that day may be, those who can envision it muster the strength to bring it closer.

Belief in redemption stands as one of those fundamental human divides. It's the difference between those who believe we're in a tunnel, though we sometimes can't see the light at the end, and those who think there is no tunnel, just a world that's unalterably dark. Those who believe in redemption retain a degree of optimism and energy to repair a world plagued by evil, even if they know they won't finish the task. Those who don't believe in redemption see an ever-broken world and surround themselves with walls that only further shut out the light of hope.

The compilers of the Haggadah certainly knew the dark times of Jewish history. But they chose to bequeath us a book that defiantly celebrates hope. Tonight we hold their shining gift in our hands. May we guard it with love and tenacity. May our Passover Seders fortify our faith in redemption. May we pass that faith down to our children. May we strengthen one another to build a world redeemed.

21

"A Remembrance of the Temple":
The Life and Times of Hillel

זֵכֶר לְמִקְדָּשׁ כְּהִלֵּל:

כֵּן עָשָׂה הִלֵּל בִּזְמַן שֶׁבֵּית הַמִּקְדָּשׁ הָיָה קַיָּם.

הָיָה כּוֹרֵךְ פֶּסַח מַצָּה וּמָרוֹר וְאוֹכֵל בְּיַחַד,

לְקַיֵּם מַה שֶּׁנֶּאֱמַר: עַל־מַצּוֹת וּמְרוֹרִים יֹאכְלֻהוּ.

A remembrance of the Temple as was the custom of Hillel. Thus did Hillel.
He made a sandwich of the Pesach offering, matzah, and bitter herbs
and ate them together to perform what has been prescribed.
"With matzot and bitter herbs they shall eat it" (Num. 9:11).
—THE PASSOVER HAGGADAH

Of the ten sages mentioned in the Haggadah, Hillel appears last. Traditionally viewed as the founder of Rabbinic Judaism, he completes an illustrious cast, each of whom has left his mark on the Seder. It's fitting that just before partaking of our own festive meal, we remember how Hillel ate his—with an earthy joy and an unforgettable knack for combining the unexpected. A number of the sages in the Haggadah lived during the later years of the Second Temple. They survived the rebellion against Rome, during which the Temple was destroyed in 70 C.E. But Hillel is the only one of the Haggadah's sages who lived out his days with the Temple still standing. In evoking Hillel, the Haggadah alludes not only to the Temple and the patriarch of Rabbinic Judaism, but also to the period before a cataclysm that would forever transform Judaism. Hillel's era was full of trials, but as long as the Temple stood, the Jewish world had an undisputed physical and spiritual center that has never been re-created, even with the establishment of Israel.

As you read parts of the Haggadah, ask your guests to point out references to the Temple. Ponder the following question.

• Why would the Haggadah want to remind us of Hillel and the Temple?

THE MEANING OF HILLEL'S SANDWICH

Read the following section on your own or during the Seder, depending on your group.

Just after the blessing over the matzah and bitter herbs, which are eaten separately, we eat them together, without a blessing, as Hillel did when the Temple stood.

First let's take a short look at the evolution of this passage and then at its significance. It does not appear in the Mishnah, the Jewish law code compiled around 200 C.E., which includes the earliest directions for the Seder. It derives from two other sources: the Tosefta, generally thought to be an early commentary on the Mishnah, and the Babylonian Talmud. When the Tosefta discusses the timing of the Seder and mentions bitter herbs, matzah, and the paschal sacrifice, it adds that "Hillel the Elder would fold together the three of them and eat them."[1]

Compiled between the the third and sixth centuries C.E., the Babylonian Talmud elaborates: "It was related of Hillel that he used to wrap them together. For it is said, 'They shall eat it with matzot and bitter herbs' (Num. 9:11) . . . [One should eat] matzot and bitter herbs together without a blessing, in memory of the Temple, as Hillel [did]."[2] We don't say a blessing over the Hillel sandwich because, since the destruction of the Second Temple, the sandwich has been missing the paschal sacrifice that had been its critical ingredient.

The Rabbis of the Talmud disagreed about whether it was permissible to combine the eating of matzah (a biblical law) with the eating of bitter herbs (a rabbinic decree). The memory of Hillel's sandwich seemed to suggest that in this case biblical and rabbinic decrees *could* be combined into a single commandment. Out of respect for the sages who opposed such a combination, however, the Seder would forever also include the ritual of eating each separately—a compromise that satisfied all sides and one that we have honored on the night of Passover for more than fifteen hundred years!

What is the significance of this passage? What might it be trying to tell us? If you look closely at the Haggadah, you'll see that after the section that recounts the plagues, when we sing *Dayyenu,* references to the Temple begin to appear. The last verse of *Dayyenu* reads: "If He had brought us into the land of Israel, but had He not built for us the chosen Temple, it would have been enough for us." Some commentators believe that *Dayyenu's* fifteen traditional verses correspond to the fifteen steps going up to the Temple that the Levites and priests ascended.

Why with the singing of *Dayyenu* does the Temple appear? In terms of the Haggadah's structure, telling the story of the Exodus is preceded and followed by reminders that redemption from Egypt is not just the story of a one-time event, but the prototype for Israel's history in relationship to God. Just before we begin the midrashic exposition of the enslavement and redemption from Egypt, we recite, "In every generation they rise up to destroy us, but the Holy One, blessed be He, rescues us from their hands."

Dayyenu follows the part of the Haggadah in which we remember the plagues. When we've finished recounting the plagues, we've reached the last act in the story of leaving Egypt. *Dayyenu* marks the completion of our liberation from Egypt. And only now specific references begin to surface about the "new Egypt," the loss of the Temple, and the exile from Israel. Thus, immediately after reciting the blessing over the matzah and bitter herbs, we eat a special sandwich as Hillel did "in remembrance of the Temple" in Jerusalem. In eating a Seder sandwich with just two of Hillel's three ingredients, we bear witness to the fact that Passover remains meaningful even without the Temple.

Hillel sandwiched the matzah, bitter herbs, and the paschal sacrifice into a "super" symbol, and the composers of the Haggadah reinterpreted those symbols for a new context. As we combine matzah and bitter herbs, we participate in transforming and extending the meaning of the ancient symbols of the Exodus.

No longer do matzah and bitter herbs represent simply ancient Egypt. They have become metaphors for all the Egypts, all the exiles in which we as a people have found ourselves over the millennia. If God brought us out of that first Egypt, then God can bring us out of other Egypts, too. If God represents the power that allows a people to find what it takes to move beyond the narrow straits, then a people that overcame that first Egypt can overcome other Egypts as well. When we eat Hillel's sandwich of matzah and bitter herbs we express our faith in redemption as an ongoing process that can be as real for us today as it was for our ancestors.

Because the Seder as we know it developed in response to the destruction of the Second Temple, it makes sense to look back at that period, at the Temple, and at the life and work of Hillel the Elder. Through this short passage about Hillel's sandwich, the composers of the Haggadah have created a special link between Hillel and the Temple. This link extends back for almost two thousand years, and it will continue as long as Jews celebrate Passover.

A LEGENDARY LEADER

Read this on your own.

Like those of many great figures of ancient history, Hillel's life and teachings remain shrouded in legends, elaborated and colored as they were passed down. But we know what our tradition says about this illustrious sage, and that is certainly worth pondering. In Hillel's character we find a vibrant portrait of the values our tradition holds dear. This portrait of Hillel as a man of peace becomes more vivid when contrasted with that of Herod, the King of Judea, an example of the murderous, paranoid tyrant with whom we have become all too familiar in the twentieth century.[3]

Hillel was born in the middle of the first century C.E., a period when Rome's increasing political and cultural domination represented a powerful challenge to the Jewish future. In 37 B.C.E., Rome installed Herod as King of Judea, a tyrant whose long rule would continue until 4 C.E. Herod seized control of the priesthood, appointing high priests as he wished. Although Herod considered himself a Jew, he was a puppet of Rome and determined to bring Roman culture into Israel. He knew enough to avoid building Roman temples in Jewish cities, but, according to Josephus (c. 38–100 C.E.), the Jewish historian, he could not resist placing the hated Roman eagle over the entrance to the Jewish Temple he rebuilt in Jerusalem.[4] In the face of widespread Jewish revulsion, he built amphitheaters throughout the country. For entertainment, spectators could watch men who had been sentenced to death fight off lions. Taxes to pay for Herod's lavish building program and military exploits fell on an increasingly restive and impoverished population.[5] Fearing rebellion, Herod created a virtual police state. Josephus put it this way:

> People everywhere talked against him . . . and [Herod] took away the opportunities they might have to disturb him, and enjoined them to be always at work; nor did he permit the citizens either to meet together, or to walk or eat together, but watched everything they did, and when any were caught, they were severely punished . . . many . . . both openly and secretly were put to death; and there were spies set everywhere . . . oftentimes [Herod] himself took the habit of a private man, and mixed among the multitude, and made trial of what opinion they had of his government . . . he required that they should be obliged to take an oath of fidelity to him, and at the same time compelled them to swear that they would bear him good will. . . .[6]

Against this turbulent backdrop, the life and legend of Hillel unfolded. Rabbinic literature preserves a picture of a saintly man whose wisdom, patience, and humility represented the antithesis of the brutal Herod.

Tradition holds that Hillel was born in Babylonia to a deeply religious family. He traveled to Jerusalem to study with Shemayah and Avtalyon, the greatest sages of the era. Most of their teachings have been lost, but the few that have survived give us a taste of what Hillel may have learned from them. For example, they disagreed about why God split the Red Sea for the Israelites. Shemayah said it occurred because of Abraham's faith in God long before. Avtalyon taught that "the faith with which *they* [the Israelites] have in Me is deserving that I should divide the sea for them."[7] Far from concern about an event in the distant past, this debate expressed questions about what would bring about the deliverance of their *own* community from increasingly difficult times.

Two teachings of these sages speak volumes about their perilous times. Shemayah taught: "Love work; despise lordliness; and do not become overly familiar with the government." Avtalyon taught: "Scholars, be cautious with your words, for you may incur the penalty of exile and be banished to a place of evil."[8]

Many tales grew up about Hillel's poverty and his passion for learning. The Talmud tells us:

> Every day he used to work and earn . . . [a day laborer's wage] half of which he would give to the guard at the House of Study, the other half being spent for his food and for that of his family. One day he found [no work] and the guard . . . would not permit him to enter. He climbed up and sat upon the window [an opening in the roof] to hear the words of the living God from the mouth of Shemayah and Avtalyon—They say that day was the eve of Sabbath in the winter solstice and snow fell down upon him from heaven. When the dawn rose, Shemayah said to Avtalyon: "Brother Avtalyon, on every day this house is light and today it is dark, is it perhaps a cloudy day?" They looked up and saw the figure of a man in the window. They went up and found him covered by . . . snow. They removed him, bathed and anointed him, and placed him opposite the fire and they said: "This man deserves that the Sabbath be profaned on his behalf."[9]

To support his family, Hillel worked as a woodcutter, but he remained impoverished. After his studies he seems to have returned to Babylonia. But Hillel was not destined to remain a poor scholar on the fringe of Jewish history. Sometime after his teachers died, Hillel returned to Jerusalem. One year, Passover was to fall on the Sabbath. Incredibly, religious authorities were unable to answer a straightforward question: If the holiday falls on the Sabbath, should the Passover sacrifice be postponed? Their inability to answer a fairly straightforward question was a sign of the low point to which the Jewish community had fallen. They turned to the sage from Babylonia for an answer. Hillel explained that the paschal sacrifice need not be put off any more than the many other sacrifices that regularly occurred on the Sabbath.[10]

Hillel's influence on the development of Judaism long outlived him. According to tradition, the dynasty that led the Jewish community in Israel from about 30 B.C.E. until 425 C.E. traced its lineage to Hillel. His life and work helped transform and preserve the Jewish religion. As the sages said, "In ancient times when the Torah was forgotten from Israel, Ezra came up from Babylon and established it. [Some of] it was again forgotten and Hillel the Babylonian came up and established it."[11] Some went further and compared Hillel to Moses:

> Both lived 120 years. Moses spent forty years in Pharaoh's palace and then left his native land; forty years in Midian in preparation for his career of leadership and then he led his people for forty years. Hillel left Babylonia for the land of Israel at forty; forty years he spent in study; forty years he served as the spiritual leader of his people.
> —SIFREI ON DEUTERONOMY 34:7, LATE-THIRD-CENTURY MIDRASH[12]

Hillel's death captured the essence of his life:

> Once when the Rabbis were met in the upper chamber of Gurya's house at Jericho, a *bat kol,* a voice from heaven, was heard, saying: "There is one amongst you who is worthy that the Shekhinah [the Divine Presence] should rest on him as it did on Moses, but his generation does not merit it." The sages present set their eyes on Hillel the Elder. And when he died, they lamented and said: "Alas, the pious man, the humble man, the disciple of Ezra [is no more]."
> —BABYLONIAN TALMUD, SANHEDRIN 11A,
> COMPILED BETWEEN 200 AND 500 C.E.

HILLEL'S TEACHINGS

Read the following statements by Hillel aloud.
Keep the questions below in mind and discuss them after the reading.

Hillel lived from the middle of the first century B.C.E. into the next century. His approach to life and his personality stand as a legacy of equal, if not greater, importance than his generally lenient approach to law. His search for understanding took him far beyond the traditional house of study.

> It was said of Hillel that he had not neglected any of the words of the sages but had learned them all. He had studied all manners of speech, even the utterance of mountains, hills, and valleys, the utterance of trees and plants, the utterance of beasts and animals. . . .
>
> —BABYLONIAN TALMUD, SOFERIM 16:9,
> TRACTATE COMPILED MID-EIGHTH CENTURY

- What is the Talmud saying about wisdom, and perhaps about God when it refers to the range of Hillel's studies? Is there an environmental message here?

Hillel believed that the purpose of life was not just to ensure one's own comfort, but to repair the world and to bring about peace. Here are several of the most memorable teachings the Mishnah attributes to Hillel:[13] "If I am not for myself, who will be for me? And if I am for myself alone, what am I? And if not now, when?" "The more Torah, the more life. The more study, the more wisdom. The more advice, the more understanding. The more charity, the more peace." "Be among the disciples of Aaron, loving peace and pursuing peace, loving people and bringing them closer to Torah." "Do not separate yourself from the community . . . In a place where there is no man, strive to be one."

- Which of Hillel's statements is most important to you and why?

- How are these teachings relevant to the Jewish people today?

- Which one of these statements has the most relevance to your life now? Would you have said the same thing a number of years ago?

- Aaron presided over the building of the Golden Calf. What does Hillel's comment imply about the lengths to which one may go to pursue peace? What is the difference between loving peace and pursuing peace? How is that difference relevant today?

• Are there tensions between the two elements of the last dictum? If
so, how would you reconcile them? To which would you give
greater weight?

Even when asked provocative or seemingly impossible questions, Hillel
managed to reach out:

It happened that a certain heathen came before Shammai and said to
him, "Convert me to Judaism on the condition that you teach me the
whole Torah while I stand on one foot." Thereupon Shammai repulsed
the heathen with the builder's measuring rod that was in Shammai's
hand. When the heathen went before Hillel, he said to the heathen,
"What is hateful to you, do not to your neighbor: That is the whole
Torah, while the rest is the commentary therefore; go and learn it."

—BABYLONIAN TALMUD, SHABBAT 31A,
COMPILED BETWEEN 200 AND 500 C.E.

• If you were asked to explain the essence of Judaism in a few sentences what might you say? Hillel could have answered the heathen
with the famous verse from Leviticus 19:18, "Love your neighbor as
yourself." Why do you think he chose to respond with a negative
formulation of that verse?

THE TALMUD ON THE DESTRUCTION OF THE TEMPLE

You may want to read this historical overview on your own or summarize it
for your guests before reading aloud and discussing the passage on page 298
from the Talmud that explains the cause of the Second Temple's destruction.

Because the Haggadah refers to the Temple numerous times and alludes to its
destruction, the Seder is an appropriate time to consider some of what our tradition has had to say about what caused that fateful event in the year 70 C.E.

The matter becomes all the more poignant when Josephus reminds us that
the siege of Jerusalem began during the festival of Passover. The number of Jews

lost in the siege was so enormous (Josephus claims more than one million) because the pilgrims had "come together from the whole country for the Feast of Unleavened Bread and had suddenly been caught up in the war, so that first the overcrowding meant death by pestilence, and later hunger took a heavier toll."[14]

Direct Roman rule of Judea began in 6 C.E., and, with it, resentment toward Rome mushroomed. Rome's occasional crucifixion of Jewish rebels only stoked the fires of revolt. Messianism hung thickly in the air. Many believed that a war against the evil empire would bring the Messiah. In 65 C.E., the Roman general Cestius marched on Jerusalem with the Twelfth Legion to suppress the incipient rebellion. After a few days of fighting, Cestius realized that the battle for Jerusalem would take longer than anticipated and that his forces were not supplied for a lengthy campaign. A few weeks before Hanukkah, he decided to retreat to Caesarea for the winter. Emboldened by his flight, Jewish forces attacked his army, killing nearly six thousand Roman troops. This stunning defeat persuaded Rome that the Judeans must be crushed. The victory convinced more and more Judeans that they could defeat Rome as the Maccabees had defeated the Seleucid Greeks in 165 B.C.E. That miscalculation among Jewish zealots sealed the fate of Judea. Even so, at many points during the ensuing war, Rome would have accepted Jewish surrender without insisting on the Temple's destruction. That sorry eventuality must be attributed to the Judeans, who clung either to their fantasy of defeating Rome or to their dream of ushering in the Messiah.

Rather than place the blame for the Second Temple's destruction on Rome, the sages of the rabbinic period assigned responsibility to factions within the Jewish community, if not the community in its entirety. For example, one well-known passage from the Talmud ascribes the Temple's destruction to groundless hatred, *sinat chinam*. Even though people "occupied themselves with Torah," groundless hatred prevailed. What is groundless hatred? When people "eat and drink together, then thrust each other through with the daggers of their tongue!"[15]

According to Josephus, "groundless hatred" resulted in more than verbal assault. The question of whether to rebel against Rome produced a virtual civil war. Dialogue between the parties completely broke down. Zealots did their best to stir up the younger generation for war. The elders, who foresaw the disaster, could only wring their hands. Those who spoke for peace were murdered.

Ananus, the high priest, urged the people to overthrow the zealots and make peace with Rome. He compared living under the zealots to slavery in Egypt. The zealots soon cut Ananus to shreds.

> Every town was seething with turmoil and civil war, and as soon as the Romans gave them a breathing-space they turned their hands against each other. Between advocates of war and lovers of peace there was a fierce quarrel. First of all in the home, family unity was disrupted by partisan bitterness; then the nearest kinsmen severed all ties of blood, and attaching themselves to men who thought as they did lined up on opposite sides. Faction reigned everywhere, the revolutionaries and jingoes with the boldness of youth silencing the old and the sensible. They began one by one and all plundering their neighbors, then forming themselves into companies they extended their brigandage all over the country, so that in lawless brutality the Romans were not worse than the victims' own countrymen—in fact those who were robbed thought it far preferable to be captured by the Romans.[16]

The zealots defied Rome in every conceivable manner, even when it required tampering with long established religious traditions to do so. Josephus writes that in 66 C.E., one of the zealots who served as a governor at the Temple suddenly "persuaded the ministers of the Temple not to accept the gift or offering from a foreigner. This it was that made war with Rome inevitable; for they abolished the sacrifices offered for Rome and Caesar himself, and in spite of the earnest appeals of the chief priests and prominent citizens not to cancel the customary offerings for the government, they would not give in."[17]

Read the following paragraph and the passage from
the Talmud aloud and discuss the questions that follow.
This will make for an interesting pre-Seder discussion.

Compiled between the years 200 and 500 C.E., the Talmud (Gittin 55b–57a) describes its own fascinating but tragic version of the events that contributed to the Temple's destruction. Rabbi Zechariah ben Avkulas, who plays a critical role near the end of the story, appears only once again, and very inconsequentially, in the Talmud and just once in the midrash where this story is also recounted.[18]

> Rabbi Johanan [active in Israel between 250 and 290] said: "What illustrates the verse, 'Happy is the man who is always anxious, but he who hardens his heart shall fall into misfortune'" (Proverbs 28:14).
>
> The destruction of Jerusalem came through a Kamza and a Bar Kamza [literally, "a locust" and "the son of a locust"] . . . in this way. A certain man had a friend, Kamza, and an enemy, Bar Kamza. He once made a party and said to his servant, "Go and bring Kamza." The man went and brought Bar Kamza. When the host found him there he said, "See, you tell tales about me; what are you doing here? Get out." Said Bar Kamza: "Since I am here, let me stay, and I will pay you for whatever I eat and drink."
>
> He said, "I won't." "Then let me give you half the cost of the party." "No," said the host. "Then let me pay for the whole party." He still said, "No." And he took Bar Kamza by the hand and put him out. Said Bar Kamza, "Since the Rabbis were sitting there and did not stop him, this shows that they agreed with him. I will go and inform against them, to the [Roman] Government." He went and said to the Emperor, "The Jews are rebelling against you." He said, "How can I tell?" He said to him: "Send them an offering and see whether they will offer it [on the altar]." So he sent with him a fine calf. While on the way he made a blemish on its upper lip, or as some say on the white of its eye, in a place where we [Jews] count it a blemish but the [Romans] do not. The Rabbis were inclined to offer it in order not to offend the Government. Said Rabbi Zechariah ben Avkulas to them: "People will say that blemished animals are offered on the altar." They then proposed to kill Bar Kamza so that he should not go and inform against them, but Rabbi Zechariah ben Avkulas said to them, "Is one who makes a blemish on consecrated animals to be put to death?"

Rabbi Johanan thereupon remarked: "Through the scrupulousness [literally, 'humility'] of Rabbi Zechariah ben Avkulas our House has been destroyed, our Temple burnt and we ourselves exiled from our land . . . It has been taught: Note from this incident how serious a thing it is to put a man to shame, for God espoused the cause of Bar Kamza and destroyed His House and burnt His Temple."

• What contemporary situations does this story bring to mind?

• What can we learn from this story?

• How would you apportion responsibility for the outcome of the story?

• Who do you think bears the greatest share of responsibility?

• Whose heart seems to have been hardened in this tale?

22

Elijah's Transformation: From Zealot to Folk Hero

שְׁפֹךְ חֲמָתְךָ אֶל־הַגּוֹיִם אֲשֶׁר לֹא יְדָעוּךָ
וְעַל־מַמְלָכוֹת אֲשֶׁר בְּשִׁמְךָ לֹא קָרָאוּ...

Fill Elijah's goblet and the fourth cup. The leader fills Elijah's goblet or passes it round the table so that every participant can add some wine from his or her own cup . . . We open the door for Elijah (usually a child is given this privilege) as we rise and recite:[1]
Pour out Your wrath upon the nations that do not know You, upon the governments which do not call upon Your name. For they have devoured Jacob and desolated his home. Pour out Your wrath on them; may Your blazing anger overtake them, destroy them from under the heavens of the Lord (Psalms 79:6–7, 69:25, and Lamentations 3:66).
—THE PASSOVER HAGGADAH

Upon completing the blessing after the Passover meal, we reach one of the Seder's most memorable rituals—pouring the Cup of Elijah and opening the door for the prophet, hoping that he will have arrived to usher in the Messiah. In welcoming Elijah, we evoke one of Jewish folklore's most beloved figures.

In the context of the Seder, Elijah also evokes the figure of Moses, whose role in the Exodus has been strikingly minimized by the compilers of the Haggadah. But Elijah's spirit is with us more often than just at the Seder.

301

A traditional circumcision evokes the prophet through the Chair of Elijah, an empty chair placed to the right of the child, a custom that reaches back some twelve hundred years, if not more.[2] Elijah's relationship with the newborn continues: he serves as the guardian of infants for the first thirty days of life. According to the Talmud, "When a man weds a wife who is right for him, Elijah kisses him. . . ."[3] At the conclusion of every Sabbath we sing *"Eliyahu Hanavi,"* a song that urges Elijah to bring the Messiah with him speedily and in our time. Some modern Haggadot have added this song to the Seder. In the grace after every meal (*Birkat Ha-Mazon*) we ask the Compassionate One to "send Elijah the Prophet, may he be remembered for good, to us so he may bring us good tidings of salvations and consolations."

In addition to these prescribed occasions, countless tales recount Elijah's legendary appearances over the ages. The variations of these often-miraculous tales are legion, but many revolve around the theme of an old man wrapped in his mantle who mysteriously appears to teach an ethical lesson, impart hope to those in despair, or aid the destitute.

> Ask your Seder participants to discuss what "opening the door for Elijah" means to them. Ask some of your senior participants to share their childhood recollections about Elijah and the Seder.

ELIJAH COMES TO THE SEDER

Read the section below aloud or on your own.

Elijah's connection with the Seder offers a wonderful example of Jewish tradition's evolution. The Babylonian Talmud holds that Elijah will *not* come during the Sabbath or on the eve of festivals. His appearance would naturally lead to special preparations that might then interfere with the proper observance of the Sabbath or festival.[4] Regardless, a tenth-century midrash declared that Elijah would indeed appear on Passover eve.[5] The Jewish people's yearning for salvation clearly overwhelmed earlier concerns that might bar Elijah from appearing at the Seder, the redemptive moment par excellence.

We don't know precisely when the rituals associated with Elijah were added to the Ashkenazic Seder, but the consensus seems to be during the Middle Ages, some time after the Crusades. At around the same time, it also became customary to recite the malediction "Pour out Your wrath . . ." upon opening the door.

Scholars believe that the practice of opening the door for Elijah may have developed from an earlier custom of leaving the door ajar throughout the entire Seder to fulfill the biblical injunction that the night of Passover was "for the Lord a night of vigil to bring them out of the land of Egypt" and it should be "one of vigil for all the children of Israel throughout the ages" (Ex. 12:42).

Moses Isserles (c. 1530–1572), the great Polish commentator, held that when Jews opened their doors in foreign lands and recited the passage above, it expressed their faith that God would protect them and that Passover had indeed remained a night of vigil on God's part: "And for the merit of this faith the Messiah will come and 'pour out his wrath' upon the deniers of God."[6] But Isserles made no mention of Elijah. By contrast, the Maharal of Prague (c. 1525–1609) taught that opening the door and preparing Elijah's Cup gave concrete expression to an undying faith in the ultimate redemption.[7]

In many quarters, opening the door on Passover eve doubtless demanded faith. Throughout Europe, Passover had become an especially dangerous season for Jews. Accusations of blood libel—that Jews secretly crucified Christian children and used their blood to make matzah—were rampant. In the face of this peril, Jewish folklore taught that it was none other than Elijah who came to defend communities beset by charges of blood libel.[8] The Bible (II Kings 2:12) calls Elijah "the chariot of Israel, and its horsemen." God's prophet would stand ready to protect his people wherever danger lurked.[9]

ELIJAH'S CUP

Read the section below aloud or on your own.

The customary Cup of Elijah is also a relatively late addition to the Seder, first written about in the fifteenth century.[10] Elijah's presence at the Seder may have reflected a response to a growing sense of vulnerability, and some believe that it also attested to a quickening faith that messianic times were imminent. In explaining the late addition of Elijah's Cup to the Seder, Rabbi Menachem M. Schneerson (1902–1994), the late Lubavitcher Rebbe, said: "This custom is an expression of the Jewish people's belief in the coming of Mashiach and in the coming of Eliyahu, who will herald the imminent Redemption. The nearer we approach the time of the Redemption, the more keenly is this faithful anticipation felt in the heart of every Jew. This is why the above custom came to light and became widespread in recent generations, even though we do not find tangible evidence of it in earlier days."[11]

That mounting vulnerability and heightened messianism should occur at the same time makes perfect sense: The venerable concept of the birth pangs of the Messiah welded them together forever. According to ancient tradition, suffering signified the pain that would precede the Messiah.[12]

Why do we evoke Elijah's spirit before beginning the last four psalms of the Hallel (Psalms 115–118)? One reason is that we have just invoked his name in the *Birkat Ha-Mazon,* the blessing after the meal. But this question raises a related one. During the Seder we read the Hallel's six psalms. The Haggadah has us recite two before and four after the meal. Why? The Hallel's first two psalms, Psalms 113 and 114 (particularly Psalm 114), address themes of the Exodus from Egypt. The Hallel's last four psalms are understood as referring to the future messianic redemption. In this light, introducing those psalms with the invocation of Elijah, herald of the Messiah, makes perfect sense.[13]

THE BIBLICAL ELIJAH

Read the following story about Elijah the Prophet and lead a discussion on the questions that follow.

According to tradition, Elijah lived during the ninth century B.C.E. The Bible tells his story in the First and Second Book of Kings. His zealous opposition to idol worship led Elijah into bitter conflict with King Ahab and Queen Jezebel. Jezebel, a Phoenician princess, came from a country that worshiped Baal. Ahab built a temple for her god in Israel so that people could worship both Baal and the God of Israel. The struggle between Elijah and the royal house reached a peak when Elijah challenged the prophets of Baal to a showdown at Mount Carmel.

Elijah said, "'How long will you keep hopping between two opinions? If the Lord is God, follow him; and if Baal, follow him!' But the people answered him not a word" (I Kings 18:21).

Elijah designed the ultimate test to reveal the true God. He and 450 of Baal each brought animals to sacrifice. The true god would cause fire from heaven to consume the sacrifices.

The prophets of Baal prayed and called to their god, but nothing happened. "Elijah mocked them, saying, 'Shout louder! After all, he is a god. But he may be in conversation, he may be detained, or he may be on a journey, or perhaps he is asleep and will wake up.' So they shouted louder, and gashed themselves with knives and spears, according to their practice, until blood streamed over them" (I Kings 18:27–28). Still nothing.

Then Elijah prepared his sacrifice. "Then the fire from the Lord descended and consumed the burnt offering . . . When they saw this, all the people flung themselves on their faces and cried out: 'The Lord, alone is God; the Lord, alone is God.' Then Elijah said to them, 'Seize the prophets of Baal; let not a single one of them get away.' They seized them, and Elijah brought them down to the [brook] of Kishon and slaughtered them there" (I Kings 18:38–40).

When Jezebel found out that Elijah ordered the people to kill the prophets of Baal she tried to hunt him down and kill him. Despite the miracle at Mount Carmel, many of the people sided with Jezebel. Feeling abandoned and full of despair, Elijah wanted to die. God told him to journey through the desert for forty days and forty nights to Mount Horeb (another name for Mount Sinai). When he arrived, Elijah went into a cave and spent the night.

The word of the Lord came to him. He said to him, "Why are you here, Elijah?" He replied, "I am moved by zeal for the Lord, the God of Hosts, for the Israelites have forsaken Your covenant, torn down Your altars, and put Your prophets to the sword. I alone am left, and they are out to take my life." "Come out," He called, "and stand on the mountain before the Lord." And lo, the Lord passed by. There was a great and mighty wind, splitting mountains and shattering rocks by the power of the Lord; but the Lord was not in the wind. After the wind—an earthquake; but the

Lord was not in the earthquake. After the earthquake—fire; but the Lord was not in the fire. And after the fire—a still, small voice.

—I KINGS 19:9–12

Realizing that great fiery miracles don't necessarily produce lasting spiritual change, Elijah understood that closeness to God comes more easily through an intimate, quiet, personal encounter. Elijah's spirit revived. God told Elijah to anoint a new king over Israel and to train Elisha to become the Prophet's eventual successor.

Together they continued the fight against idol worship. By the time Elijah had grown old, Elisha had become a wise and powerful prophet. At the Jordan River, "Elijah took his mantle and, rolling it up, he struck the water; it divided to the right and left, so that the two of them crossed over on dry land . . . As they kept on walking and talking, a fiery chariot with fiery horses suddenly appeared and separated one from the other; and Elijah went up to heaven in a whirlwind. Elisha saw it and cried out, 'My father, my father, the chariot of Israel, and its horsemen!'" (II Kings 2:12).

Over the centuries, Elijah became a great hero of Jewish lore and legend. In rabbinic tales, Elijah frequently offered his opinions on the intricacies of Jewish law. When legal questions were too difficult for the sages to resolve, they said, "Let the matter stand" (*teiku*). This was said to mean "the Tishbite (Elijah) will resolve difficulties and problems," or *Tishbi yetaretz kushyot u-va'ayot* (the first letter of each word spells *teiku*).

Elijah also returned to help the sages at difficult points in their lives. Some of these tales involve Rabbi Akiva and his teacher Rabbi Eliezer, two of the most important sages mentioned in the Haggadah.

Rabbi Akiva could afford only a bed of straw for Rachel, his new bride, to sleep upon. Elijah appeared before their hut dressed as a beggar, crying out for a bit of straw for *his* wife's bed.[14] Seeing that, Akiva and Rachel felt better about sleeping on straw. And it was Elijah who appeared to Eliezer and convinced him to leave the family farm and pursue his dream of studying Torah in Jerusalem. When Rabbi Eliezer died, Rabbi Akiva, his student, began his eulogy with these words, *"My father, my father, the chariot of Israel, and its horsemen."*[15] And when Akiva died at the hands of Hadrian's torturers, Elijah bore his body to a burial cave and thence to "the heavenly academy."[16]

Jewish tradition gradually transformed Elijah from a zealot to a peacemaker. No longer the slayer of heathen prophets, Elijah comes to give us hope and direction when we stand at the crossroads and, most important, brings peace and healing to a broken world.

Rabbi Joshua said, "Elijah will not come to judge between those who are ritually clean or unclean, but to remove those who have come to power through force and to bring near those who have been cast away by force. . . ." The sages say neither to remove nor to bring near, but to make peace in the world. For it is said, "Lo, I will send to you Elijah the Prophet before the coming of the awesome, fearful day of the Lord. And he shall turn the heart of the parents to the children and the hearts of the children to their parents . . ." (the Mishnah, Eduyot 8:7, quoting Malachi 3:23–24).

Tonight we pray that Elijah will help us resolve our disputes with one another; enable us to open our hearts to one another; and bring peace to Israel, to her neighbors, and to all places filled with fear and hatred.

- Why do you think Jewish tradition transformed Elijah from a zealot to a peacemaker?

- What is the meaning of the idea that messianic times are associated with Elijah's turning "the heart of the parents to the children and the hearts of the children to their parents"?

- Ancient midrashim and contemporary scholars alike have discovered many similarities between Elijah and Moses.[18] How many parallels can you find between their careers? How might you explain these similarities? How are Moses and Elijah different?

THE ELIJAH PUZZLE

You may want to read this yourself, or you can use it as the basis for a discussion.
Read the two paragraphs below and then ask your guests this question:
Why do you think that Elijah, of all the figures in the Bible, became the
most popular figure in Jewish folklore? You may want to bring some
of the answers to the question below into the discussion.

Why Elijah became the most popular figure in Jewish folklore has puzzled more
than a few scholars. Of all the biblical figures who could have laid claim to this
role, Elijah seems one of the least likely. A man whose family the Bible never
mentions, Elijah even reacts coldly when Elisha, his newly chosen disciple, wants
to kiss his father and mother good-bye before starting his apprenticeship with the
prophet (I Kings 19: 20).[19] Elijah was overly zealous, a champion of God rather
than of his people. And for this, the third-century midrash, the *Mekhilta of Rabbi
Ishmael,* chides him:

> Thus you find that there were three types of prophets. One [Jeremiah]
> insisted upon the honor due the Father [God] as well as the honor due
> the son [Israel]; one [Elijah] insisted upon the honor due the Father
> without insisting upon the honor due the son; one [Jonah] insisted
> upon the honor due the son without insisting upon the honor due the
> Father . . . Elijah insisted upon the honor due the Father, but did not
> insist on the honor due the son, as it is said: "And he [explained to God
> why he had fled to Mount Horeb, saying] I am moved by the zeal for
> the Lord, the God of Hosts, for the Israelites have forsaken Your
> covenant. . . ."[20]

So how did Elijah become the superhero of Jewish folklore?

Elijah's qualifications for this role are rooted in the Bible. Along with Enoch
(Gen. 5:21–24), Elijah is one of the two figures the Bible describes as having risen
directly to heaven without dying. "A fiery chariot with fiery horses suddenly
appeared . . . and Elijah went up to heaven in a whirlwind" (II Kings 2:11). And
this certainly must have caught the eye of the author of Malachi (sixth century
B.C.E.), who envisioned God sending down the errant Elijah "before the coming

of the great and awesome day of the Lord" (Malachi 3:22).

Yet scholars believe that this alone does not account for Elijah's folkloric status. Here are several other explanations.

- Enoch had been so strongly identified with non-Jewish apocalypticism that Jewish tradition sought to downplay his significance by elevating that of Elijah.[21]

- Elijah's unusual role is a function of his unique name, in Hebrew *Eliyahu* (אֵלִיָּהוּ) It is the only name in the Bible that includes the two divine names: El, as in Elohim (God), and YHWH (Lord), doubling the *hey*.[22] Befitting his name, Elijah, in the contest with the prophets of Baal, calls on God to demonstrate that "YHWH is Elohim" (I Kings 18:37). Jewish thought has long accorded the creation and continued existence of the world to a balance between the divine attributes of judgment associated with Elohim and the mercy associated with YHWH. The Elijah of legend uniquely combines these.[23] Tales of Elijah often depict him bestowing mercy upon the down and out and judgment upon the high and mighty.

- Elijah's special role at ceremonies such as circumcision and the Passover Seder serves as a kind of punishment for his excessive zeal. Elijah complained to God that the people of Israel had abandoned the covenant (*brit*) and, except for *himself,* they had all turned to idol worship. Joseph Telushkin teaches that "he who sees himself as the last Jew is fated to bear constant witness to the eternity of Israel, to be present when every male Jewish child enters the covenant, and when every Jewish family celebrates the Seder . . . Elijah stands in a long line of despairing Jews who erroneously have prophesied the end of the Jewish people."[24]

- "Elijah confronts the age-old choice between faithfulness to, and betrayal of, the ancient covenant, and he is alone during that confrontation. This is the crisis-situation of every prophet in Israel. It is, moreover, the situation of every Jew in extremis, when, looking around for allies in his desperate struggle for survival in faithfulness, he finds, like Elijah, none but the God of the covenant Himself."[25] It is the universalism of Elijah's choice and the uniqueness of his response—his willingness to subject God to a win or lose test—that makes Elijah Judaism's hero par excellence.

MODELING THE POTENTIAL TO CHANGE

Read the following passage aloud.

Let's consider one more way to understand Elijah's unrivaled folkloric status. Elijah's ascent to heaven without dying endows him, of course, with certain qualities of eternality. Yet it's ironic that Elijah of all people achieves eternal life—ironic because, after fleeing the troops Jezebel has sent to kill him, Elijah implores God to *take* his life. God eventually refuses the request and tells Elijah to "go, return [*shuv*] toward Damascus. . . ." (I Kings 19:15) and to find a disciple. The midrash explains God's displeasure with Elijah: "Elijah ought to have gone to the place in which his forefathers stood [Horeb, another name for Sinai] and prayed for mercy for Israel; he did not do so. God said to him, 'You have prayed for yourself; go return [*shuv*] toward Damascus. . . .'"[26] God is telling Elijah that his career as a prophet is drawing to a close, so he must change course. God instructs Elijah, the religious zealot, to do *teshuvah*, to abandon his self-righteousness and turn back to the world of ordinary human beings.

In terms of his own spiritual journey, Elijah has not reached the end of the road. In fact, he never will. But he knows where he's headed—back to humanity, over and over again. Eternal life assures Elijah plenty of time to ponder and mend his ways. By messianic times, Elijah, who seems to have had such little understanding of relations between parents and children, will become the one who brings about parent-child reconciliation: "And he shall turn [*heyshiv*, from the same root as *shuv*] the heart of the parents to the heart of the children, and the heart of the children to their parents . . ." (Malachi 3:24).

Elijah's story epitomizes the potential for eternal growth and change. Elijah makes the long journey from misanthrope to philanthrope. The prophet who once rejected humanity continuously reappears to enlighten those who have lost their way, to aid the weak and vulnerable. It's not punishment. It's a privilege. Elijah remembers what it was like to be lost, to feel all alone, to feel stuck in a narrow place [*maytzar, Mitzrayim,* Egypt]. He knows the heart of the stranger, because he was one. Elijah embodies the transformation of painful memories into godly behavior: "God . . . upholds the cause of the fatherless and the widow, and befriends the stranger, providing him with food and clothing. You too shall befriend the stranger, for you were strangers in the land of Egypt" (Deut. 10:17–20). Having overcome the bitterness of his own isolation, Elijah makes helping the downtrodden his mission. "Elijah becomes the Jewish alter-ego, the symbol for the whole people; exiled and tortured, but alive and hopeful."[27]

Redemption may involve salvation from external sources of oppression, but it also involves our own spiritual journey toward ultimate truth. Elijah's transformation reminds everyone around the Seder table that we, too, are free to continue our journeys.

Menachem Mendel (1787–1859), the Hasidic Rebbe of Kotsk, said, "We err if we believe that Elijah the Prophet comes through the door. Rather he must enter through our hearts and souls."[28]

THE MIRROR: A TALE OF ELIJAH AND THE SEDER

The Israel Folktale Archives at Haifa University has collected close to six hundred stories about Elijah the Prophet, more than any other figure. Read the following tale aloud at your Seder and discuss the questions below.

A pious and wealthy Jew asked his rabbi, "For about forty years I have opened the door for Elijah every Seder night waiting for him to come, but he never does. What is the reason?" The rabbi answered, "In your neighborhood there lives a very poor family with many children. Call on the man and propose to him that you and your family celebrate the next Passover in his house, and for this purpose provide him and his whole family with everything necessary for the eight Passover days. Then on the Seder night Elijah will certainly come." The man did as the rabbi told him, but after Passover he came to the rabbi and claimed that again he had waited in vain for Elijah. The rabbi answered: "I know very well that Elijah came on the Seder night to the house of your poor neighbor. But of course you could not see him." And the rabbi held a mirror before the face of the man and said, "Look, this was Elijah's face that night."[29]

• What is this tale's message about how to bring the Messiah?

• What is the significance of the fact that the man has been waiting for forty years for Elijah to come?

• How should this revelation of Elijah influence the wealthy man?

• If acting according to the attributes of Elijah reveals the prophet, does acting according to the attributes of God reveal God?

"POUR OUT YOUR WRATH" VERSUS "GIVE UP ANGER"

Here we contrast two alternatives for the passage to be read while opening the door for Elijah. Read the paragraphs that follow and lead a discussion on the questions below.

According to traditional Haggadot, upon completing the blessing after the meal and before reciting Psalm 115, it is customary to recite a passage that begins, "Pour out Your wrath. . . ." This was added to the Haggadah in the Middle Ages, possibly during the period of the Crusades, a time of great suffering for European Jewry. According to Ashkenazic tradition, it is customary to recite these words upon opening the door for Elijah the Prophet, herald of the Messiah. In modern times, various Haggadot have omitted some or all of this passage or have offered alternative readings.

In addition to the traditional passage, *The Open Door*, a Haggadah published by the Reform Movement, includes the alternative below. Note that in traditional Haggadot, the first passage functions as an introduction to the remainder of the Hallel (Psalms 115–118), which in part addresses themes of God's punishing Israel's idol-worshiping enemies and subsequently redeeming Israel.

From the traditional Haggadah:

Pour out Your wrath upon the nations that do not know You, upon the governments which do not call upon Your name. For they have devoured Jacob and desolated his home. Pour out Your wrath on them; may Your blazing anger overtake them, destroy them from under the heavens of the Lord.

—PSALMS 79:6–7, 69:25, AND LAMENTATIONS 3:66

From *The Open Door:*

Give up anger, abandon fury, put aside your wrath; it can only harm. The call to violence shall no longer be heard in your land, nor the cry of desolation within your borders. If your enemy is hungry, give him bread to eat. If she is thirsty, give her water to drink. For when compassion and truth meet, justice and peace kiss.

—PSALMS 37:8, ISAIAH 60:18, PROVERBS 25:21, AND PSALMS 85:11[30]

- Which of these passages do you prefer as a reading for opening the door for Elijah? Why?

- Are there times when it might be appropriate to vent, at least verbally, one's vengeful feelings? Similarly, are there situations in which it is unrealistic and unhealthy to "give up anger" and to feed your enemy?

- How do these passages relate to the Talmudic dictum (Sanhedrin 72a), "If one comes to kill you, rise up early to kill him?"

- Given our world today, are we better served by calling on God to support us as we strike down our enemies or as we give them bread to eat? Is there a time when both might be appropriate?

23

The Exodus from Egypt: The Question of Archeology

וַיִּבֶן עָרֵי מִסְכְּנוֹת לְפַרְעֹה אֶת־פִּתֹם וְאֶת־רַעַמְסֵס.

And they built garrison cities for Pharaoh: Pithom and Ramses (Exodus 1:11).
—THE PASSOVER HAGGADAH

In 2001, David Wolpe, a Conservative rabbi from Los Angeles, delivered a Passover sermon that many found shocking. He interpreted the holiday in light of the fact that most archeologists believe that if there were an Exodus at all, it bore little resemblance to the biblical version of the story.

After more than a century of research, archeologists have found no record of an identifiable Israelite population that resided in ancient Egypt during the period when the Exodus was to have occurred. Nor have they uncovered in the desert any of the expected remains of a migration involving a large number of people over a forty-year period. Moreover, questions have emerged about whether the people of Israel developed outside the land of Canaan, invaded that territory, and then made it their home. Recent discoveries have led many archeologists to conclude that Israel may have emerged predominantly, though not exclusively, from *within* the land of Canaan.

In this chapter, we'll take a brief look at the Exodus as a story and as history, then examine five approaches to understanding the meaning of the saga in light of questions concerning its historical accuracy.

- What difference, if any, does it make if we relate to the Exodus as a story rather than as history?

- Can the underlying truths of the biblical Exodus remain valid even if we question the historical nature of certain elements of the story?

- What are the story's most significant truths or lessons?

- Why might we feel more comfortable questioning the literal claim that God created the heavens and the earth in six days than questioning the historical truth of the biblical Exodus?

HISTORY AND STORY

Depending on the nature of your group, you may want to take
turns reading aloud what follows. Ask your guests to keep the above
questions in mind and, if you have not already done so,
discuss them when you finish the reading.

My father was a wandering Aramean. He went down to Egypt few in numbers and sojourned there; but there he became a great and very populous nation. The Egyptians dealt harshly with us and oppressed us; they imposed heavy labor upon us (Deut. 26:5–6). So they set taskmasters over them to oppress them with forced labor; and they built garrison cities for Pharaoh: Pithom and Ramses . . . (Ex. 1:11). Pharaoh decreed, "You shall no longer provide the people with straw for making bricks . . ." (Ex. 5:7).

Like many great epics, the story of the Exodus may well contain core facts, however distantly remembered or artfully refracted. Although archeologists have questioned certain elements of the tale, they have also discovered evidence of some events that probably did occur.[1]

There is evidence that in ancient times people from Canaan journeyed to Egypt, where they sold members of their families into slavery in exchange for grain during all-too-frequent famines. Some of those slaves actually rose to power and established the Hyksos Dynasty that ruled Egypt from 1800 to 1550 B.C.E. Its capital was near Goshen, where Jacob and his family of shepherds reportedly settled. The Hyksos were remembered in Egyptian lore as "shepherd kings." The Hyksos were driven from power and exiled by a Pharaoh named Ahmose; one inscription accused the Hyksos of "ruling without Ra," the Egyptian sun god. Moses' name, which means "begotten" or "brought forth," is clearly Egyptian and resembles the names of many pharaohs—Ahmose, begotten by the moon, Ramses, begotten by the sun god, and so on.

A few centuries later, ancient sources report the devastation Egypt suffered when one of its Pharaohs attempted to force monotheism upon the Egyptians: "The temples of the gods and goddesses were desolated . . . their holy places were about to disintegrate having become rubbish heaps . . . The land was in grave disease. The gods have forsaken this land."[2] The epidemic that swept Egypt was called the "Canaanite" illness.

About a hundred years after this religious revolution was reversed, Ramses II embarked upon a massive construction campaign, conscripting large numbers of Semitic slaves to carry it out. He rebuilt the ancient Hyksos capital, renamed it Ramses, and erected a store city at Pithom. One tomb painting from an earlier period depicts Canaanite slaves making bricks and complaining about the absence of straw, as described in Exodus.[3]

A papyrus from this era speaks of the nighttime escape into the desert of a small number of slaves from Pharaoh's palace. It also includes orders to the border guards to retrieve them. There may well have been similar escapes by other small groups of slaves.

The Bible's account of the Israelites' wandering in the desert describes their yearning for "the cucumbers, the melons, the leeks, the onions, and the garlic" they ate for free in Egypt (Num. 11:5). Writing in about 440 B.C.E., Herodotus, the Greek historian, recorded a now-lost inscription he observed on the base a pyramid built more than a thousand years before the traditional dating of the Exodus: "There is a notice in Egyptian script on the pyramid about how much was spent on radishes, onions, and garlic for the laborers. . . ."[4]

Thus, the story of the Exodus may be "true" in the sense that its general contour and many of its details correlate to real events that happened to real people. But those people may not have been Israelites, and the scale of those events may have been far smaller than that recounted in the Bible.

So how did the Exodus from Egypt become an Israelite story? Imagine that over the centuries countless numbers of Canaanites went down into Egypt as slaves and gradually identified their hopes with legends of the Hyksos slaves who rose to rule Egypt. Those old Hyksos tales were slowly interwoven with the stories of more recent migrants who became slaves to Pharaoh. Later, small groups of these slaves repeatedly escaped into the desert, where they encountered followers of YHWH.

This "Exodus group" brought their memories and stories north, where they found favor in the eyes of Israelites. They told of their slavery in Egypt, of plagues brought by God upon the Egyptians, of their miraculous escape to the desert. They told of the encounter with their new God, YHWH, who had brought them forth and whom they had come to revere. The Israelites who heard these memories were a people composed mostly of migrants to hilltop towns from Canaanite cities that had fallen on hard times. They had already known Egypt's domineering hand and were no strangers to the cycle of famine and servitude. As the eminent scholar Baruch Halpern concludes, "Small wonder [the Israelites] were also the most receptive to a cult myth [brought by the Exodus group] conditioned on the assumption of escaping bondage to the Egyptians."[5]

FIVE SAGE PERSPECTIVES ON THE EXODUS AND HISTORY

Given that the biblical narrative of the Exodus cannot be read as a history book, how are we to relate to our founding story? It's a question that deserves an answer. Below you'll find five responses. Choose one or two to read aloud for discussion.

When I read the Haggadah on the eve of Passover . . . the spirit of Moses . . . hovers before me and lifts me out of this nether world . . . I care not whether this man Moses really existed; whether his life and its activity really corresponded to our traditional account of him; whether he was really the savior of Israel and gave his people the Torah in the form in which it is preserved among us and so forth . . . We have another Moses of our own, whose image has been enshrined in the hearts of the Jewish people for generations, and whose influence on our national life has never ceased from ancient times to the present day . . . For even if you succeeded in demonstrating conclusively that the man Moses never existed, or that he was not such a man as we supposed, you would not thereby detract one jot from the historical reality of the ideal Moses—the Moses who has been our leader not only for forty years in the wilderness of Sinai, but for thousands of years in all the wildernesses in which we have wandered since the Exodus.

—AHAD HA-'AM ("ONE OF THE PEOPLE"), PEN NAME OF ASHER HIRSCH GINSBERG (1856–1927), HEBREW ESSAYIST AND ZIONIST LEADER[6]

There can be no certainty of arriving . . . at "what really happened." However, even if it is impossible to reconstitute the course of the events themselves, it is nevertheless possible to recover much of the manner in which the people participating experienced those events. We become acquainted with the meeting between this people and a vast historical happening that overwhelmed it. We become conscious of the saga-creating ardor with which the people received the tremendous event and transmitted it to a molding memory . . . The meeting of a people with events so enormous that it cannot ascribe them to its own plans and their realization, but must perceive in them deeds performed by heavenly powers, is of the genuine substance of history. Insofar as the saga begins near the event, it is the outcome and record of this meeting.

—MARTIN BUBER (1878–1965), PHILOSOPHER, THEOLOGIAN, AND ZIONIST LEADER[7]

The biblical appeal to remember . . . has little to do with curiosity about the past. Israel is told only that it must be a kingdom of priests and a holy people (Ex. 19:6); nowhere is it suggested that it become a nation of historians . . . It is above all God's acts of intervention in history, and man's responses to them, be they positive or negative, that must be recalled . . . For the real danger is not so much that what happened in the past will be forgotten, as the more crucial aspect of *how* it happened. "And it shall be, when the Lord your God shall bring you into the land which He swore unto your fathers, to Abraham, to Isaac, and to Jacob, to give you great and goodly cities, which you did not build, and houses full of all good things, which you did not fill, and cisterns hewn out, which you did not hew, vineyards and olive-trees, which you did not plant, and you shall eat and be satisfied—then beware lest you forget the Lord who brought you out of the land of Egypt, out of the house of bondage [*beit avadim*]" (Deut. 6:10–12).

—YOSEF HAYIM YERUSHALMI (1932–),
SCHOLAR OF MEDIEVAL AND
MODERN JEWISH HISTORY[8]

For generations, Pesach has been passed down as history: Moses, the ten plagues, the parting of the Sea of Reeds, the miraculous deliverance. Our ancestors recited the story of the Exodus to affirm their belief that it was true and to derive faith in the God who made it happen.

In our time, most of us tell the Seder tale as sacred story rather than as historical record; we are skeptical of miracles; we are troubled by the moral implications of plague and punishment; and we seek a God commensurate with our enlarged vision of the liberation of all peoples.

Is this story true? No, not if we mean an accurate account of events that happened more or less the way they are told. But our ancestors, those who wrote the Bible and those who wrote the Haggadah, did not write history; they wrote of their experience of a Power greater than themselves that stood for freedom and against oppression.

They used myth and poetic language, couched in the context of their world of experience.

We do not live in that world, but we are the extension of the family that the Exodus created—the Jewish people. We do not tell the story of the Exodus because it is historically accurate; we tell the story because it is *our* story and we need to recover and uncover the eternal ideas that this story conveys. We take this story seriously but not literally. Pesach is the way the Jewish people celebrate, affirm, wrestle with, and work for freedom as our human destiny.

—RABBI RICHARD HIRSH (1953–), DIRECTOR
OF THE RECONSTRUCTIONIST
RABBINICAL ASSOCIATION[9]

Why should a rabbi come before a congregation on the first day of Passover and say the story you told last night at the Seder might be just a story? There is only one good reason and nothing else will justify it. It is that our rabbis insist that the seal of God is truth and that you do not serve God if you do not seek truth. It is no honor to the God who created our minds not to use them . . . If you want to pray to God you want to pray out of your faith, which means a combination of your reason and your emotion, out of the depths of your soul, and you cannot do that by closing your eyes. . . .

The story that you told at your Seder has inspired people who were searching for freedom and liberation for thousands of years. And the paradox of it is that they searched for freedom and for liberation so that they could proclaim truth, not hide it—so that their spirit could soar, so that they could be free, so they could build their religion on a foundation of what is real, on the soil of what you find, not solely on the ground of their imaginations. Ralph Waldo Emerson . . . wrote that "God gives every human being a choice between truth and repose. Take one," he said, "you cannot have them both." And the Jewish people has never had repose. And we have never had it because we have always sought truth. *"Avadim hayinu l'pharaoh b'mitzrayim."* We were slaves to Pharaoh in Egypt. We know what it is to be slaves. We know what it is not to have freedom. That is true.

Does it matter if that sense comes to us from something that happened 3,000 years ago or 2,000 years ago? Not at all . . . I have never been in Egypt, but I know what it is to leave. If you sat at the Seder table and you felt like a slave, and you ate the matzah and you sang the songs and you were free by the time your Seder was over, then it is true. Then you don't need to be afraid of the findings of the scientists or the archeologists because in your soul it is true. Pesach has been proved true in virtually every generation of the Jewish people. Are there not people sitting in this congregation this morning who were, in a manner of speaking, slaves, and sitting here this morning are free? Don't tell me that Pesach is not true.

—RABBI DAVID WOLPE (1958–), CONSERVATIVE RABBI
AND SPIRITUAL LEADER OF SINAI TEMPLE IN WEST LOS ANGELES,
IN AN EXCERPT FROM HIS SERMON ON THE
FIRST DAY OF PASSOVER, 2001[10]

Abraham Joshua Heschel wrote, "As a report about revelation the Bible itself is *a midrash*," not a text "in systematic theology."[11] The same can be said about the Bible as a report about history. Its intent is to teach the deepest truths of the human spirit, not to serve as a textbook of ancient history. What does the biblical Exodus want us to learn? That we must never lose faith that evil can be overcome, no matter how deeply entrenched; that the struggle for freedom is intrinsically worthy; that though we may feel terribly weak in the face of adversity, on the most fundamental level we are not alone; and that it is our responsibility to use memories of our suffering not to inflict our wounds on others, but to build a more just world.

Proving the historical truth of the Exodus depends on digging up tangible artifacts from the ground. Discovering the spiritual truths of the Exodus depends on opening your heart to the story.

APPENDIX I
—
CHAPTER TEN OF MISHNAH PESACHIM, THE NIGHT OF PASSOVER[1]

The Mishnah was compiled in about 200 C.E. by Judah the Prince. It contains the oldest description of how Passover was celebrated following the destruction of the Second Temple in 70 C.E.

Depending on your group, you might consider reading this aloud before your Seder. Make a copy for each of your guests. Read each mishnah and ask for one or two reactions or comments. Note that the Mishnah does not make clear distinctions between the Passover offering that occurred prior to the Temple's destruction and the Passover Seder that replaced the sacrificial offering.

- What does it feel like to read these ancient instructions of the Passover Haggadah?
- What seem to be the major differences between the Mishnah and the Haggadah?

Mishnah 10:1 On the eve of Passover, close to [the time of] *minchah* [the daily afternoon offering], a person should not eat until it gets dark. Even a poor person in Israel should not eat until [he] reclines. [Those who serve] should not give him fewer than four cups of wine even if [the funds] come from the charity plate.

Mishnah 10:2 [They] poured for him the first cup [of wine]. The House of Shammai say, "[He] says the blessing over the day [the festival] and afterward [he] says the blessing over the wine." And the House of Hillel say, "[He] says the blessing over the wine and afterward [he] says the blessing over the day."

Mishnah 10:3 [They] served—[he] dips the lettuce [*chazeret*, the vegetable used for the bitter herbs] before he reaches the bread condiment. [They] served him unleavened bread and lettuce and *charoset,* even though the *charoset* is not a [biblical] commandment. And in the Temple [they] serve him the carcass of the Passover offering.

Mishnah 10:4 [They] poured for him the second cup—and here the child asks, and if the child lacks intelligence, his father instructs him. How is this night different from all [other] nights? For on all the [other] nights we dip once, this night twice. For on all the [other] nights we eat leavened and unleavened bread, this night we eat only unleavened. For on all the [other] nights we eat meat roasted, steamed, or cooked [in a liquid, boiled], this night only roasted. According to the child's intelligence, his father instructs him. [He] starts [reading] with the disgrace [section of the Bible] and ends with glory; and [he] expounds from, "My father was a wandering Aramean" [Deut. 26:5], until he finishes the entire portion.

Mishnah 10:5 Rabban Gamaliel said, "Whoever did not say these three things on Passover did not fulfill his obligation: *Pesach* [the Passover offering], *matzah* [unleavened bread], and *merorim* [bitter herbs]." *Pesach*—because the Omnipresent skipped over the house of our ancestors in Egypt. *Merorim*—because the Egyptians embittered the lives of our ancestors in Egypt. *Matzah*—because they were redeemed. Therefore we are obligated to give thanks, to praise, to glorify, to crown, to exalt, to elevate the One who did for us all these miracles and took us from slavery to freedom, and let us say before him: Hallelujah [Psalm 113].

Mishnah 10:6 Up to what point does he recite [the Hallel]? The House of Shammai say, "Until 'as a happy mother of children'" [the end of Psalm 113]. And the House of Hillel say, "Until 'the flinty rock into a fountain'" [the end of Psalm 114]. And [he] seals with redemption. [He ends with a blessing formula with the motif of redemption.] Rabbi Tarfon says, "Who has redeemed us and redeemed our ancestors from Egypt and brought us to this night"—and [he] does not seal [with a concluding formula]. Rabbi Akiva says, "[One adds to the blessing:] 'Thus O Lord, our God and God of our ancestors, bring us in peace to the approaching festivals which are coming to meet us, happy in the building of Your city [so as] to eat from the Passover and festive offerings whose blood will reach the wall of Your altar with favor, and let us thank You for our redemption. Praised are You, O Lord, Who redeemed [or "redeems"] Israel.'"

Mishnah 10:7 [They] poured for him the third cup [of wine]—[he] says the blessing over his food. [At] the fourth [cup]—[he] finishes the Hallel [through Psalm 118] and says over it the blessing over the song. Between the four cups, if [he] wants to drink [further] he may drink. Between the third and the fourth, [he] should not drink.

Mishnah 10:8 After [eating from] the Passover offering, [they] do not end with *afikomen* [revelry]. [If they] fell asleep: [if it was] some of them—[they] may eat [again because the remaining individuals of the group, who stayed awake, maintained the group] and [if it was] all of them—[they] may not eat [again]. Rabbi Yossi says, "If [they] dozed—[they] may eat [again]. And if [they] slumbered—[they] may not eat [again]."

Mishnah 10:9 The concluding mishnah addresses the appropriate recitation of blessings for the Passover and festival offerings in Temple times.

APPENDIX II

—

WHAT IS MIDRASH?

From ancient to modern times, midrash has embodied one of Judaism's most vibrant modes of wisdom, wondering, and creativity. The term derives from the biblical Hebrew *lidrosh*—"to search," "to seek," "to examine," or "to investigate." Later, midrash (plural: midrashim) came to signify elaboration with the intent of discovering deeper meanings or new questions behind the plain meaning of the text. The Haggadah abounds with midrash. Its phrase-by-phrase elaboration on Deuteronomy 26:5–8 ("My father was a wandering Aramean . . .") is a classic example. The debate among Rabbis Yossi the Galilean, Eliezer, and Akiva about the "true" number of plagues visited upon the Egyptians is another. Often midrash uses one biblical text to interpret another, in the process shedding new light on both. As you might expect, the miraculous events surrounding the Exodus from Egypt became the focus of enormous midrashic speculation. But remember: Midrash is meant to make a point, to stretch your thinking, not necessarily to be taken literally.

APPENDIX III

—

DIRECTIONS FOR ART MIDRASH PROJECTS

Midrash involves the process of uncovering new meaning in familiar texts or concepts. Here you can use a simple art project to explore what particular ideas or passages from the Haggadah mean to your Seder participants. Try this before your Seder begins. Distribute sheets of colored paper and glue sticks to each of your guests. Some scissors would be helpful but are not necessary.

Read aloud the particular passage that will serve as the basis for your art midrash project. Ask everyone to spend about twenty minutes making a collage that expresses something important to him or her about an idea the passage raises.

Explain that the collages can be representational or completely abstract, using shape and color to express feelings of or about one of the transitions. When you have finished, ask a few of your guests to hold up their collages, one at a time. Ask others to make a brief comment on what they think the collage may be saying. Then ask the creator of the collage to explain what he or she had in mind. Remember, the goal of this art midrash project is to explore our ideas, not to see who is the "best" artist.

Those interested in learning more about this approach may want to look at Jo Milgrom's *Handmade Midrash* (Philadelphia: Jewish Publication Society, 1992).

APPENDIX IV

—

BLESSING FOR THE NEW MOON

To be recited when the moon can be seen clearly, preferably outdoors. This blessing may be recited until the point in the month when the moon begins to wane. (See chapter 7, note 19 for more details.) The first paragraph below is from the Talmud (Sanhedrin 42a) and dates from between the third and sixth centuries. The complete service for blessing the moon begins with Psalm 148:1–6. It concludes with Psalms 121, 150, a selection from the Talmud about the blessing and then Psalm 67.

Blessed are You, Lord our God, Sovereign of the universe, whose utterance created the heavens, the breath of His mouth all their hosts. Order and regularity He gave them so they will not deviate from their tasks. Joyfully and gladly they do the will of their Master, who does truth, whose deed is true. He told the moon to renew its crown of glory over those [He] sustained from the womb, so that like the moon, in the future, they too, will be renewed to glorify of His dominion. Blessed are you God, who renews the moons.

(*Recite the following verses three times.*)

Blessed is your Molder, blessed is your Maker, blessed is your Master, blessed is your Creator.

(*Stand on toes as if dancing when reciting this verse.*)

Just as I dance toward You but cannot touch you, so may all my enemies be unable to touch me with evil.

Terror and dread descend upon them; through the might of Your arm they are as still as stone (Ex. 15:16, from the song the Israelites sang after crossing the Red Sea).

David, King of Israel, lives and endures.*

(*Participants exchange greetings:*)

David melech Yisrael chai v'kayam.

Shalom aleikhem, peace be with you!

Aleikhem shalom, peace be with you!

(*Recite three times.*)

May we and all Israel have a favorable omen and good fortune. Amen.

Siman tov u'mazal tov y'hei lanu u'l'chol Yisrael. Amen.

Hark! My beloved! There he comes, leaping over the mountains, bounding over hills. My beloved is like a gazelle or like a young stag. There he stands behind our wall, gazing through the window, peering through the lattice (Song of Songs 2:8–9).**

---

* The Talmud (Rosh Hashanah 25a) attributes these words to Judah the Prince, compiler of the Mishnah. He used them as a watchword to verify that his order to sanctify the new moon had been carried out. In Psalms 89:36–38 God promises that rule of the House of David shall be as enduring as the sun and the moon.

** The Song of Songs—traditionally read following the Seder and subsequently in synagogue during the festival—is often interpreted as an allegory of God's love for the Jewish people that was revealed in the redemption from Egypt. Here, the passage expresses hope for the ultimate messianic redemption.

ABBREVIATIONS AND ABBREVIATED TITLES USED IN THIS BOOK
—

ABBREVIATIONS FOR BOOKS OF THE BIBLE

Genesis: Gen.

Exodus: Ex.

Leviticus: Lev.

Numbers: Num.

Deuteronomy: Deut.

Ecclesiastes: Eccl.

Joshua: Jos.

Jeremiah: Jer.

OTHER ABBREVIATIONS AND ABBREVIATED TITLES

BT: Babylonian Talmud.

EJ: *Encyclopedia Judaica*. Jerusalem: Keter Publishing House, 1972.

Etz Hayim: Etz Hayim Torah and Commentary. New York: The Rabbinical Assembly/The United Synagogue of Conservative Judaism, 2001.

Fox: *The Schocken Bible: The Five Books of Moses*. Translated by Everett Fox. New York: Schocken Books, 1995.

Hagadah Shelemah: Kasher, Menachem. *Hagadah Shelemah*. Jerusalem: Torah Shelemah Institute, 1967 (Hebrew).

Haggadah of the Sages: Safrai, Shmuel, and Safrai Ze'v. *The Haggadah of the Sages*. Jerusalem: Carta, 1998 (Hebrew).

Haggadah: Sources and History: Goldschmidt, E. Daniel. *The Passover Haggadah: Sources and History*. Jerusalem: The Bialik Institute, 1960 (Hebrew).

Legends: Ginzberg, Louis. *Legends of the Jews.* Philadelphia: Jewish Publication Society, 1968.

Mekhilta of Rabbi Ishmael: Mekhilta of Rabbi Ishmael. Translated by Jacob Z. Lauterbach. Philadelphia: Jewish Publication Society, 1949.

New Studies in Shemot: Leibowitz, Nehama. *New Studies in Shemot.* Jerusalem: The Joint Authority for Jewish Zionist Education, 1993.

Passover and Easter: Passover and Easter: Origin and History to Modern Times. Edited by Paul F. Bradshaw and Lawrence Hoffman. Notre Dame, Ind.: University of Notre Dame Press, 1999.

Pirke de Rabbi Eliezer: Friedlander, Gerald. *Pirke de Rabbi Eliezer.* New York: Sepher-Hermon Press, 1916; 1981.

Ramban: *Ramban (Nachmanides): Commentary on the Torah.* Translated by Charles B. Chavel. New York: Shilo Publishing House, 1973.

Scholar's Haggadah: Guggenheimer, Heinrich. *The Scholar's Haggadah.* Northvale, N.J.: Jason Aronson, 1998.

NOTES

—

Chapter 1—Long Road from Slavery to Freedom

1. *Haggadah: Sources and History,* pp. 7–9.
2. Isaac Mendelsohn, *Slavery in the Ancient Near East: A Comparative Study of Slavery in Babylonia, Assyria, Syria, and Palestine from the Middle of the Third Millennium to the End of the First Millennium* (New York: Oxford University Press, 1949), p. 1.
3. Antonia Loprieno, "Slaves," in *The Egyptians,* ed. Sergio Donadoni, trans. Robert Bianchi (Chicago: University of Chicago Press, 1997), p. 202.
4. Ibid. pp. 204–205.
5. Donald B. Redford, *Egypt, Canaan and Israel in Ancient Times* (Princeton: Princeton University Press, 1992), p. 209.
6. Loprieno, p. 208.
7. Moshe Weinfeld, *Social Justice in Ancient Israel and in the Ancient Near East* (Jerusalem: The Magnes Press/The Hebrew University, 1995), p. 142.
8. Chilperic Edwards, *The Hammurabi Code: And the Sinaitic Legislation,* 3rd ed. (London: Watts, 1921), paragraph 16.
9. BT, Gittin 45a, watered this down in the sense that the fugitive slave was to be brought to court and ordered to sign a promissory note to his former owner for the amount of that slave's value.
10. John Winthrop, "City on a Hill." On the web at www.mtholyoke.edu/acad/intrel/winthrop.htm. For clarity, the spelling of Winthrop's original speech has been rendered into modern English
11. Charles Chauncey, "A Discourse on the Good News from a Far Country," in *The Pulpit of the American Revolution: Or the Political Sermons of the Period of 1776,* ed. John Wingate Thornton (Boston: Gould and Lincoln, 1860), p. 129.
12. Letter from John Adams to Abigail Adams, August 14, 1776, in *The Adams Family Papers,* on the web at www.masshist.org/digitaladams/aea/letter/.

13. Articles I, section 2, and IV, section 2. Of note, the framers avoided using any form of the word "slave" in the Constitution.

14. Samuel Elliot Morrison, *The Oxford History of the American People,* vol. 1, (New York: Penguin Books, 1972), p. 384.

15. Abraham Lincoln, *His Speeches and Writings,* ed. Roy P. Basler (New York: Da Capo Press, 1946), p. 489.

16. Martin Luther King Jr., "The Quest for Justice," on the web at www.nobel.se/peace/laureates/1964/king-lecture.html.

17. This analysis reflects the influence of Michael Walzer, *Exodus and Revolution* (New York: Basic Books, 1985).

18. Frantz Fanon, *The Wretched of the Earth* (New York: Grove Press, 1961/1968), pp. 39, 53.

19. This analysis reflects the teachings of Rabbi Irving Greenberg, "Judaism as an Exodus Religion: Passover," in *The Jewish Way: Living the Jewish Holidays* (New York: Summit Books, 1988), chapter 2.

20. BT, Shabbat 31a.

21. See note 12.

22. Mary Prince, *History of Mary Prince, A West Indian Slave* (London: Westly and Davis, 1831), in *The Classic Slave Narratives,* ed. Henry Louis Gates Jr. (New York: Penguin Books, 1987), pp. 191, 214.

23. *The Union Kommando in Auschwitz,* ed. Lore Shelley (Lanham, Md.: University Press of America, 1996), pp. 83–84.

24. Available on the web at frwebgate.access.gpo.gov/cgi-bin/getdoc.cgi?dbname=106_senate_hearings&docid=f:69751.wais.

25. Aristotle, *Politics,* trans. Benjamin Jowett, book 3, part 4 on the web at www.eserver.org/philosophy/aristotle/politics.txt.

26. *The Historical Review of Pennsylvania,* attributed to Benjamin Franklin (Philadelphia: E. Olmsted and W. Power, 1812).

27. Abraham Lincoln, *His Speeches and Writings,* ed. Roy P. Basler (New York: Da Capo Press, 1946), p. 473.

28. Elizabeth Cady Stanton and Susan B. Anthony, *The Elizabeth Cady Stanton—Susan B. Anthony Reader: Correspondence, Writings, Speeches,* ed. Ellen Carol DuBois (Boston: Northeastern University Press, 1981), p. 154.

29. Mohandas K. Gandhi, *The Essential Gandhi: An Anthology,* ed. Louis Fischer (New York: Random House, 1962), pp. 165, 173.

30. David Ben-Gurion, *Netzach Yisrael* (Tel Aviv: Ayanot, 1964), p. 25. Quoted on p. 2 of "Israel's Grand Strategy: Ben-Gurion and Israel's Next Great Debate" by Shai Feldman, delivered at the Colloquium of the Woodrow Wilson International Center for Scholars, Washington, D.C., June 15, 1988.

31. Martin Luther King Jr., "The Birth of a New Nation," Montgomery, Alabama, on the web at www.mlkonline.com/mlkhome.html.

32. Nelson Mandela, *Long Walk to Freedom: The Autobiography of Nelson Mandela* (Boston: Little, Brown and Company, 1994), p. 554. Thanks to Nadera Shalhoub Keverkian for bringing this to my attention.

33. See EJ, vol. 6, pp. 51–55, under *"dina de-malkhuta dina."*

34. Bertram W. Korn, "Jews and Negro Slavery in the Old South, 1789–1865," in *Publications of the American Jewish Historical Society,* vol. 50, 1960–1961, pp. 198–199.

35. This question became controversial in the early 1990s, when publications of the Nation of Islam grossly exaggerated the Jewish role in slavery. See Eli Faber, *Jews, Slaves and the Slave Trade: Setting the Record Straight* (New York: New York University Press, 1998), and Saul S. Friedman, *Jews and the American Slave Trade* (New Brunswick, N.J.: Transaction Publishers, 1998).

36. Kevin Bales, *Disposable People: New Slavery in the Global Economy* (Berkeley: University of California Press, 1999). The American Anti-Slavery Group's "Modern Day Slavery Fact Sheet" is on the web at www.iabolish.com/today/factsheet.htm.

Chapter 2—The Four "Questions"

1. Sephardic and Yemenite Haggadot include the same questions in the following order: dipping, matzah, bitter herbs, reclining.

2. Nehama Leibowitz, *Studies on the Haggadah,* eds. Yitshak Reiner and Shmuel Peerless (New York: Lambda Publications, 2002), p. 29.

3. *Haggadah: Sources and History,* pp. 10–13. *Haggadah of the Sages,* pp. 112–115.

4. *Haggadah of the Sages,* p. 113.

5. *Abarbanel Haggadah,* ed. Shlomo Fox, trans. Yisrael Isser Zvi Herczeg (New York: Mesorah Publications, 1990), p. 31.

6. Plato, "The Symposium," in *The Works of Plato,* trans. Benjamin Jowett (New York: Modern Library, 1928), p. 338.

7. Quoted in Sigmund Stein, "The Influence of Symposia Literature on the Literary Form of the Pesach Haggadah," in *Journal of Jewish Studies,* vol. 8, nos 1 and 2, 1957,

p. 19. See also Baruch M. Bokser, "A Jewish Symposium?" in *The Origins of the Passover Seder* (Berkeley: University of California Press, 1984), chapter 5.

8. See Joseph Tabory, "Towards a History of the Paschal Meal," in *Passover and Easter,* pp. 67–68.

9. Bokser, "A Jewish Symposium?" p. 68.

10. Ibid., Appendix A: "Roasted Meat or Sacrifices after 70 C.E.?"

11. Tabory, "Towards a History," p. 71.

12. *Haggadah: Sources and History,* pp. 77–78. This manuscript is available online at oldsite.library.upenn.edu/cajs/geniza/ (See folio 4b for this question.)

Chapter 3—Two Haggadot in One

1. BT, Pesachim 116a. Rav and Shmuel's discussions on the Mishnah formed a central component of the Gemarah, which was compiled through about the year 500. Together, the Mishnah and the Gemarah comprise the Talmud. Actually, there are two Talmuds, one compiled in Babylonia and the other in the land of Israel. The version of Rav's statement that appears in the Haggadah uses a different term for idol worship (*avodah zarah*) than the standard Vilna edition of the Babylonian Talmud (*gilulim*). Manuscripts of the Talmud include many variations of the exchange between Rav and Shmuel, some attributing their positions to different sages. See *Hagadah Shelemah,* pp. 20 and 22.

2. The passage was added in the nineteenth century. See *Scholar's Haggadah,* p. 362.

3. The translation of the passage from Joshua follows that of the Davka Soncino Classics, CD-ROM version.

4. Genesis Rabbah 42:8, a midrash from the fifth century C.E.

Chapter 4—The Five Sages' Seder

1. Mishnah, Avot 2:12.

2. Mishnah, Avot 2:15; BT, Shabbat 153a.

3. Ecclesiastes Rabbah 5:4.

4. *The Fathers According to Rabbi Nathan,* trans. Judah Goldin (New Haven: Yale University Press, 1955), p. 74.

5. Ibid. p. 34.

6. Mishnah, Berachot 1:5.

7. Mishnah, Avot 2:21.

8. Mishnah, Makkot 1:10.

9. Jerusalem Talmud, Nedarim 9:4; Genesis Rabbah 34:14.

10. Song of Songs Rabbah 2:38.

11. BT, Berachot 61b.

12. BT, Sanhedrin 101a and 68a.

13. EJ, vol. 8, p. 351.

14. Rather than interrupt the conversation with footnotes, I've included all sources here. "Rabbi Akiva began" . . . Exodus Rabbah 1:12. "Rabbi Eliezer lamented" . . . Midrash Seder Eliyahu Rabbah, p. 151. "Akiva continued" . . . Song of Songs Rabbah 1:45. "Since the day that the Temple was destroyed" . . . Mishnah Sotah 9:12. "Suffering is precious". . . BT, Sanhedrin 101a. "Everything is foreseen" . . . Mishnah, Avot 3:19. "Rabbi Eliezer explained" . . . Midrash on Proverbs 13:3. "Rabbi Tarfon said" . . . Mishnah, Avot 2:21. "The entire Torah is based on justice" . . . Exodus Rabbah 30:19. "Then Moses returned" . . . Exodus Rabbah 5:22. "Rabbi Akiva then said something astounding" . . . Exodus Rabbah 5:22. "Master of the universe" . . . Midrash on Psalms 44:1. "Elijah will not come" . . . Mishnah Eduyot 8:7.

Chapter 5—The Four Children

1. Mishnah, Pesachim 10:4.

2. The four verses usually associated with the injunction to tell your children about the story of the Exodus are Ex. 12:26, 13:8, 13:14; and Deut. 6:20. However, Ex. 10:1–2 also contains a similar injunction that refers to God's hardening of Pharaoh's heart. The Haggadah's discomfort with this theme may account for the omission of this verse from its treatment of the Four Children. (See chapter 6.)

3. *Mekhilta of Rabbi Ishmael Piskha,* 18:118–131, vol. 1, pp. 166–167.

4. *Haggadah: Sources and History,* pp. 22–29; Jerusalem Talmud, Pesachim 10:4.

5. See *Haggadah: Sources and History,* pp. 22–29; *Scholar's Haggadah,* pp. 268–278. In a personal communication, Rabbi Burton L. Visotzky argues that *otanu* likely reflected an alternative, pre-Masoretic biblical text.

6. According to this view, the Seder was at one point a "messianic meal," the chief ritual of which was eating the *afikomen,* which some claim should be translated as "the coming one." This may have inspired the Eucharist. See David Daube, "He That Cometh," St. Paul's Lecture, October 1966 (an obscure publication, but an influential article).

7. Joseph Tabory, "Towards a History," in *Passover and Easter,* p. 73.

8. Abraham Joshua Heschel, *God in Search of Man* (New York: Farrar, Straus and Giroux, 1955), pp. 337, 341. Thanks to Rabbi Michael Paley for teaching me about Heschel's insight in relation to the Four Children.

9. Numbers Rabbah 8:4, a collection of midrashim from the ninth century C.E. or earlier.

10. *The Breslov Haggadah,* ed. Yehoshuah Starret (Jerusalem: Breslov Research Institute, 1989), p. 47.

11. Samson Raphael Hirsch, *The Collected Writings,* vol. 1 (New York: Phillip Feldheim, 1984), pp. 61–62.

12. Menachem M. Schneerson, *Likkutei Sichot: An Anthology of Talks,* vol. 3 (Brooklyn: Kehot Publication Society, 1987), pp. 110–119.

13. *The Journey Continues: The 1997 Ma'yan Passover Haggadah,* eds. Tamara Cohen, Sue Levi Elwell, Debbie Friedman, and Ronnie M. Horn (New York: Ma'yan: The Jewish Women's Project—The JCC of the Upper West Side, 1997), pp. 18–19.

Chapter 6—Hardening Pharaoh's Heart

1. The first section of this chapter uses the translation of the Pentateuch by Fox.

2. The Fox translation of the Pentateuch is faithful to the Hebrew, which actually uses variants of three distinct verbs to describe Pharaoh's emotional state. Some translations don't capture this nuance. Where Fox uses YHWH, I have substituted "Adonai," because it is easier to read aloud.

3. The identity of the fourth plague is unclear. The term *arov* literally means "mixture" and is generally interpreted as swarms of insects or wild beasts.

4. For modern Bible scholarship on this subject, see Brevard S. Childs, *The Book of Exodus: A Critical, Theological Commentary* (Philadelphia: Westminster Press, 1974), p. 174; David M. Gunn, "The 'Hardening of Pharaoh's Heart': Plot, Character and Theology in Exodus 1–14," in *Art and Meaning: Rhetoric in Biblical Literature,* eds. David J. A. Clines, David M. Gunn, and Alan J. Hauser (Yorkshire, U.K.: Sheffield, 1982), pp. 72–96. For a clear schematic analysis of this motif, see Walter C. Kaiser, *Toward Old Testament Ethics* (Grand Rapids, Mich.: Zondervan, 1983), pp. 252–256.

5. Maimonides, "The Eighth Chapter," in *Ethical Writings of Maimonides,* ed. Raymond L. Weiss (New York: Dover Publications, 1975), pp. 89–90.

6. Neil Gillman, *Sacred Fragments: Recovering Theology for the Modern Jew* (Philadelphia: Jewish Publication Society, 1990), p. 191.

7. *New Studies in Shemot (Exodus),* vol. 1, p. 156.

8. Aviva Gottlieb Zornberg, *The Particulars of Rapture: Reflections on Exodus* (New York: Doubleday, 2001), pp. 104–105.

9. Thanks to Rabbi Gordon Tucker bringing this text to my attention. The translation is Rabbi Tucker's. See Arnold B. Ehrlich, *Mikra Ki-Pheshuto: The Bible According to Its Literal Meaning,* vol. 1 (New York: KTAV Publishing House, 1969), p. 151 (Hebrew).

10. Jonah 4:11.

11. Jack Miles, *God: A Biography* (New York: Vintage Books, 1996).

12. *Pirke de Rabbi Eliezer,* pp. 341–342.

Chapter 7—The Festival of Spring

1. *Mekhilta of Rabbi Ishmael, Piskha* 17:100, vol. 1, p. 149. Passover often occurs on the first full moon after the vernal equinox, but due to the periodic insertion of an extra month into the Jewish calendar, it sometimes falls on the second full moon after the equinox.

2. Oded Borowski, *Agriculture in Iron Age Israel* (Winona Lake, Ind.: Eisenbrauns, 1987), p. 88.

3. Irving Greenberg, *The Jewish Way: Living the Holidays* (New York: Summit Books, 1988), p. 60.

4. Mirce Eliade, *The Myth of the Eternal Return* (New York: Pantheon Books, 1954), pp. 89, 95.

5. Stephen J. Gould, *Time's Arrow: Time's Cycle* (Cambridge: Harvard University Press, 1987), pp. 10–19.

6. Eliade, *The Myth of the Eternal Return,* p. 156

7. The blessing comes from BT, Sanhedrin 42a.

8. Mirce Eliade, *Patterns in Comparative Religion* (Cleveland: Meridian Books, 1963), pp. 155, 176.

9. Eliade, *The Myth of the Eternal Return,* p. 95.

10. Hayyim Schauss, *The Jewish Festivals: From Their Beginnings to Our Own Day,* (New York: Union of American Hebrew Congregations, 1938), p. 39.

11. Scholarly inquiry into the origins of Passover is in part derived from subtle variations in the description of the festival in the Bible. For a good overview of these differences see *Etz Hayim,* pp. 1456–1459.

12. See Schauss, *The Jewish Festivals,* pp. 38–43.

13. Borowski, *Agriculture in Iron Age Israel,* pp. 158–161.

14. J. B. Segal's *The Hebrew Passover: From the Earliest Times to A.D. 70* (London: Oxford University Press, 1963) provides the basis for this section on the relationship between Passover and ancient New Year's festivals.

15. Johannes Pedersen, *Israel: Its Life and Culture,* vols. 3 and 4 (London: Oxford University Press, 1940), p. 384.

16. See Glen J. Taylor, "Yahweh and the Sun: Biblical and Archeological Evidence for Sun Worship in Ancient Israel," in *Journal for the Study of the Old Testament: Supplement Series* 111 (1993): p. 91.

17. Commentary on BT, Pesachim 116a.

18. Eileen Abrams, "Grow Your Own—Barley, That Is!" in *Ecology and the Jewish Spirit: Where Nature and the Sacred Meet,* ed. Ellen Bernstein (Woodstock, Vt.: Jewish Lights Publishing, 1998), pp. 157–159.

19. According to Jewish law, it is permissible to recite the blessing over the new moon at any point in the month—when the full moon is clearly visible—until the full moon begins to wane. Due to the complexities of the Jewish calendar, the full moon sometimes occurs before the fifteenth of a Hebrew month. In that case, it would not be appropriate to recite the blessing for the new moon on Passover because the moon would already have begun to wane. The easiest way to make sure you can bless the new moon on the first Seder is to check Ezras Torah on the web at www.ezrastorah.org/nisan.htm.

20. *Kol Haneshamah: Shabbat Vehagim* (Wyncote, Pa.: The Reconstructionist Press, 1996), p. 332. This is actually only about half of the prayer.

21. BT, Shabbat 118b.

22. Philo, *The Special Laws,* vol. 7, ed. F. H. Colson (Cambridge: Harvard University Press, 1937), pp. 399–405.

23. Bachya ben Joseph Ibn Paquda, *Duties of the Heart,* trans. Moses Hyamson (Jerusalem: Boys Town Publishers, 1962), p. 171.

24. Maimonides, "Mishne Torah," in *A Maimonides Reader,* ed. Isadore Twersky (New York: Behrman House Publishers, 1972), pp. 45–46.

25. Rebbe Nachman of Breslav, "*Likkutei MoHaRan:* Rabbi Nachman's Wisdom," in *A Garden of Choice Fruit: 200 Classic Jewish Quotes on Human Beings and the Environment,* ed. David E. Stein (Wyncote, Pa.: Shomrei Adamah, 1991), p. 56.

26. Heschel, *God in Search of Man,* pp. 34, 36.

27. From the website of the Coalition for the Environment and Jewish Life, www.coejl.org/learn/je_schorsch.shtml.

Chapter 8—The Exodus as a Personal Spiritual Journey

1. See pages 36–38. This illustrates Rav's vision of where the journey leads—the end of days: a time of uninterrupted mystical cleaving to God.

2. See "Pathways of the Prophets—Life in the Fast Lane," an audiotape by Rabbi Yisrael Reisman (available through Yeshiva Tiferes Yisroel, 1271 East 35th Street, Brooklyn, NY 11210).

3. Isaiah Horowitz, *Shnei Luchot Ha-Brit, Matzah Shmurah,* 1. *Judaic Classics II.* Davka CD-ROM version (Hebrew).

4. Joel Ziff, *Mirrors in Time: A Psycho-Spiritual Journey through the Jewish Year* (Northvale, N.J.: Jason Aronson, 1996), p. 73.

5. *The Breslov Haggadah,* ed. Yehoshua Starret (Jerusalem: Breslov Research Institute, 1989), p. 54.

6. Martin Buber, *Tales of the Hasidim,* vol. 1 (New York: Schocken Books, 1947), p. 313.

7. Quoted in *Kol Haneshamah: Shabbat Vehagim: The Reconstructionist Prayer Book* (Wyncote, Pa.: The Reconstructionist Press, 1996), p. 284.

8. Warren Kenton, *Kabbalah and Exodus* (Bath, England: Gateway, 1988).

9. See Isaiah Horowitz, *Shnei Luchot Ha-Brit, Masechet Pesachim, Matzah Shmurah,* 2. *Judaic Classics Library II.* Davka CD-ROM version (Hebrew). These ideas led to the inclusion in many Ashkenazic Haggadot of a passage from Ezekiel (16:6) mentioning circumcision. See *Scholar's Haggadah,* p. 42.

10. Yehudah Leib Alter, *The Torah Commentary of the Sefat Emet,* trans. and inter. Arthur Green (Philadelphia: Jewish Publication Society, 1998), p. 390.

11. *Mekhilta of Rabbi Ishmael, Beshalach* 6:32, vol. 1, p. 234.

12. BT, Sotah 37a.

13. Martin Buber, *Moses: The Revelation and the Covenant* (Atlantic Highlands, N.J.: Humanities Press International, 1988), p. 75.

14. The Song at the Sea, the Bible's first song, begins with *aleph* (*ashir,* "I will sing . . ."), the first letter of the Hebrew alphabet. As Lawrence Kushner notes, "*Aleph* has no sound. Only the sound you make when you begin to make every sound . . . The most basic words there are begin with the most primal sound there is." Lawrence Kushner, *The Book of Letters: A Mystical Aleph-bait* (Woodstock, Vt.: Jewish Lights Publishing, 1990), pp. 21–23.

15. There is some question as to whether the term *shira* in the context of this song refers to a musical song or a spoken form of poetry. See *The Anchor Bible: Exodus 1–18,* ed. William C. Propp (New York: Doubleday, 1998), p. 508.

16. Heschel, *God in Search of Man,* pp. 46–47, 281.

17. BT, Pesachim 118a.

18. *The Breslov Haggadah,* p. 58. See also Joseph B. Soloveitchik, "Redemption, Prayer and Talmud Torah," in *Tradition,* 17:2, Spring 1978, p. 56.

19. Abraham Joshua Heschel, *Man Is Not Alone* (Philadelphia: Jewish Publication, 1951), p. 153.

Chapter 9—Enslaved in Egypt

1. *Seder Olam Rabbah,* with translation and commentary by Heinrich W. Guggenheimer (Northvale, N.J.: Jason Aronson, 1998), pp. 37–41.

2. *Mekhilta of Rabbi Ishmael, Pischa* 14:60, vol. 1, p. 112.

3. Moshe Weinfeld, "The Covenant of Grant in the Old Testament and in the Ancient Near East," in *Journal of the American Oriental Society,* vol. 90, 1970, pp. 184–203.

4. See Rabbi David Silber, "The Passover Haggadah—The Wandering Aramean," audiotape from the Drisha Institute, 131 West 86th Street, New York, NY 10024 (www.drisha.org/programs/tape.htm).

5. BT, Sotah 11a.

6. Thanks to Rabbi Gilbert Rosenthal for raising these issues.

7. *New Studies in Shemot,* pp. 1–11; Mordechai Winiarz, "The Reasons for the Bondage," in *The Yeshiva University Haggadah,* eds. Steven F. Cohen and Kenneth Brander (New York: Yeshiva University, 1985), pp. 48–52.

8. Genesis Rabbah 45:1.

9. Ramban, Genesis 16:6, pp. 173–174, 213.

10. Yair Zakovitch, *And You Shall Tell Your Son: The Concept of the Exodus in the Bible* (Jerusalem: Magnes Press/Hebrew University, 1991), pp. 15–45.

11. Ovadia Sforno, *Commentary on the Torah,* trans. Raphael Pelcovitz (Brooklyn: Mesorah Publications, 1997), p. 281.

12. Yitzchak Arama, *Akeydat Yitzchak,* vol. 2, trans. Eliyahu Munk (Jerusalem: Lambda Publishers, 2001), p. 304.

13. *New Studies in Shemot,* pp. 7–8.

14. E.g., Ecclesiastes Rabbah 9:18.

15. Numbers Rabbah 13:3 makes a similar point about Joseph. The BT, Chullin 60b, seems palpably dismayed that the tale of Joseph's treatment of the Egyptians was even included in the Torah.

16. *Or HaChayim* on Genesis 47:15; *Judaic Classic Library II,* Davka, CD-ROM version (Hebrew). Thanks to Elie Kaunfer for pointing out the common verb used to describe the shrewdness of both Joseph and Pharaoh.

17. For some reason, in this context, *avadim* is generally translated as "bondmen," "servants," or "serfs," instead of "slaves." *Avadim* can certainly carry all those meanings, but in this particular context "slave" seems most appropriate.

18. The Midrash, which specializes in finding relationships between similar wordings in dif-

ferent texts, remains amazingly silent on the connection between *v'hayinu avadim l'pharaoh* (Gen. 47:25) and *avadim hayinu l'pharaoh* (Deut. 6:21). For one of the rare contemporary comments on this, see Zakovitch, p. 39 (see note 7). On the general paucity of comment on Joseph's "reign," see W. Gunther Plaut, "The Trace of Joseph: A Commentary on Genesis 47:13–27," in *CCAR Journal,* 9:6, October 1961, pp. 29–32, 40.

19. *Etz Hayim,* p. 288.

20. BT, Shabbat 10b.

21. *The Talmud: Steinsaltz Edition,* vol. 21, Sanhedrin part 7 (New York: Random House, 1999), p. 36.

22. Zohar, Shemoth, Section 2, p. 12b. Elsewhere the Zohar (Bereshit, section 1, 142a) also sets the stolen blessing on Passover, but evinces little sympathy for Esau's tears. Genesis Rabbah (67:4) also highlights the grave consequences of Jacob's theft of his brother's blessing.

23. *Pirke de Rabbi Eliezer,* pp. 236–237. The midrash expands on the fact that the blessing Isaac gave to Jacob and Esau both referred to "the dew of heaven" (Gen. 27:28, 40), and that the recitation of the Prayer for Dew occurs on the first day of Passover.

Chapter 10—"Strangers in a Land Not Theirs"

1. *New Studies in Shemot,* p. 380.

2. BT, Shabbat 31a.

3. Rabbi Lester Bronstein points out that the same verbs for "crying out" and "heeding" in this verse also appear in Deut. 26:7, part of the Haggadah's principal text for telling the story of the Exodus. God will heed the cry of the stranger just as God heard our cry in Egypt.

4. Thanks to Ariella Sidelsky for her help with the composition of this blessing.

5. Chaim Weizmann, *Trial and Error* (New York: Harper and Brothers, 1949), pp. 461–462.

6. *The Sikkuy Report: 2001–2002,* available on the web at www.sikkuy.org.il.

7. *Statistical Abstract of Israel,* available on the web at www.cbs.gov.il/shnatonenew.htm (tables 3.10 and 8.35).

8. "The Official Summation of the Or Commission Report, September 1, 2003." On the web at www.haaretz.co.il.

9. "Selected Indices of Tolerance in Israeli Society." Findings of a Public Opinion Survey conducted by the Dahaf Institute under the Direction of Dr. Mina Tzemach. Available on the web at http://www.vanleer.org.il/eng/upload/.houseoftoler/survey.html.

10. David Grossman, *Sleeping on a Wire: Conversations with Palestinians in Israel* (New York: Farrar, Straus and Giroux, 1993), p. 308.

11. Quoted in Shlomo Avineri, *The Making of Modern Zionism* (New York: Basic Books, 1981), p. 164

Chapter 11—"In Every Generation . . ."?

1. This passage begins with the Hebrew word *v'hi*, literally, "and she." Most commentators hold that the pronoun refers to the promise in the previous paragraph. Zvi Yehudah Kalisher (1795–1874) suggested that *v'hi*, "and she," refers to the Shekhinah, the feminine aspects of God's immanence, often said to accompany Israel in exile. See Mayer Irwin Gruber, "The Jewish Goddess in an Orthodox Haggadah," in *Conservative Judaism*, 38:3, 1986, pp. 62–65.

2. See Rabbi Silber, "The Passover Haggadah."

3. *Haggadah of the Sages*, p. 271.

4. Steven M. Cohen, *Content or Continuity: The 1989 National Survey of American Jews* (New York: American Jewish Committee, 1991), p. 67.

5. Ana-Maria Rizzuto, *The Birth of the Living God: A Psychoanalytic Study* (Chicago: University of Chicago Press, 1979).

6. Anthony Flew, "Divine Omnipotence and Human Freedom," in *New Essays in Philosophical Theology*, eds. Anthony Flew and Alasdair MacIntyre (London: SCM Press, 1955), p. 144.

7. Joseph Albo, *Sefer Ha-Ikarim*, vol. 2 (The Book of Principles), trans. Isaac Husik (Philadelphia: Jewish Publication Society, 1929), p. 206.

8. Elliot N. Dorff, *Knowing God: Jewish Journeys to the Unknowable* (Northvale, N.J.: Jason Aronson, 1992), p. 130.

9. Ibid., pp. 130, 148.

10. Anson Laytner, *Arguing with God: A Jewish Tradition* (Northvale, N.J.: Jason Aronson, 1998), pp. 16–23.

11. Joseph Heinemann, *Prayer in the Talmud* (Berlin: Walter de Gruyter, 1977), p. 205.

12. Mishnah, Ta'anit 3:8.

13. For an excellent discussion that refers to many of these texts, see Marvin Fox, "Theodicy and Anti-Theodicy in Biblical and Rabbinic Literature," in *Theodicy*, ed. Dan Cohn-Sherbok (Lewiston, Maine: The Edwin Mellon Press, 1997), pp. 33–49.

14. Mishnah, Berachot 9:2.

15. Martin Buber, *Tales of the Hasidim*, vol. 1 (New York: Schocken Books, 1947), pp. 212–213.

16. *The Jewish Moral Virtues,* eds. Eugene B. Borowitz and Frances Weinman Schwartz (Philadelphia: Jewish Publication Society, 1999), p. 300.

17. Emmanuel Levinas, "To Love the Torah More Than God," in *Loving the Torah More Than God?* ed. Franz Jozef Van Beek (Chicago: Loyola University Press, 1989), pp. 37–38.

18. Heschel, *Man Is Not Alone,* p. 151.

19. Richard Rubinstein, *After Auschwitz* (New York: Bobbs-Merrill Company, 1966), pp. 152–153.

20. David Weiss Halivni, *The Book and the Sword: A Life of Learning in the Shadow of the Holocaust* (New York: Westview Press, 1996), p. 3, unnumbered.

21. Joseph B. Soloveitchik, "*Kol Dodi Dofek:* It Is the Voice of My Beloved That Knocketh," in *Theological and Halakhic Reflections on the Holocaust,* ed. Bernard H. Rosenberg (Hoboken, N.J.: KTAV Publishing, 1992), p. 54.

22. Harold S. Kushner, *When Bad Things Happen to Good People* (New York: Schocken Books, 1981), pp. 53, 55.

23. Eliezer Berkovitz, *Faith after the Holocaust* (New York: KTAV Publishing House, 1973), p. 158.

24. Milton Steinberg, *Basic Judaism* (New York: Harcourt, Brace and World, 1947), p. 48.

25. Lawrence Kushner, *God Was in This Place and I, i Did Not Know* (Woodstock, Vt.: Jewish Lights Publishing, 1991), p. 122.

26. David Biale, *Power and Powerless in Jewish History* (New York: Schocken Books, 1986), p. 210.

Chapter 12—"Go Out and Learn . . ."

1. *Haggadah: Sources and History,* p. 30.

2. Mishnah, Sotah 7:1 and Bikkurim 3:7.

3. Moshe Weinfeld, *Deuteronomy and the Deuteronomic School* (Oxford, U.K.: Clarendon Press, 1972), pp. 32–34.

4. See Rabbi Silber, "The Passover Haggadah."

5. David Daube, "He That Cometh," St. Paul's Lecture, London, October 1966, p. 12.

6. Nehama Leibowitz, *New Studies in Devarim/Deuteronomy* (Jerusalem: The Joint Authority for Jewish Zionist Education, 1993), p. 374.

7. E.g., Deuteronomy Rabbah, 3:17 and 11:4.

8. See Michael Avioz, "The Fifth Question: Why Is Moses Missing?" (on the web at

www.biu.ac.il/JH/Eparasha/metzora/avi.html#fn4) and Avigdor Shinan, "Why Is Moshe Rabenu Not Mentioned in the Passover Haggadah?" in *Amudim,* 39, 1991, pp. 172–174. (Hebrew). Some also explain Moses' absence as an outgrowth of conflicts with the Karaites in the ninth and tenth centuries. See Bezalel Narkiss, *The Golden Haggadah* (Rohnert Park, Calif.: Pomegranate Artbooks, 1997), p. 9.

9. Baruch M. Bokser, *The Origins of the Seder: The Passover Rite and Early Rabbinic Judaism* (Berkeley: University of California Press, 1984). Bokser analyzes the evolution of the Seder as a response to the Temple's destruction. He notes (p. 72) that, for the Rabbis, "Study became the highest form of piety and a ritual in its own right. The Mishnah's requirement to expound the formulaic account of Jewish history, set out in Deuteronomy 26:5ff, reflects this new dimension of study and distinct type of encounter with the biblical text."

10. BT, Menachot 110a.

11. Joseph B. Soloveitchik, "The Nine Aspects of the Haggadah," in *The Haggadah of Yeshiva University,* eds. Steven F. Cohen and Kenneth Brander (Jerusalem: Koren Publishers, 1985), p. 8.

12. These terms appear in Genesis 31:41, 42, and 32:5. See Rabbi Silber, "The Passover Haggadah."

13. The grammatical details need not concern us here. See Leibowitz, *Studies in Deuteronomy,* pp. 269–273.

14. *Haggadah: Sources and History,* pp. 30–35.

15. *Hagadah Shelemah,* p. 125.

16. *Or HaChayim on Deuteronomy* 26:5, Davka, CD-ROM version (Hebrew).

17. Menachem Kasher, *Torah Shelemah,* vol. 8 (Jerusalem: Torah Shelemah Institute, 1944), pp. 243–44 (Hebrew).

18. *Mekhilta of Rabbi Ishmael, Beshalach* 7:113, p. 251.

19. See, for example, the Sarajevo Haggadah (c. 1350) or the Ashkenazi Haggadah (c. 1450). Also see *Haggadah of the Sages,* p. 146, note 1, and p. 275.

20. Maimonides, Mishne Torah, Hilchot Chametz U' Matzah, 7:2.

21. Weinfeld, *Deuteronomy and the Deuteronomic School,* pp. 206–207.

22. Gerhard von Rad, *Old Testament Theology: The Theology of Israel's Historical Tradition,* vol. 1 (New York: Harper & Row, 1962), p. 122. See also Lawrence A. Hoffman, *Beyond the Text: A Holistic Approach to Liturgy* (Bloomington: Indiana University Press, 1987), chapter 5.

Chapter 13—Women of the Exodus

1. Exodus Rabbah 1:12 and BT, Sotah 11b (sometimes attributed to Rabbi Avira).

2. BT, Pesachim 116a. Akiva's midrash quotes the Song of Songs (8:5): "Under the apple tree I roused you; it was there your mother conceived you, there she bore you."

3. This is based on David Arnow, "Yocheved's Lesson: Decisive Action Is in Order When the World Seems Upside Down," in *Forward,* March 29, 2002.

4. The song is: "And You Shall Say: 'It Is the Sacrifice of Passover.'"

5. Tal Ilan, *Integrating Women into Second Temple History* (Tubingen: Mohr Siebeck, 1999), chapter 1.

6. Theodore Friedman, "The Shifting Role of Women, from the Bible to Talmud," in *Judaism,* 36:4, Fall 1987, p. 479; "Yocheved's Lesson," 487; Eileen Schuller, "Women of the Exodus in Biblical Retellings of the Second Temple Period," in *Gender Difference in Ancient Israel,* ed. Peggy L. Daly (Minneapolis: Fortress Press, 1989), pp. 178–194.

7. Blake Layerle, "Meal Customs in the Greco-Roman World," in *Passover and Easter,* especially pp. 43–45. If there was indeed a trend toward excluding women from symposia, this was an element of Hellenism the Rabbis were not prepared to accept when it came to the Seder. Women's participation in the Seder is indicated from a number of sources. A pre-Talmudic legal code known as the Tosefta (Pesachim 10:4) states that "a man is commanded to make his children and his wife happy on the holiday. With what does he make them happy? With wine . . ." The BT (Pesachim 116a) indicates that if a man's son cannot ask the four questions, his wife should.

8. Judith Plaskow, *Standing Again at Sinai: Judaism from a Feminist Perspective* (San Francisco: Harper, 1991), p. 1.

9. This "synthetic midrash" combines material from the following sources: Exodus Rabbah 1:15, 1:26, 18:3; Leviticus Rabbah 1:3; BT, Sotah 12a–13a; *Mekhilta of Rabbi Ishmael, Shirata* 10:64, p. 81; *Midrash HaGadol* 2:14, as quoted in *Legends,* vol. 2, p. 270; *Derech Eretz Zuta,* as quoted in *Legends,* vol. 5, pp. 95–96. Notwithstanding the references to first born sons in Ex. 4:23 and 13:12, the Bible is ambiguous as to whether the tenth plague, slaying of the Egyptian firstborn, killed just males as is commonly understood. The legend that Pharaoh's daughter, Bitya, was spared the last plague because she rescued Moses from the Nile reflects a midrashic tradition that this plague struck both males and females. See for example *Pesikta Rabbati* 17:5 (W.G. Braude, p. 368) and the Shulchan Aruch (470:1). Thanks to Alvan and Elie Kaunfer for bringing these two sources to my attention.

10. Suzanne Scholz, "The Complexities of 'His' Liberation Talk: A Literary Feminist

Reading of the Book of Exodus," in *Exodus to Deuteronomy: A Feminist Companion to the Bible* (Second Series), eds. Athalya Brenner and Carole R. Fontaine (Sheffield, U.K.: Sheffield Academic Press, 2000), pp. 26–27.

11. Ramban (Gen. 2:9), pp. 70–71. Also see Maimonides, *Guide of the Perplexed,* ed. Sholomo Pines (Chicago: University of Chicago Press, 1963), pp. 23–26, part 1 chapter 2.

12. Martin Buber, "The Tree of Knowledge," in *On the Bible,* ed. Nahum Glatzer (Syracuse: Syracuse University Press, 2000), p. 21.

13. Exodus Rabbah 18:6.

14. Fox. All four of these passages have been ascribed to the J source, an author thought to have lived in Judea between 848 and 722 B.C.E. See Richard Elliott Friedman, *Who Wrote the Bible?* (New York: Harper & Row, 1987), pp. 246–251. Common authorship suggests that the use of these terms expresses a subtle, but intentional, linkage of Eden and Exodus.

15. BT, Sotah 11b, compares the posture of a birthing woman to that of a potter. In quoting Jeremiah 18:3 in which the prophet describes God as a potter, the Talmud points to the godliness of women's role in procreation.

16. This "synthetic midrash" combines material from the following sources: BT, Sotah 13a; Genesis Rabbah 94:9; Exodus Rabbah 5:13; Deuteronomy Rabbah 11:7; and Ecclesiastes Rabbah 9:28. For Serakh's words to Jacob, see *Midrash HaGadol,* ed. Mordecai Margulies (Jerusalem: Mosad HaRav Kook, 1947), p. 766, on Genesis 45:26. For the confrontation between Serakh and ben Zakkai, see Jacob Neusner, *Pesikta de-Rav Kahana: An Analytical Translation,* vol. 1 (11:13) (Atlanta: Scholars Press, 1987). For two excellent and comprehensive treatments of Serakh, see "Serah bat Asher: The Transformative Power of Aggadic Invention," in Leila Leah Broner, *From Eve to Esther: Rabbinic Reconstructions of Biblical Women* (Louisville: Westminster John Knox Press, 1994), pp. 42–60; and Rachel Adelman, "Serakh bat Asher: Songstress, Poet, and Woman of Wisdom," in *Torah of Our Mothers,* eds. Ora Wiskind Elper and Susan Handelman (New York: Urim Publications, 2000), pp. 218–243. See also Aviva Gottlieb Zornberg, *The Beginning of Desire: Reflections on Genesis* (New York: Doubleday, 1995), pp. 280–283.

17. The midrash elaborates on the actions of a bold and "clever woman" described in II Samuel 21.

18. Phyllis Trible, "Bringing Miriam Out of the Shadows," in *Bible Review* 5:1, February 1989, p. 23.

19. Moses Isserles, gloss on the Shulchan Aruch (299:10), the great sixteenth-century legal code.
20. The lyrics pertaining to Miriam were composed by Leila Gal Berner.
21. *ArtScroll Tanakh* (New York: Mesorah Publications, 1996).
22. Thanks to Riva Silverman for many of these insights.

Chapter 14—The Ten Plagues

1. The identity of the fourth plague is unclear. The term *arov* literally means "mixture" and is generally interpreted as swarms of insects or wild beasts.
2. Although the above list of the plagues may sound familiar, identifying the ten plagues in the Book of Exodus is not so simple. Indeed, Psalms 78 and 105 enumerate seven plagues, each with a slightly different list. Rabbi Yehuda's acronym asserts the primacy of this particular enumeration of the plagues. For an excellent treatment of the plagues, including their literary structure, see Nachum M. Sarna, *Exploring Exodus* (New York: Schocken Books, 1986), chapter 4.
3. *Torat Chaim* vol. on Exodus (7:24) (Jerusalem: Mossad Harav Kook, 1993), p. 83 (Hebrew). *Etz Hayim* (p. 362) supports this position. Regarding the fourth plague, it comments: "For the first time, a clear distinction is made between the Egyptians and the Israelites."
4. Ramban, Exodus 8:18.
5. *Hagadah Shelemah*, pp. 126–127. The interpretation of the significance of "sixteen" is also from Kasher and attributed to Jacob ben Asher, known as the Tur.
6. *The Yeshiva University Haggadah*, p. 19. The attribution to Abarbanel's Haggadah commentary, *Zevach Pesach*, is widespread but appears erroneous. Goldschmidt (*Passover Haggadah,* Tel Aviv: Schocken, 1947, p. 22) attributes this interpretation to Samson Raphael Hirsch and Edouard Baneth. Baneth writes: "[The wine] is removed because each plague that our persecutors suffered to bring about our freedom diminished the joy of our liberation . . . The custom breathes the spirit of the essence of Judaism." Baneth, *Der Sederabend* (Berlin: M. Poppelauer, 1904), p. 28. Thanks to Peter Reimold for translating the German.
7. *Legends,* vol. 3, pp. 22–25. Midrash *Va-Yosha,* pp. 39–40.
8. *Yalkut Shimoni* on *Emor,* 654, quoted in *The Book of Legends,* no. 111 (*Sefer Ha-Aggadah*), eds. Hayim Nahman Bialik and Yehoshua Hana Ravnitzky, trans. William G. Braude (New York: Schocken Books, 1992), p. 499.
9. Franz Rozenzweig, *The Star of Redemption* (Notre Dame: Notre Dame Press, 1985, 1921), p. 317.

10. See also Samuel E. Lowenstamm, *The Evolution of the Exodus Tradition* (Jerusalem: Magnes Press/Hebrew University, 1992), pp. 111–128.

11. *New Studies in Shemot,* pp. 170–177. Leibowitz (p. 171) mentions that these ten references to knowing the Lord correspond to the Ten Commandments given to the Israelites. For a midrashic treatment, see *Pesikta Rabbati* (Piskha 21:20), trans. William G. Braude (New Haven: Yale University Press, 1968), pp. 446–447.

12. This is the first time in the Bible that God speaks through a human intermediary and the first time God seeks to overcome human skepticism. See Jack Miles, *God: A Biography,* pp. 102–103.

13. Exodus 8:6; 8:18; 9:14; 9:29.

14. For a fascinating discussion of whether Pharaoh eventually comes to know God, see Zornberg, *The Particulars of Rapture,* p. 152.

15. H. H. Schmid, "Creation, Righteousness, and Salvation," in *Creation in the Old Testament,* ed. Bernhard W. Anderson (Philadelphia: Fortress Press, 1984), p. 105.

16. It has been argued that the plagues involved a chain of natural events. Occasional super-floods washed down red microorganisms from the Ethiopian highlands, upsetting the ecology of the Nile. Frogs sought higher ground, etc. See Greta Hort, "The Plagues of Egypt," in *Zeitschrift Für Die Alttestamentliche Wissenchaft* vol. 69, 1957, pp. 84–103, and vol. 70, 1958, pp. 48–59 (English). Many scholars have rejected this approach, because the relevant biblical passages are thought to derive from different sources and because the plagues as recounted in Psalms 78 and 105 differ in number and sequence from those in Exodus (and from each other). This suggests distinct oral traditions about the plagues that would not fit with the naturalistic explanation of the plagues as they occur in Exodus. See Propp, ed. *The Anchor Bible: Exodus 1–18,* p. 347.

17. S.G.F. Brandon, *Creation Legends of the Ancient Near East* (London: Hodder and Stoughton, 1963), pp. 16–17.

18. Exodus Rabbah 22:1. A related version of this midrash appears in BT, Sotah 11a.

19. Mishnah, Avot 5:1. Ziony Zevit, "Three Ways to Look at the Ten Plagues," in *Bible Review* 6:3, June 1990, p. 23. These pronouncements refer to the ten occurrences of *vay-omer* ("and He said") in the context of God's creation of the cosmos in Genesis. In the Bible, precise identification of some of the things most taken for granted, such as the ten plagues and the Ten Commandments, proves challenging. So, too, with the ten utterances of creation. Zevit lists the following: Genesis 1:3, 6, 9, 11, 14, 20, 24, 26, 28, 29.

20. This material comes primarily from three sources: Ziony Zevit, "The Priestly Redaction and Interpretation of the Plague Narrative in Exodus," in *The Jewish*

Quarterly Review 66:4, April 1976, pp. 193–211; Ziony Zevit, "Three Ways to Look at the Ten Plagues" (see note 19); and Terrence E. Fretheim, part III "The Plagues," in *Exodus* (Louisville: John Knox Press, 1991).

21. This appears in several psalms, such as 74 and 80, in Job 26:1–13, and in sections of Isaiah, including 51:9–10.

Chapter 15—Rabban Gamaliel

1. *Haggadah: Sources and History*, p. 52.

2. Material on Gamaliel comes from the following sources: Shamai Kanter, *Rabban Gamaliel II: The Legal Traditions* (Chico, Calif.: Scholars Press, 1980); *Brown Judaica Series*, 8; Judah Goldin, "On the Account of the Banning of Rabbi Eleazer ben Hyrqanus: An Analysis and Proposal," *Studies in Midrash and Related Literature*, eds. Barry L. Eichler and Jeffrey H. Tigay (Philadelphia: Jewish Publication Society, 1988), pp. 283–297; Judah Nadich, *The Legends of the Rabbis: Volume II* (Northvale, N.J.: Jason Aronson, 1994).

3. Israel J. Yuval, "Easter and Passover As Early Jewish-Christian Dialogue," in *Passover and Easter*, pp. 98–124.

4. Jonathan Sacks, *The Chief Rabbi's Haggadah* (New York: HarperCollins, 2003), p 87. Thanks to Nigel Savage for bringing this to my attention.

5. For example, the *Mekhilta of Rabbi Ishmael* (*Pischa* 16:96) includes virtually the same statements by Ben Zoma with no reference to Elazar Ben Azariah.

6. BT, Chagigah 5b.

Chapter 16—Reliving the Exodus

1. Thanks to Nigel Savage of Hazon for teaching me about the relationship between this prayer and the Exodus.

2. *Legends*, vol. 2, p. 375 and vol. 5, p. 439. This combines three sources: The *Mekhilta of Rabbi Ishmael* (*Masechet Pischa* 13 on Exodus 12:34); *Mekhilta of Rabbi Shimon bar Yochai* (24); and the *Targum Yerushalmi* on Exodus 12:34.

Chapter 17—Israel and the Haggadah

1. Thanks to Rabbi Gordon Tucker for bringing this issue to my attention.

2. Scholars differ as to Rashi's stance on the fifth cup, referred to in some manuscripts of the Talmud. Goldschmidt (*Haggadah: Sources and History*, p. 66) believes that Rashi based his position on the fact that the Mishnah only mentions four cups of wine and therefore Rashi "emended" versions of the Talmud referring to a fifth cup as simply erroneous.

Guggenheimer (*Scholar's Haggadah,* p. 367) asserts that Rashi merely preferred the version of the Talmud associated with the ancient Babylonian academy of Pumbedita, which held to four cups, over that of Sura, which allowed an optional fifth cup.

3. The concept first finds expression in the Babylonian Talmud (Ta'anit 5a). "The Holy One, blessed be He, said, 'I will not enter the heavenly Jerusalem until I can enter the earthly Jerusalem.' Is there then a heavenly Jerusalem? Yes; for it is written, 'Jerusalem [is] built up like a city knit together'" (Psalms 122:3). Here, the heavenly Jerusalem is not a substitute for the earthly city, but will in fact be built only *after* God restores the mundane city.

4. Song of Songs Rabbah 2:20.

5. Benjamin Segal, *Returning: The Land of Israel as a Focus in Jewish History* (Jerusalem: Department of Education and Culture of the World Zionist Organization, 1987), p. 124.

6. Ibid. p. 131.

7. For the omission in Saadiah's Haggadah, see *Haggadah of the Sages,* p. 280. Thanks to Rabbi Gilbert Rosenthal for suggesting this line of inquiry.

8. Joseph B. Soloveitchik, "The Nine Aspects of the Haggadah," in *The Yeshiva University Haggadah,* p. 11.

9. For the former view, see Irving Greenberg, *The Jewish Way* (New York: Summit Books, 1988), pp. 56, 424. For the latter, see Shlomo Riskin, "Lesson of the Haggadah in Our Present War Against Terror." *Shabbat Hadagol Drasha,* 2002. CD-ROM by Ohr Torah Stone Institutions, (212) 935-8672. As Rabbi Riskin pointed out in a personal communication, the notion of drinking a cup without the traditional blessing over wine is common in Sephardic practice, which includes that blessing only for the first and third cups.

10. Joseph Tabory, *The Passover Ritual throughout the Generations* (Israel: Hakibbutz Hameuchad Publishing, 1996), p. 330 (Hebrew).

11. Menachem Kasher, *The Israel Passover Haggadah* (New York: The Sentry Press, 1962), p. 334. The *Shulchan Arukh* (481:1), an authoritative legal code from the sixteenth century, renders a fifth cup optional.

12. See Tabory, *The Passover Ritual throughout the Generations,* pp. 323–341.

13. Theodore Herzl, *Altneuland,* trans. Paula Arnold (Haifa: Haifa Publishing Company, 1960), p. 156. Thanks to Madeleine Arnow for bringing this to my attention.

14. For a discussion of Kasher and the fifth cup see, *Studies on the Haggadah from the Teachings of Nechama Leibowitz,* eds. Yitshak Reiner and Shmuel Peerless (New York: Urim Publications, 2002), p. 11.

15. Riskin, "Lessons of the Haggadah."

16. Leonard S. Cahan, ed., *Siddur Sim Shalom* (New York: Rabbinical Assembly/United Synagogue of Conservative Judaism, 1998), p. 149.

17. Kasher, *Israel Passover Haggadah*, p. 335.

18. Amos Elon, *Herzl* (New York: Schocken Books, 1986), p. 16.

19. *The Jewish Case Before the Anglo-American Committee of Inquiry on Palestine: Statement and Memoranda* (Jerusalem: The Jewish Agency for Israel, 1947), p. 65.

20. Mishnah, Pesachim 10:6.

21. *New York Times*, August 29, 2003, p. 8

Chapter 18—The Restoration of Wonder

1. The JPS Tanakh translates *moftim* as "portents." In this chapter, I've followed the Artscroll rendering: "wonders."

2. Thanks to Rabbi Lester Bronstein for pointing this out.

3. Yair Zakovitch, *The Concept of the Miracle in the Bible* (Tel Aviv: MOD Books, 1991), pp. 9–20. See also *Divine Intervention and Miracles in Jewish Theology*, ed. Dan Cohn-Sherbok (Lewiston, Maine: The Edwin Mellon Press, 1996).

4. Moshe Weinfeld, *Social Justice in Ancient Israel and in the Ancient Near East* (Jerusalem: The Magnes Press/The Hebrew University, 1995), pp. 14–15.

5. Thanks to Rabbi Alfredo Borodowski for pointing out this disagreement between Gersonides and Abarbanel.

6. David Hume, *Enquiries Concerning the Human Understanding and Concerning the Principles of Morals,* ed. L. A. Selby-Bigge (London: Oxford University Press, 1966, 1902), pp. 114–115, note 1. Although Hume did not rule out the possibility of miracles, he believed their probability to be extremely low: The test is whether false testimony of the miraculous would be more miraculous than the event itself (p. 116).

7. *The Random House Dictionary of the English Language* (New York: Random House, 1987).

8. BT, Shabbat 32a.

9. Jerusalem Talmud, Berachot 5:2, as quoted in Ephraim Urbach, *The Sages: Their Concepts and Beliefs* (Cambridge: Harvard University Press, 1975), p. 112.

10. Mishnah, Berachot 9:1. The Gemarah (Berachot 54a) illustrates this with reference to the place where the Israelites crossed the Red Sea.

11. BT, Niddah 31a.

12. BT, Chullin 90b.

13. As quoted in Urbach, *The Sages,* pp. 111–112.

14. Buber, *Tales of the Hasidim,* vol. 2, p. 315.

15. Heschel, *God in Search of Man,* p. 46.

16. BT, Pesachim 109a.

17. Maimonides, *The Guide of the Perplexed,* trans. Shlomo Pines (Chicago: The University of Chicago Press, 1963), Book 2, chapter 6, pp. 263–264.

18. Ramban (vol. on Exodus 13:6) pp. 172, 174.

19. Benedict de Spinoza, *A Theologico-Political Treatise,* trans. R.H.M. Elwes (New York: Dover Publications, 1951), p. 91.

20. Umberto Cassuto, *A Commentary on the Book of Exodus* (Jerusalem: The Magnes Press/Hebrew University, 1967), pp. 167–168.

21. Heschel, *God in Search of Man: A Philosophy of Judaism,* p. 49. Chapter 4, "Wonder," is an absolute gem.

22. Robert N. Goldman, *Einstein's God* (Northvale, N.J.: Jason Aronson, 1997), p. 24.

23. Michael Graetz, "Metaphors for God," in *Conservative Judaism,* 51:2, Winter 1999, p. 69.

24. Abraham Joshua Heschel, *The Prophets* (Philadelphia: Jewish Publication Society, 1955), p. 186.

25. Lawrence Kushner, "Opening Your Eyes," in *The Book of Miracles: A Young Person's Guide to Jewish Spirituality* (Woodstock, Vt.: Jewish Lights, 1997), pp. 15–18.

26. Vol. 1, p. 214.

27. Vol. 2, p. 21.

Chapter 19: "From Darkness to Great Light"

1. *Haggadah of the Sages,* p. 159.

2. The increase from one to five phrases may parallel the Haggadah's midrashic elaboration of the plagues, which also increase by a ratio of five to one.

3. *Haggadah of the Sages,* p. 281; *Scholar's Haggadah,* p. 67.

4. Commentaries have been condensed and paraphrased from the following sources: *The Abarbanel Haggadah,* ed. and trans. Yisrael Isser Zvi Herczeg and Shlomo Fox (Brooklyn: Mesorah Publications, 1990), p. 102; *The Vilna Gaon Haggadah,* ed. and trans. Yisrael Isser Zvi Herczeg (Brooklyn: Mesorah Publications, 1993), p. 78; Jacob Ben Jacob Moses, *Haggadah shel Pesach: 'Im Perush Ma'aseh Nisim* (Jerusalem: Hadrat Yerushalayim, 1990), p. 80; Maharal of Prague, *Divrai Negidim* (Judaic Classics, Davka

CD-ROM version, Hebrew), p. 117. Also see Eliezer Ginsberg, *Shiras Yehudah: Pesach Haggadah* (Brooklyn: Mesorah Publications, 1994), pp. 135–136.

5. Esther Rabbah 8:7.

6. Midrash on Psalms, Psalm 107.

7. Michael Strassfeld, *The Jewish Holidays* (New York: Harper & Row, 1985), p. 197. There are many other Passover/Purim parallels. BT (Shabbat 88a) asserts that at Sinai the Israelites accepted the Torah under divine coercion. They accepted it freely only with the events of Purim. Thanks to David Goshen for bringing this text to my attention.

8. The passage plays a critical role in Matthew 4:16. Jesus fulfills Isaiah's promise as he spreads his light to those who walked in darkness before his coming.

9. E.g., BT, Kiddushin 15b.

10. Leviticus (26:34–35, 43) and BT, Shabbat 33a, prescribe exile as the punishment for violating the laws of the sabbatical year and the Jubilee.

11. Acts 26:17–18; Colossians 1:12–14; I Peter 2:9–10.

12. Shlomo Pines, "From Darkness into Great Light," in *The Collected Works of Shlomo Pines,* vol. 4 (Jerusalem: Magnes Press/Hebrew University, 1996), pp. 3–10. Pines suggests that Joseph and Aseneth may have inspired Melito and the Mishnaic passage in the Haggadah. See also Israel J. Yuval, "Easter and Passover As Early Jewish-Christian Dialogue," in *Passover and Easter,* pp. 98–124.

13. *On Pascha: Melito of Sardis,* trans. Alistair Stewart-Sykes (New York: St. Vladimir's Seminary Press: Crestwood, 2001), verse 68.

14. H.F.D. Sparks, "Joseph and Aseneth" (8:10–11), in *The Apocryphal Old Testament,* trans. Mark Goodacre (New York: Oxford University Press, 1984), on the web at www.bham.ac.uk/theology/goodacre/aseneth/translat.htm.

Chapter 20—"Blessed Are You . . . Who Redeemed Us"

1. Maimonides, "Epistle to Yemen," in *A Maimonides Reader,* ed. Isadore Twersky (Philadelphia: Behrman House, 1972), pp. 459–460.

2. Gershom Scholem, *Sabbatai Sevi: The Mystical Messiah* (Princeton: Princeton University Press, 1973), p. 652.

3. Ibid., pp. 459, 460. Shabbetai Zevi's breaking Jewish law upset some; others found justification for it in rabbinic statements, such as this one in BT, Shabbat 151b: "Rabbi ben Eliezer [active in the late second century] said: 'In the messianic era, there is neither merit nor guilt.'"

4. Buber, *Tales of the Hasidim,* vol. 1, pp. 78–79.

5. David G. Roskies, *The Literature of Destruction* (Philadelphia: Jewish Publication Society, 1989), pp. 403–404.

6. EJ, vol. 14, p. 1. The two principal Hebrew words associated with redemption derive from two roots, *pey-dalet-hey* and *gimel-alef-lamed*. Both can be associated with either human or divine agency. The first is more general and does not imply any special relationship between redeemer and redeemed. The second refers to the next of kin "who acts to maintain the validity of his extended family group by preventing any breaches form occurring within it" (p. 1).

7. Weinfeld, *Social Justice in Ancient Israel,* p. 141.

8. Ibid., p. 80.

9. Ibid., pp. 15, 88, 81.

10. David Daube, *The Exodus Pattern in the Bible* (London: Faber and Faber, 1963), chapter 5.

11. In Egypt, the first known appearance of the term "slave" occurs in a religious context, "servant of god." The reference dates from the Old Kingdom, between 2630 and 2213 B.C.E. See Antonio Loprieno, "Slaves," in *The Egyptians,* ed. Sergio Donadoni (Chicago: University of Chicago Press, 1997), p. 195.

12. *Pischa,* 5:14, vol.1, p. 34.

13. *Pikudei,* 9 (Warsaw version).

14. Jacob Neusner, *The Talmud of the Land of Israel: A Preliminary Translation and Explanation,* vol. 13 (Chicago: University of Chicago Press, 1991), pp. 476–477. This and the following excerpts from the Jerusalem Talmud come from the same source. For Neusner's interpretation, see p. 589, note 20.

15. Mordecai M. Kaplan, *The Meaning of God in Modern Jewish Religion* (New York: Berhman's Jewish Book House, 1937), pp. 45, 52–54.

16. Martin Buber, *On the Bible* (Syracuse: Syracuse University Press, 2000), p. 12.

17. Heschel, *God in Search of Man,* pp. 312–313, 380.

18. Abraham Isaac Kook, *"Orot,"* in *The Zionist Idea,* ed. Arthur Hertzberg (New York: Atheneum Books, 1959), pp. 420, 425. Thanks to Rabbi Michael Paley for bringing this selection to my attention.

19. David Arnow, "In Every Generation, Finding Redemption in the Seder," in *Forward,* April 18, 2003. It is reprinted here with permission.

20. Maimonides, *"Mishne Torah:* The Laws of Kings and Wars 12:5," in *A Maimonides Reader,* ed. Isadore Twersky (New York: Behrman House, 1972), pp. 225–226.

Chapter 21—"A Remembrance of the Temple"

1. Tosefta, Pesachim 2:22.
2. BT, Pesachim 115a.
3. For how little we know about the historical Hillel, see Jacob Neusner, "The Figure of Hillel: A Counterpoint to the Problem of the Historical Jesus," *Judaism in the Beginning of Christianity,* chap. 4 (Philadelphia: Fortress Press, 1984).
4. Flavius Josephus, *Wars of the Jews,* in *The Life and Works of Flavius Josephus,* trans. William Whiston (New York: Holt, Rinehart and Winston, 1973), p. 663 (1:33:2).
5. For a history of the period, see Solomon Zeitlin, *The Rise and Fall of the Judean State: Volume II, 37 B.C.E. to 66 C.E.* (Philadelphia: Jewish Publication Society, 1967), and Shaye J. D. Cohen, *From the Maccabees to the Mishnah* (Philadelphia: Westminster Press, 1987).
6. Flavius Josephus, *Antiquities of the Jews,* in *The Life and Works of Flavius Josephus,* p. 471 (15:10:4).
7. *Mekhilta of Rabbi Ishmael, Beshalach* 4:60, vol. 1, p. 220.
8. Mishnah Avot 1:10–11.
9. BT, Yoma 35b.
10. Rabbinic literature includes three versions of the story: Tosefta, Piskha 4:3; Jerusalem Talmud, Pesachim 6:1; and BT, Pesachim, 66a.
11. BT, Sukkot 20a, quoted in Judah Nadich, p. 203.
12. This and all of the following references can be found in Nadich, *The Legends of the Rabbis: Volume I,* pp. 201–212.
13. Mishnah, Avot (Ethics of the Fathers), 1:14, 2:8, 1:12, 2:5–6.
14. Flavius Josephus, *The Jewish War,* trans. G. A. Williamson; rev. E. Mary Smallwood (London: Penguin Books, 1981), p. 371.
15. BT, Yoma 9b.
16. Flavius Josephus, *The Jewish War,* pp. 243–244.
17. Flavius Josephus, ibid., p. 164. There were widely shared rules among Jews and non-Jews alike as to the nature of defects that would render an animal unfit for sacrifice. See Saul Lieberman, *Hellenism in Jewish Palestine* (New York: Jewish Theological Seminary of America, 1950), pp. 153–163.
18. BT, Shabbat 143a. Lamentations Rabbah's version of this story (4:3) notes that Avkulas was present at the dinner and could have prevented the host from offending his would-be guest but refrained from doing so.

Chapter 22—Elijah's Transformation

1. *Passover Haggadah: The Feast of Freedom* (New York: The Rabbinical Assembly, 1982), p. 101. There is enormous variation in how contemporary Haggadot refer to Elijah's cup. For a discussion of how modern Haggadot approach this passage, see Debra Reed Blank, "*Sh'fokh Hamatkha* and *Eliyahu* in the Haggadah: Ideology in Liturgy" in *Conservative Judaism*, 40:2, Winter 1987/1988, pp. 73–86.

2. The earliest reference to Elijah's presence at circumcisions is found in the eighth-century midrash *Pirke de Rabbi Eliezer*, chap. 29, pp. 213–214.

3. Derekh Eretz Rabbah 1 (one of the "minor" tractates of the BT), quoted in *The Book of Legends*, eds. H. N. Bialik and Y. H. Ravnitzky, trans. William G. Braude (New York: Schocken Books, 1992), p. 617, no. 32.

4. BT, Pesachim 13a.

5. Exodus Rabbah 18:12: "Why does He call it 'a night of watching'? (Ex. 12:47). Because, on that night, He performed great things for the righteous, just as He had wrought for Israel in Egypt. On that night, He saved Hezekiah, Hananiah and his companions, Daniel from the lions' den, and on that night Messiah and Elijah will be made great" [or revealed, as some readings suggest].

6. *Hagadah Shelemah*, p.180. (Shulchan Aruch, Orach Chayim, 480, the Order of the Fourth Cup.) Isserles brings this interpretation in the name of Rabbanu Israel Bruna (mid-fifteenth century, known as the Mahariv). The Shulchan Aruch makes no specific mention of any of the rituals associated with Elijah. See also *Scholar's Haggadah*, p. 366.

7. Judah Loew Ben Bezalel, the Maharal of Prague, *Divrai Nigidim* (Noble Words), p. 155, Judaic Classics, Davka CD-ROM version (Hebrew).

8. Yisroel Yaakov Klapholtz, part II, chap. 9, "Elijah Saves from a Blood Libel," in *Stories of Elijah the Prophet* (B'nei B'rak, Israel: Pe'er Hasefer Publishers, 1973).

9. See A. M. Beek, "The Chariots and the Horsemen of Israel," in *Oudtestamentische Studien*, vol. 17, 1972, pp. 1–10. Beek observes that Elisha's curious designation of Elijah as "Israel's chariots and its horsemen" evokes imagery of the Exodus from Egypt in which references to Pharaoh's pursuit of Israel with his chariots and horsemen occur six times in the fourteenth chapter of Exodus alone.

10. *Scholars Haggadah*, pp. 365–366.

11. Menachem Mendel Schneerson, *From Exile to Redemption: Chassidic Teachings of the Lubavitcher Rebbe and the Preceding Rebbeim of Chabad*, vol. 1 (Brooklyn: Kehot Publication Society, 1992), p. 99.

12. BT, Sanhedrin 98b.

13. BT, Pesachim 118a.

14. BT, Nedarim 50a.

15. BT, Sanhedrin 68a.

16. Midrash Eileh Ezkerah, a martyrology from early medieval times, some of which is read on the afternoon of Yom Kippur. See David G. Roskies, *The Literature of Destruction: Jewish Responses to Catastrophe* (Philadelphia: Jewish Publication Society, 1988), p. 64.

17. Mishnah Eduyot 8:7.

18. For an excellent discussion of this, see Rabbi David Silber, "Moses and Elijah: A Study in Leadership," audiotape from the Drisha Institute. *Pesikta Rabbati* (Piskha 4), a collection of midrashim from the sixth to seventh centuries C.E., includes the definitive rabbinic comparison between Moses and Elijah. It lists dozens of similarities. *Pesikta Rabbati,* vol. 1, ed. and trans. William G. Braude (New Haven: Yale University Press, 1968), pp. 1, 82–88.

19. To Elisha's request, Elijah replies, "Go return. What have I done to you?" (I Kings 19:20). Rashi interprets this as follows: "**Go return** from following me, for **what have I done to you** that you should follow me?"

20. *Mekhilta of Rabbi Ishmael, Piskha* 1:88–97, vol. 1, pp. 8–9.

21. Dov Noy, "Forward," in *Tales of Elijah,* ed. Peninah Schram (Northvale, N.J.: Jason Aronson, 1997), p. xiv.

22. Ibid., p. xv.

23. See Genesis Rabbah (12:15) for the balance between justice and mercy. The *Zohar* (Shemoth, section 2, p. 216b), the mystical text from the thirteenth century, provides an intriguing interpretation of the *Sh'ma,* Judaism's credal statement on the unity of God: "The words, 'the Lord our God' [YHWH—*Elohainu*] are to reunite God's attributes . . . This is the method of avowing the unity of God practiced by Rab Hamnuna the Venerable, who learnt it from his father, who had it from his master, and so on, till it came from the mouth of Elijah."

24. Joseph Telushkin, *Biblical Literacy* (New York: William Morrow and Company, 1997), pp. 257–258.

25. Emile Fackenheim, *Encounters between Judaism and Modern Philosophy* (New York: Basic Books, 1973), p. 9. Thanks to Rabbi Gordon Tucker for bringing this to my attention.

26. Midrash Zuta Song of Songs 8:4, quoted in Aharon Wiener, *The Prophet Elijah in the Development of Judaism* (London: Routledge & Kegan Paul, 1978), pp. 48–49.

27. Gerson D. Cohen, *Studies in the Variety of Rabbinic Cultures* (Philadelphia: Jewish Publication Society, 1991), p. 35.

28. Yitzchak Sender, *The Commentator's Pesach* (New York: Feldheim Publishers, 1996), p. 220.

29. Wiener, *The Prophet Elijah*, p. 139. The tale is attributed to a Hasidic circle in Israel.

30. *The Open Door: A Passover Haggadah*, ed. Sue Levi Elwell (New York: Central Conference of American Rabbis, 2002), pp. 85–87.

Chapter 23—The Exodus from Egypt

1. In addition to cited works, this essay synthesizes material from the following sources: *Exodus: The Egyptian Evidence*, eds. Ernest S. Frerichs and H. Lesko, eds. (Winona Lake, Ind.: Eisenbrauns, 1997); Ronald Hendel, "The Exodus in Biblical Memory," in *Journal of Biblical Literature*, 120:4, 2001, pp. 601–622; Donald B. Redford, "An Egyptological Perspective on the Exodus Narrative," in *Egypt, Israel, Sinai: Archaeological and Historical Relationships in the Biblical Period*, ed. Anson F. Rainey (Tel Aviv: Tel Aviv University Press, 1987); Nahum M. Sarna, "Israel in Egypt: The Egyptian Sojourn and the Exodus," in *Ancient Israel*, rev. ed. Hershel Shanks (Washington, D.C.: Biblical Archaeological Society, 1999); Hershel Shanks, "Did the Exodus Really Happen?" in *Moment*, vol. 102, October 2001, pp. 62–65.

2. Jan Assmann, *Moses the Egyptian: The Memory of Egypt in Western Monotheism* (Cambridge: Harvard University Press, 1997), p. 27.

3. *The Rise of Ancient Israel*, ed. Hershel Shanks (Washington, DC: Biblical Archeology Society, 1992), color plate II, facing p. 22.

4. Herodotus, *The Histories*, trans. Robin Waterfield (New York: Oxford University Press, 1998), p. 145.

5. Baruch Halpern, "The Exodus from Egypt: Myth or Reality," in *The Rise of Ancient Israel*, p. 106.

6. Ahad Ha-'Am, "Moses" (1904), in *Selected Essays of Ahad Ha-'Am*, trans. Leon Simon (New York: Atheneum, 1970), pp. 308–309.

7. Buber, *Moses*, p. 16.

8. Yosef Hayim Yerushalmi, *Zakhor: Jewish History and Jewish Memory* (Seattle: University of Washington Press, 1982), pp. 10–11.

9. Richard Hirsh, "Is This Story True?" in *A Night of Questions: A Passover Haggadah*, eds. Joy Levitt and Michael Strassfeld (Elkins Park, Pa.: Reconstructionist Press, 2000), p. 21.

10. Transcribed from an audiotape supplied by Sinai Temple.

11. Heschel, *God in Search of Man*, p. 185.

Appendix I—Chapter Ten of Mishnah Pesachim, The Night of Passover

1. Baruch M. Bosker, *The Origins of the Seder*, pp. 29–32. Bokser's translation is based on the Kaufmann manuscript of the Mishnah, which dates from the thirteenth century. This manuscript is considered the best such manuscript and lacks additions from the Gemarah or the Haggadah that have found their way into the "standard" Mishnah.

SELECT BIBLIOGRAPHY

—

Alter, Judah Aryeh Leib. *The Language of Truth: The Torah Commentary of the Sefat Emet.* Translated and interpreted by Arthur Green. Philadelphia: Jewish Publication Society, 1998.

Anisfeld, Sharon Cohen, Tara Mohr, and Catherine Spector, eds. *The Women's Seder Sourcebook: Rituals and Readings for Use at the Passover Seder.* Woodstock, Vt.: Jewish Lights Publishing, 2003.

————. *The Women's Passover Companion: Women's Reflections on the Festival of Freedom.* Woodstock, Vt.: Jewish Lights Publishing, 2003.

Babylonian Talmud, Midrash Rabbah, and the *Zohar.* Davka CD-ROM version. Soncino Translation.

Bokser, Baruch M. *The Origins of the Seder: The Passover Rite and Early Rabbinic Judaism.* Berkeley: University of California Press, 1984.

————. "Changing Views of Passover and the Meaning of Redemption According to the Palestinian Talmud." *Journal of the Association for Jewish Studies,* 10:1 (Spring 1985): 1–18.

Borowski, Oded. *Agriculture in Iron Age Israel.* Winona Lake, Ind.: Eisenbrauns, 1987.

Bradshaw, Paul F., and Lawrence H. Hoffman, eds. *Passover and Easter: Origin and History to Modern Times.* Notre Dame, Ind.: University of Notre Dame Press, 2000.

Brumberg-Kraus, Jonathan. "Meals as Midrash: A Survey of Ancient Meals in Jewish Studies Scholarship." On the web at acunix.wheatonma.edu/jkraus/articles/MealsasMidrash.htm.

Buber, Martin. *Moses: The Revelation and the Covenant.* Translated by Michael Fishbone. Atlantic Highlands, N.J.: Humanities Press International, 1988.

Cassuto, Umberto. *A Commentary on the Book of Exodus.* Translated by I. Abrahams. Jerusalem: Magnes Press, 1967.

Cohen, Jeffrey M. *Let My People Go: Insights to Passover and the Haggadah.* Northvale, N.J.: Jason Aronson, 2002.

Cohen, Nachman. *The Historical Haggadah.* Yonkers, N.Y.: Torah Lishmah Institute, 2002.

Daube, David. *The Exodus Pattern in the Bible.* London: Faber and Faber, 1963.

Feinstein, David. *The Laws of Passover.* Brooklyn: Mesorah Publications, 2000.

Fredman, Ruth Gruber. *The Passover Seder.* New York: New American Library, 1983.

Gaster, Theodor H. *Festivals of the Jewish Year: A Modern Interpretation and Guide.* New York: Morrow Quill Paperbacks, 1978.

Ginsberg, Harold Louis. *The Israelian Heritage of Judaism.* New York: The Jewish Theological Society of America, 1982.

Ginzberg, Louis. *Legends of the Jews.* Philadelphia: Jewish Publication Society, 1963.

Goldschmidt, E. Daniel. *The Passover Haggadah: Its Sources and History.* Jerusalem: The Bialik Institute, 1960 (Hebrew).

Goodman, Amy and Philip, eds. *Passover Anthology.* Philadelphia: Jewish Publication Society, 2003.

Greenberg, Irving. *The Jewish Way: Living the Holidays.* New York: Summit Books, 1988.

Greenberg, Sidney, and Pamela Roth, eds. *In Every Generation: A Treasury of Inspiration for Passover and the Seder.* Northvale, N.J.: Jason Aronson, 1998.

Guggenheimer, Heinrich. *The Scholar's Haggadah: Ashkenazic, Sephardic, and Oriental Versions.* Northvale, N.J.: Jason Aronson, 1998.

Haggadat Torah Chaim. Jerusalem: Mossad Harav Kook, 1998 (Hebrew).

Hamolka, Walter. "God Is Thy Rescue As the Central Message of the Seder Ritual." *European Judaism,* 30:2 (Autumn 1997): 72–85.

Hauptman, Judith. "How Old Is the Haggadah?" *Judaism,* 51:1 (Winter 2002): 3–18.

Hoffman, Lawrence A. *Beyond the Text: A Holistic Approach to Liturgy.* Bloomington: Indiana University Press, 1987.

Isaac, Benjamin, and Aharon Oppenheimer. "The Revolt of Bar Kochba: Ideology and Modern Scholarship." *Journal of Jewish Studies,* 36:1 (Spring 1985): 33–60.

Kasher, Menachem. *Hagadah Shelemah.* Jerusalem: Torah Shelemah Institute, 1967 (Hebrew).

Klein, Mordell. *Passover.* Jerusalem: Keter Books, 1973.

Leibowitz, Nehama. *New Studies in Shemot.* Jerusalem: World Zionist Organization, 1986.

Lieber, David L., and Jules Harlow, eds. *Etz Hayim: Torah and Commentary.* Philadelphia: Jewish Publication Society, 2001.

Maimonides. *Mishneh Torah: The Laws of Chametz and Matzah.* Translated by Eliyahu Touger. New York: Moznaim Publishing Corporation, 1988.

Mekhilta of Rabbi Ishmael. Translated by Jacob Z. Lauterbach. Philadelphia: Jewish Publication Society, 1949.

Mihaly, Eugene. "The Passover Haggadah as PaRaDiSe." *CCAR Journal,* 13:5 (April 1966): 3–27.

Nachmanides. *Ramban (Nachmanides): Commentary on the Torah.* Translated by Charles B. Chavel. New York: Shilo Publishing, 1974.

Nadich, Judah. *The Legends of the Rabbis: Volume 2: The First Generation After the Destruction of the Temple and Jerusalem.* Northvale, N.J.: Jason Aronson, 1994.

———. *Rabbi Akiva and His Contemporaries.* Northvale, N.J.: Jason Aronson, 1998.

Olitzky, Kerry M. *Preparing Your Heart for Passover: A Guide for Spiritual Readiness.* Philadelphia: Jewish Publication Society, 2003.

Pirke de Rabbi Eliezer. Translated by Gerald Friedlander. New York: Sepher-Hermon Press, 1981.

Propp, William C. *Exodus 1–18: A New Translation with Introduction and Commentary.* (Anchor Bible, Volume 2) New York: Anchor, 1999.

Raphael, Chaim. *A Feast of History: The Drama of Passover Through the Ages.* New York: Gallery Books, 1972.

Safrai, Shmuel, and Ze'v Safrai. *The Haggadah of the Sages.* Jerusalem: Carta, 1998 (Hebrew).

Sarna, Nahum M. *Exploring Exodus: The Origins of Biblical Israel.* New York: Schocken Books, 1996.

Schauss, Hayyim. *The Jewish Festivals: A Guide to Their History and Observance.* New York: Schocken Books, 1996.

Segal, J. B. *Hebrew Passover from the Earliest Times to A.D. 70.* London: Oxford University Press, 1963.

Silber, David. "The Passover Haggadah/The Wandering Aramean." New York: Drisha Institute Tape Project (audiotape), 1994. Available at www.drisha.org.

Soloveitchik, Joseph B. "Redemption, Prayer, Talmud, Torah." *Tradition,* 17:2 (1978): 55–72.

Stein, Siegfried. "The Influence of the Symposia Literature on the Literary Form of the Haggadah." *Journal of Jewish Studies,* 7:1 and 2 (1957): 13–44.

Strassfeld, Michael. *The Jewish Holidays: A Guide and Commentary.* New York: Harper & Row, 1985.

Tabory, Joseph. *The Passover Ritual throughout the Generations.* Tel Aviv, Israel: Hakibbutz Hameuchad Publishing House, 1996 (Hebrew).

Urbach, Ephraim E. *The Sages: Their Concepts and Beliefs.* Cambridge: Harvard University Press, 1987.

Walzer, Michael. *Exodus and Revolution.* New York: Basic Books, 1985.

Wolfson, Ron. *Passover: The Family Guide to Spiritual Celebration,* 2nd. Ed. Woodstock, Vt.: Jewish Lights Publishing, 2003.

Ziff, Joel. *Mirrors in Time: A Psycho-Spiritual Journey through the Jewish Year.* Northvale, N.J.: Jason Aronson, 1997.

Zornberg, Avivah Gottlieb. *The Particulars of Rapture: Reflections on Exodus.* New York: Image Books, 2002.

HAGGADOT OF INTEREST

Birnbaum, Philip. *The Passover Haggadah.* New York: Hebrew Publishing Company, 1976.

Cohen, Steven F., and Kenneth Brander, eds. *Yeshiva University Haggada.* New York: KTAV Publishing House, 1988.

Cohen, Tamara R. *The Journey Continues: The Ma'yan Passover Haggadah.* New York: May'an: The Jewish Women's Project, 2000.

Dishon, David, and Noam Zion. *A Different Night: The Family Participation Haggadah.* Jerusalem: Shalom Hartman Institute, 1997. (See also Dischon and Zion, *Leader's Guide to the Family Participation Haggadah.*)

Elias, Joseph. *Haggadah.* New York: Mesorah Publications, 2000.

Elwell, Sue Levi, ed. *The Open Door: A Passover Haggadah.* New York: Central Conference of American Rabbis, 2002.

Geffen, David, ed. *American Heritage Haggadah.* Jerusalem: Gefen Books, 1997.

Glatzer, Nahum H. *The Passover Haggadah.* New York: Schocken Books, 1984.

Herczeg, Yisrael I., ed. *Abarbanel Haggadah: The Passover Haggadah with the Commentary of Don Issac Abarbanel (Artscroll Mesorah Series).* Translated by Shlomo Fox. New York: Mesorah Publications, 1990.

————. *Haggadah: Vilna Gaon, Artscroll Mesorah Series.* New York: Mesorah Publications, 1999.

Hirsch, Samson R. *The Hirsch Haggadah.* New York: Phillip Feldheim, 1989.

Kasher, Menachem M. *Israel Passover Haggadah.* New York: Sentry Press, 1950.

Leibowitz, Nechama, and Yitshak Reiner, eds. *Studies on the Haggadah: From the Teachings of Nechama Leibowitz.* New York: Urim Publications, 2002.

Levitt, Joy, and Michael Strassfeld, eds. *A Night of Questions: A Passover Haggadah.* Elkins Park, Pa.: Jewish Reconstructionist Federation, 2000.

Mykoff, Moshe, ed. *The Breslov Haggadah.* Translated by Yehoshua Starret. Jerusalem and New York: Breslov Research Institute, 1989.

Rabbinowicz, Rachel Anne. *Passover Haggadah: The Feast of Freedom.* New York: United Synagogue Book Service, 1982.

Riskin, Shlomo. *The Passover Haggadah: With a Traditional and Contemporary Commentary.* New York: KTAV Publishing House, 1984.

Sacks, Jonathan. *The Chief Rabbi's Haggadah.* London: HarperCollins, 2003.

INDEX

—

Aaron, 182, 218, 226
Abarbanel, Isaac, 192, 262
Abbreviations, 329–330
Abraham, 120, 126, 160, 228, 280; descendants of, 200, 232; fifth cup and, 235, 237; Sodom and Gomorrah and, 143–144; promise and fulfillment, 157–158; *See also* Abram
Abram, 116–118, 230; *See also* Abraham
Afikomen, defined, 60
Aggadah, defined, 65
Agnon, S.Y., 236
Ahab (King), 304
Ahad Ha-'Am. *See* Ginsberg, Asher Hirsch
Ahmose (Pharaoh), 317
Akiva (Rabbi), xvii, 324; Bar Kochba rebellion and, 46; B'nei B'rak Seder seating and, 210; Elijah and, 306; his teachings and death, 46; Five Sages' Seder, 43, 44–46; plagues and, 159, 325; second cup of wine, blessing, 239
Altneuland (Herzl), quotation, 235
Amalek, 126
American Anti-Slavery Group, The, 24
Amidah, 207
Ananus (high priest), 297
Anger and wrath, 312, 313
Anthony, Susan B., 18
Arama, Yitzchak, 121
Arba Kushiot, defined, 26
Archaeology. *See* Exodus, archaeology and
Aristotle, 17
Ark of the Covenant, 40, 226
Art midrash activities, 38–39, 95, 260; directions, 326
Aseneth, 269
Asher, 178, 179
Attar, Chayim ben (Attar, Chaim Ibn) Moshe, 122, 164
Augustine (Saint), 141
Aviv, defined, 88

B

Baal, 304–305, 309
Baal Shem Tov, 272
Barak, Ehud, 135
bar Chalafta, Shimon (Rabbi), 278
Bar Kamza and Kamza, story, 298
Bar Kochba rebellion, 1, 46, 49, 232, 239
Benaiah (Rabbi), 280
ben Avkulas, Zechariah (Rabbi), 298, 299
ben Azariah, Elazar (Rabbi): B'nei B'rak Seder seating and, 210; designated Sabbaths to preach, 209; Five Sages Seder, 43, 44–46; flour and Torah statement, 38; miracle of white hair, 208–209
ben Bezalel, Budah Loew (Maharal of Prague), 262
ben Eliezer, Jeremiah (Rabbi), 245–246
Ben-Gurion, David: Anglo-American Committee of Inquiry and, 238; on government by force, 19
ben Joseph, Messiah, 284
ben Pedat, Eliezer (Rabbi), 246–247
ben Yitzhak, Shlomo. *See* Rashi
ben Zakkai, Yochanan (Rabbi): Eliezer and, 44–45; Red Sea teachings, 180, 181; revolt against Romans and, 207; Yavne academy and, 207
Ben Zoma, 210, 211
Berkovitz, Eliezer, 151
Bethuel, 162
Biale, David, 152
Bibliodrama, 215; "Knocking in the Night," 220–221; "To Stay or to Leave?" 221–222
Bill of Rights, 18
Birkat Ha-Mazon, 304
Birth of the Living God, The (Rizzuto), 141
Bitter herbs: blessing over, 288, 324; Hillel's sandwich and, 288–290; purpose at Passover, 205; re-enacting Egypt march, 224
Bitya, 174, 175, 178, 180, 345
Blessings, natural world and, 96–99

Blood: in creation/plague narratives, 201–202; plagues and, 186–187, 191; as symbol at circumcision, 187; "The Last Night in Egypt" and, 219
Blood libel, 303
B'nei B'rak Seder: background, 50–52; discussion questions, 55; Exodus story and, 52; reconstructed conversation, 52–55; seating, 210; *See also* Five Sages' Seder
Bockmuehl, Markus, xxiv
Boils, ten plagues and, 191
Bondage and redemption, 261, 262, 263, 264, 267–268
Buber, Martin, 111, 177, 283, 319

C

Cairo Geniza, 139
Caleb, 175, 226
Cassuto, Umberto, 251
Cattle blight: ten plagues and, 191; "The Last Night in Egypt" and, 219
Cestius (Roman general), 296
Chacham (wise child), 63, 64
Chad Gadya, 236, 273, 286
Chag HaAviv, defined, 85, 94
Chair of Elijah, 302
Chanokh (Rabbi), 248
Charoset, 31, 112, 170, 323
Chattel slavery, defined, 22
Children, engaging in Seder, 26–28
"Christian Haggadah," 268
Contract slavery, defined, 23
"Covenant of the Pieces," 116–118
Creation: de-creation and, 200–201; myths, plagues and, 198–203; myths, ten utterances and, 201
Crossing over: discussion questions, 41; taking responsibility and, 39–41
Crossing Red Sea, 110–112; Israelite dissension and, 255–257; judgment of Egyptian horses and drivers and, 255; miracles and, 254
Cup of Elijah, 185, 301, 303–304

D

Darkness: great light and, 261, 262, 263, 264, 266–267; ten plagues and, 191; "The Last Night in Egypt" and, 219
David (King), 180, 206, 209, 263, 327
Dayyenu, 234, 289
Debt bondage, defined, 23
Declaration of Independence (American), 18
Declaration of Independence (Israeli), 19, 135
De-creation, and plagues, examples, 200–201

Destruction of Temple, 295–299
Deuteronomy: Exodus version of redemption compared, 158–159; Pilgrims' Prayer and, 154–155, 168; Sinai omission, 168
Deuteronomy Rabbah (midrash), 186, 343, 346
Discussion questions: destruction of Temple, 299; God's covenant with Abraham, 118; anger and wrath, 313; blood and water, 187; B'nei B'rak Seder, 55; Chapter Ten of *Mishnah Pesachim,* 323; in creation and plague narratives, 202; crossing over, 41; Elijah, 307, 308, 312; Exodus, archaeology and, 316; Exodus, reliving, 215, 220, 221, 222; Festival of Spring, 87; Four Children, 59–60, 61–63; "From darkness to great light," 260, 261, 262; fruits of Egypt and Israel, 226, 227; Gamaliel, Rabban, II, 210, 211; God, 138–139, 142–143; Greek influences on Seder, 30; Hillel (sage), 288, 294–295; House of Laban, 162; Israel, Haggadah and, 231; Joseph, 124–125; Kamza and Bar Kamza story, 299; legal and religious authority, 48–49; miracles, 246–247, 249–253, 256, 257; Miriam's Well legend, 182–183; Passover perspectives, 37–38; Pharaoh's hardening heart, 72; Pilgrims' Prayer, 156–157; plagues, 195, 198; redemption, 274, 278–280, 281–282; self-criticism, 127; Serakh, 180–181; slavery and freedom, 2–3, 13, 22, 23, 124–125; spilling wine from cup, 192; strangers, 130, 133, 136, 221; ten plagues, 190, 191; wandering Aramean, 162–163, 221
Divine miscalculations, 196
Dome of the Rock, 240
Dorff, Elliot, 141–142
Duran, Shimon ben Tzemach. *See* Rashbetz

E

Ecclesiastes Rabbah (midrash), 100, 340, 346
Eden. *See* Garden of Eden
Egypt: fruits of, symbolism, 226–227; Garden of Eden, compared, 178; march from, reenacting, 223
Egyptian Book of the Dead, The, 201
Ehrlich, Arnold, 79
Einstein, Albert, 252
Eliezer (Rabbi): on annulling God's decrees, 44; banned from community, 46–48; B'nei B'rak Seder seating and, 210; Elijah and, 306; Five Sages Seder, 43, 44–46; Gamaliel, Rabban, II and, 48; on legal/religious authority, 47–48; on miracles, 245; plagues debate, 325; *Unetaneh Tokef* prayer and, 44

Elijah (*Eliyahu Hanavi*): Baal and, 304–305; basis for folkloric status, 309–310; Chair of, 302; cup of, 185, 301, 303–304; discussion questions, 307, 308, 312; Enoch and, 308, 309; faithfulness to ancient covenant and, 309–310; as model for change, 310–311; opening door for, 302, 303; special ceremonial role, 309; transformation of, 301–313; unique name, 309

"*Eliyahu Hanavi,*" 185, 302

Elijah's Cup, 185, 301, 303–304

Elisha, 306

Eliyahu, coming of, 303–304. *See also* Elijah

Emerson, Ralph Waldo, 321

Empathy, vengeance vs., 8–12

Encyclopedia Judaica, 273, 284

Enoch, 308, 309

Esther, 172, 265, 266

Eve, 176–178

Exodus and women, The: biblical references, 170, 171, 173, 174, 176, 278–279; in Exodus (book of), 177–178; in Genesis, 176–178; Haggadah version, 169–170, 172–173; midrash and Talmud versions, 173–176; Miriam's Cup, 183

Exodus, book of: attire for Exodus journey, 94; circumcision and paschal sacrifice, 108; depiction of God, 82, 140; fifth cup and, 235; four cups of wine, meaning, 231; horse/driver and, 257; Israel enslavement, 115, 118, 227; Israelites yearning for Egypt, 9; "knowing God," 193–195; "Let my people go," 17; Moses, Pharaoh and, 105, 194, 256, 257; Moses, Ten Commandments and, 10; paradigms of faith, 202–203, 222; Pharaoh's hardening heart and, 72; plagues and, 79, 197–198; procreation and redemption, 278–279; references to color, 248; Song of the Sea and, 252; specified time for Passover, 87–88; strangers, 131; "The Last Night in Egypt" and, 218; *See also* Exodus from Egypt

Exodus Rabbah (midrash), 76, 107, 108, 109, 111, 120, 147, 197, 198, 220, 254

Exodus, reliving the: 213–224; discussion questions, 215, 221, 222; rationale for, 213–214; setting stage, 214–215; supplies, 214; "The Last Night in Egypt," 216–220; timing, 214

Exodus, from Egypt: archaeology and, 315–322; circumcision and paschal sacrifice, 277; crossing Red Sea, 110–112; cultural milieu, 276; date and meaning, relationship, 88; drowning of Pharaoh's troops, 11, 81, 197; early American leaders and, 7; Egypt as motif, 138; explained, xxiii, 37, 51, 103–106, 113–114, 117–118; first song and,

111–112; five sages and, 43, 318–322; fixed biblical account, xvi; Four Children and, 58; Four Questions and, 29; freedom and, xvii; God of, 81, 140; God's thirty-nine-year sentence, 226; Great Seal of United States and, 13; meaning related to time, 89–90; milestones, 106–109; miracles and, 247–248; moral confusion and, 80; The Passover Haggadah and, xv, xviii, xix, xxii; Passover origin and, 92–93; Pharaoh's hardening heart and, 71; plagues, 79, 247; rebellion against Moses and Aaron, 226; rebellion-liberation pattern, 9; redemption and, 193, 271–272; reliving. *See* The Exodus, reliving; slavery/freedom and, 2–3, 13, 276; storytelling principles, xvi, 85–87; suffering as strangers and, 130; three critical experiences, 117; Torah vs. Haggadah, 60–63; women and. *See* The Exodus and women; *See also* Exodus (book of)

F

Faith: Israelites and, 195–197; parting Red Sea and, 196

Fanon, Frantz, 10

Festival of Matzot, 92

Festival of Shavuot, 154

Festival of Spring, 85–87

Festivity and mourning, 261, 262, 263, 264, 265–266

Fifth cup, 231–235, readings, 236–238

Firstborn, slaying of: gender of, 345; "Knocking in the Night," 220–221; ten plagues and, 191

First song, 111–112

Five Sages' Seder, 210–211; basis and message, 49–50; sages identified, 43, 44; *See also* B'nei B'rak Seder

Four Children: background and versions, 58; Breslov Haggadah version, 66; discussion questions, 59–60, 61–63; feminist version, 68–69; Haggadah quotation, 57; Hirsch version, 66–67; Schneerson version, 67–68; Torah vs. Haggadah, 60–63; wise vs. wicked child, 57, 59–60

Four Questions: as *Arba Kushiot*, 26; explained, 25–32; Haggadah and, 230, 234; paradox of Seder and, 29

Fox, Everett, 87, 177

Franklin, Benjamin, 18

Freedom. *See* Slavery and freedom

Free the Slaves (organization), contact information, 24

Free will, hardening of Pharaoh's heart and, 76–78

Frogs: in creation and plague narratives, 202; ten plagues and, 191; "The Last Night in Egypt" and, 219

"From darkness to great light," 259–269; art midrash activity, 260; Ashkenazic, Sephardic, and Yemenite interpretations, 261; cultural milieu, 268–269; defined, 266–267; discussion questions, 260, 261, 262; five key phrases, 261–264; sources and evolution, 264–268

Fruits of Egypt and Israel, 226–228

G

Gabriel (angel), 193

Gamaliel, Rabban, II (Gamaliel), 324; deposed, 209; designated Sabbaths to preach, 209; discussion questions, 210, 211; eighteen benedictions, 207; Eliezer and, 48; Haggadah references, 210; historic overview, 206–207; and Joshua (Rabbi) debate, 208; minimum Passover duties, 205; Seder traditions and, 207; struggles, 207–210

Gandhi, Mohandas K., 18–19

Gaon, Amram, 261

Gaon, Netronai, 261

Gaon, Saadiah, 233

Gaon (Vilna), 235. *See also* Zalman, Elijah ben Solomon (Vilna Gaon)

Garden of Eden, 176–178

Geonim, defined, xxiv

Genesis Rabbah (midrash), 147, 246, 334

George III (King), as freedom's enemy, 6

Gersonides, 159

Gillman, Neil, 77

Ginsberg, Asher Hirsch, 319

God—A Biography (Miles), 82

God: arguing with, 143–145; challenge by Job, 144–145; contradictory concepts, 141–142; court with Jeremiah, 144; discussion questions, 138–139, 142–143; of Exodus, 82, 140; as Haggadah central character, 139–140; heart of, softening, 80–83; as interventionist, 140; modern perspectives, 148–152; role in Jewish history, 137–139; sin of Golden Calf and, 144

God in Search of Man: A Philosophy of Judaism, 283

Golden Calf, 82, 144, 196

Goldschmidt, E.D., xxv. *See also The Passover Haggadah: Its Sources and History*

Goshen, land of, 191

Graetz, Michael, 253

Great Seal of United States, 7, 12–13

Grossman, David, 135

H

Hagar, 120

Haggadah: Ashkenazic, xvii, xxv; defined, xv; sources and evolution, xiii, xxiv–xxv, 33–38; "When Two Sages Disagree," 33–38

Hail: ten plagues and, 191; "The Last Night in Egypt" and, 219; *See also* Seventh plague

ha-Kappar, Eliezer (Rabbi), 277

Halakhah, defined, 64–65

Halivni, David Weiss, 150

Hallel, 193, 231, 235, 260, 281, 304, 324

Haman, 126, 265, 266

Handmade Midrash (Milgrom), 326

Hasidic masters, 66, 68, 101, 105, 106, 109, 148, 248, 272, 311

Hebron, 240

Helbo (Rabbi), 232

Herod (King of Judea), 290–291

Herzl, Theodore, 235, 238, 284

Heschel, Abraham Joshua, 101, 149, 248, 252, 254, 283, 322

Hillel: House of, 209, 323, 324; school of, 207

Hillel (sage), 287–299; compared to Moses, 293; discussion questions, 288, 294–295; on empathy, 12; as patriarch of Rabbinic Judaism, 287–288; teachings, 293–295

Hirsch, Samson Raphael, 67

Hirsh, Richard, 321

Holocaust, 11, 139, 141, 221, 238

Honi the Circle Drawer, 145

Horseradish, reliving Exodus and, 214–215

House of Laban, 160–162

Human Rights Watch, 24

Hume, David, 243, 244

Hyksos (Dynasty, people), 317, 318

I

Ibn Ezra, 191

Ibn Paquda, Bachya ben Joseph, 100

Insects: ten plagues and, 191; "The Last Night in Egypt" and, 219

Intifada, first, xiii

Intifada, second, 135

Introduction to the Talmud and Midrash, dating of Rabbinic literature and, xxiii–xxiv

Isaac, 235, 237, 280

Ishmael (Rabbi), 255

Israel: discussion questions, 231; enslavement in Egypt, 115–116, 118–122; four virtues and, 277–278; fruit and vegetable puzzle activity, 226–229; fruits of, symbolism, 226–227; Haggadah references, 225, 229–231, 232–234; Northern vs. Southern Kingdom festivals, 92

Israeli-Arab citizens, 134–135
Isserles, Moses, 183, 303

J
Jabotinsky, Vladimir, 136
Jacob, 178, 179, 228, 317; House of Laban and, 160–162, 164; journey, descent of Israel and, 227; redemption and, 280
Jacoby, Jonathan, xiii
Jeremiah, 144, 267–268
Jerusalem Talmud, four cups of wine and, 279–280, 281
Jezebel (Queen), 304, 305
Johanan (Rabbi), 245, 298, 299
Joseph and Aseneth, 269
Joseph: Aseneth and, 269; discussion questions, 124–125; dreams of plenty and famine, 122–123; Pharaoh and, 123–124, 179, 228; protection of Israelites, 124; slavery and, 122–125; as son of Jacob, 179, 180
Josephus, 291, 295, 296, 297
Joshua (Rabbi), 255; B'nei B'rak Seder seating and, 210; Five Sages' Seder, 43, 44–46, 49; Rabban Gamaliel II and, 208, 209; Rabbi Ishmael and, 255
Josiah (King), 92, 155
Journey Continues, The: The 1997 Ma'yan Passover Haggadah, 68
Judah, 34–38
Judah (the Prince), 323, 327

K
Kabbalah, 66, 67, 105, 109
Kamza and Bar Kamza story, 298, 299
Kaplan, Mordecai M., 282
Kasher, Menachem, 164, 236, 237
King, Martin Luther, Jr., 8, 19–20, 283
Kiryat Arba, 240
Kook, Abraham Isaac, 284
Korach, miracles and, 243
Kushner, Harold S., 151
Kushner, Lawrence, 151, 254

L
Laban, 160–162, 164
Law court prayers, 145
Lazarus, Emma, 18
Legal and religious authority, 47–49
Leibowitz, Nehama, 78, 121, 194
Lekha Dodi, 253
"Let My People Go," 224
Levinas, Emmanuel, 149

Levinger, Moshe (Rabbi), 239
Levi Yitzhak (of Berditchev), 148
Lice: ten plagues and, 191; "The Last Night in Egypt" and, 219
Lincoln, Abraham, 18
Locusts, ten plagues and, 191
Lubavitcher Rebbe. *See* Schneerson, Menachem Mendel (Rabbi)
Luria, Isaac, 67

M
Maharal (of Prague), 235, 303
Maimonides, Moses, 27, 32, 77, 101, 166, 233, 235, 249, 272, 285
Malachi, 308
Mandela, Nelson, 20
Matzah: blessing over, 288, 324; in concentration camps, 285; Hillel's sandwich and, 288–290; purpose at Passover, 205; reenacting march from Egypt and, 223, 224; reliving Exodus and, 214–215
maytzarim. See Mitzrayim
Mekhilta, defined, 255
Mekhilta of Rabbi Ishmael, 58, 255, 278, 308
Melito (Bishop of Sardis), 268
Mendel, Menachem (Hasidic Rebbe of Kotsk), 311
Messiah (*Mashiach*), 38, 60, 151, 205, 238, 268, 272, 284, 285, 296, 303, 304; *See also* ben Joseph, Messiah
Messianism, 238–240
Michael (angel), 193
Midrash, defined, 325
Midrash Rabbah, xxv
Milgrom, Jo, 326
Miracles, 241–257; ambivalence about, 245; Bible on, 242–244; David Hume on, 243, 244; defined, 243, 244; discussion questions, 246–247, 249–253, 256, 257; of God's redemption, 241–242; Moses and, 243; sages on, 244–247
Miriam, 178, 180, 181–185; legend of well, 182–183, 186; "The Last Night in Egypt" and, 217
Miriam's Cup: Cup of Elijah and, 185; Exodus/women and, 183; redemption and, 184; ritual, 183–185
Mishkan, defined, 226
Mishnah: approaches to Seder, xvi–xvii, 154; defined, xvi; Deuteronomy and, 159, 162, 230–231; Exodus and, 154, 156; Four Questions origin, 31–32; *Haggadah* sources and, xxiv; wine and, 279–281
Mishnah Pesachim, Chapter Ten, 323–324

Mitzrayim, xxii, 228, 229

Moellin, Jacob ben Moses, 192

Moses, xxi; Abraham Lincoln and, 7; arguing with God, 52, 54, 143, 144, 147; barred from Promised Land, 182; in basket, 126; burning bush and, 107, 196; challenging Pharaoh, 8; Covenant of the Pieces and, 117; crossing Red Sea, 110; five books of, 125; four daughters and, 68; freedom and, 19; frustration with followers, xxii; Golden Calf and, 82; Haggadah and, 81, 157, 166–167; Herzl dream and, 238; Hillel (sage) and, 293; Joshua as successor, 39; meaning, 105, 317; miracles and, 243; Miriam and, 181–183; parting Red Sea, 7, 11, 13; Pharaoh's hardening heart and, 73–76, 256; plagues and, 108; rebellion against, 226; rod, 167; Serakh and, 179–180; suffering and, 147; swallowing snakes and, 80; Ten Commandments and, 9–10; "The Last Night in Egypt" and, 217–220; as true prophet of God, 159; Yocheved, mother, 178

Mount Carmel, 305

Mount Horeb. *See* Sinai

Mourning and festivity, 261, 262, 263, 264, 265–266

N

Nachman, Rebbe (of Breslov),66, 101

Nachmanides, 120, 177, 191, 250

Nachshon, 110–111

Nasi (head) of Sanhedrin, 206, 209, 210

Nes, defined, 243

Neusner, Jacob, 280

"New Israel," 6

New Israel Fund, xiii

New moon blessing, 90–91, 96–97, 327–328, 338

The 1997 Ma'yan Passover Haggadah, 183

1973 War in Suez Canal, 253

Numbers Rabbah (midrash), 177, 283, 319

O

"On that day," meaning, 209

Open Door, The, 312

Oppression: absence of wonder and, 248; B'nei B'rak Seder and, 51–55; oppressed as oppressors, 12; vengeance vs. empathy and, 11

P

Parsley (*karpas*), xx, 33, 87, 95, 96

Passover: ancient New Year rituals and, 93–94; blessings, 96–99; as calendar based, 93–94; celebration tradition, xv, 219; collective empathy and, 11; contemporary emphasis, 94–95; dew and, 97, 127; dialogue, xviii; as Festival of Spring, 85–87; as fusion of ancient festivals, 91–92; offering, purpose, 206; perspectives, 34–38, 232; specified time for, 85, 87–88; taking responsibility and, 39–41

Passover Haggadah: Its Sources and History, The (Goldschmidt); 329, 331, 333, 335, 343, 344, 349

"Pauper's dish," 279

Pesach offering, 92, 225, 324

Pharaoh, xxi; ancient New Year rituals and, 93; Bitya, daughter, 178; B'nei B'rak Seder and, 50, 53–54; defiance of, 106–108; drowning of army, 11, 81, 197; fear of Israelites and, 118; as freedom's enemy, 6; Joseph and, 122–125, 228; Laban and, compared, 164; liberation from, 51; male children death decree, 138, 153, 219; modern symbols, 10; plagues and, 79; repentance at Red Sea, 83; slavery and, 7–8, 33, 37, 61, 122, 230, 285, 321; symbolism, 12–13, 105–106, 109; "The Last Night in Egypt" and, 216–220; warnings, 82

Pharaoh's heart, hardening of, 80, 140, 255; Bible references, list, 73–76; discussion questions, 72; exclusion from Haggadah, 81; Exodus and, 71–72; free will and, 76–78

Philo (of Alexandria), 100

Pilgrims' Prayer: activity, 155; background and versions, 154; Deuteronomy and, 155, 168; discussion questions, 156–157; expounding on, benefits, 160; Haggadah and, 157–160, 167; received law absence, 169

Pirke de Rabbi Eliezer (midrash), 82, 127, 341, 356

Plagues: Akiva and, 159; creation myths and, 199–203; discussion questions, 195, 198; Exodus (book of) and, 79, 247; knowing God and, 193–197; morality of, 197–198; Moses and, 108; Pharaoh/Laban, compared, 79; seventh, 78–79; "The Last Night in Egypt" and, 218–219

Plutarch, 29–30

Post-Temple Passover, Greek symposium and, 29

Potential to change, Elijah as model, 310–311

Puah, 178, 180

Purim, xix, 265, 266

R

Rabban, defined, 206

Rabbinic literature, xxiii–xxiv

Rachel (biblical), 161

Rachel (wife of Akiva), 46, 50, 52, 53, 306

Ramses, as name, 317

Ramses II, 315

Ramses III, 4

Ramses IV, 275–276

Rasha, 63, 64

Rashbetz, 163
Rashi, 76, 162, 231, 235
Rav, Haggadah of, Passover, Mishnah and, 36–38
Rav Papa, 246
Redemption: ancient Near East view, 275–277; biblical view, 274–275; coming of Eliyahu and, 304; Messiah and, 304; defined, 273–274; dimensions of, 273–274; discussion questions, 274, 278–280, 281–282; Exodus from Egypt as, 193, 271–272; Final, 284; four cups of wine and, 279–281; four elements, 280; fruits of Egypt and Israel and, 227; Haggadah and, 167; invoking Elijah, 184; of Israelites, perspectives, 277–279; paradox, faith and hopelessness, 285–286; procreation and, 278–279; Ramses IV and, 275–276; Seder of, 271–286; spilling wine from cup and, 192; symbols of salvation, 273; twentieth-century views, 281–284; water and blood as mediums, 186–187
Responsibility, taking, 39–41
Reuven and Shimon, 254
Riskin, Shlomo, 237
Rizzuto, Ana-Maria, 141
Roots, symbolism, 228
Rubenstein, Richard, 149

S
Sabbath, justifications, 202–203
Sarah, 120
Sarajevo Haggadah (illustrated), 165
Schneerson, Menachem Mendel, 68, 304
Scholz, Suzanne, 176
Schorsch, Ismar, 102
Second Temple, Jewish revolt and burning of, 207, 232, 296
Seder: ancient timing, 85; challenges, xxi–xxiii; concepts of God and, xxiii; defined, xxii; Elijah and, 302–303; engaging children, 26–28; Exodus and, xxii, 159; fifteen traditional elements, xxii; five sages and, 159; four cups of wine, meaning, 231; Four Questions, 25–32, 159; goals, xv, xxi; Maggid section, 3; of redemption, 271–286; structure, Greek symposium and, 269; suggestions for leaders, xxi–xxv; this book as resource, xix–xx; *See also specific topics*
Segal, Benjamin, 232
Self-criticism, 125–127
September 11 (2001), 51, 221
Serakh: discussion questions, 180–181; Exodus and, 178–181; genealogies, 178; Moses and, 179–180; parting Red Sea and, 180
Seventh plague, 78–79
Sex slavery, defined, 23

Sforno, Ovadia, 121
Shammai, 295
Shammai, school of, 207
Shavuot, 86, 154, 233
Shekhinah, defined, 293
Shemayah and Avtalyon (sages), 291–292
Shiphrah, 171, 178, 180
Shmoneh Esrei, 207
Shmuel, Haggadah of, Passover, Mishnah and, 36–38
"Sign," meanings of, 243
Sikkuy: Association for Advancement of Civic Equality in Israel, 135
Sinai, 112; as destination of Exodus, xxiii, 227; Deuteronomy history without, 168; Four Children and, 64; Moses as leader, 319; Mount, 47, 226, 305, 306; redemption and, 277; revelation of Torah, 40, 47, 121, 154, 233–234, 277; standing before, 106; women and, 68
Six-Day War, 240
Slave labor, Egyptian pyramids and, 4
Slavery and freedom, 261, 262, 263, 264–265; between 200 and 500 C.E., 1; activities, 2, 24; biblical law, 4; contemporary and historical similarities, 6–8; current forms of slavery, 22–23; discussion questions, 2–3, 13, 22, 23, 118–119, 124–125; Egyptian law, 4; Exodus and, 2–3, 13, 276; Hammurabi's laws, 5; historic statements on freedom, 17–19; Israel enslavement in Egypt, 115–116, 118–122, 160, 230; Joseph and, 122–125; meaning of Exodus and, 113–114; readings, 2; redemption and, 285; sample slave narratives, 14–17; Seder activities and, 1–3, 13–14; slavery, defined, 22; Ten Commandments and, 5; vengeance vs. empathy and, 8–12
Sodom and Gomorrah, 143
Solomon, 263
Soloveitchik, Joseph B., 150, 233
Song of Songs, 182, 232, 327
Song of Songs Rabbah (midrash), 182, 334, 335, 350
Song of the Sea, 252, 272
Sorrow and joy, 261, 262, 263, 264, 265
Spinoza, Baruch, 250
Spira, Israel, 285
Statue of Liberty inscription, 18
Steinberg, Milton, 151
Stemberger, Gunter, xxiv
Strack, H. L., xxiv
Strangers: Arab citizens of Israel and, 134–136; biblical passages referencing, 131–133; discussion questions, 130, 133, 136, 221; empathy for, 130–133; just treatment basis, 129–130; original blessing, 133–134; suffering as, 130

Suffering, 130, 146, 147, 192–193
Sukkot, 193

T
Taking responsibility. *See* Responsibility, taking
Tanchuma (midrash), 279
Tarfon, 43, 44–46, 210, 231
Tefilat Ha-derekh. See Wayfarer's Prayer
Temple Mount Faithful, 240
Ten Commandments, 5, 9–10
Ten Martyrs, 150
Ten plagues, 320; discussion questions, 190, 191; Exodus (book of) and, 190; extended midrashic treatment, 189–190; identified, 191; Israelites and, 191; Seder ritual, 189; ten utterances and, 201
Ten utterances, 201
Third Temple, 240
Time: Exodus relevance, 88–90; Passover relevance, 85–92
Trible, Phyllis, 181

U
Unleavened bread. *See* Matzah
Uzza (angel), 193

V
"Vengeance vs. Empathy," 8–12

W
Wandering Aramean, 230, 316, 324; discussion questions, 162–163, 221; identified, 162; interpretations, 162–164; story of, 157–158
Water, 186–187
Wayfarer's Prayer, 214, 223
Wine: fifth cup, 234–235, 236; four vs. five cups, 231; redemption promises and, 235–236; Seder spilling of, 189, 191, 192; third/fourth cups, procedure, 324
Wolpe, David, 315, 322
Wonder, restoration of, 247–249
Wrath and anger, 312

Y
Yannai (Rabbi), 245
Yerushalmi, Yosef Hayim, 320
Yochanan (Rabbi), 280
Yocheved, 178, 180, 216
Yom Ha Bikurim, defined, 154
Yossi (the Galilean, Rabbi), 166, 325

Z
Zalman, Elijah ben Solomon (Vilna Gaon), 263
Zevi, Shabbetai, Jewish law and, 272
Zion: beauty of, 232; as Israel, 225, 229; longing for, 238; as messianic Jerusalem, 233; redemption and, 273, 275
Zman Herutanu, defined, 94
Zohar, xxv, 126, 127
Zornberg, Aviva, 78, 348

PERMISSIONS

—

"Is This Story True?" by Richard Hirsh, from *A Night of Questions: A Passover Haggadah*, © 2000 by the Reconstructionist Press, Elkins Park, PA. Used with permission of the Reconstructionist Press.

Translation of the "Prayer for Dew," *Kol Haneshamah: Shabbat Vehagim*, © 1994 by the Reconstructionist Press, Elkins Park, PA. Used with permission of the Reconstructionist Press.

"Metaphors for God," by Michael Graetz, *Conservative Judaism*, volume 51, number 2, Winter 1999, pp. 69–70, © by The Rabbinical Assembly, reprinted with permission.

"A Prayer for Peace," Siddur Sim Shalom, used with permission of the Rabbinical Assembly.

"Tending Our Cosmic Oasis," by Ismar Schorsch. Used with permission of the Coalition on the Environment and Jewish Life (www.coejl.org).

"The Four Daughters," by Tamara Ruth Cohen, Rabbi Sue Levi Elwell, and Ronnie Horn. Reprinted with permission from *The Journey Continues: The Ma'yan Passover Haggadah*, 1997.

Mir'yam Han'viah, © 1989 by Leila Gal Berner, from *The Ma'yan Passover Haggadah*, 1997. Used with permission of the composer.

Kos Miryam Ritual, Composed by Matia Rania Angelou and Janet Berkenfield, © Matia Rania Angelou. Used with permission of Matia Rania Angelou. Matia Rania Angelou credits Stephanie Loo with inspiring the creation of this ritual.

"Opening Your Eyes," from *The Book of Miracles* by Lawrence Kushner, © 1987 by the UAHC Press. Reprinted with permission of the UAHC Press.

"Sermon for the First Day of Passover 2001," by Rabbi David Wolpe. Used with permission of Rabbi Wolpe.

Page from the Sarajevo Haggadah, © Zemaljski Musej Bosne I Hercegovine Sarajevo (The National Museum of Bosnia and Herzegovina in Sarajevo). Reproduced with permission of the copyright holder.

Chapter 10 of Mishnah Pesachim (the Kaufmann Manuscript), translated by Baruch Bokser. *The Origins of the Seder: The Passover Rite and Early Rabbinic Judaism*, by Baruch Bokser, © 1984 by the Regents of the University of California. Reprinted with permission of the University of California Press.

"Give up anger . . . ," alternative to *Sh'fokh chamatkha*. *The Open Door: A Passover Haggadah*, © 2002 by the Central Conference of American Rabbis. Selections are used with permission of the Central Conference of American Rabbis.

The Book and the Sword: A Life of Learning in the Shadow of Destruction by David Weiss Halivni. © 1996 by Perseus Books Group. Reproduced with permission of Perseus Books Group, via Copyright Clearance Center.

Notes

Notes

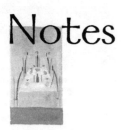

Notes

About Jewish Lights

People of all faiths and backgrounds yearn for books that attract, engage, educate, and spiritually inspire.

Our principal goal is to stimulate thought and help all people learn about who the Jewish People are, where they come from, and what the future can be made to hold. While people of our diverse Jewish heritage are the primary audience, our books speak to people in the Christian world as well and will broaden their understanding of Judaism and the roots of their own faith.

We bring to you authors who are at the forefront of spiritual thought and experience. While each has something different to say, they all say it in a voice that you can hear.

Our books are designed to welcome you and then to engage, stimulate, and inspire. We judge our success not only by whether or not our books are beautiful and commercially successful, but by whether or not they make a difference in your life.

For your information and convenience, at the back of this book we have provided a list of other Jewish Lights books you might find interesting and useful. They cover all the categories of your life:

Bar/Bat Mitzvah	Life Cycle
Bible Study / Midrash	Meditation
Children's Books	Parenting
Congregation Resources	Prayer
Current Events / History	Ritual / Sacred Practice
Ecology	Spirituality
Fiction: Mystery, Science Fiction	Theology / Philosophy
Grief / Healing	Travel
Holidays / Holy Days	Twelve Steps
Inspiration	Women's Interest
Kabbalah / Mysticism / Enneagram	

Stuart M. Matlins, Publisher

Or phone, fax, mail or e-mail to: **JEWISH LIGHTS** Publishing
Sunset Farm Offices, Route 4 • P.O. Box 237 • Woodstock, Vermont 05091
Tel: (802) 457-4000 • Fax: (802) 457-4004 • www.jewishlights.com
Credit card orders: **(800) 962-4544** (8:30AM–5:30PM ET Monday–Friday)
Generous discounts on quantity orders. SATISFACTION GUARANTEED. Prices subject to change.

Bar/Bat Mitzvah

The Bar/Bat Mitzvah Memory Book
An Album for Treasuring the Spiritual Celebration
By Rabbi Jeffrey K. Salkin and Nina Salkin
A unique album for preserving the spiritual memories of the day, and for recording plans for the Jewish future ahead. Contents include space for creating or recording family history; teachings received from rabbi, cantor, and others; mitzvot and *tzedakot* chosen and carried out, etc.
8 x 10, 48 pp, Deluxe Hardcover, 2-color text, ribbon marker, ISBN 1-58023-111-X **$19.95**

Bar/Bat Mitzvah Basics: A Practical Family Guide to Coming of Age Together
Edited by Helen Leneman. Foreword by Rabbi Jeffrey K. Salkin.
6 x 9, 240 pp, Quality PB, ISBN 1-58023-151-9 **$18.95**

For Kids—Putting God on Your Guest List: How to Claim the Spiritual
Meaning of Your Bar or Bat Mitzvah *By Rabbi Jeffrey K. Salkin*
6 x 9, 144 pp, Quality PB, ISBN 1-58023-015-6 **$14.95** *For ages 11–12*

Putting God on the Guest List:
How to Reclaim the Spiritual Meaning of Your Child's Bar or Bat Mitzvah
By Rabbi Jeffrey K. Salkin 6 x 9, 224 pp, Quality PB, ISBN 1-879045-59-1 **$16.95**

Tough Questions Jews Ask: A Young Adult's Guide to Building a Jewish Life
By Rabbi Edward Feinstein 6 x 9, 160 pp, Quality PB, ISBN 1-58023-139-X **$14.95** *For ages 13 & up*
Also Available: **Tough Questions Jews Ask Teacher's Guide**
8½ x 11, 72 pp, PB, ISBN 1-58023-187-X **$8.95**

Bible Study/Midrash

Hineini in Our Lives: Learning How to Respond to Others through 14 Biblical
Texts, and Personal Stories *By Norman J. Cohen*
6 x 9, 240 pp, Hardcover, ISBN 1-58023-131-4 **$23.95**

Ancient Secrets: Using the Stories of the Bible to Improve Our Everyday Lives
By Rabbi Levi Meier, Ph.D. 5 /2 x 8 /2, 288 pp, Quality PB, ISBN 1-58023-064-4 **$16.95**

Moses—The Prince, the Prophet: His Life, Legend & Message for Our Lives
By Rabbi Levi Meier, Ph.D. 6 x 9, 224 pp, Quality PB, ISBN 1-58023-069-5 **$16.95**;
Hardcover, ISBN 1-58023-013-X **$23.95**

Self, Struggle & Change: Family Conflict Stories in Genesis and Their Healing Insights
for Our Lives *By Norman J. Cohen* 6 x 9, 224 pp, Quality PB, ISBN 1-879045-66-4 **$16.95**

Voices from Genesis: Guiding Us through the Stages of Life
By Norman J. Cohen 6 x 9, 192 pp, Quality PB, ISBN 1-58023-118-7 **$16.95**

Congregation Resources

Becoming a Congregation of Learners: Learning as a Key to Revitalizing
Congregational Life *By Isa Aron, Ph.D. Foreword by Rabbi Lawrence A. Hoffman.*
6 x 9, 304 pp, Quality PB, ISBN 1-58023-089-X **$19.95**

Finding a Spiritual Home: How a New Generation of Jews Can Transform the
American Synagogue *By Rabbi Sidney Schwarz*
6 x 9, 352 pp, Quality PB, ISBN 1-58023-185-3 **$19.95**

Jewish Pastoral Care: A Practical Handbook from Traditional & Contemporary
Sources *Edited by Rabbi Dayle A. Friedman*
6 x 9, 464 pp, Hardcover, ISBN 1-58023-078-4 **$35.00**

The Self-Renewing Congregation: Organizational Strategies for Revitalizing
Congregational Life *By Isa Aron, Ph.D. Foreword by Dr. Ron Wolfson.*
6 x 9, 304 pp, Quality PB, ISBN 1-58023-166-7 **$19.95**

Children's Books

Because Nothing Looks Like God
By Lawrence and Karen Kushner
What is God like? The first collaborative work by husband-and-wife team Lawrence and Karen Kushner introduces children to the possibilities of spiritual life. Real-life examples of happiness and sadness invite us to explore, together with our children, the questions we all have about God, no matter what our age.
11 x 8½, 32 pp, Full-color illus., Hardcover, ISBN 1-58023-092-X **$16.95** *For ages 4 & up*

Also Available: **Because Nothing Looks Like God Teacher's Guide**
8½ x 11, 22 pp, PB, ISBN 1-58023-140-3 **$6.95** *For ages 5–8*

Board Book Companions to *Because Nothing Looks Like God*
5 x 5, 24 pp, Full-color illus., SkyLight Paths Board Books, **$7.95** each *For ages 0–4*

What Does God Look Like? ISBN 1-893361-23-3
How Does God Make Things Happen? ISBN 1-893361-24-1
Where Is God? ISBN 1-893361-17-9

The 11th Commandment: Wisdom from Our Children
by The Children of America
"If there were an Eleventh Commandment, what would it be?" Children of many religious denominations across America answer this question—in their own drawings and words.
8 x 10, 48 pp, Full-color illus., Hardcover, ISBN 1-879045-46-X **$16.95** *For all ages*

Jerusalem of Gold: Jewish Stories of the Enchanted City
Retold by Howard Schwartz. Full-color illus. by Neil Waldman.
A beautiful and engaging collection of historical and legendary stories for children. Each celebrates the magical city that has served as a beacon for the Jewish imagination for three thousand years. Draws on Talmud, midrash, Jewish folklore, and mystical and Hasidic sources.
8 x 10, 64 pp, Full-color illus., Hardcover, ISBN 1-58023-149-7 **$18.95** *For ages 7 & up*

The Book of Miracles: A Young Person's Guide to Jewish Spiritual Awareness
By Lawrence Kushner. All-new illustrations by the author.
6 x 9, 96 pp, 2-color illus., Hardcover, ISBN 1-879045-78-8 **$16.95** *For ages 9–13*

In Our Image: God's First Creatures
By Nancy Sohn Swartz
9 x 12, 32 pp, Full-color illus., Hardcover, ISBN 1-879045-99-0 **$16.95** *For ages 4 & up*

From SKYLIGHT PATHS PUBLISHING

Becoming Me: A Story of Creation
By Martin Boroson. Full-color illus. by Christopher Gilvan-Cartwright.
Told in the personal "voice" of the Creator, a story about creation and relationship that is about each one of us. In simple words and with radiant illustrations, the Creator tells an intimate story about love, about friendship and playing, about our world—and about ourselves.
8 x 10, 32 pp, Full-color illus., Hardcover, ISBN 1-893361-11-X **$16.95** *For ages 4 & up*

Ten Amazing People: And How They Changed the World
By Maura D. Shaw. Foreword by Dr. Robert Coles. Full-color illus. by Stephen Marchesi.
Black Elk • Dorothy Day • Malcolm X • Mahatma Gandhi • Martin Luther King, Jr. • Mother Teresa • Janusz Korczak • Desmond Tutu • Thich Nhat Hanh • Albert Schweitzer • This vivid, inspirational, and authoritative book will open new possibilities for children by telling the stories of how ten of the past century's greatest leaders changed the world in important ways.
8½ x 11, 48 pp, Full-color illus., Hardcover, ISBN 1-893361-47-0 **$17.95** *For ages 7 & up*

Where Does God Live? *By August Gold and Matthew J. Perlman*
Using simple, everyday examples that children can relate to, this colorful book helps young readers develop a personal understanding of God.
10 x 8½, 32 pp, Full-color photo illus., Quality PB, ISBN 1-893361-39-X **$8.95** *For ages 3–6*

Children's Books
by Sandy Eisenberg Sasso

Adam & Eve's First Sunset: God's New Day
Engaging new story explores fear and hope, faith and gratitude in ways that will delight kids and adults—inspiring us to bless each of God's days and nights.
9 x 12, 32 pp, Full-color illus., Hardcover, ISBN 1-58023-177-2 **$17.95** *For ages 4 & up*

But God Remembered
Stories of Women from Creation to the Promised Land
Four different stories of women—Lillith, Serach, Bityah, and the Daughters of Z—teach us important values through their faith and actions.
9 x 12, 32 pp, Full-color illus., Hardcover, ISBN 1-879045-43-5 **$16.95** *For ages 8 & up*

Cain & Abel: Finding the Fruits of Peace
Full-color illus. by Joani Keller Rothenberg
Shows children that we have the power to deal with anger in positive ways. Provides questions for kids and adults to explore together.
9 x 12, 32 pp, Full-color illus., Hardcover, ISBN 1-58023-123-3 **$16.95** *For ages 5 & up*

God in Between
Full-color illus. by Sally Sweetland
If you wanted to find God, where would you look? This magical, mythical tale teaches that God can be found where we are: within all of us and the relationships between us.
9 x 12, 32 pp, Full-color illus., Hardcover, ISBN 1-879045-86-9 **$16.95** *For ages 4 & up*

God's Paintbrush
Wonderfully interactive, invites children of all faiths and backgrounds to encounter God through moments in their own lives. Provides questions adult and child can explore together.
11 x 8½, 32 pp, Full-color illus., Hardcover, ISBN 1-879045-22-2 **$16.95** *For ages 4 & up*

Also Available: **God's Paintbrush Teacher's Guide**
8½ x 11, 32 pp, PB, ISBN 1-879045-57-5 **$8.95**

God's Paintbrush Celebration Kit
A Spiritual Activity Kit for Teachers and Students of All Faiths, All Backgrounds
Additional activity sheets available:
8-Student Activity Sheet Pack (40 sheets/5 sessions), ISBN 1-58023-058-X **$19.95**
Single-Student Activity Sheet Pack (5 sessions), ISBN 1-58023-059-8 **$3.95**

In God's Name
Full-color illus. by Phoebe Stone
Like an ancient myth in its poetic text and vibrant illustrations, this award-winning modern fable about the search for God's name celebrates the diversity and, at the same time, the unity of all people.
9 x 12, 32 pp, Full-color illus., Hardcover, ISBN 1-879045-26-5 **$16.95** *For ages 4 & up*

Also Available as a Board Book: **What Is God's Name?**
5 x 5, 24 pp, Board, Full-color illus., ISBN 1-893361-10-1 **$7.99** *For ages 0–4 (A SkyLight Paths book)*

Also Available: **In God's Name video and study guide**
Computer animation, original music, and children's voices. 18 min. **$29.99**

Also Available in Spanish: **El nombre de Dios**
9 x 12, 32 pp, Full-color illus., Hardcover, ISBN 1-893361-63-2 **$16.95** *(A SkyLight Paths book)*

Noah's Wife: The Story of Naamah
When God tells Noah to bring the animals of the world onto the ark, God also calls on Naamah, Noah's wife, to save each plant on Earth. Based on an ancient text.
9 x 12, 32 pp, Full-color illus., Hardcover, ISBN 1-58023-134-9 **$16.95** *For ages 4 & up*

Also Available as a Board Book: **Naamah, Noah's Wife**
5 x 5, 24 pp, Full-color illus., Board, ISBN 1-893361-56-X **$7.95** *For ages 0–4 (A SkyLight Paths book)*

For Heaven's Sake: Finding God in Unexpected Places
9 x 12, 32 pp, Full-color illus., Hardcover, ISBN 1-58023-054-7 **$16.95** *For ages 4 & up*

God Said Amen: Finding the Answers to Our Prayers
9 x 12, 32 pp, Full-color illus., Hardcover, ISBN 1-58023-080-6 **$16.95** *For ages 4 & up*

Current Events/History

The Story of the Jews: A 4,000-Year Adventure—A Graphic History Book
Written & illustrated by Stan Mack
Through witty, illustrated narrative, we visit all the major happenings from biblical times to the twenty-first century. Celebrates the major characters and events that have shaped the Jewish people and culture.
6 x 9, 288 pp, illus., Quality PB, ISBN 1-58023-155-1 **$16.95**

The Jewish Prophet: Visionary Words from Moses and Miriam to Henrietta Szold and A. J. Heschel   *By Rabbi Michael J. Shire*   6½ x 8½, 128 pp, 123 full-color illus., Hardcover, ISBN 1-58023-168-3 **$25.00**

Shared Dreams: Martin Luther King, Jr. & the Jewish Community
By Rabbi Marc Schneier. Preface by Martin Luther King III.
6 x 9, 240 pp, Hardcover, ISBN 1-58023-062-8 **$24.95**

"Who Is a Jew?": Conversations, Not Conclusions   *By Meryl Hyman*
6 x 9, 272 pp, Quality PB, ISBN 1-58023-052-0 **$16.95**

Ecology

Ecology & the Jewish Spirit: Where Nature & the Sacred Meet
Edited by Ellen Bernstein   6 x 9, 288 pp, Quality PB, ISBN 1-58023-082-2 **$16.95**

Torah of the Earth: Exploring 4,000 Years of Ecology in Jewish Thought
Vol. 1: Biblical Israel: One Land, One People; Rabbinic Judaism: One People, Many Lands
Vol. 2: Zionism: One Land, Two Peoples; Eco-Judaism: One Earth, Many Peoples
Edited by Rabbi Arthur Waskow
Vol. 1: 6 x 9, 272 pp, Quality PB, ISBN 1-58023-086-5 **$19.95**
Vol. 2: 6 x 9, 336 pp, Quality PB, ISBN 1-58023-087-3 **$19.95**

Grief/Healing

Against the Dying of the Light: A Parent's Story of Love, Loss and Hope
By Leonard Fein
In this unusual exploration of heartbreak and healing, Leonard Fein chronicles the sudden death of his 30-year-old daughter and shares the hard-earned wisdom that emerges in the face of loss and grief.
5½ x 8½, 176 pp, Hardcover, ISBN 1-58023-110-1 **$19.95**

Grief in Our Seasons: A Mourner's Kaddish Companion   *By Rabbi Kerry M. Olitzky*
4½ x 6½, 448 pp, Quality PB, ISBN 1-879045-55-9 **$15.95**

Healing of Soul, Healing of Body: Spiritual Leaders Unfold the Strength & Solace in Psalms   *Edited by Rabbi Simkha Y. Weintraub, C.S.W.*
6 x 9, 128 pp, 2-color illus. text, Quality PB, ISBN 1-879045-31-1 **$14.95**

Jewish Paths toward Healing and Wholeness: A Personal Guide to Dealing with Suffering   *By Rabbi Kerry M. Olitzky. Foreword by Debbie Friedman.*
6 x 9, 192 pp, Quality PB, ISBN 1-58023-068-7 **$15.95**

Mourning & Mitzvah, 2nd Edition: A Guided Journal for Walking the Mourner's Path through Grief to Healing   *By Anne Brener, L.C.S.W.*
7½ x 9, 304 pp, Quality PB, ISBN 1-58023-113-6 **$19.95**

The Perfect Stranger's Guide to Funerals and Grieving Practices
A Guide to Etiquette in Other People's Religious Ceremonies   *Edited by Stuart M. Matlins*
6 x 9, 240 pp, Quality PB, ISBN 1-893361-20-9 **$16.95**   *(A SkyLight Paths book)*

Tears of Sorrow, Seeds of Hope: A Jewish Spiritual Companion for Infertility and Pregnancy Loss   *By Rabbi Nina Beth Cardin*
6 x 9, 192 pp, Hardcover, ISBN 1-58023-017-2 **$19.95**

A Time to Mourn, A Time to Comfort: A Guide to Jewish Bereavement and Comfort   *By Dr. Ron Wolfson*   7 x 9, 336 pp, Quality PB, ISBN 1-879045-96-6 **$18.95**

When a Grandparent Dies: A Kid's Own Remembering Workbook for Dealing with Shiva and the Year Beyond   *By Nechama Liss-Levinson, Ph.D.*
8 x 10, 48 pp, 2-color text, Hardcover, ISBN 1-879045-44-3 **$15.95**   *For ages 7–13*

Abraham Joshua Heschel

The Earth Is the Lord's: The Inner World of the Jew in Eastern Europe
5½ x 8, 128 pp, Quality PB, ISBN 1-879045-42-7 **$14.95**

Israel: An Echo of Eternity *New Introduction by Susannah Heschel*
5½ x 8, 272 pp, Quality PB, ISBN 1-879045-70-2 **$19.95**

A Passion for Truth: Despair and Hope in Hasidism
5½ x 8, 352 pp, Quality PB, ISBN 1-879045-41-9 **$18.99**

Holidays/Holy Days

7th Heaven: Celebrating Shabbat with Rebbe Nachman of Breslov
By Moshe Mykoff with the Breslov Research Institute
Based on the teachings of Rebbe Nachman of Breslov. Explores the art of consciously observing Shabbat and understanding in-depth many of the day's traditional spiritual practices.
5⅛ x 8¼, 224 pp, Deluxe PB w/flaps, ISBN 1-58023-175-6 **$18.95**

The Women's Passover Companion
Women's Reflections on the Festival of Freedom
Edited by Rabbi Sharon Cohen Anisfeld, Tara Mohr, and Catherine Spector
A groundbreaking collection that captures the voices of Jewish women who engage in a provocative conversation about women's relationships to Passover as well as the roots and meanings of women's seders.
6 x 9, 352 pp, Hardcover, ISBN 1-58023-128-4 **$24.95**

The Women's Seder Sourcebook
Rituals & Readings for Use at the Passover Seder
Edited by Rabbi Sharon Cohen Anisfeld, Tara Mohr, and Catherine Spector
This practical guide gathers the voices of more than one hundred women in readings, personal and creative reflections, commentaries, blessings, and ritual suggestions that can be incorporated into your Passover celebration as supplements to or substitutes for traditional passages of the haggadah.
6 x 9, 384 pp, Hardcover, ISBN 1-58023-136-5 **$24.95**

Creating Lively Passover Seders: A Sourcebook of Engaging Tales, Texts & Activities
By David Arnow, Ph.D.
7 x 9, 416 pp, Quality PB, ISBN 1-58023-184-5 **$24.99**

Hanukkah, 2nd Edition: The Family Guide to Spiritual Celebration
By Dr. Ron Wolfson. Edited by Joel Lurie Grishaver.
7 x 9, 240 pp, illus., Quality PB, ISBN 1-58023-122-5 **$18.95**

The Jewish Family Fun Book: Holiday Projects, Everyday Activities, and Travel Ideas
with Jewish Themes *By Danielle Dardashti and Roni Sarig. Illus. by Avi Katz.*
6 x 9, 288 pp, 70+ b/w illus. & diagrams, Quality PB, ISBN 1-58023-171-3 **$18.95**

The Jewish Gardening Cookbook: Growing Plants & Cooking for
Holidays & Festivals *By Michael Brown*
6 x 9, 224 pp, 30+ illus., Quality PB, ISBN 1-58023-116-0 **$16.95**;
Hardcover, ISBN 1-58023-004-0 **$21.95**

Passover, 2nd Edition: The Family Guide to Spiritual Celebration
By Dr. Ron Wolfson with Joel Lurie Grishaver
7 x 9, 352 pp, Quality PB, ISBN 1-58023-174-8 **$19.95**

Shabbat, 2nd Edition: The Family Guide to Preparing for and Celebrating the Sabbath
By Dr. Ron Wolfson 7 x 9, 320 pp, illus., Quality PB, ISBN 1-58023-164-0 **$19.95**

Sharing Blessings: Children's Stories for Exploring the Spirit of the Jewish Holidays
By Rahel Musleah and Michael Klayman
8½ x 11, 64 pp, Full-color illus., Hardcover, ISBN 1-879045-71-0 **$18.95** *For ages 6 & up*

Inspiration

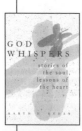

God in All Moments
Mystical & Practical Spiritual Wisdom from Hasidic Masters
Edited and translated by Or N. Rose with Ebn D. Leader
Hasidic teachings on how to be mindful in religious practice and how to cultivate everyday ethical behavior—*hanhagot*.
5½ x 8½, 192 pp, Quality PB, ISBN 1-58023-186-1 **$16.95**

The Dance of the Dolphin: Finding Prayer, Perspective and Meaning in the Stories
of Our Lives *By Karyn D. Kedar* 6 x 9, 176 pp, Hardcover, ISBN 1-58023-154-3 **$19.95**

The Empty Chair: Finding Hope and Joy—Timeless Wisdom from a Hasidic Master,
Rebbe Nachman of Breslov *Adapted by Moshe Mykoff and the Breslov Research Institute*
4 x 6, 128 pp, 2-color text, Deluxe PB w/flaps, ISBN 1-879045-67-2 **$9.95**

The Gentle Weapon: Prayers for Everyday and Not-So-Everyday Moments—
Timeless Wisdom from the Teachings of the Hasidic Master, Rebbe Nachman of Breslov
Adapted by Moshe Mykoff and S. C. Mizrahi, together with the Breslov Research Institute
4 x 6, 144 pp, 2-color text, Deluxe PB w/flaps, ISBN 1-58023-022-9 **$9.95**

God Whispers: Stories of the Soul, Lessons of the Heart *By Karyn D. Kedar*
6 x 9, 176 pp, Quality PB, ISBN 1-58023-088-1 **$15.95**

An Orphan in History: One Man's Triumphant Search for His Jewish Roots
By Paul Cowan. Afterword by Rachel Cowan. 6 x 9, 288 pp, Quality PB, ISBN 1-58023-135-7 **$16.95**

Restful Reflections: Nighttime Inspiration to Calm the Soul, Based on Jewish Wisdom
By Rabbi Kerry M. Olitzky & Rabbi Lori Forman
4½ x 6½, 448 pp, Quality PB, ISBN 1-58023-091-1 **$15.95**

Sacred Intentions: Daily Inspiration to Strengthen the Spirit, Based on Jewish Wisdom
By Rabbi Kerry M. Olitzky and Rabbi Lori Forman
4½ x 6½, 448 pp, Quality PB, ISBN 1-58023-061-X **$15.95**

Kabbalah/Mysticism/Enneagram

Seek My Face: A Jewish Mystical Theology
By Dr. Arthur Green
This classic work of contemporary Jewish theology, revised and updated, is a profound, deeply personal statement of the lasting truths of Jewish mysticism and the basic faith claims of Judaism. A tool for anyone seeking the elusive presence of God in the world. 6 x 9, 304 pp, Quality PB, ISBN 1-58023-130-6 **$19.95**

Zohar: Annotated & Explained
Translation and annotation by Dr. Daniel C. Matt. Foreword by Andrew Harvey, SkyLight Illuminations series editor.
Offers insightful yet unobtrusive commentary to the masterpiece of Jewish mysticism that explains references and mystical symbols, shares wisdom of spiritual masters, and clarifies the *Zohar*'s bold claim: We have always been taught that we need God, but in order to manifest in the world, God needs us.
5½ x 8½, 160 pp, Quality PB, ISBN 1-893361-51-9 **$15.95** *(A SkyLight Paths book)*

Cast in God's Image: Discover Your Personality Type Using the Enneagram and Kabbalah
By Rabbi Howard A. Addison
7 x 9, 176 pp, Quality PB, Layflat binding, 20+ journaling exercises, ISBN 1-58023-124-1 **$16.95**

Ehyeh: A Kabbalah for Tomorrow *By Dr. Arthur Green*
6 x 9, 224 pp, Hardcover, ISBN 1-58023-125-X **$21.99**

The Enneagram and Kabbalah: Reading Your Soul *By Rabbi Howard A. Addison*
6 x 9, 176 pp, Quality PB, ISBN 1-58023-001-6 **$15.95**

Finding Joy: A Practical Spiritual Guide to Happiness *By Dannel I. Schwartz with Mark Hass*
6 x 9, 192 pp, Quality PB, ISBN 1-58023-009-1 **$14.95**; Hardcover, ISBN 1-879045-53-2 **$19.95**

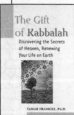

The Gift of Kabbalah: Discovering the Secrets of Heaven, Renewing Your Life on Earth
By Tamar Frankiel, Ph.D.
6 x 9, 256 pp, Quality PB, ISBN 1-58023-141-1 **$16.95**; Hardcover, ISBN 1-58023-108-X **$21.95**

The Way Into Jewish Mystical Tradition *By Lawrence Kushner*
6 x 9, 224 pp, Hardcover, ISBN 1-58023-029-6 **$21.95**

Life Cycle

Parenting

The New Jewish Baby Album: Creating and Celebrating the Beginning of a Spiritual Life—A Jewish Lights Companion
By the Editors at Jewish Lights. Foreword by Anita Diamant. Preface by Sandy Eisenberg Sasso.
A spiritual keepsake that will be treasured for generations. More than just a memory book, *shows you how—and why it's important*—to create a Jewish home and a Jewish life. Includes sections to describe naming ceremony, space to write encouragements, and pages for writing original blessings, prayers, and meaningful quotes throughout.
8 x 10, 64 pp, Deluxe Padded Hardcover, Full-color illus., ISBN 1-58023-138-1 **$19.95**

The Jewish Pregnancy Book: A Resource for the Soul, Body & Mind during Pregnancy, Birth & the First Three Months
By Sandy Falk, M.D., and Rabbi Daniel Judson, with Steven A. Rapp
Includes medical information on fetal development, pre-natal testing and more, from a liberal Jewish perspective; prenatal *Aleph-Bet* yoga; and ancient and modern prayers and rituals for each stage of pregnancy.
7 x 10, 208 pp, Quality PB, b/w illus., ISBN 1-58023-178-0 **$16.95**

Celebrating Your New Jewish Daughter: Creating Jewish Ways to Welcome Baby Girls into the Covenant—New and Traditional Ceremonies
By Debra Nussbaum Cohen 6 x 9, 272 pp, Quality PB, ISBN 1-58023-090-3 **$18.95**

The New Jewish Baby Book: Names, Ceremonies & Customs—A Guide for Today's Families *By Anita Diamant* 6 x 9, 336 pp, Quality PB, ISBN 1-879045-28-1 **$18.95**

Parenting As a Spiritual Journey: Deepening Ordinary and Extraordinary Events into Sacred Occasions *By Rabbi Nancy Fuchs-Kreimer*
6 x 9, 224 pp, Quality PB, ISBN 1-58023-016-4 **$16.95**

Embracing the Covenant: Converts to Judaism Talk About Why & How
Edited and with introductions by Rabbi Allan Berkowitz and Patti Moskovitz
6 x 9, 192 pp, Quality PB, ISBN 1-879045-50-8 **$16.95**

The Guide to Jewish Interfaith Family Life: An InterfaithFamily.com Handbook
Edited by Ronnie Friedland and Edmund Case 6 x 9, 384 pp, Quality PB, ISBN 1-58023-153-5 **$18.95**

Making a Successful Jewish Interfaith Marriage: The Jewish Outreach Institute Guide to Opportunities, Challenges and Resources
By Rabbi Kerry Olitzky with Joan Peterson Littman 6 x 9, 176 pp, Quality PB, ISBN 1-58023-170-5 **$16.95**

The Perfect Stranger's Guide to Wedding Ceremonies
A Guide to Etiquette in Other People's Religious Ceremonies *Edited by Stuart M. Matlins*
6 x 9, 208 pp, Quality PB, ISBN 1-893361-19-5 **$16.95** *(A SkyLight Paths book)*

How to Be a Perfect Stranger, 3rd Edition
The Essential Religious Etiquette Handbook
Edited by Stuart M. Matlins and Arthur J. Magida
The indispensable guidebook to help the well-meaning guest when visiting other people's religious ceremonies.
A straightforward guide to the rituals and celebrations of the major religions and denominations in the United States and Canada from the perspective of an interested guest of any other faith, based on information obtained from authorities of each religion. Belongs in every living room, library, and office.
6 x 9, 432 pp, Quality PB, ISBN 1-893361-67-5 **$19.95** *(A SkyLight Paths book)*

Divorce Is a Mitzvah: A Practical Guide to Finding Wholeness and Holiness When Your Marriage Dies *By Rabbi Perry Netter. Afterword by Rabbi Laura Geller.*
6 x 9, 224 pp, Quality PB, ISBN 1-58023-172-1 **$16.95**

A Heart of Wisdom: Making the Jewish Journey from Midlife through the Elder Years
Edited by Susan Berrin. Foreword by Harold Kushner. 6 x 9, 384 pp, Quality PB, ISBN 1-58023-051-2 **$18.95**

So That Your Values Live On: Ethical Wills and How to Prepare Them
Edited by Jack Riemer and Nathaniel Stampfer 6 x 9, 272 pp, Quality PB, ISBN 1-879045-34-6 **$18.95**

Meditation

The Handbook of Jewish Meditation Practices
A Guide for Enriching the Sabbath and Other Days of Your Life
By Rabbi David A. Cooper
Easy-to-learn meditation techniques for use on the Sabbath and every day, to help us return to the roots of traditional Jewish spirituality where Shabbat is a state of mind and soul. 6 x 9, 208 pp, Quality PB, ISBN 1-58023-102-0 **$16.95**

Discovering Jewish Meditation: Instruction & Guidance for Learning an Ancient Spiritual Practice *By Nan Fink Gefen, Ph.D.* 6 x 9, 208 pp, Quality PB, ISBN 1-58023-067-9 **$16.95**

A Heart of Stillness: A Complete Guide to Learning the Art of Meditation
By Rabbi David A. Cooper
5½ x 8½, 272 pp, Quality PB, ISBN 1-893361-03-9 **$16.95** *(A SkyLight Paths book)*

Meditation from the Heart of Judaism: Today's Teachers Share Their Practices, Techniques, and Faith *Edited by Avram Davis*
6 x 9, 256 pp, Quality PB, ISBN 1-58023-049-0 **$16.95**

Silence, Simplicity & Solitude: A Complete Guide to Spiritual Retreat at Home
By Rabbi David A. Cooper
5½ x 8½, 336 pp, Quality PB, ISBN 1-893361-04-7 **$16.95** *(A SkyLight Paths book)*

Three Gates to Meditation Practice: A Personal Journey into Sufism, Buddhism, and Judaism *By Rabbi David A. Cooper*
5½ x 8½, 240 pp, Quality PB, ISBN 1-893361-22-5 **$16.95** *(A SkyLight Paths book)*

The Way of Flame: A Guide to the Forgotten Mystical Tradition of Jewish Meditation
By Avram Davis 4½ x 8, 176 pp, Quality PB, ISBN 1-58023-060-1 **$15.95**

Ritual/Sacred Practice

The Jewish Dream Book
The Key to Opening the Inner Meaning of Your Dreams
By Vanessa L. Ochs with Elizabeth Ochs; Full-color Illus. by Kristina Swarner
Vibrant illustrations, instructions for how modern people can perform ancient Jewish dream practices, and dream interpretations drawn from the Jewish wisdom tradition help make this guide the ideal bedside companion for anyone who wants to further their understanding of their dreams—and themselves.
8 x 8, 120 pp, Full-color illus., Deluxe PB w/flaps, ISBN 1-58023-132-2 **$16.95**

The Rituals & Practices of a Jewish Life: A Handbook for Personal Spiritual Renewal *Edited by Rabbi Kerry M. Olitzky and Rabbi Daniel Judson*
6 x 9, 272 pp, illus., Quality PB, ISBN 1-58023-169-1 **$18.95**

The Book of Jewish Sacred Practices: CLAL's Guide to Everyday & Holiday Rituals & Blessings *Edited by Rabbi Irwin Kula and Vanessa L. Ochs, Ph.D.*
6 x 9, 368 pp, Quality PB, ISBN 1-58023-152-7 **$18.95**

Science Fiction/ Mystery & Detective Fiction

Mystery Midrash: An Anthology of Jewish Mystery & Detective Fiction
Edited by Lawrence W. Raphael. Preface by Joel Siegel.
6 x 9, 304 pp, Quality PB, ISBN 1-58023-055-5 **$16.95**

Criminal Kabbalah: An Intriguing Anthology of Jewish Mystery & Detective Fiction
Edited by Lawrence W. Raphael. Foreword by Laurie R. King.
6 x 9, 256 pp, Quality PB, ISBN 1-58023-109-8 **$16.95**

More Wandering Stars: An Anthology of Outstanding Stories of Jewish Fantasy and Science Fiction *Edited by Jack Dann. Introduction by Isaac Asimov.*
6 x 9, 192 pp, Quality PB, ISBN 1-58023-063-6 **$16.95**

Wandering Stars: An Anthology of Jewish Fantasy & Science Fiction
Edited by Jack Dann. Introduction by Isaac Asimov.
6 x 9, 272 pp, Quality PB, ISBN 1-58023-005-9 **$16.95**

Spirituality

The Alphabet of Paradise: An A–Z of Spirituality for Everyday Life
By Rabbi Howard Cooper
In twenty-six engaging chapters, Cooper spiritually illuminates the subjects of our daily lives—A to Z—examining these sources by using an ancient Jewish mystical method of interpretation that reveals both the literal and more allusive meanings of each. 5 x 7¾, 224 pp, Quality PB, ISBN 1-893361-80-2 **$16.95** *(A SkyLight Paths book)*

Does the Soul Survive?: A Jewish Journey to Belief in Afterlife, Past
Lives & Living with Purpose *By Rabbi Elie Kaplan Spitz. Foreword by Brian L. Weiss, M.D.*
Spitz relates his own experiences and those shared with him by people he has worked with as a rabbi, and shows us that belief in afterlife and past lives, so often approached with reluctance, is in fact true to Jewish tradition.
6 x 9, 288 pp, Quality PB, ISBN 1-58023-165-9 **$16.95**; Hardcover, ISBN 1-58023-094-6 **$21.95**

First Steps to a New Jewish Spirit: Reb Zalman's Guide to
Recapturing the Intimacy & Ecstasy in Your Relationship with God
By Rabbi Zalman M. Schachter-Shalomi with Donald Gropman
An extraordinary spiritual handbook that restores psychic and physical vigor by introducing us to new models and alternative ways of practicing Judaism. Offers meditation and contemplation exercises for enriching the most important aspects of everyday life. 6 x 9, 144 pp, Quality PB, ISBN 1-58023-182-9 **$16.95**

God in Our Relationships: Spirituality between People from the
Teachings of Martin Buber *By Rabbi Dennis S. Ross*
On the eightieth anniversary of Buber's classic work, we can discover new answers to critical issues in our lives. Inspiring examples from Ross's own life— as congregational rabbi, father, hospital chaplain, social worker, and husband— illustrate Buber's difficult-to-understand ideas about how we encounter God and each other. 5½ x 8½, 160 pp, Quality PB, ISBN 1-58023-147-0 **$16.95**

The Jewish Lights Spirituality Handbook: A Guide to Understanding,
Exploring & Living a Spiritual Life *Edited by Stuart M. Matlins*
What exactly is "Jewish" about spirituality? How do I make it a part of my life? Fifty of today's foremost spiritual leaders share their ideas and experience with us.
6 x 9, 456 pp, Quality PB, ISBN 1-58023-093-8 **$19.99**; Hardcover, ISBN 1-58023-100-4 **$24.95**

Bringing the Psalms to Life: How to Understand and Use the Book of Psalms
By Dr. Daniel F. Polish
6 x 9, 208 pp, Quality PB, ISBN 1-58023-157-8 **$16.95**; Hardcover, ISBN 1-58023-077-6 **$21.95**

God & the Big Bang: Discovering Harmony between Science & Spirituality
By Dr. Daniel C. Matt 6 x 9, 216 pp, Quality PB, ISBN 1-879045-89-3 **$16.95**

Godwrestling—Round 2: Ancient Wisdom, Future Paths
By Rabbi Arthur Waskow 6 x 9, 352 pp, Quality PB, ISBN 1-879045-72-9 **$18.95**

One God Clapping: The Spiritual Path of a Zen Rabbi *By Rabbi Alan Lew with Sherril Jaffe*
5½ x 8½, 336 pp, Quality PB, ISBN 1-58023-115-2 **$16.95**

The Path of Blessing: Experiencing the Energy and Abundance of the Divine
By Rabbi Marcia Prager 5½ x 8½, 240 pp., Quality PB, ISBN 1-58023-148-9 **$16.95**

Six Jewish Spiritual Paths: A Rationalist Looks at Spirituality *By Rabbi Rifat Sonsino*
6 x 9, 208 pp, Quality PB, ISBN 1-58023-167-5 **$16.95**; Hardcover, ISBN 1-58023-095-4 **$21.95**

Soul Judaism: Dancing with God into a New Era
By Rabbi Wayne Dosick 5½ x 8½, 304 pp, Quality PB, ISBN 1-58023-053-9 **$16.95**

Stepping Stones to Jewish Spiritual Living: Walking the Path Morning, Noon,
and Night *By Rabbi James L. Mirel and Karen Bonnell Werth*
6 x 9, 240 pp, Quality PB, ISBN 1-58023-074-1 **$16.95**; Hardcover, ISBN 1-58023-003-2 **$21.95**

There Is No Messiah... and You're It: The Stunning Transformation of Judaism's
Most Provocative Idea *By Rabbi Robert N. Levine, D.D.*
6 x 9, 192 pp, Hardcover, ISBN 1-58023-173-X **$21.95**

These Are the Words: A Vocabulary of Jewish Spiritual Life *By Dr. Arthur Green*
6 x 9, 304 pp, Quality PB, ISBN 1-58023-107-1 **$18.95**

Spirituality/Lawrence Kushner

The Book of Letters: A Mystical Hebrew Alphabet
Popular Hardcover Edition, 6 x 9, 80 pp, 2-color text, ISBN 1-879045-00-1 **$24.95**
Deluxe Gift Edition with slipcase, 9 x 12, 80 pp, 4-color text, Hardcover, ISBN 1-879045-01-X **$79.95**
Collector's Limited Edition, 9 x 12, 80 pp, gold foil embossed pages, w/limited edition silkscreened print, ISBN 1-879045-04-4 **$349.00**

The Book of Miracles: A Young Person's Guide to Jewish Spiritual Awareness
All-new illustrations by the author
6 x 9, 96 pp, 2-color illus., Hardcover, ISBN 1-879045-78-8 **$16.95** *For ages 9–13*

The Book of Words: Talking Spiritual Life, Living Spiritual Talk
6 x 9, 160 pp, Quality PB, ISBN 1-58023-020-2 **$16.95**

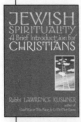

Eyes Remade for Wonder: A Lawrence Kushner Reader
Introduction by Thomas Moore
6 x 9, 240 pp, Quality PB, ISBN 1-58023-042-3 **$18.95;** Hardcover, ISBN 1-58023-014-8 **$23.95**

God Was in This Place & I, i Did Not Know
Finding Self, Spirituality and Ultimate Meaning
6 x 9, 192 pp, Quality PB, ISBN 1-879045-33-8 **$16.95**

Honey from the Rock: An Introduction to Jewish Mysticism
6 x 9, 176 pp, Quality PB, ISBN 1-58023-073-3 **$16.95**

Invisible Lines of Connection: Sacred Stories of the Ordinary
5½ x 8½, 160 pp, Quality PB, ISBN 1-879045-98-2 **$15.95**

Jewish Spirituality—A Brief Introduction for Christians
5½ x 8½, 112 pp, Quality PB Original, ISBN 1-58023-150-0 **$12.95**

The River of Light: Jewish Mystical Awareness
6 x 9, 192 pp, Quality PB, ISBN 1-58023-096-2 **$16.95**

The Way Into Jewish Mystical Tradition
6 x 9, 224 pp, Hardcover, ISBN 1-58023-029-6 **$21.95**

Spirituality/Prayer

Pray Tell: A Hadassah Guide to Jewish Prayer
By Rabbi Jules Harlow, with contributions from Tamara Cohen, Rochelle Furstenberg, Rabbi Daniel Gordis, Leora Tanenbaum, and many others
A guide to traditional Jewish prayer enriched with insight and wisdom from a broad variety of viewpoints—from Orthodox, Conservative, Reform, and Reconstructionist Judaism to New Age and feminist. Offers fresh and modern slants on what it means to pray as a Jew, and how women and men might actually pray. 8½ x 11, 400 pp, Quality PB, ISBN 1-58023-163-2 **$29.95**

My People's Prayer Book Series
Traditional Prayers, Modern Commentaries
Edited by Rabbi Lawrence A. Hoffman
Provides diverse and exciting commentary to the traditional liturgy, helping modern men and women find new wisdom in Jewish prayer, and bring liturgy into their lives.

Each book includes Hebrew text, modern translation, and commentaries from all perspectives of the Jewish world.
Vol. 1—The *Sh'ma* and Its Blessings
7 x 10, 168 pp, Hardcover, ISBN 1-879045-79-6 **$23.95**
Vol. 2—The *Amidah*
7 x 10, 240 pp, Hardcover, ISBN 1-879045-80-X **$24.95**
Vol. 3—*P'sukei D'zimrah* (Morning Psalms)
7 x 10, 240 pp, Hardcover, ISBN 1-879045-81-8 **$24.95**
Vol. 4—*Seder K'riat Hatorah* (The Torah Service)
7 x 10, 264 pp, Hardcover, ISBN 1-879045-82-6 **$23.95**
Vol. 5—*Birkhot Hashachar* (Morning Blessings)
7 x 10, 240 pp, Hardcover, ISBN 1-879045-83-4 **$24.95**
Vol. 6—*Tachanun* and Concluding Prayers
7 x 10, 240 pp, Hardcover, ISBN 1-879045-84-2 **$24.95**
Vol. 7—Shabbat at Home
7 x 10, 240 pp, Hardcover, ISBN 1-879045-85-0 **$24.95**

Spirituality/The Way Into... Series

The Way Into... Series offers an accessible and highly usable "guided tour" of the Jewish faith, people, history and beliefs—in total, an introduction to Judaism that will enable you to understand and interact with the sacred texts of the Jewish tradition. Each volume is written by a leading contemporary scholar and teacher, and explores one key aspect of Judaism. *The Way Into...* enables all readers to achieve a real sense of Jewish cultural literacy through guided study.

The Way Into Encountering God in Judaism   *By Neil Gillman*
6 x 9, 240 pp, Hardcover, ISBN 1-58023-025-3 **$21.95**

Also Available: **The Jewish Approach to God: A Brief Introduction for Christians**
By Neil Gillman 5½ x 8½, 192 pp, Quality PB, ISBN 1-58023-190-X **$16.95**

The Way Into Jewish Mystical Tradition   *By Lawrence Kushner*
6 x 9, 224 pp, Hardcover, ISBN 1-58023-029-6 **$21.95**

The Way Into Jewish Prayer   *By Lawrence A. Hoffman*
6 x 9, 224 pp, Hardcover, ISBN 1-58023-027-X **$21.95**

The Way Into Torah   *By Norman J. Cohen*
6 x 9, 176 pp, Hardcover, ISBN 1-58023-028-8 **$21.95**

Spirituality in the Workplace

Being God's Partner
How to Find the Hidden Link Between Spirituality and Your Work
By Rabbi Jeffrey K. Salkin. Introduction by Norman Lear.
6 x 9, 192 pp, Quality PB, ISBN 1-879045-65-6 **$17.95**

The Business Bible: 10 New Commandments for Bringing Spirituality & Ethical
Values into the Workplace   *By Rabbi Wayne Dosick*
5½ x 8½, 208 pp, Quality PB, ISBN 1-58023-101-2 **$14.95**

Spirituality and Wellness

Aleph-Bet Yoga
Embodying the Hebrew Letters for Physical and Spiritual Well-Being
By Steven A. Rapp. Foreword by Tamar Frankiel, Ph.D., and Judy Greenfeld. Preface by Hart Lazer
7 x 10, 128 pp, b/w photos, Quality PB, Layflat binding, ISBN 1-58023-162-4 **$16.95**

Entering the Temple of Dreams
Jewish Prayers, Movements, and Meditations for the End of the Day
By Tamar Frankiel, Ph.D., and Judy Greenfeld
7 x 10, 192 pp, illus., Quality PB, ISBN 1-58023-079-2 **$16.95**

Minding the Temple of the Soul
Balancing Body, Mind, and Spirit through Traditional Jewish Prayer, Movement, and
Meditation   *By Tamar Frankiel, Ph.D., and Judy Greenfeld*
7 x 10, 184 pp, illus., Quality PB, ISBN 1-879045-64-8 **$16.95**
Audiotape of the Blessings and Meditations: 60 min. **$9.95**
Videotape of the Movements and Meditations: 46 min. **$20.00**

Spirituality/Women's Interest

Lifecycles, Vol. 1: Jewish Women on Life Passages & Personal Milestones
Edited and with introductions by Rabbi Debra Orenstein
6 x 9, 480 pp, Quality PB, ISBN 1-58023-018-0 **$19.95**

Lifecycles, Vol. 2: Jewish Women on Biblical Themes in Contemporary Life
Edited and with introductions by Rabbi Debra Orenstein and Rabbi Jane Rachel Litman
6 x 9, 464 pp, Quality PB, ISBN 1-58023-019-9 **$19.95**

Moonbeams: A Hadassah Rosh Hodesh Guide *Edited by Carol Diament, Ph.D.*
8½ x 11, 240 pp, Quality PB, ISBN 1-58023-099-7 **$20.00**

ReVisions: Seeing Torah through a Feminist Lens *By Rabbi Elyse Goldstein*
5½ x 8½, 224 pp, Quality PB, ISBN 1-58023-117-9 **$16.95**

White Fire: A Portrait of Women Spiritual Leaders in America
By Rabbi Malka Drucker. Photographs by Gay Block.
7 x 10, 320 pp, 30+ b/w photos, Hardcover, ISBN 1-893361-64-0 **$24.95** *(A SkyLight Paths book)*

Women of the Wall: Claiming Sacred Ground at Judaism's Holy Site
Edited by Phyllis Chesler and Rivka Haut
6 x 9, 496 pp, b/w photos, Hardcover, ISBN 1-58023-161-6 **$34.95**

The Women's Haftarah Commentary: New Insights from Women Rabbis on
the 54 Weekly Haftarah Portions, the 5 Megillot & Special Shabbatot
Edited by Rabbi Elyse Goldstein 6 x 9, 544 pp, Hardcover, ISBN 1-58023-133-0 **$39.99**

The Women's Torah Commentary: New Insights from Women Rabbis on the 54
Weekly Torah Portions *Edited by Rabbi Elyse Goldstein*
6 x 9, 496 pp, Hardcover, ISBN 1-58023-076-8 **$34.95**

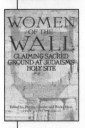

The Year Mom Got Religion: One Woman's Midlife Journey into Judaism
By Lee Meyerhoff Hendler
6 x 9, 208 pp, Quality PB, ISBN 1-58023-070-9 **$15.95**; Hardcover, ISBN 1-58023-000-8 **$19.95**

See Holidays for *The Women's Passover Companion: Women's Reflections on
the Festival of Freedom* and *The Women's Seder Sourcebook: Rituals &
Readings for Use at the Passover Seder.*

Travel

Israel—A Spiritual Travel Guide: A Companion for the Modern Jewish Pilgrim
By Rabbi Lawrence A. Hoffman 4¾ x 10, 256 pp, Quality PB, illus., ISBN 1-879045-56-7 **$18.95**
Also Available: **The Israel Mission Leader's Guide** ISBN 1-58023-085-7 **$4.95**

12 Steps

100 Blessings Every Day
Daily Twelve Step Recovery Affirmations, Exercises for Personal Growth &
Renewal Reflecting Seasons of the Jewish Year
By Rabbi Kerry M. Olitzky. Foreword by Rabbi Neil Gillman.
Using a one-day-at-a-time monthly format, this guide reflects on the rhythm of
the Jewish calendar to help bring insight to recovery from addictions and com-
pulsive behaviors of all kinds. Its exercises help us move from *thinking* to *doing*.
4½ x 6½, 432 pp, Quality PB, ISBN 1-879045-30-3 **$14.99**

Recovery from Codependence: A Jewish Twelve Steps Guide to Healing Your Soul
By Rabbi Kerry M. Olitzky 6 x 9, 160 pp, Quality PB, ISBN 1-879045-32-X **$13.95**

Renewed Each Day: Daily Twelve Step Recovery Meditations Based on the Bible
By Rabbi Kerry M. Olitzky and Aaron Z.
Vol. 1—Genesis & Exodus:
6 x 9, 224 pp, Quality PB, ISBN 1-879045-12-5 **$14.95**
Vol. 2—Leviticus, Numbers & Deuteronomy:
6 x 9, 280 pp, Quality PB, ISBN 1-879045-13-3 **$14.95**

Twelve Jewish Steps to Recovery
A Personal Guide to Turning from Alcoholism & Other Addictions—Drugs, Food,
Gambling, Sex...
By Rabbi Kerry M. Olitzky and Stuart A. Copans, M.D. Preface by Abraham J. Twerski, M.D.
6 x 9, 144 pp, Quality PB, ISBN 1-879045-09-5 **$14.95**